The Working Landscape

D0209068

Urban and Industrial Environments
Series editor: Robert Gottlieb, Henry R. Luce Professor of Urban and Environmental Policy, Occidental College

For a complete list of books published in this series, please see the back of the book.

The Working Landscape
Founding, Preservation, and the Politics of Place

Peter F. Cannavò

The MIT Press
Cambridge, Massachusetts
London, England

© 2007 Massachusetts Institute of Technology

All rights reserved. No part of this book may be reproduced in any form by any electronic or mechanical means (including photocopying, recording, or information storage and retrieval) without permission in writing from the publisher.

MIT Press books may be purchased at special quantity discounts for business or sales promotional use. For information, please email special_sales@mitpress.mit .edu or write to Special Sales Department, The MIT Press, 55 Hayward Street, Cambridge, MA 02142.

This book was set in Sabon on 3B2 by Asco Typesetters, Hong Kong.
Printed and bound in the United States of America.

Printed on Recycled Paper.

Library of Congress Cataloging-in-Publication Data

Cannavò, Peter F.
The working landscape : founding, preservation, and the politics of place / Peter F. Cannavò
    p.   cm. — (Urban and industrial environments)
Based on the author's Ph.D. thesis, Harvard University, 2000.
Includes bibliographical references (p.   ) and index.
ISBN-13: 978-0-262-03364-0 (hardcover : alk. paper)
ISBN-13: 978-0-262-53292-1 (pbk. : alk. paper)
1. Land use—Government policy—United States. 2. Sustainable development—United States. 3. Human geography—United States. 4. Political ecology—United States. 5. Regional planning—United States—Citizen participation.
I. Title. II. Title: Politics of place.
HD205.C36   2007
333.730973—dc22   2006031788

10 9 8 7 6 5 4 3 2 1

To Helen, Maja, and Peri

Contents

Preface and Acknowledgments

In the fall of 1997 my wife Helen and I paid a final visit to her childhood home in Grand Forks, North Dakota. That April, after a brutal winter marked by eight major blizzards, the Red River of the North had overflowed its banks, flooding Grand Forks and forcing the evacuation of almost the entire population. My in-laws, whose basement had been flooded, were able to clean up and make repairs, but they had had enough of North Dakota winters. The blizzards and flood of 1996–1997 had been the last straw. They had sold the house and were moving to Florida. Although Helen had lived in the East for many years, the fact that she would never again come home to Grand Forks was painful.

Her sorrow was but a dim flicker of the enormous loss experienced by many Grand Forks residents. Although my in-laws gave up their house voluntarily, for others there was no choice. Low-lying areas along the Red River would be converted into green space to restore a natural floodplain. The homes would be condemned, bought by the city, and razed.

We walked around Lincoln Park, one of these doomed, deserted neighborhoods, and saw an eerie landscape. Like a scene out of a post-apocalyptic science fiction movie, block after block of tidy, suburban-style homes, the embodiment of the American Dream, all of them damaged but many still upright, stood silent and boarded up. On many of the condemned houses, the owners had spray-painted messages, epitaphs for an existence washed away. One house bore a message all the more poignant because of its simplicity: THIS WAS A HOME.

I thought of those houses and their exiled inhabitants when in August 2005 large sections of the Gulf Coast, including New Orleans, were devastated by Hurricane Katrina. More than a million people were displaced. For many New Orleaneans, there would probably not be any home to return to as the city considered converting especially flood-prone neighborhoods into open space.

The victims of natural disasters experience an extreme form of displacement in which they are uprooted not only from a physical house and neighborhood, but also from social networks associated with these places. Displacement is not just the result of natural disasters. War, land expropriation, ethnic cleansing, and massive infrastructure projects have displaced whole populations around the world. In the United States, urban renewal programs during the 1950s, 1960s, and 1970s displaced hundreds of thousands of city dwellers, many of them African-Americans or white ethnics, and demolished historic neighborhoods throughout the country. Today, municipalities, eager to bring in private development and increase tax revenues, wield the power of eminent domain to remove homeowners and small businesses. Gentrification drives low- and moderate-income residents out of booming cities.

Displacement also occurs in a subtler way. Although individuals may not be forced out of a place they inhabit, work in, or like to visit, that place can change so radically as to become more or less unfamiliar or even hostile. This happens when employers move to another town and local prosperity is replaced by economic decline, as has happened to old industrial cities like Syracuse, New York, where I now live. It also happens when a place is ruined by natural disaster, ecological degradation, or unchecked exploitation of resources, as when clear-cutting razes an old-growth forest or when, after 9/11, parts of New York City were blanketed with potentially toxic dust and individuals felt unsafe even in the their own homes. A place can also be radically transformed when sprawl or other development eliminates historic structures, farms, forests, or natural habitats. Finally, rising global temperatures may radically alter many natural landscapes beyond recognition.

Several years ago, Helen and I were driving in my hometown of Manhasset, Long Island. I distractedly took a wrong turn and found myself on a completely unfamiliar street with expensive new homes. After a few disorienting moments, I realized with a visceral combination of shock, sorrow, and anger that we were in what had been Manhasset Woods. This was a small forest where my brother Joe and I had gone on many childhood adventures, often accompanied by our dog, Samba. Although I hadn't been to Manhasset Woods in many years and no longer even lived in Manhasset, the little forest seemed to be a given, an essential part of my town and its character. I never even thought much about who owned it or what they planned to do with it. It seemed a fixture in the landscape, an indispensable touch of wild nature in an otherwise built-out suburb. When I realized the woods were gone, I felt as if a piece of my world had been torn away from me. Manhasset has not seemed quite the same since.

Many of these examples of displacement and transformation of the landscape are manifestations of what I describe in this book as a crisis of place facing the United States and perhaps much of the rest of the world. Rampant development, unsustainable exploitation of resources, environmental degradation, and the commodification of places are ruining built and natural landscapes, disconnecting people from their surroundings, and threatening individuals' fundamental sense of place. Meanwhile, preservationists, including many environmentalists, respond with a hard-line, counterproductive stance that rejects virtually any change in the landscape. I offer an alternative to this polarized, often deadlocked politics of place by proposing a regional, democratic approach to land-use policy. Such an approach, which I call *the working landscape*, attempts to embrace, within a regional context, both the useful transformation of places—what I call *founding*—and the preservation of their character.

Like most first books by academics, this one was long in the making and grew out of my doctoral dissertation. The origins of this project in fact go all the way back to my two years at Princeton University's Woodrow Wilson School, where I received a Master in Public Affairs in 1992. There I studied domestic environmental policy and became increasingly interested in land-use issues, including the debate over logging of the old-growth forest in the Pacific Northwest, one of the main case studies in this book.

My interest in land-use issues and in the concept of place itself merged with my interest in political theory when I began a doctoral program in Harvard's Department of Government. Drawing on political theory and then geography, I began to develop a deeper conceptual understanding of place and space.

Meanwhile, my desire to write on land-use issues was enhanced by six developments, in addition to the evolving Northwest timber debate, that have profoundly shaped the content of this book. The first was the growth of the environmental justice movement, which challenged environmentalism's traditional anti-urban bias and often single-minded focus on wilderness. It brought minorities and working-class people into the environmental movement and championed a participatory democratic approach to land use. The second was the explosion of sprawl with the recent housing boom that began in the 1990s. Landscapes were obliterated with little regard for preservationist values. Communities and government seemed powerless to fend off sprawl, even as individuals mourned the loss of familiar surroundings and even as inner cities suffered disinvestment while the countryside was paved over. The third was the rise of New Urbanism, a deeply flawed but still promising approach that offers higher-density, mixed-use planning as an alternative to sprawl. The fourth was the collaborative conservation movement, an effort—based largely in the American West—to bring local environmentalists and resource interests together to democratically manage watersheds and other ecological regions and try to combine ecosystemic values with continued harvesting of resources. Fifth, there was the 9/11 tragedy, particularly the brutal attack on the World Trade Center. As someone who had worked in Lower Manhattan and had grown up just outside of New York City, the destruction of the Twin Towers affected me on a deeply personal level. Moreover, the rebuilding of Ground Zero offered me a fascinating opportunity for observing how we conceptualize place and approach land-use politics. Finally, there was Hurricane Katrina and the crisis of displacement that followed. Katrina occurred after I had completed the first draft of this book. However, one should not underestimate the significance of this event as an indication of the profound importance of place, an importance underscored by loss.

My ideas were also fundamentally shaped by a development in my own field of study. This was the rise of the environmental political theory, or EPT, community in the United States, a process with which I was closely involved. Through the work of John Meyer, Timothy Luke, and others, including myself, what had been a scattered group of scholars working outside the mainstream of political theory became a community of academics meeting regularly, sharing ideas, and profoundly influencing one another's research and teaching. Today we have both a workshop and a section at the annual meeting of the Western Political

Science Association. Our gatherings have also been joined by EPT scholars from as far away as the United Kingdom and Australia. We have, as a community of scholars, worked to reverse the scandalous neglect of environmental politics by mainstream political theorists. We have also interrogated the unexamined assumptions and principles of environmentalism, in the interests of intellectual curiosity and honesty and out of a desire to generate a more philosophically robust basis for ecological responsibility. This critical stance underlies the arguments in this book.

All of the aforementioned experiences, issues, events, and intellectual threads have found their way into this volume. However, what has shaped this book even more profoundly is the incredible support and assistance I have received from so many people over so many years. Since the roots of this book go back to my time at Princeton, I would like to thank the instructors there who nurtured my interest in environmental and land-use politics: Clinton Andrews, Hal Feiveson, Frank von Hippel, Michael Danielson, Steve Brechin, and especially Julian Wolpert, who gave me enormous encouragement and got me interested in geography. At Harvard as well I received invaluable assistance, support, and criticism from my instructors. I am especially indebted to my dissertation committee. Dennis Thompson was my intellectual conscience, steering me away from excessive jargon and toward focus and philosophical rigor. Jill Frank was a thorough, careful reader and commentator who encouraged me to develop concepts and principles out of my case studies rather than try to fit the case studies to predetermined ideas. Jill was also a mentor who provided an enormous amount of advice on writing a dissertation, navigating the job market, and combining parenthood with an academic career. Michael Sandel, my committee chair, has been an intellectual inspiration since my undergraduate days. His constant enthusiasm for my project meant a great deal. My entire approach in both the dissertation and the book is ultimately indebted to his guidance as my advisor and to his civic republican perspective on politics and society. Faculty members Bonnie Honig and Pratap Mehta, each of whom ran the Department of Government's political theory colloquium, also provided valuable commentary on selected chapters that I presented. Finally, I owe thanks to my former undergraduate advisor, Claire Laporte, who urged me to stay in graduate school during my stressful first year.

I also benefited tremendously from the unparalleled intellectual environment and nurturing camaraderie provided by my fellow graduate students, many of whom made specific comments on my work. Here I would like to especially thank Michaele Ferguson, Sharon Krause, Patchen Markell, Sankar Muthu, Ben Berger, Chris Willemsen, Jennifer Pitts, Andy Sabl, Tamara Metz, Danielle Allen, and Thad Williamson. Michaele deserves special mention as a generous, loyal friend and a constant intellectual foil throughout my graduate days and over the years since. I also owe a good deal to my 1997–98 graduate fellowship at Harvard's Edmond J. Safra Foundation Center for Ethics. There I had a wonderful, challenging year of heady seminars with the other graduate fellows—Nien-he Hsieh, Samantha Power, Evan Charney, and Angela Smith—and with the director of the graduate fellowship, Arthur Applbaum.

While writing the dissertation, I also greatly benefited from the willingness of Michael Anderson of the Wilderness Society, Jerry Franklin of the University of Washington, Linda Hagen of the U.S. Small Business Administration, Nels Hanson of the Washington Farm Forestry Association, John Poppino of the Oregon Small Woodlands Association, and Rex Storm of Associated Oregon Loggers to answer my many questions about forestry.

My transition from graduate student to professional academic was in large part facilitated by my fellow EPT scholars, who showed interest in my work long before I even had a complete dissertation draft. I am particularly indebted to those who read and commented on numerous bits and pieces of the dissertation and book (often in the form of conference papers): John Meyer, David Schlosberg, John Barry, Tim Luke, Harlan Wilson, Sheri Breen, Kim Smith, Kerry Whiteside, Robyn Eckersley, Bill Chaloupka, Amy Lovecraft, Bob Paehlke, Susan Liebell, Joe Bowersox, Joel Kassiola, Breena Holland, Sandra Hinchman, David Camacho, and Mark Brown. John Meyer, a good friend, has provided especially valuable comments as well as career advice. He, David Schlosberg, and John Barry deserve special thanks for having read through the entire first draft of this book and offering voluminous and enormously helpful comments. This book also shows the profound influence of their scholarship. I cannot thank the three of them enough. Tim Luke, Harlan Wilson, Kerry Whiteside, Robyn Eckersley, Bill Chaloupka, and Joel Kassiola, senior scholars in EPT, have been important mentors. Tim also prodded me to read more geography. Kim Smith deserves special mention for always urging me to be more productive and for enriching my perspective on place through her own innovative scholarship.

Several colleagues at Hamilton College and at the College of William and Mary have also graciously read sections of this work and offered comments along the way: Margie Thickstun, Joel Schwartz, Rob Martin, Steve Orvis, Nick Tampio, Carlos Yordan, and Mike Tierney. Thanks also go to my students whose research projects over the years exposed me to new dimensions of the politics of place: Bob Diehl, Carla Fabrizi, Brian Alward, Marian Lyman, Amara McCarthy, Matt Marks, Nick Mirick, James Pulliam, Jennifer Rose, Noelle Short, Elena Filekova, Andrew Graham, Toby Nanda, Jonathon Peros, and Emily Wasley. Peter Oppenheimer, my oldest friend, regularly e-mailed me articles relevant to my project. Special thanks go to Dawn Woodward for handling the enormous task of photocopying and mailing drafts of the book. Our babysitters Pamela Montressor and Arlayne Searle have been saviors in freeing up time for me to complete this project.

At MIT, I would like to thank the environmental and political science acquisitions editor, Clay Morgan, for his comments, his faith in my project, and his infinite patience in dealing with my infinite missed deadlines. I would also like to thank Senior Editor Katherine Almeida for her own patience and for guiding the book through the production process, my copy editor, Ruth Haas, for her innumerable and invaluable substantive and stylistic comments, and Bob Gottlieb, the editor of the Urban and Industrial Environments series, for his comments on my prospectus.

Turning to those nearest and dearest to me, anything I say will be inadequate for all they have done, but I will try my best. My parents, Salvator and Gaetana, instilled in me a love of ideas and of nature and an unwillingness to accept injustice in the world. Both of them, who are educators, bear a good deal of responsibility for my financially unwise interest in an academic career. They are still a constant source of encouragement. My sister Fran and my brother Joe have been loving siblings, inspirations in terms of character and professional accomplishment, and intellectual partners who have shaped my ideas and values in subtle ways that I probably won't ever fully appreciate. Fran, who lives in the Boston area, was a selfless rock during my graduate school years, even using her

day off from work to babysit my daughter Maja and free up some productive time for me when our nanny took several weeks off. She, along
with my brother-in-law Tom and their children Tad and Kate, always
welcomed me into their home, had me over for innumerable dinners,
and helped me out during the numerous small crises of graduate school,
whether it was a shortage of cash or of self-confidence. My in-laws, Phil
and Trudy Jacoby, were also loving and supportive. My mother-in-law
Trudy deserves special thanks for having actually read through the enormous tome that was the dissertation; she has been looking forward to the
book version. Phil passed away quite suddenly in 2001. I will forever
miss him and also miss his willingness to challenge me on my decidedly
un-libertarian views on property rights.

Finally, to my wife, Helen Jacoby, and my daughters, Maja and Pier-
ina ("Peri"), I dedicate this book. Their love has sustained me throughout. Helen has gone the extra distance many, many times over, picking
up more than her share of household and childcare responsibilities whenever deadlines approached, even though she was often exhausted from
her busy job as a physician. She has been my most important companion
and best friend, and has used her incredibly sharp mind to push me to
refine my ideas and temper my habit of making sweeping, unfounded
generalizations. She has been with me for over twelve years of this process, since the end of my graduate coursework, and has given her enormous love and support unconditionally.

My two girls arrived during key points in the evolution of this book
and my academic career. I finished my dissertation during Maja's first
year, and Peri came along during my first year at Hamilton. Despite the
pressure of simultaneously writing a book and teaching at a liberal arts
college, I have done my best to be fully involved in their lives, from
changing diapers to preparing lunches and dinners to building snowmen
to going on hikes. The book would have probably been done a lot earlier
had I put work before family, but in return I have proudly helped two
incredibly wonderful kids grow up and have received from them a love
that has kept me grounded, put my professional life in proper perspective, and also made me powerfully aware of what this project is really
about—maintaining our direct engagement with those who share and
enliven the places that we inhabit. This engagement with our fellow
inhabitants is an important aspect of what it means to be fully human.

The Working Landscape

Introduction
The Phantom Roads of Utah

The culture of good place-making, like the culture of farming, or agriculture, is a body of knowledge and acquired skills. It is not bred in the bone, and if it is not transmitted from one generation to the next, it is lost.

—James Howard Kunstler, *The Geography of Nowhere*

What Defines Wilderness?

If you are hiking in the canyons of southern Utah and happen upon some rock with tire markings and oil stains, you are no longer in the wilderness. At least that is what some local governments in the state would like you to believe.[1] A rather curious debate arose in Utah after President Bill Clinton gave limited protection to 1.7 million acres of federal land in the state by establishing the Grand Staircase-Escalante National Monument in 1996. The debate was over what constituted a "road."

Clinton's action was unpopular in Utah. Many residents feared that the monument designation was a first step toward satisfying environmentalists' demands for even more stringent protection of 5.7 million acres in Utah.[2] Through congressional legislation, the lands could be given national park status or, even worse from the standpoint of many residents, declared federally protected wilderness, resulting in the loss of most or even all economic uses of the land.

Local governments and Utah's congressional delegation, arguing that the federal Wilderness Act of 1964 defined wilderness as roadless, claimed that lands potentially slated for wilderness designation were already traversed by thousands of roads. Environmentalists, surveying the supposed roads, argued that many were no more than cattle paths, disturbed ground left by offroad vehicles, or footpaths. Determined to reinforce their claims of a vast road network, local officials, the *New York Times* reported, began to "send out bulldozers to widen some of the trails into roads."[3]

The use of creative but bizarre contrivances to exploit legal loopholes is nothing new. Neither is conflict over resource and wilderness issues, especially in the American West. In fact, what is interesting about the phantom roads of Utah is how the seemingly unusual tactics of calling a trail a road to prevent a wilderness designation are so thoroughly unsurprising. County officials in Utah were simply taking advantage of how American culture commonly defines "wilderness."

The Wilderness Act defines "wilderness" as existing "in contrast with those areas where man and his own works dominate the landscape." A wilderness area is one "where the earth and its community of life are untrammeled by man, where man himself is a visitor who does not remain," a place that, among other things, "generally appears to have been affected primarily by the forces of nature, with the imprint of man's work substantially unnoticeable" (section 2, paragraph c).

Certainly, a rude trail does not "dominate the landscape"; county officials also based their arguments and road improvements on federal law that allows private rights-of-way over established roads going through public land. Of course, this does not resolve the question of whether these trails are indeed roads. There is also a deeper issue here: Why might the barest hint of a road in any way disqualify an area from being considered as "wilderness"? Relatedly, why does the Wilderness Act draw such a hard distinction between the domain of human beings and the domain of nature?

The Wilderness Act, the environmentalists and Clinton administration officials who sought to preserve the Utah canyonlands, and Utah's opponents of wilderness status all subscribe to an infamous distinction, that between "nature"—as in biological, ecological, and geophysical systems, entities, and relationships unchanged by human action—and "culture"—the relationships, things, and ideas created by human beings. I introduce this distinction as a prelude to a related distinction that forms a key theme of this book.

The nature–culture distinction has been vigorously challenged in recent decades in both the social sciences and the humanities. More recently, critics have challenged the continued reliance on this distinction in environmental thought and ideology.[4] A number of environmental historians and social and political theorists have pointed out that the natural and the cultural are thoroughly intermixed—especially given the profound influence that human beings have exerted on the biosphere—and that trying to untangle them is to make untenable distinctions in our lived experience. Yet the nature–culture divide persists in popular environmental discourse and contemporary environmental policy debates, as the events in Utah indicate. The existence or nonexistence of a road somehow defines a place as either culture or nature, with no middle category.

I do not want to rehearse the debate over the nature–culture dichotomy. I bring it up because I am interested in another, somewhat related distinction that is much less studied but that is also implicit in the debate about Utah's "roads." What I have in mind is the distinction between two ways of interacting with our spatial environment, i.e., with the places around us. In her discussion of how we interact with the places we call home, Iris Marion Young identifies two activities, founding and preservation.[5] Here, I would like to elaborate on her framework and develop a more systematic account of how founding and preservation apply to places and to what I call "the practice of place."

Founding and Preservation

We can found places—i.e., create new places or significantly change existing ones—or we can preserve places—i.e., refrain from altering places or perhaps maintain them according to some notion of their defining character. Often we think of these two activities as fundamentally opposed: founding promotes change and preservation promotes stability. Land-use politics, including environmental politics, upholds this notion of an opposition between founding and preservation. This is why it is so unsurprising that officials in Utah decided to conjure up a bunch of roads. The roads define the difference between two incompatible approaches to land use. If there are no roads, the canyonlands are still wilderness and can be preserved in an "untrammeled" state. Once there are roads, though, the land has been opened up to resource extraction and land development; i.e., to founding. It is no longer eligible for preservation because it has lost its original character and is now in the process of being altered. It must go into some other category besides wilderness, the domain of that which is both natural and preserved. Perhaps that other category is "civilization" or something more specific, like "real estate." Land in this category is available as a resource or commodity that can be developed with relatively little regard for its ecological value.

Journalist Michael Pollan writes, "Essentially we have divided our country in two, between the kingdom of wilderness, which rules about 8 percent of America's land, and the kingdom of the market, which rules the rest." We preserve pristine wild places, while the rest of our landscape is "written off as fallen, lost to nature" and handed "over to the jurisdiction of that other sacrosanct American ethic: laissez-faire economics."[6] To paraphrase, wilderness is the domain of preservation and the market is the domain of founding. We can either preserve or found, but we can't do both to the same place.

The conflict between founding and preservation might then seem to be just another conflict between culture and nature. After all, my examples seem to show that that which is part of civilization, or culture, is worked on, changed, i.e., founded and refounded by human beings, while that which is considered part of nature is meant to be kept from human interference and preserved. This is a view to which many people subscribe. It is interesting, though, that issues of founding versus preservation go beyond traditional environmental politics and also apply to controversies over built places.

For example, in the Battle Road section of Minuteman National Historical Park in Massachusetts, the National Park Service has erased virtually all marks of history since the Battle of Concord in 1775 so as to recreate the landscape of the Revolutionary era. To many, this has meant eradicating a rich legacy of 200 years and creating a glorified theme park.[7] To the Park Service, it has meant a restorative effort to preserve the area's essential but threatened character, which is as a landscape of the American Revolution. The later buildings did not "taint" Minuteman Park enough to disqualify it from preservation, as the roads threatened to do with the Utah canyons, but the offending structures could not remain. The Park Service has tried to create an island of strict preservation, a frozen snapshot of 1775. The region around the park, which also has great historical significance, enjoys little or no protection and has experienced an eruption of development and sprawl that has seriously threatened the area's character. The park boundary is thus one between founding and preservation.

A distinction between founding and preservation maps onto the distinction between culture and nature to the degree that both distinctions contrast the altered and the given. However, as the example of Minuteman National Park suggests, the distinction between founding and preservation can also apply to built or settled landscapes. Yet it is no more valid to establish separate realms for founding and preservation than it is to radically separate culture and nature.

In this book I argue that the presumed incompatibility between founding and preservation presents a serious obstacle to resolving land-use disputes and is a major cause of these disputes. In my discussion, I focus on land-use politics and conceptions of place in the United States, although my discussion is certainly applicable to other parts of the industrialized and developing worlds. I contend that in the United States, an overemphasis on founding to the exclusion of preservation has led to land-use approaches that are destructive of particular places and important social and ecological values associated with these places. The response to such land-use problems has often been of a hard-line preservationist variety, rejecting any alteration of the landscape as illegitimate. The result is a tug-of-war between founding and preservation.

There are some serious casualties in this conflict. Democratic deliberation among competing interests over land use is undermined because each side argues for either founding or preservation without compromise and cannot afford to give opposing voices a hearing.

More fundamentally, the initial overemphasis on founding and the ensuing either/or conflict between founding and preservation threaten an important human activity, the practice of *place*. This is the practice through which we conceptually and/or physically reconstruct our spatial environment into coherent, distinctive locales, or places. It is inevitable that the practice of place is an arena of conflict because the character and configuration of places are always subject to debate as different parties approach places from different perspectives. However, the current conflict in our land-use politics also involves a distortion of the practice of place.[8]

Although founding and preservation seem to be incompatible, both are integral to the practice of place. All places are founded. In other words, all places are human creations in that we must at least interpret, if not reconstruct, what is given by nature. Human beings do not invent the physical, spatial world, but we pick out features that define particular places and draw boundaries to distinguish one place from other places; this is true even when we identify places in a wilderness landscape. We also found places in more concrete ways. We physically alter the landscape, for example, by cultivating a field or building structures or roads.

At the same time, we found places in the expectation that they will be lasting. Young emphasizes that after founding a home, there comes the work of homemaking, of maintaining or preserving one's abode. We want homes and other places to provide enduring, reliable functions or uses. Moreover, some places may have special ecological, historical, or cultural significance that would be destroyed if these places changed too much. Other places may provide a basis for community or family life, religious worship, social rituals, political practices, or economic relationships. In some cases, places may be so important to an individual or community that their preservation takes on a profound moral importance. Finally, we also rely on places to provide enough coherence and stability in our spatial environment so that we can reliably navigate our surroundings and understand the spatially mediated relationships connecting us with our physical environment—both natural and built—and with one another. Therefore, we must in some measure preserve what we have founded.

Yet preservation is never absolute. Although we might preserve significant aspects of particular places, we also alter our environment to suit our changing needs, values, and ends. Protecting places from all change would be an exercise in geographic taxidermy; it would render places lifeless. Therefore, over time, we change the character or dimensions of places to a greater or lesser degree. In some cases we may even create entirely new places where the old ones once stood.

The total prevention of change, even if we desired it, is not possible. For example, efforts by federal and state forest managers in the twentieth century to prevent or put out forest fires created conditions for even greater changes and damage. The attempts to stop a regularly occurring natural disturbance led to the build-up of fuels and contributed to severe and extensive conflagrations. In other words, ecological as well as social forces change places even when we want these places to stay exactly as they are. As changes occur, we need to adapt to the new landscapes that emerge. Adaptation may even entail creating or delineating new places in the landscape. Yet despite all of these changes, we still seek some stability in our spatial environment.

Over time then, we both alter and maintain all places, although the balance between change and stability will vary from place to place. Furthermore, we do not simply found and then preserve, but are always changing and preserving different aspects of a place. Founding and preservation exist in a dynamic tension and balance. The practice of place thus involves both founding and preservation. Even though these two activities are inevitably in tension, they are both necessary to the practice of place. They must be integrated so that they constantly interact. To privilege either founding or preservation to the exclusion of the other is to create a dysfunctional relationship with our spatial environment. To try to compromise between founding and preservation, say by dividing the landscape between them, is also problematic. Founding and preservation are distinct, yet they must both be present and must exist in a kind of dynamic interplay and tension.

In the United States we see a destructive, unrestrained pursuit of founding, an endeavor nourished by political and intellectual currents peculiar to modernity and postmodernity. Over the past century, governments, developers, property owners, and investors have abruptly altered or erased places without regard to their ecological and social significance and complexity. They have created a landscape that is increasingly bereft of stability and also emptied of complex meaning, one that is akin to abstract space and is alienating and illegible to those inhabiting it. While founding is an essential human activity, this is a narrow, crude, even debased form of founding. It does not aim to create something lasting, but to transform the landscape for short-term financial or political gain. A good founder, by contrast, must also be a preservationist.

The response to this debased, short-sighted approach to founding has been an uncompromising preservationism on the part of many, although certainly not all environmentalists, as well as other opponents of development and other founding activities. Rather than trying to balance and integrate founding and preservation, antidevelopment forces, motivated by an understandable desire to protect the proverbial "last great places" have drawn a hard line on further changes in the landscape or have offered rigid blueprints for future land-use management. Both sides, the "founders" and the preservationists, have advanced uncompromising agendas that have left little room for mutual engagement or deliberation. The resulting either/or polarization between founding and preservation overlooks the complexity of human beings' relationship to their surroundings and leads political actors to articulate simplistic, unreasonable, divisive, rigid, and thus intolerant and antidemocratic positions.

This may help explain the intractability of land-use politics in the United States. Daniel Kemmis remarks that in conflicts between environmentalists and resource interests in the American West, "the parties have the power to veto each other's initiatives, but none has the ability to create successful initiatives."[9] The deadlock in part stems from mobilization and countermobilization by environmentalists and backlash forces like the Wise Use movement, and from the pendulum swings in national politics that lend support first to one side and then the other. The two sides are sufficiently matched to drag out the conflict, although prodevelopment interests arguably have the upper hand in terms of political and economic power. The conflict is also bogged down by ideological deadlock. The antagonists in these debates are so ideologically polarized between founding and preservation that they are often unable to offer anything but diametrically opposed views and impossible dilemmas for land-use policy or, at best, unsatisfying compromises that partition the landscape.

Summary of the Book

The aim of this book is twofold: First, I criticize contemporary land-use practices and politics and their problematic orientation to the practice of place. I argue that contemporary approaches to land use have generated a crisis of place.[10] Although I criticize the extremes of both founding and preservation, most of my criticism is aimed at the former extreme. It is an excessive, crude approach to founding that has precipitated the crisis of place and done the most direct violence to places. The preservationist response has heightened the crisis by creating ideological deadlock and preventing constructive solutions.

I should acknowledge here that I am somewhat defending preservation as the neglected half of the duo. This defense of preservation also derives from an additional concern that I briefly touch on in this book. I am concerned about a tendency I have observed among my fellow academics, particularly those who, like me, identify themselves as political progressives. They tend to disparage notions of preservation and stability as static and reactionary, and consider attributing value to a place as a dangerous launching pad for parochialism; exclusion; and even racism, violence, and genocide (see chapters 1 and 5). When I presented earlier versions of the chapters that form this book at academic conferences, I often found myself almost apologizing for my defense of preservation.

This antipreservationism in the academy may be the result of a rootlessness that comes with chasing teaching jobs around the country or around the world. Or it may come from a healthy awareness of how attempts to draw boundaries and assign places have led to rank inequalities and unchallenged tyrannies. Certainly the preservationist defense of place-based stability is not without its dangers. Defense of place *can* promote exclusion, parochialism, reactionary values, and even ethnic cleansing and violence.

Nevertheless, attachment to some place, together with some measure of stability in our spatial environment, is necessary for a fully human life. We are physical, embodied beings who need to navigate, make sense of, and feel some measure of security in our spatial world. We need some enduring coherence in our environment and we need to have some familiar, comfortable places that we call "home." Otherwise, it becomes difficult to make sense of our surroundings, our relationships with others, and even our own identities. Our existence becomes rootless and we feel alienated in some measure from our own physical environment. The traumatic impacts of displacement on the hundreds of thousands of victims of Hurricane Katrina in the fall of 2005 are testimony to what happens when one loses one's home and one's place. Finally, I would argue that the exclusionary, repressive abuses of preservationism can be avoided, not by disdaining preservation per se, but by pursuing democratic processes that give voice to all inhabitants and users of a place and to all perspectives on that place.

This leads me to my second main objective, which is to offer a theoretical and practical approach to place that can get us beyond the crisis of founding and preservation. This framework, which I term "the working landscape," embraces both founding and preservation and also calls for more democratic governance of places. One might see similarities between my approach and the notion of sustainable development or, even more so, what green political theorist John Barry terms "collective ecological management."[11]

In chapter 1 I begin by investigating the meaning of place, both as a thing and as a practice. I draw upon geography and political and social philosophy. I discuss the relationship between founding and preservation and how both are necessary to the practice of place. I also defend place against views that the concept is becoming obsolete in an era of globalization and information technology. At the same time I acknowledge that the practice of place is indeed threatened, but emphasize that this is a troubling, unwelcome development. I discuss this crisis more fully in chapter 5.

In chapters 2–4 I begin my critique of contemporary land-use practices and politics through three case studies. These are (1) the debate over logging versus preservation of old-growth forests in the Pacific Northwest; (2) the problem of sprawl; and (3) the rebuilding of New York City's former World Trade Center site, or Ground Zero, after the terrorist attack of September 11, 2001. The three case studies show how today's problematic approach to place plays out in a variety of settings—wilderness, the urban/suburban/rural interface, and the urban built environment—and in three prominent land-use issues today.

The first case study, the Northwest forest debate, starkly shows the contemporary conflict between founding and preservation as timber interests and environmentalists square off over whether to log what many regard as a magnificent wilderness, the last remnants of the region's old-growth forests. Each side's understanding of humanity's relationship with forests and with nature in general encourages an uncompromising embrace of either founding or preservation. At the same time, the opposing perspectives in the logging debate are complex enough to suggest some important underlying commonalities between the opposing sides and the possibility of transcending the founding–preservation dichotomy and developing a better approach to place.

The second case, the issue of sprawl, also shows a conflict between founding and preservationist perspectives. More important, the issue highlights the consequences that an unrestrained, crude, commodity-oriented founding can have for both our built and our rural landscapes and, more fundamentally, our ability to understand and navigate our spatial environment. The response to sprawl often takes the form of either extreme preservationist antigrowth movements or, more recently, New Urbanism and its unsatisfactory combination of extreme founding and extreme preservationism.

The third case, Ground Zero, presents another conflict between founding and preservation. Those who want to redevelop the former World Trade Center site as commercial office space to maximize financial revenue are engaged in a crude, narrow, founding endeavor, one that shows commonalties with the Twin Towers' original construction. On the other hand, the friends and family of the 9/11 victims have overemphasized preservation. They have understandably argued that memorializing 9/11 and its victims should more or less determine land use at the site. It thus seems that the resulting landscape will be an unsatisfying partition between the two camps. However, there has been a third, more promising constituency in play, one that attempts to both balance and integrate founding and preservation. This group, composed of local residents and civic groups, has tried to create a mixed-use neighborhood that also memorializes 9/11, a neighborhood with a healthy combination of life and remembrance. However, this third group has to a considerable degree been marginalized, in part because of the lack of a truly democratic redevelopment process.

Chapter 5 returns to the crisis of place introduced in chapter 1. I outline how place has been undermined in the modern era by philosophical, political, and economic perspectives and practices that push founding to destructive extremes. Since roughly the seventeenth century, places have been simplified into something a bit closer to abstract space, turned into commodities, destroyed and reassembled almost at will, and ultimately threatened with obsolescence by electronic communication networks. I present the environmental movement as a leading defender of the value of place. However, I also point out an overly preservationist strain among some environmentalists. My main example is the bioregionalism advocated by Kirkpatrick Sale.[12] One of my fundamental criticisms is that such environmentalists see the human founding of places as almost an illegitimate interference with nature's order and instead urge us to discover a preexisting geography in nature. This emphasis on discovery rather than founding is fundamentally at odds with how human beings actually inhabit the world.

In chapter 6 I argue for regional, democratic governance as the best framework for integrating founding and preservation. Regional government, on the level of a watershed or metropolitan area, best fits the geographic scale at which a high density of important human and ecological relations are carried out. It is best able to capture externalities between neighboring communities, overcome the disempowerment of local communities that results from municipal fragmentation, and bring together and coordinate a diversity of places, perspectives, and demographic groups in a way that can promote comprehensive, long-term land-use planning that integrates founding and preservation. I also maintain that a regional approach, or any approach for integrating founding and preservation, must be based on democratic processes, including elected regional government, and offer some scope for democratic participation at the local or neighborhood level. A democratic approach to land use, which has largely been absent even in ostensibly democratic societies, is necessary because it better enables a broad range of constituencies and views, including those more inclined to either founding or preservation, to enter public debate and help shape a more balanced, integrated approach to place. Governance structures that exclude democratic deliberation are much more to likely to push a radical founding or preservationist agenda.

The concept of an elected regional government admittedly remains a controversial idea that has been fully tried in only one place in the United States, the Portland, Oregon, metropolitan region, and even here, as I discuss, regionalism is now profoundly threatened. However, despite these obstacles, regionalism is increasingly favored by many academics, activists, and policy makers.[13] My own work underscores the attractiveness of regional government by arriving at regionalism from the ground up, i.e., through an analysis and defense of place as an important practice and through consideration of the requirements for a successful practice of place.

The final substantive chapter, chapter 7, presents a set of specific policy recommendations for the working landscape. Although I am critical of the dominant approaches to the practice of place, there are nevertheless a number of promising initiatives in the political arena. These can be found in the work of public officials, nonprofits, activists, and new environmental political movements like collaborative conservation and environmental justice. These initiatives are dispersed throughout the political and policy arenas, but they can be gathered into an agenda for the three landscape types that reflect my three case studies and are themselves essential elements of the regional landscape: wilderness and rural areas, the urban/suburban/rural interface, and cities.

Finally, I conclude with an admittedly somber postscript. Drawing upon the experience of Hurricane Katrina in the fall of 2005, I argue that any attempt to rescue the practice of place is ultimately contingent on a solution to another problem, that of global climate change. Katrina's aftermath of exile and homelessness for many Gulf Coast residents may be a preview of a more generalized worldwide crisis of displacement if we do not try to mitigate climate change now.

The quote by James Howard Kunstler at the beginning of this introduction points to a seeming paradox in our contemporary relationship with our spatial environment. We continue to create places, but increasingly lead a "placeless" existence. Our places themselves promote placelessness. What can it mean to speak of placeless places? What Kunstler is saying is that we can create places in a nominal sense, but that this does not make us good practitioners of place. There are better and worse ways of creating places, and the better ways, I would argue, balance and integrate founding and preservation and involve the democratic participation of the affected community. Our crisis of place may be traceable to the decline of the practice of place. This book was written in the hope that a better understanding of the practice of place might help us to overcome this crisis.

1

Place: Founding and Preservation

The Obsolescence of Place?

It has become almost a truism nowadays to speak of the decisive conquest of time and space by globalization and the information age. Terms and phrases like "deterritorialization," "time-space compression,"[1] and the "end of geography"[2] are the order of the day. Human activity is increasingly defined in terms of networks and flows rather than locations.[3] Organizational, cultural, and other social formations leapfrog geographic boundaries and distances. We have, the familiar argument goes, entered a new era, indeed a new stage of human evolution, in which physical location is becoming profoundly irrelevant.

The institutions and transactions of global capital are dissolving the coherence, distinctiveness, and stability of individual places. The nation-state as a territorial unit is itself under assault from numerous, decentered, nonstate actors and forces.[4] The exercise of political and economic power has less and less to do with physical proximity. Communities of interest based on lifestyle, age, profession, and ideology are taking precedence over communities of place.[5] Finally, human activity is increasingly conducted in the dematerialized, deterritorialized, virtual world of cyberspace.

The elimination of time and space constraints has literally transformed the fabric of daily life. Geographer John Rennie Short remarks, "One of my suits was designed by Italians, made in Yugoslavia from Australian wool and sold by a Swedish company with outlets across Europe and North America."[6] The diverse origins of Short's suit only seem to underline the meaninglessness of the individual locales where it was assembled. Physical place, the argument goes, has become obsolete.

Peter Gordon and Harry Richardson exult, "The revolution in information processing and telecommunications is accelerating the growth and dispersion of both economic activities and population, possibly moving towards the point where 'geography is irrelevant'." They note that "[r]apid advances in telecommunications are now accelerating the decentralization trends set in motion by the advent of the automobile." The authors conclude, "Proximity is becoming redundant."[7]

Of course, not all manifestations of the "end of geography" could be deemed even remotely positive. The terrorist attacks of September 11, 2001 on the World Trade Center and the Pentagon may have been the quintessential symbol of time-space compression. Mohamed Atta, one of the ringleaders of the Al Qaeda attacks of September 11, 2001, was born in Cairo, carried a Saudi passport, studied urban planning in Hamburg, trained as a terrorist in Afghanistan, went to flight school in Florida, plotted with fellow 9/11 hijackers in Spain, New Jersey, Nevada, and Maryland, and flew from Portland, Maine, to board American Airlines flight 11 in Boston and then crash it into the North Tower of New York City's World Trade Center. In fact, in just the fifteen months leading up to the World Trade Center attack, Atta managed to visit, among other places, Prague; Madrid; Norman, Oklahoma; Virginia Beach; Boston; New York City; Las Vegas; Portland, Maine; and various locales in New Jersey, Maryland, Georgia, and Florida.

On 9/11, the lives, ideologies, and actions of Atta and his fellow terrorists collided with almost three thousand doomed people in the northeastern United States, many of whom were employed in channeling capital through global investment networks or in projecting American military might around the world. The terrorists' weapon of choice was the preeminent symbol of international mobility, the jetliner. Doomed passengers on airplanes or occupants of the World Trade Center were able to use cell phones and e-mails to communicate with loved ones miles away, even though they faced imminent death in their trapped bodies. In the aftermath of 9/11, the United States dispatched military forces, not to fend off invaders on American shores, but to distant places like Afghanistan, Iraq, Somalia, and the Philippines. One can go even further in seeing 9/11 as symbolic of time-space compression: Oil revenues made Saudi Arabia a leading source of funding for terrorism.[8] The use of oil and other fossil fuels is warming the Earth and, among other impacts, rapidly melting sea ice and glaciers in the Arctic and profoundly disrupting the region's cultures.[9] In understanding 9/11, it seems to be not so much a matter of the proverbial connecting of the dots as it is of there no longer being any separate dots at all.

Even if we were to focus strictly on the positive aspects of time-space compression, we would still be hard pressed to speak of the "end of geography" as a peaceful event. In fact, it is profoundly jarring. As geographer David Harvey has remarked, we are living in a period of considerable disruption in the relationship between human beings and the places around them.[10] One might speak, as I did in the introduction, of a contemporary crisis of place.

To characterize a situation as disruptive or call it a crisis is not necessarily to condemn it. One might welcome placelessness as a necessary, even if unsettling, transition. From this standpoint, any attempt to cling to the importance of place, whether as a condition or a value, is at best nostalgic and at worst reactionary. This view does not mean embracing terrorism or climate change. However, it does mean embracing the technological and social changes that have made possible the fatal journeys of Atta and his accomplices and have enabled the transport of massive amounts of oil from the Middle East and elsewhere for environmentally destructive combustion in Americans' sport utility vehicles.

Among those who welcome placelessness, at least two views are prevalent in the academy. The first is a market-oriented, information age utopianism reflected in Gordon and Richardson's vision of technological liberation from geography.[11] The second view is associated with postmodernism. Postmodernists tend to reject narratives of technological progress or deliverance, but they do see placelessness, dislocation, mobility, or nomadism as liberating. Geographer Tim Cresswell observes, "Place, roots, and authenticity are hardly the favored characteristics of postmodern theorists. Indeed, postmodernist worlds are worlds in which nothing is certain or fixed, and where fixity appears, it is as an illusion."[12] Notions of place as fundamental to human experience run afoul of the antiessentialist, postmodern view of the self as a fragmented, unstable collection of traits and attachments, none having any necessary priority in the construction of individual identity. To favor place as a value is to challenge the freedom, openness, and multiplicity of the self that comes with mobility, with being nomadic.

To postmodernists, the affirmation of stable, coherent places and geographically rooted identities is nostalgic, reactionary, and dangerous. To them, the yearning for place is a misguided quest for clear, policed boundaries to community; for depoliticized social unity; for "authentic" locales and communities with uncontested, static meanings; and for the exclusion of outside influences and internal and external differences.[13]

However, it is hard to ignore the value of place and physical proximity. Spatial proximity, physical presence, and existence in a shared place afford myriad interactions that help sustain friendships, sexual relationships, families, communities, workplaces, teams, activist networks, and religious congregations. Individuals who are connected only remotely, through print or mass media or cyberspace, cannot provide one another with the physical dimensions of companionship; with the subtle visual cues of facial expression and body language; with a common shared sense of membership in a locality; or with help at a moment's notice when the power goes out, when someone is injured, when one needs to borrow a tool, or when one has to run an errand and needs someone trustworthy to watch the kids.

Reid Ewing, responding to Gordon and Richardson, argues that "electronic communications are (and probably always will be) imperfect substitutes for the kind of rapid face-to-face communications made possible by cities. There is a texture and subtlety to face-to-face exchanges that cannot be reproduced electronically."[14] Even software developer and information age guru Esther Dyson comments on the continued primacy of "the community of physical presence" over electronic interactions like telecommuting, which she sees as "overrated": "in the end, people like physical proximity ... you need the body language, you need the bandwidth, and whether it's just pheromones or what have you ... we're still human beings. We're still physical."[15]

Furthermore, in order to function in our spatial surroundings and effectively interact with other persons and other organisms that share our physical space, our surroundings must in some measure be stable, coherent, and legible. We must be able to make sense of and navigate the places around us. We must even be able to feel at home and grounded in, and identify with, a few special places that we inhabit, work in, or frequently visit.

Certainly, physical location does not define the totality of human activities and self-perceptions. However, to deny the importance of place is to indulge in absurdity, to overlook what it means to be an embodied human being. To the degree that place and proximity remain fundamental to human existence, contemporary threats to place are deeply troubling. At risk is our ability to comprehend, navigate, and feel connected to the physical, spatial world.

A number of writers recognize the importance of place and the danger inherent in the crisis of place. Castells sees the "space of places" as threatened by the "space of flows". In other words, the global realm of information and capital flows is disrupting place-based and historically situated social relationships, yet he also maintains that physical location remains a central determinant of the lives of the overwhelming majority of humanity.[16] He consequently describes a disturbing, schizophrenic dissonance between individuals' lived experience in physical place and the increasing (un)reality of their lives being structured by globalized interactions over which they have little control and with which they have little tangible connection. Castells sees in contemporary politics an attempt, with both positive and negative implications, to defend place-based connections, activities, and identities against such a threat.[17]

Harvey speaks of "a quest for visible and tangible marks of identity . . . in the midst of fierce space-time compression" and notes that "there is still an insistent urge to look for roots in a world where image streams accelerate and become more and more placeless."[18] In regard to environmental problems, Mark Sagoff says, "Much of what we deplore about the human subversion of nature—and fear about the destruction of the environment—has to do with the loss of places we keep in shared memory and cherish with instinctive and collective loyalty."[19]

The contemporary crisis of placelessness does not mean that all places are being annihilated and that the world is becoming a single, undifferentiated locale. Short, rejecting the "end of geography" thesis, notes that globalization is connecting the world through economic and cultural transactions but is also magnifying differences between global cities and nearby rural areas. He notes that Sydney is becoming more like Los Angeles, but less like Australia's Outback.[20] Meanwhile, nationalism, community consciousness, and the assertion of ethnic identity push back against globalization and time-space compression.[21] Even among those areas caught up in globalization, there is differentiation as places try to market their particularities to attract investment.[22]

However, I would argue that while differentiation persists and distinct places survive, all places and place attachments are increasingly vulnerable to, and destabilized by, global forces and time-space compression, as we will see in chapter 5. Differentiation among places is increasingly a product of the increasing vulnerability of places as they market themselves to, react against, or are marginalized by globalization. We still have places, but we are losing the capacity to effectively practice place, as I will argue. Our relationships with our surroundings are being radically disrupted. Physical space is increasingly shaped by forces beyond our understanding and made incomprehensible, even alien. This is not only a cultural crisis, but also a political crisis, indeed a crisis of democracy in that it involves decisions by powerful economic and governmental actors. It is also a normative crisis in that the threat to place endangers an important human good.

Defining Place

What is place? The term *place* commonly signifies a kind of entity or object, specifically a coherent, enduring location in physical space. More precisely, a place is a physically distinct parcel of relative stability in space and time,[23] a local congealing of the flow of matter over time.[24] This parcel, need not have a proper name. It must, though, have identifiable physical characteristics that distinguish it from its surroundings. It must also have at least rough spatial bounds and persist with some continuity of character over a period of time.

A place is not simply a container for things and relationships. There is no preexisting space for the contents of a place. Rather, a place is an aggregation of things and relationships—human and nonhuman, social and ecological—that are tangibly cohering, at least for a time.[25] Without those constituents, nothing is there. The parcel *is* the contents.

Places vary in dimensions and character. They also may be built or wild. Examples of places include kitchens and planets, street corners and continents, old-growth forests and city neighborhoods.

Places are not frozen in time. They are ever-changing, the product of dynamic social and ecological interactions. Places are both the products and the spatial embodiment of these interactions. Although places are in part made up of the world's natural material, the creation and identification of something as a defined place as place is inevitably a process of social construction. Thus Henri Lefebvre speaks of the production of space. Similarly, Castells describes the spatial world as a material product, as the expression and embodiment of society.[26] The production of places, to paraphrase the title of Lefebvre's book *The Production of Space*, is a fundamental social practice, even though it engages natural systems as well.

Given that places are the creation and embodiment of social and ecological dynamics, this aggregation of things we call a place exists as a process, as Harvey emphasizes.[27] Places are temporarily created out of flows: of people; of natural and artificial objects and substances; of energy; of ecological and social relations and organizational arrangements; of cultural interpretations, symbols, and practices.[28] What we recognize as a particular place is a moment of relative stability in some of these constituents.

Coherence and Stability

Though he emphasizes the dynamic, processual character of places, Harvey also tells us that we inhabit a world not only of flows but of things.[29] Things are created by processes.[30] Our experience of the world consists of both processes and enduring, coherent things or "permanences."[31] Places themselves are things. They have "relative stability in both their bounding, and their internal ordering of processes, creating space, for a time. Such permanences come to occupy a piece of space in an exclusive way (for a time) and thereby define a place—their place—(for a time). The process of place formation is the process of carving out 'permanences' from the flow of processes creating spatio-temporality."[32] Thus, all places are in flux, but "some places are more in flux than others, and some more permanent and securely bounded than others."[33]

Places are not random collections of things that come together, but are internally differentiated objects that have some organic structure and coherence. Jane Jacobs, writing about one sort of place, a city, instructively describes it as a coherent whole of interrelated elements that presents an organized complexity.[34] Organized complexity involves myriad subtle interactions among elements and between the whole and its parts.[35] A system of organized complexity achieves a dynamic but coherent internal structure—the whole can be regarded as not only organized but as self-organizing.[36] One might speak of not only a built environment like a city but also a natural assemblage or ecosystem, for example an old-growth forest, as exhibiting organized complexity. Even a simple room or a street corner or a clearing around a tree has a certain internal structure that is defined by the relative position of objects, by how these objects and their placement affect one another, and by how the objects interact with physical forces and living organisms both inside and outside that place.

Consequently, while places are dynamic entities embedded in space and time, they have some distinct and enduring character. The concept of place is meaningless without some notion of stability, boundedness, and even structure. Allan Pred says that places involve "the material continuity both of the people who participate in that process [of place] and of any natural and humanly made objects employed in time-space specific practices."[37]

Recall that a place exists as a "moment" of stability in a larger flux. Within the flux of spatiotemporal change, certain elements remain for a while at a specific location, providing enough continuity and structure for a place to be recognized. A place's moment of existence should be long enough so that the place in question shapes our conception or map of our surroundings and/or how we repeatedly navigate those surroundings. If I stay in someone's guest room for a few days, unpack my suitcase, rearrange the furniture a bit, and put a book I am reading on the night table, I have created a new place. At the other extreme, a place's moment can last for what to us seems an eternity. Continents are recognizable places, retaining a rough stability of shape, topography, and location for long periods of time even though they ultimately change through plate tectonics. The Earth itself is a place, enduring in rough stability of form for billions of years.

Place versus Space

It is important to distinguish place from space.[38] Place is concrete and particular. Space, by contrast, is an abstract entity, pure extension and dimension. Space is quantitative, not qualitative. When we think of a parcel of space, we do not think of its particular constituents so much as its measurements. We can delineate space through geometry and quantity, dividing it into neatly defined portions. The concept of space is also marked by universality; spatial dimensions are unvarying across location. A cubic foot of space is a cubic foot of space anywhere. Yet space is purely conceptual; it does not actually exist without its contents. Lefebvre thus remarks, "Space considered in isolation is an empty abstraction."[39] We might also regard the concept of space as a conceptual foil for or negation of place, as a kind of negative ideal that places can tend toward, especially as they lose their internal richness.

Places as Embedded

Unlike a neat parcel of space, the dimensions of a particular place are often uncertain, even if we try to contain that place within jurisdictional boundaries. No place is fully self-contained and isolated from its environment.[40] Every place is embedded in a larger matrix of places. Every place is shaped by external forces. The boundaries of places are porous, ambiguous, and fluid.[41] All places interact with and in some way blend into the places around them through social and ecological relations, water and energy conduits, transport systems, and telecommunications networks.[42]

The indeterminacy of boundaries is heightened in the case of larger places. As more and more relationships interpenetrate and constitute a place, the demarcations with the rest of the world become ever more indistinct and subject to conflicting interpretation. Where does New York City begin and end? How is it distinct from its surrounding metropolitan area? From the rest of the urbanized Eastern Seaboard? Are formal political boundaries enough to define New York City? Why do people from Long Island, Westchester, and even northeastern New Jersey and southwestern Connecticut often say that they are from "New York"? Similarly, where does a forest begin? Where does an *old-growth* forest begin? What are the boundaries of the relevant ecosystem? Do these boundaries also include marine environments inhabited by anadromous fish that spend part of their lives under the protective shade of old-growth conifers?

Further complicating matters is the fact that one place will itself consist of many identifiable places. New York City consists of five boroughs and scores of neighborhoods, districts, blocks, and street corners. The forested region of the Pacific Northwest consists of a variety of individual forests, forest types, watersheds, and topographical features.

At the same time, though, for a place to have any coherence, it must have some approximate boundaries. Places are defined not just by what they embrace but by what they exclude. To see a place as entirely porous is to see no place at all, for in the extreme it has no bounds.

Finally, I should also emphasize that places are not only spatially but also temporally embedded. A place and its changes are part of a larger, dynamic story. The character and possibilities of a place inevitably reflect the historical forces that created that place.

Places as Loci of Activities, Experiences, and Values

Different places facilitate different activities and yield different experiences and values. Most obviously, places are functional; we rely upon them to satisfy needs. Yet place is most fully understood as something experienced.[43] Places, Lefebvre suggests, are the spatial form of lived experience.[44] The experience of place is of course an embodied one.[45] The structure and spatial position of our bodies shapes our experience of our surroundings.[46] Differences in bodily types—size, shape, sex, maturity, physical ability or disability—are even among the factors that produce different perspectives on places.[47]

Places generate profound experiences and elicit a variety of responses.[48] Places may instruct, delight, awe, fascinate, terrify, alienate, elicit reverence or revulsion, or embody a set of values or taboos. Places may be sublime, charming, picturesque, depressing, mysterious, sacred, nostalgic, familiar, scary, alienating, or exotic. They may reflect historical experiences or future aspirations. Places may offer a pleasing contrast to or refuge from what is around them. They may be predictable and subject to our control or they may be commanding presences that reflect, embody, or symbolize awe-inspiring forces. Or, they may even be dangerous or hostile. We often take some places, such as a warehouse, a stretch of road, or a motel room, for granted as a background for our activities. Yet even the most seemingly inconsequential place has significance for someone.[49] For a particular individual or community, some places will have special social or ecological significance, whether positive or negative. Some places we may wish to preserve or restore; others, we may want to escape or even destroy.

The positive or negative character of a particular place is frequently contested. In general, the qualities of places are subject to debate. During the era of urban renewal, what was a slum for public housing and development agencies was often a thriving urban neighborhood for its inhabitants and shopkeepers. Environmentalists honor old-growth forests with the title of "ancient," while timber interests describe such forests as "decadent." Visitors and residents also have starkly different perceptions and evaluations of a place.[50] Tourists may see a forest as a wilderness that ought to be preserved from logging, while local inhabitants might see that same forest as an important source of timber and livelihood.

The valence of a place will often change over time. The highways, concrete plazas, parking lots, and austere high rises built as proud monuments to progress during the mid-twentieth century are now for many people the architectural equivalent of a polyester leisure suit, although they are a lot harder to toss into the back of the closet or the trash. Places of dread, such as concentration camps, slave markets, and Ground Zero, because of their history, have become important symbols and artifacts in the collective life and identity of a community or people that suffered there.

Places may also provide a focal point for the expression and transmission of moral and cultural values or objectives. Wilderness can promote a love of the outdoors and aesthetic and spiritual appreciation of, and even respect for, nature. Farms can promote the virtues of hard work and personal independence. Monumental architecture may instruct or even indoctrinate. Public squares and parks may help inculcate communitarian and civic values. Commercial development may encourage consumerism. Places with dark histories may be preserved to warn of evils to be eradicated or to sustain the identity of a victimized community. In fact, places may be so important in defining one's world and identity that their significance entails a set of moral obligations regarding their care and preservation. In this case, rather than simply providing a vehicle for the transmission of values, places themselves become the objects of moral consideration. I will say more on this below.

A Map of the World

Through the activity of place and through these many responses to places, we create a stable, meaningful map in which we can feel at home.[51] To call the world "home" is not to say that we want the world itself, or every place within it, to have the same familiarity, comfort, security, or predictability as ideally is afforded by one's personal domicile. Such a world would be monotonous and overly constraining. The world should contain a diversity or plurality of places having different characters and uses and promoting different goods or values. From the standpoint of any individual or community, most of these places are unknown, perhaps alien or forbidding or frightful. They provide a horizon of challenge, contrast, and possibility and even offer resources for creatively subverting and revising that which is familiar.

What the overall map does is provide some pattern—political, cultural, geographical, and ecological—indicating how different places stand in relation to one another, even if that sets up a contrast that puts many places into the realm of the unfamiliar or unknown. One's map of the world is not without a standpoint. It is always drawn from a mental and physical vantage point.[52]

Each individual will typically have a set of places that are more or less familiar. Some of these, usually the places where one lives, works, visits often, went to school, or grew up, will be most familiar and even have the status of home. Beyond the familiar will be places that one has visited, that one knows about but has never seen, and then places that are more or less unknown. Although the map is geographic, the places on it are colored with varying sorts of meaning and significance. The map also has an implicit history. One's knowledge and impressions of places contain some story about how those places got there and evolved and about how one has related to those places over time. When a person has a strong familiarity with a particular place or set of places, including their complexity, small details, aesthetic qualities, and history, and when that person is actively involved in sustaining that place or places, we may say that that person has a strong sense of place.

What is familiar and unfamiliar on the map is only partly a function of physical proximity. In a world characterized by increased mobility, one may be much more familiar with a place many miles away than some place a few blocks down. However, in conveying where the familiar and unfamiliar places are and whether these are near or far, the map enables one to understand and navigate the proximal environment.

One's map also shapes one's sense of self by situating someone in this world and illuminating their relation to their surroundings and their relation to others who share the world. Moreover, in shaping one's sense of self, the map helps shape one's moral values and ends.[53]

The map gives the world a certain pattern and coherence. Someone making their way in the world can plan their actions and behavior in relation to that map. As one familiarizes oneself with new places while frequenting others less and less, the map changes. Some places become more prominent while others fade into unfamiliarity or take on new significance.

To return to my earlier point, with such a map one can feel at home in the world. To feel at home is to see enough familiarity, stability, security, and coherence in the world so that one can reliably pursue ends and projects and draw some guidance from one's surroundings rather than have to continuously renegotiate and make sense of them.[54] This does not require that every place be friendly or comforting or benign. In a world in which one feels at home, the unfamiliar and the challenging play a key role, by facilitating personal development, appealing to repressed parts of the self and liberating one from stifling or oppressive routines, norms, and surroundings. Furthermore, in an ecologically and socially diverse planet, most places will inevitably be unfamiliar and challenging and in many cases even dangerous and hostile. Yet one must have some spatial pattern by which to approach the unfamiliar and some secure ground from which to make forays beyond one's own horizons and frontiers.

Over time though, one may come to feel more at home in previously alien or threatening places. This may come about by visiting or residing in such places, abandoning prejudices against those living there, expanding one's moral horizons, and cultivating a greater respect for difference. Unfamiliarity or danger may also be overcome in less respectful, peaceful, or democratic ways, through conquest or the forcible suppression of difference.

However, one can never eliminate all alienness, otherness, or threat in the world's places. One can never eliminate the relative contrast between the familiar and unfamiliar. Otherwise, one's map would lose much of its coherence. In fact, inhabitants of one place, in seeking to preserve the identity of their own locale may even exaggerate or invent the threatening aspect of the world beyond their borders.

The Concept of "Home"

To feel at home in the world also requires that one have at least one place that is home in the more traditional sense, where one feels a fairly predictable familiarity and security and even a strong measure of control. Home in this sense usually pertains to one's private space, one's personal domicile. Here one can be both vulnerable and empowered. One can sleep, eat, undress, make love, go to the bathroom, wash, nurture, play, argue, and read, write, and watch whatever one likes, while excluding most unwelcome visitors or intrusions.

A home ideally provides one's most familiar, legible, and stable place. It is where we might exercise the most control and have the most security.[55] It is an indispensable resting place from the rigors of the outside world. It is a place where one can evaluate encounters with difference and danger on the outside and reflect on one's new horizons and sense of self. For Iris Marion Young, home carries a core positive meaning as the anchor for a sense of agency and a shifting and fluid identity.[56] In a somewhat similar vein, geographer Yi-Fu Tuan says that attachment to a homeland appears to be universal. "It is not limited to any particular culture and economy. It is known to literate and nonliterate peoples, hunter-gatherers, and sedentary farmers, as well as city dwellers." Such a place nourishes. It is "permanent and hence reassuring to man, who sees frailty in himself and change and flux everywhere."[57]

The condition of homelessness is so inhumane because it leaves an individual constantly and utterly exposed and vulnerable to the world. Whether living on the streets or in a shelter, the homeless person is constantly subject to the threat of crime, harassment by law enforcement agents, control by social service agencies, and hostility from passers-by.

Yet, in keeping with contemporary rejection of the value of place, the concept of home is often maligned, largely by feminist and postmodern theorists, as privileged and exclusionary of outsiders, as providing a refuge for patriarchal domestic tyranny, and as involving a false sense of security that masks troubling political questions about society at large. From this viewpoint, the longing for a relatively unproblematic *home-ground* involves the false universalization of an aspiration that is in fact available, if at all, only to those with political, economic, or sexual privilege.[58]

Certainly, home life has not lived up to the ideal I have sketched here, especially given class, race, and gender privilege.[59] For battered or dominated spouses or partners, for abused or neglected children, and for many live-in domestic workers, a domicile promises no security or empowerment and provides only vulnerability in the form of subordination. Under such conditions and for such persons, home can be a supremely threatening and destructive place, not only because of the physical danger, but also because they expect or yearn for home to be exactly the opposite and it instead becomes a cruelly false refuge. Home can also be, as critics have maintained, a way of excluding difference and enjoying material comforts and luxuries through the exploitation of outsiders who are kept away, in their own neighborhoods or countries, and are only allowed on the premises to perform labor. More recently, in the wake of 9/11, the notion of home has been used to justify a siegelike state of fear in the United States. Threats to the "homeland" have become a mantra used by President George W. Bush, other elected officials, and the right-wing media to justify a war of aggression in Iraq, the abusive treatment of military detainees and other enemy combatants, harassment or imprisonment of Muslims, and suppression of dissenting opinions.[60]

However, these abuses are not intrinsic to the concept of home. As Young argues, home can support struggles against oppressive structures and practices and be a place of liberation. Home can provide a refuge from oppressive, homogenizing cultural, economic, and political forces, a space for resistance where "different, more humane social relations can be lived or imagined," and a secure, stable ground for maintaining and nurturing one's identity and political agency.[61] Young quotes bell hooks: "Historically, African American people believed that the construction of a homeplace, however, fragile and tenuous (the slave hut, the wooden shack), had a radical political dimension. Despite the brutal reality of racial apartheid, of domination, one's homeplace was the one site where one could freely confront the issue of humanization, where one could resist."[62]

However, a conception of home as purely private space and refuge should not be exaggerated. Life even within one's home is subject to cultural and legal norms, as well as standards of health and safety.

Feminists rightly politicized home and the private sphere, challenging the protection of domestic, patriarchal tyranny that notions of privacy had provided. Furthermore, the private aspect of one's domicile does not stretch nearly as far as the legal boundaries of one's private property. Much of what we call private property is part of a larger, public network of places (recall that every place is embedded in a larger matrix of places). For example, one's front lawn and backyard and the outer walls of one's house are really an integral part of the larger neighborhood. Inspectors, meter readers, mail carriers, delivery services, schoolchildren raising money, police with warrants, and even neighbors taking a shortcut may come onto one's property. One's house, as Lefebvre notes, is also literally permeated by wires, cables, water and sewage pipes, gas lines, and broadcast signals that connect it to the outside.[63]

Moreover, many places that are often regarded as private are not so, and attempts to wall them off are deeply problematic. To extend the bounds of the private home outward to create policed, sealed-off enclaves such as gated communities is to commit a kind of violence against the broader community and its landscape.[64] The erection of gates unilaterally withdraws a piece of the landscape from the public. Such gates need not be physical. In rural areas, the enforcement of property boundaries on large landholdings can cut off long-standing public access to hunting, fishing, and recreation.

Ecological interrelationships and interdependencies indeed call into question the whole notion of land as private property. Gary Varner notes that "[i]ncreasingly, taking an ecological view of land forces us to treat it as a public resource that individuals hold only in a stewardship (or trust) capacity. Any and every piece of land is involved in diverse ecological processes, and any and every form of land use affects these processes to some extent."[65]

At the same time, one may also take a more expansive view of the bounds of one's home place. As Young observes, what one calls home may spill over into the surroundings, such as the block or neighborhood or the front stoop of one's apartment building.[66] In short, the outer boundaries of home, like most boundaries, are indistinct. However, the concept of home as domicile requires some core of personal space under the control of its inhabitants.

Place as a Practice

We have been speaking of place as a thing. We can also speak of it as an activity or practice—the practice of creating, interpreting, and maintaining places. The practice of place enables us to make sense of, and situate ourselves in, the spatial world. The very act of inhabiting, working in, visiting, or even just describing a particular place involves us in the practice of place. This is a practice in which all of us, as spatially situated, physical beings, are involved. It is also an activity that fundamentally involves the exercise of political and economic power. The practice of place is complex, and I won't try to describe it in full. I want to focus on how this practice involves two key elements, the founding of places and their preservation.[67]

The practice of place is always an ongoing process. There is never a moment when a place is finally and fully completed. Rather, there is a continuous interplay between the founding and transformation of places on the one hand and the preservation of places' important qualities on the other. This ongoing process that animates a place is shaped by political and cultural conflict and the exercise of power.

Founding

People must found places. The natural world does not come with defined places. Certainly, nature and its topography precede the founding of places, but any conception of the world as a terrain of defined places is inevitably the product of our interpretations, descriptions, labels, and transformations of what is given us by nature. Elements of the landscape blend into one another, and organisms and natural forces traverse landscapes and ecosystems, making physical boundaries indistinct and in flux.[68] Human beings must read the terrain in some fashion and at the very least delineate somewhat defined, reasonably enduring and coherent locales.[69] In other words, places as places are human constructs.[70] No place is simply found; every place is also founded. Sack thus describes place as both physical and cultural.[71]

As Tuan emphasizes, the creation of places involves not only physical effort but also descriptive words.[72] The founding of places requires at the very least some sort of description that singles out and organizes the features of one's surroundings. Tuan says that "although speech alone cannot materially transform nature, it can direct attention, organize insignificant entities into significant composite wholes, and in so doing, make things formerly overlooked—and hence invisible and nonexistent—visible and real."[73] However, one does not just "read" or talk about the landscape in all its detail. Human beings overlay their surroundings with inevitably selective interpretations. Indeed, no description of a place can capture every detail and object in that location. Description highlights the qualities most prominent to the senses or most significant in terms of some set of concerns. It distinguishes relationships among things and delineates spatial assemblages and boundaries.

Individual places can thus be created without effecting any physical change in the landscape.[74] Tuan says, "Speech is a component of the total force that transforms nature into a human place. But speech can be an effective force acting alone or almost alone."[75] This is revealed in how even so-called natural places are human constructs, founded through description. Certainly, the physical terrain preceded humanity. However, the division of nature into more or less coherent places is the result of human interpretation. For example, Tuan notes that hunter-gatherer societies are often described as living out in nature. However, "they live in a deeply humanized world," he points out. "Outsiders say 'nature,' because the environment seems barely touched. Insiders see 'homeplace'—an environment that is familiar to them, not because they have materially transformed it but because they have named it. It is their place—their world—through the casting of a linguistic net."[76]

The Mississippi watershed, as a clearly delineated area, was created through naming:

French explorers in the seventeenth century carried the word "Mississippi" (of Algonquian origin) all the way from the source of the river in Minnesota to its mouth on the Gulf. In time, "Mississippi" displaced all other names (both Indian and Spanish) that applied to only limited stretches of the river.... The name "Mississippi River," henceforth, evoked an image of a vast hydrological system; the name can be said to have created the system by making the entire river, and not just the parts visible to observers on the ground, accessible to consciousness.[77]

Through naming, human beings mark out a particular landscape, deciding on its distinctive characteristics and the boundaries that separate it from its surroundings.[78]

The Mutual Founding of Place and Identity

In founding places, individuals or groups also found or shape their own identities. Places are not merely an environment or background; they help determine who we are.[79] This point is powerfully made by Hannah Arendt. "The things of the world," she says, "have the function of stabilizing human life"; "men, their ever-changing nature notwithstanding, can retrieve their sameness, that is, their identity, by being related to the same chair and the same table."[80]

In the course of interacting with their spatial environment, individuals formulate, pursue, and revise their ends and activities.[81] Thus, in relying upon and also contending with the things and places that fill the world, individuals singly and collectively shape their life stories and aspirations; their routines and societal connections; their sense of limits and possibilities; their conception of how the world is organized; and their values, affiliations, and loyalties. Our personality and consciousness are conditioned, explains geographer Allan Pred, by an ongoing, endless interplay between the paths we negotiate through space and time on the one hand and the projects we undertake on the other. As we move from project to project, we accumulate experiences, reflect on our circumstances, revise our goals in response to spatial and temporal constraints and meanings embedded in our environment, and so shape our own personality and consciousness.[82] Such interactions help define individual—and also communal—identities.[83] When things and places are in a relatively stable configuration, as with Arendt's chair and table, human identities are themselves stabilized.[84]

However, the stability of places and identities is not unqualified. Once we found them, places do not become inert. Human beings transform things and places, particularly as needs, practices, values, and ends change. As things and places change, they in turn change those who interact with them. Consequently, although places help shape and stabilize our identities, in the long run places and persons are mutually constitutive, shaping one another over time.[85] We are born into places, but we inevitably change their character to a greater or lesser degree[86] and then these places change us. Given these dynamics, places are always in varying degrees both stable and in flux.[87]

In this ongoing process, the boundaries between person and place are not absolute. I am really a part of the places I inhabit or visit and more a part of those places with which I closely interact and identify. A place is in some ways an extension of the self and the self is a manifestation of that place. Edward Casey describes the relationship between place and selfhood in some detail.[88] According to Casey, this "relationship ... is not just one of reciprocal influence." Place and self are each "essential to the being of the other. In effect, there is *no place without self and no self without place.*"[89] Places only exist because we found them, and our founding of places creates a context in which our identities unfold.

What mediates between self and place, says Casey, borrowing from Pierre Bourdieu, is habitus.[90] A habitus is a "settled disposition or 'habitude'." The self is created by a core of habitudes that incorporate and continue at psychical and physical levels one's experience in particular places.[91] A habitus is not merely the "solidified deposition of past actions or a mere disposition to future actions."[92] Rather, it is something we put into action in the course of inhabiting the world, action that Casey calls "habitation."[93] A habitus is settled, but not frozen; we can revise it over time.[94]

A habitus develops through the medium of the body, the physical and mental entity through which we interact with the place-world.[95] Casey describes two ways in which body and place interact. Through the body, we go out to meet the place-world, and our encounter with this world is shaped by the bilateral, erect structure of the body, particularly the axes of up/down, front/back, right/left. Places in turn imprint themselves on us, both on our physical bodies and on our minds and memories.[96] The human subject then expresses the particularities of the place in which he or she has spent time.[97] Such close identification or connection between person and place comes about through a number of concrete activities, such as habitation, work, recreation, spiritual or aesthetic appreciation, and even personal tragedy.

Is Founding a Conscious Act?

The concept of founding may imply a conscious act. Indeed, foundings are often conscious and deliberate. Explorers or migrants come upon a topographic feature and name it, a farmer surveys land for clearing, a city dedicates a park or monument, a government declares an area to be protected wilderness, builders and architects plan and execute a new development, a painter chooses a landscape as an artistic subject, an ecologist marks out the bounds of an ecosystem, a forestry agency opens an area to timber-cutting.

One of the most momentous, deliberate foundings of place is the creation or geographic transformation of a nation or other political entity. Declarations of independence, revolutions, constitutional conventions, conquests and annexations, partitions, and the planning and building of cities are all political foundings. Founding is often celebrated in political theory, whether the creation of a "city in speech" in Plato's *Republic*, the social contract in Thomas Hobbes's *Leviathan* and in John Locke's *Second Treatise of Government*, or the communist revolution anticipated by Karl Marx and Friedrich Engels. Political philosophers have at times imagined an individual, heroic founder, such as Niccolò Machiavelli's Prince or Jean-Jacques Rousseau's Great Legislator.

However, the founding of a place need not be entirely conscious, nor must it be a discrete event. A place can gradually take shape through use, its existence only half-consciously recognized. For example, if a couple decides to have a picnic in the park, they might choose a flat, grassy area under a large maple tree. The following week they might return to picnic at the same spot, and then do the same a week later. Sooner or later they have recognized the area as their regular picnic spot. What was once a nondescript area becomes for them a coherent place and even one with considerable importance in the narrative and character of their relationship. That same couple might have a favorite restaurant. The restaurant staff tends to seat them at a particular table. At first, the two people are hardly aware of the particularities of their table. Gradually, however, it becomes their special table—a defined place—and they seek it out. A farmer clearing land may gradually and only half-consciously adjust her overall plans as she encounters obstacles in the land such as boulders and tree roots. A small number of immigrants settle in a neighborhood and then begin inviting friends and relatives to come over and move into the area. Over time, a distinctive ethnic enclave has grown up around them. Moreover, a new place can also gradually develop in a way that departs from its founders' intentions. Thus New York City's Times Square, evolved from a piece of real-estate speculation to become America's public square.[98]

At some point in all these processes, however, there are moments in which founding is quite conscious—when lovers decide that this is their picnic spot or special table and they regularly return to it, when a farmer surveys her land and decides what areas to clear, when the inhabitants of an ethnic neighborhood realize that they have created a community and become conscious of its bounds and internal geography, and when people begin to intentionally gather at Times Square for celebrations. At these moments, a place is fully recognized and delineated and it can be said to have fully come into existence.

Founding as a Collective, Contested Project

When individuals or groups of individuals found places, whether unconsciously or deliberately, gradually or at a stroke, their actions reflect their own perspectives as place founders. Political theorists' visions of individual, heroic founders notwithstanding, place founding is generally a collective act involving a number of people who have some relation to a place.

Founders may disagree about the character of the place that is being founded and even whether a place should be founded at all. Thus, conflict attends nation building; environmentalists and resource-extractive industries square off over wilderness designation; builders, interest groups, citizens, and elected officials vie over development projects; neighborhoods resist diversification or gentrification; and political communities fight over shared boundaries.

Founded in a matrix of human difference, or plurality, places are inevitably sites of contestation.[99] Geographer Doreen Massey speaks of "space as the sphere in which distinct narratives co-exist."[100] According to Arendt, our words and deeds—such as the actions by which we might found places—are inherently social; they go on directly between persons and reflect the condition of human plurality.[101] In a world in which we share territory, any act of founding a place, whether carried out by an individual or a group, inevitably affects others and initiates a kind of dialogue with them. In this dialogue, the varying perspectives of other individuals or communities come into play;[102] that is, unless someone imposes an authoritarian grip on a place and its interpretation.

Thus, for an individual's conception or map of the spatial world to be functional, it must correspond in some way to the conceptions held by others. It cannot be purely subjective, but must develop at least in part through confirmation by others. If this is not the case, an individual's attempt to found places or otherwise map, inhabit, and/or affect the spatial world will be frustrated by others' conceptions and treatment of the world. Sharing the spatial world and its places thus entails some collective understanding, however tacit, vague, or temporary, as to the character of places.[103]

Often, however, such common understandings, even if they are not prevented by authoritarian planning, fail to emerge. In some cases, different groups connected to a place might simply disregard one another. For many Bostonians today, the old West End is unknown or simply forgotten. However, for the neighborhood's former residents, who were displaced by urban renewal in the 1950s and 1960s, the West End continues to exist, even as it remains invisible to others. Many former residents communicate through a quarterly newsletter, the *West Ender*.[104]

More common than mutual disregard is fundamental disagreement about the existence or character of a place. Some disagreement is inevitable and desirable because it allows places to incorporate difference and evolve according to changing perspectives. However, conflict may be so severe as to prevent any agreement or understanding that would facilitate the shared habitation, use, or care of a place. An extreme example of this is civil war, which in some cases can even divide individual neighborhoods within a city against one another. For example, the Northern Ireland city of Belfast is divided between Catholic and Protestant factions, each with their own sectarian geography of how the city ought to be organized.[105]

Founding Places, Building Communities
The collective construction of places not only situates individuals and communities in their physical environment, it also provides a spatial dimension for the organization and legibility of human relationships. The world "relates and separates men at the same time," Arendt says. It "gathers us together and yet prevents our falling over each other."[106] "To live together in the world means essentially that a world of things is between those who have it in common, as a table is located between those who sit around it."[107] Existing "between" individuals, the world

of things gives relationships spatial coherence and legibility.[108] A coherent world of places in common enables human beings to read and navigate their shared existence.

Because human relationships are to a considerable degree collectively organized around spatial arrangements of things and places, communities, strong or weak, are often realized through place. Daniel Kemmis, who draws on Arendt, notes that community arises through a common focus on something of value, and that places provide such a tangible, concrete, and publicly visible focus.[109] A table is not just a useful surface. It marks out a shared parcel of space, a place in common. Around this shared place, individuals orient themselves toward one another. One might think of a table to which a group of friends, colleagues, or family members regularly repair for a meal or a meeting, with perhaps each person in their usual place. Gatherings around the table refresh and sustain relationships and shared aims and meanings within the group, and even sustain the identities of individual members.

This is not to say that all communities must be place based, or that all places are the focus of community. Many communities take non-geographic forms, including communities of interest, ethnic diasporas, and families or former neighbors or friends who have been dispersed, like the residents of the West End. Moreover, as we have seen, a shared focus on a place may situate individuals in relationships of tense coexistence or conflict rather than community.

A Plurality of Meanings

Even when the inhabitants of a place think of themselves as a community, a place's vitality depends on there still being some plurality of meanings that individuals or groups attach to that place. When people holding a plurality of meanings live in peaceful interaction, the diversity and recombination of different perspectives profoundly enriches and enlivens a place.

This is true, for example, of urban neighborhoods that have a variety of cultures, ethnicities, businesses, income levels, households, and visitors.[110] Such diversity means that individuals will view a place differently, in terms of that place's meaning, and also in terms of how they use that place. This diversity is tangibly realized in a variety of visible activities that can all be taking place within one city block. Alternatively, one might think of a rural watershed, where over a larger area, farmers, foresters, backpackers, hunters, fishermen, guides, and townspeople, all with their respective histories and perspectives, interact with a variety of landscapes and living things and with one another.

Such complex choreographies of intentions, motions, things, and locales dazzle the mind and the eye and give a place a fine-grained texture of appearance, structure, and meaning. These choreographies generate encounters, social bonds, and conflicts, and weave stories. The various meanings and perspectives pile on, recombine, and transform themselves, giving a place a rich, living significance and enabling that place and its inhabitants to respond to changing conditions.

Refounding Places

That places can be the basis for moral commitments, identities, and communities would seem to suggest that once places are founded they do not change. Yet, as we saw, places are dynamic, changing under social and ecological influences, responding to both external forces and conditions and internal diversity and conflict. Over time, as people respond to or initiate changes in their environment, they alter or even "refound" places to suit changing circumstances. Massey says "we make, and constantly remake, the spaces and places and identities through which we live our lives."[111] Places are always unfinished.[112]

Hybridity and Fluidity: Overvalued?

Contemporary academics, particularly those loosely identified with postmodernism, take great pains to emphasize the dynamic, changing, and hybrid nature of places, particularly in a globalized world. Places are always changing. They exist as processes or in flux. Their character is always manifold and contested, their boundaries always uncertain. To think of places as unchanging or monolithic or unalloyed in character is to deny the fluidity and complexity of human attachments and identities, to deny the dynamic, even turbulent character of our spatial context, and to favor one unchanging character for each place or even places in general. To favor one character of a place is to exclude competing voices, discourses, and interpretations, often in order to support a politically hegemonic standpoint. Some critical geographers thus emphasize, for example, that all places are hybrids and all places are ephemeral.

Indeed, no place has a pure, uncontested character.[113] Every place embraces difference, contradiction, conflict, and otherness. The notion that cultures and places are hybrid "suggests [a] radical heterogeneity that disrupts notions of purity and stasis."[114] Massey sees space as disrupted and as a source of disruption. "That is, even though it is constituted out of relations, spatiality/space is not a totally coherent and interrelated system of connections."[115]

From this point of view, all is in motion; every place is fleeting,[116] as is embedded in, interpenetrated by, and made up of a multiplicity of conflicting, fluid relationships and interactions. Massey emphasizes the chaotic, incoherent, dislocating aspects of the spatial world, arguing that these are not disempowering but liberating because they leave the future "genuinely open." She says, "we inhabit an environment through which the genuinely novel may emerge."[117]

I am in many ways sympathetic to these ideas. Places, as I have noted, are marked by difference and they are in flux. Both purity and stasis, the opposites of hybridity and fluidity, have been values deployed against progressive change and against difference and those perceived as "other."

However, in the postmodern privileging of hybridity and fluidity, there is a tendency to go to the other extreme, i.e., to deny the stability and coherence of places and of place-based identities, to the point where place itself begins to disappear as a meaningful concept. For example, according to Massey, places "are not so much bounded areas as open and porous networks of social relations." She emphasizes "the lack of basis for any claims for establishing the authentic character of any particular place (whether such claims are used as the grounds for arguing for ethnic exclusivity or for opposing some unwanted development)."[118] Places are "the intersection of social activities and social relations . . . which are necessarily, by definition, dynamic, changing. There is no stable moment, in the sense of stasis, if we *define* our world, or our localities, *ab initio* in terms of change."[119]

Recall, however, that places are both interpenetrated and bounded, are characterized by flux and permanence, conflict and agreement, and diversity and commonality. Geraldine Pratt thus warns against overvaluing mobility and hybridity.[120]

Preservation

These considerations lead us to the notion that even though places are founded and refounded, the founding of places has to be balanced with their preservation. As suggested by Arendt's chair and table, places provide a sustaining, reassuring permanence that enables individuals and communities to rely on the world for usefulness, meaning, and affirmation of identities. Perpetual change or instability in places can endanger identities, communities, essential routines, the ability to make sense of the world, and even physical security, leading to extreme stress, disorientation, and a kind of existential homelessness.[121] Changes in places can also conflict with moral obligations to sustain these places. Moreover, change can wipe out the diversity and richness of a place. Founding a place therefore ought to be accompanied by preservation.

Preservationist activities include physical care and maintenance ranging from wilderness management all the way to housekeeping. Preservation can also entail the creation of protective boundaries or barriers, as when endangered ecosystems are protected from invasive species.

As with founding, preservation is also generally a collective activity. One cannot seek to preserve an area without some assent from others who inhabit or use it. Otherwise, preservationist efforts are bound to fail. Preservationists must recognize that others may disagree on what to preserve or that others may be more interested in founding activities. As with founding, collective assent may be secured through either democratic or authoritarian means.

Preservation as a Necessary Complement to Founding

While it must balance founding, preservation is also complementary to founding. Founding can be seen as an act of creativity.[122] Architecture and landscape design are generally classed as arts, and even the craft of political founding, in the person of Machiavelli's Prince or Rousseau's Legislator, can be seen as an artistic endeavor. However, founding a place, although it involves the performance of actions and possibly ceremony, is not just an evanescent creative action like a musical or theatrical performance. Rather, it is more akin to crafting a work of art, such as a painting, book, symphony, or sculpture, although the analogy breaks down somewhat when we consider that a place evolves and changes over time. Place founding creates the spatial world that human beings inhabit. Consequently, a founder, or founders, has a responsibility to create a world that, while not unchanging, has some measure of stability and reliability. For founding to involve unrestrained creativity would be to subject the world to chaos.

For example, Machiavelli's Prince is the consummate founder, employing the qualities of *virtù*, including audacity and self-sufficiency, to battle fortune and create a new principality.[123] Machiavelli's founding project aims at creating a stable society. *Virtù* acts to stabilize human affairs in the face of chaotic, capricious fortune. In his *Discourses*, Machiavelli remarks, "it is the man who uses violence to *spoil* things, not the man who uses it to *mend* them, that is blameworthy."[124] Consequently the founder's art must take account of preservation—a good founder is also a preservationist. We might also look to Arendt. In discussing the founding of a humanized world on Earth, she emphasizes the stabilizing aspect of what is founded, as I noted earlier.[125]

Does this mean that preservation is simply part of founding?[126] This is not just a semantic question, for it concerns whether founding and preservation have equal importance as aspects of the practice of place. To establish founding as the more fundamental activity would be to favor founding activities as the norm, and preservation as merely a moment of rest from founding.

The distinction between, and equal status of, founding and preservation is reflected in political thought. Both Rousseau and Machiavelli separate the arts and activities of the founder from the politics of an established society, whose stability requires a more preservationist approach. Rousseau, in *The Social Contract* warns that the Legislator should not actually rule, but must strictly be a founder.[127] Once society has been founded, then the political community lives out and maintains the Legislator's work. Rousseau might be said to take the contrast between founding and preservation to an extreme because the Legislator does nothing but found, and the resulting political community actually does little but preserve what has been created.

For his part, Machiavelli addresses founding and preservation in two separate works. The *Prince* deals with the "new prince," who must act as an amoral, dictatorial founder, while the *Discourses* focuses on statesmen with somewhat more traditional civic virtues who must maintain existing republics. However, Machiavelli describes more of a continuous interaction between founding and preservation than does Rousseau because the Prince attempts to stabilize a political society, and the republican statesmen of the *Discourses* sometimes employ political tumult and emergency powers to effect changes that bring stability to society in the long run. Machiavelli is correct to both distinguish founding and preservation *and* put them in dynamic interaction.

The Interaction Between Founding and Preservation

This dynamic interaction between founding and preservation is best brought out by Young. She does say: "as soon as the deeds of founding are accomplished, ... a new task comes into play: preservation."[128] Yet, contrary to Rousseau, preservation does not simply follow founding. Young herself acknowledges this. She actually presents an ongoing, balanced interaction between founding and preservation rather than a serial ordering of the two. In practice, one generally preserves some aspects of a place while changing others. If one wishes to preserve the place's basic character, one must maintain a place's perceived defining aspects. For example, preserving a house might mean maintaining its shape and exterior, and preserving an old-growth forest ecosystem means first of all keeping its larger trees, both living and fallen.

Preservation also entails attention to ecological and social origins and context. Though places are human constructs, they do not emerge ex nihilo. First of all, places emerge through interaction between what is given by nature, by history, and by present-day society. "A place," says Kimberly Smith, "is neither wholly natural nor wholly social; it is the product of a relationship between people and nature, coming into being as individuals interact and come to terms with the objective conditions presented by the physical (and social) world."[129]

The places we found must be ecologically, culturally, and socially functional and also enable us to make some sense of our connections with the world. Place founders must not destroy natural ecosystems or obliterate the human culture and history of an existing place. As we will see in the next three chapters, a sweepingly destructive transformation of the landscape leads to ecological problems, cultural decline, and social dysfunction.

Having a sense of place—a concept discussed earlier—helps guard against destructive behavior. As Smith discusses, this involves a sense of a place's history and possibilities.[130] It entails the realization that places are not blank slates that one may freely write on. Smith notes, "Far from being the domain of freedom, places always have their own rules and requirements; they make demands on us."[131]

Preservation does not require rigid adherence to the past. It does, however, provide the continuity between past and present that makes life a coherent story, or narrative. Activities of preservation, Young says, "give some enclosing fabric" to shifting meanings, conditions, and identities. They do so "by knitting together today and yesterday, integrating the new events and relationships into the narrative of a life, the biography of a person, a family, a people." To put it somewhat differently, "The preservation of things among which one dwells gives people a context for their lives."[132]

When properly balanced with founding, preservation actually enables new possibilities, even radical ones, to unfold. In fact, preservation of place provides individuals and communities with a sense of identity and confidence from which movements for social change can arise. As noted earlier, Young discusses how the preservation of home can provide a place for resistance by politically marginalized groups, such as African-Americans and women. Preservation conserves without being necessarily conservative. At the same time, preservation prevents founding from being an abrupt, destructive change and tempers it so that it emerges from preexisting possibilities.

Here we might look to Arendt's discussion of care and cultivation. In *Between Past and Future*, she considers the origins of the word *culture*. The term, she says, "derives from [the Latin] *colere*—to cultivate, to take care, tend and preserve—and it relates primarily to the intercourse of man with nature in the sense of cultivating and tending nature until it becomes fit for human habitation. As such, it indicates an attitude of loving care and stands in sharp contrast to all efforts to subject nature to the domination of man."[133] Building from Arendt's remarks, one might say that care allows the original or existing qualities of a place to endure and flourish, while cultivation enables new possibilities to unfold smoothly.[134] Care allows a stabilizing continuity with the past. Cultivation facilitates incremental change and adaptation.[135] By contrast, domineering, aggressive action abruptly destroys and replaces.

Moral Obligation as Basis for Preservation

Preservation may be motivated by a sense of moral obligation, a phenomenon related to the sense of place discussed earlier. Moral obligation is most likely to develop when the bounds of the self are relaxed as an individual comes to identify with a place. In identifying with a place, an individual develops a rootedness, a sense of belonging to one's surroundings that provides moral purpose. Self and place are fundamentally connected in a shared good.[136] Knowledge of that place, a sense of being at home there, and, importantly, a moral obligation to defend that place are all enmeshed with one's very sense of self. If a place becomes integral to the identity of a person or community, then the good of that place and the sense of obligation to care for that place become part of the person's or community's own good. This does not mean that moral obligations to places are unconditional. Individuals are claimed by a variety of obligations and often by more than one place. In following any obligation, one must always weigh competing ones. However, obligations to place can generate considerable pull.

Someone is most likely to feel such a connection to their home; to a territorial entity with which they are affiliated, such as a nation, region, or locality; to a place where they work or visit frequently; and to a birthplace, hometown, or ancestral home. One may even feel an obligation to preserve a place that one has only read about and seen in photos or films, if that place is integral to one's conception of the world or one's values. For example, the efforts of environmentalists to protect exceedingly remote places like the Arctic National Wildlife Refuge or Antarctica stem in part from a worldview that emphasizes the ecological importance and/or moral worth of wilderness. In regard to the sense of obligation to preserve tragic places or create memorials to past evils, such places and memorials are important, not only from a didactic point of view, but because they have become an integral part of a people's own history and identity. Consequently, to obliterate Auschwitz, the battlefield at Gettysburg, the A-Bomb Dome in Hiroshima, the House of Slaves on Senegal's Goree Island, or Ground Zero would be an act of violence against a people or community that has been shaped by that place and its tragedies and evils.[137] The idea of moral obligation to a place with which one identifies helps explain the fervor with which people fight to protect threatened neighborhoods, historic places, open spaces, and wilderness areas.

The notion of moral obligations to places has perhaps been most strenuously articulated by environmentalists. Environmentalists often see our ecological and cultural connections with natural areas and ecosystems, and with nature in general, as making the good of the natural world congruent with that of human beings. Environmentalists call on us to know, identify with and preserve natural ecosystems and features of the natural landscape, such as forests, mountains, and rivers.[138] Kirkpatrick Sale emphasizes "fully knowing the character of the natural world and being connected to it in a daily and physical way [that] provides [a] sense of oneness, of rootedness."[139] Val Plumwood speaks of identification with natural places "yielding ties often as special and powerful as those to kin, and which are equally expressed in very specific and local responsibilities of care."[140]

Overemphasizing Preservation

However, an overemphasis on preservation is just as problematic as an overemphasis on founding. Human beings interact dynamically with places, altering or refounding them in response to changing conditions. There is no single moment of founding followed by rigid adherence to what has been created; otherwise, all places would become museum pieces.[141] The narrow pursuit of preservation can harm individuals and communities dependent on a place for habitation, sustenance, or livelihood. At times preservation may also be ecologically misguided, as suggested by my example of fire suppression in the introduction.

In fact, to be successful, preservation must itself draw upon founding activities. The preservation and care of a place inevitably involves defining boundaries, selecting elements that need attention, and even changing some of a place's existing qualities so that it can be more resilient in the face of change. For example, wilderness areas require active intervention, if only to improve their resilience to the environmental impacts of human activities. Human beings set legal boundaries, provide for visitors, and pursue active management, including prescribed fires, extirpation of exotic species, and/or the restoration of predators.[142]

Complementarity and Tension at the Heart of Place

The dual importance of founding and preservation points to both a complementarity and an unavoidable tension at the heart of the practice of place. We impart meaning and coherence to the world by founding places, yet founding alters the world and disrupts our existing maps. Consequently, although we found places, we do not do so in the interests of pure and unfettered creativity, but in the expectation that what we found will provide a lasting physical environment and home rather than a world subject to continuous disruption. And yet, even as we want stability in the character of places, we would also like places to respond to changing needs, knowledge, and values.

Despite this tension, both founding and preservation are integral to the practice of place. The preservationist desire for an enduring human home leads to the care of places and respect for their ecological, historical, and cultural context and origins, while the willingness to found and refound makes the world a habitable, functional home. Founding must not destroy the meaningful world we have created or cut off our connections to nature and history. At the same time, preservation must not freeze our environment in time, turning it into an unusable, untouchable museum piece.

In the coming chapters, I discuss how in contemporary land-use politics, founding and preservation are no longer in a complementary tension, but have been set against one another so that political actors pursue one or the other end in a zero-sum game. This conflict is an outgrowth of the crisis of placelessness discussed earlier, and it has led to the debasement of the practice of place. In the next three chapters, I examine three cases of land-use politics—the old-growth forest debate in the Pacific Northwest, the problem of sprawl, and the rebuilding of Ground Zero—and how they exhibit a conflict between founding and preservation. Then I return to the crisis of placelessness and more fully examine its origins and implications. Finally, I outline a politics of place that reconciles and reintegrates founding and preservation.

2

The Northwest Timber War

It is described as a "living museum," as "the most magnificent forest on the continent and the greatest conifer forest on earth." It has been accorded the honorific of "ancient." Yet for some persons it is a workplace or "just a big old tree farm" and for others it is "decadent" and "dying." In the past, it was dubbed a "biological desert" and even compared to a slum by those who wanted to eradicate it.

The forested landscape of the Pacific Northwest, with its old-growth stands of gigantic conifers is one of America's most controversial places. Whether ancient or decadent, a magnificent forest or a biological desert, this old-growth forest is also a battlefield. It is the site of one of the most intractable, polarized, and publicized ecological controversies in the United States. The debate over whether to log or preserve the old-growth forests, unresolved since the 1970s, has been characterized by profound hostility and even violence between the contending parties.[1]

The debate is interesting for more than its prominence or vehemence. Since forests are often perceived as archetypal wild nature, our very relationship with the natural world seems to be at issue here. This underlying debate over nature suggests another fundamental issue: how we interact with our spatial environment or, more specifically, how we approach the concept of place.

There are a number of parties, positions, and issues in this debate. However, the main point of contention is whether the federally owned forests in the Northwest should be logged for timber or preserved from the chain saw. The debate is highly polarized between two camps. Former Governor of Oregon John Kitzhaber remarks that efforts to resolve the conflict and constructively manage the forests of the Northwest "have been thwarted by the conflict between those who wish to harvest timber and those who wish to preserve it, and by their distrust of each other and of the federal land-management agencies themselves. Each side in the debate operates from its own deeply entrenched positions, pointing at the other as the culprit."[2] Similarly, the *New York Times* comments that "the battle between those who want to make a profit from federal timberlands and those who want to lock business out has been as polarizing and fierce as those over abortion and gun control."[3] Moreover, the debate is further polarized because it has taken place in venues that favor adversarial stances—Congress, the courts, and the media. Under such conditions, say Joe Bowersox and Karen Arabas, "a strategic dualism is adopted, compelling the participants to take oversimplified positions fitting traditional stereotypes, such as commodity interests versus the environmental community." They also note that this polarization may prevent parties that have varying although not mutually exclusive goals and values from discovering common ground.[4]

In terms of the categories and ideas developed in chapter 1, we might say that the debate in the Pacific Northwest is one between founding—logging the old-growth forest and turning it into a commodity-producing tree farm—and preservation—maintaining the forest in its naturally given state. The debate thus reflects the polarization between founding and preservation that characterizes land-use politics today.

What is also interesting is that beneath the strident rhetoric and polarized ideologies, the positions in this debate are quite complex and in certain ways deeply ambivalent. Some of the antagonists are in closer agreement than they might readily admit. Many participants in this debate are themselves internally conflicted; they value the forest as it is and yet want timber harvesting to continue in some form.[5] Often these ideas are not consciously reconciled, even in the minds of those who hold them simultaneously. However, the complexity of the participants' perspectives points beyond the simple founding versus preservation dichotomy and suggests a more nuanced and balanced approach to place that integrates founding and preservation and sees them as complementary.

In the following sections, I outline the history and contemporary contours of the Northwest forest debate, beginning with the larger national context for this conflict. I then consider how this issue has developed into a contest between founding and preservation and how the issue also suggests possibilities for transcending this conflict.

U.S. Forest Politics

Establishment of the Forest Service

The debate over logging in the Pacific Northwest is situated within a larger historical debate over the management of American forests, particularly those on federal lands.

The spread of European settlers over the North American continent was accompanied by a wave of logging that extirpated as much as 95 percent of the pre-Columbian forest. Nineteenth-century fears of a "timber famine,"[6] as well as increasing interest in wilderness as a place of beauty and respite and a source of national character and spiritual values[7] led to efforts at forest preservation. In the 1890s, federal legislation created forest reserves out of public lands. In 1905, the U.S. Forest Service, under forester Gifford Pinchot, was established to administer the reserves, although some federal timberlands have remained in the hands of other agencies, particularly the Bureau of Land Management (BLM). Pinchot and other conservationists saw the timber companies' logging practices as short-sighted, destructive, and unsustainable. Conservationists aimed to create efficient, sustainable management of forests in order to ensure a timber supply into the future. Pinchot was opposed by forest activist John Muir, who wanted the forests kept as wilderness rather than used for timber harvesting.[8]

Pinchot's views ostensibly became the Forest Service's guiding philosophy. The agency adopted Pinchot's top-down, timber-oriented, founding ethos, but it did not honor Pinchot's long-term perspective. Instead, the Forest Service took a more short-sighted and destructive approach to timber harvesting. Forest politics ultimately became polarized between commodity-oriented and preservationist views. This debate has been especially intense since the 1970s.

The Failure of Multiple Use

The Forest Service was officially committed to a doctrine termed multiple use: forests were to be managed not only for timber, but for wildlife habitat, wilderness, watershed protection, fishing, hunting, grazing, mining, and recreation. However, following Pinchot, the agency's primary objective was timber production,[9] and outright preservation of forests would have conflicted with this focus and "can do" organizational culture.[10]

Until the mid-twentieth century, though, logging in the national forests was comparatively modest. There was enough timber flowing from private lands, and private landowners feared that competition from public lands would depress timber prices.[11] However, World War II and the postwar economic boom brought a considerable increase in timber demand, while private lands were becoming exhausted. Logging on the national forests soared. Timber production on the national forests increased from 1.5 billion board feet (bbf) in 1941 to between 11 and 12 bbf annually during the 1970s and 1980s.[12] National forests were now supplying some 25 percent of all domestic timber.[13] With increased demand, timber became even more central to the Forest Service's mission. During this period, there also emerged an "iron triangle" embracing the Forest Service, the timber industry, and Congress. Forest Service budgets were dependent on the level of the timber cut; the industry benefited from high harvests and below-cost timber sales; and congressional representatives from timber-producing regions secured votes and campaign contributions by pushing for higher cuts and higher budgets for the Forest Service.[14]

Under such conditions, Pinchot's vision of sustainable management did not survive, and multiple use also faced problems. These problems came from two directions. On the one hand, increased timber harvesting and other uses of the national forests strained the physical resource base. On the other hand, the concurrent rise of the modern environmental movement involved an increased valuation of noncommodity, wilderness-oriented "uses" of the land, including aesthetic, scientific, recreational, and spiritual values.

The Forest Service had traditionally been uncomfortable with wilderness designations because these involved a single use rather than multiple uses, minimized the Forest Service's active managerial role, and were particularly incompatible with its timber focus.[15] The Forest Service's commitment to multiple use thus turned out to be little more than a sham, with the agency's primary commitment to timber leading to explosive harvesting levels. The Forest Service was often called a "timber beast."[16]

By the 1970s, increasing pressures to log collided with growing environmental consciousness. Mounting conflict over incompatible uses was dangerously coupled with a shrinking resource base. After massive clearcuts[17] during the 1960s led to erosion, mountain slides, and severe damage to watersheds and salmon spawning streams, federal legislation was passed in 1976 to ensure multiple-use management and proper planning of forestlands. However, the legislation failed to provide clear guidelines and priorities for multiple use[18] and did little to stem the tide of clearcutting.[19]

Since the 1970s, there has been an intense national debate over how much logging ought to be permitted in the forests and, more fundamentally, over the nature and value or worth of a forest. Environmentalists and members of the scientific community, along with some Forest Service employees, have continued to raise concern over the ecological impacts of logging, especially the logging of old-growth forests and their huge, ancient trees. Reflecting the increasing popularity of the "zero cut" idea among environmentalists,[20] in 1996 the Sierra Club even voted to endorse a ban on commercial logging on all federal lands.[21]

The 1990s saw a shift away from timber harvesting as a priority for the Forest Service. Measures taken by the administration of President Bill Clinton, as well as a series of court injunctions, reduced timber output from national forests by about 70 percent over the course of the 1990s.[22] During the Clinton era, the Forest Service itself also became more ecologically oriented. In part this was due to a longer-term evolution within the Forest Service's professional orientation and organizational culture going back at least to the 1980s. There was a shift in agency employment from traditional areas like forestry, range management, and engineering to more nontraditional areas like biology, social science, and recreation.[23] The Forest Service put increasing focus on recreational needs, protection of wilderness and biodiversity, restoration of habitats and watersheds, ecologically sustainable forestry, and preservation of ecosystem health and integrity. This shift was accelerated by Clinton's appointment of Michael Dombeck, who was much more sympathetic to environmental goals, as agency chief.[24]

In his final days in office, Clinton issued a sweeping executive order that prohibited the building of logging roads, commercial logging, and oil and gas development in almost one-third of the national forest system.[25] Days later, Dombeck banned the logging of old-growth timber on national forest lands.[26]

However, President George W. Bush, backed by the timber industry and by many timber-state members of Congress, has pushed the Forest Service back toward a traditional timber focus.[27] Bush has sought to relax provisions under the 1976 National Forest Management Act (NFMA) that require environmental assessments and impose environmental restrictions, including measures to protect wildlife, when national forests develop fifteen-year management plans.[28] He tried to abandon Clinton's road-building ban by giving governors discretion over whether or not to open up roadless areas in their states, though a federal judge reinstated the ban in September, 2006.[29]

Bush also used a series of devastating western fires and fears of a "forest health crisis" to push through the 2003 Healthy Forests Restoration Act, which increased logging activities under the rationale of thinning forests to reduce fuel loads, prevent fire danger, and salvage fire-damaged timber.[30] The Act reduced environmental reviews and judicial oversight of forest management and led to the felling of large, healthy trees.[31] In the highly polarized debate over forest health, many environmentalists, justifiably alarmed at the prospect of a return to the old days, took a hard line even against thinning projects that were arguably necessary for good forest management.[32] Finally, the Administration has caused alarm by increasingly outsourcing Forest Service functions to private contractors.[33]

Despite the Bush administration's more traditional timber focus, many observers say that it is unlikely that federal timber harvests will return to the levels of the 1970s and 1980s. Much of the old growth is gone, the Forest Service has arguably gone through an enduring shift away from its earlier timber orientation, the agency's timber operations are increasingly focused on thinning and fire prevention, and budget cuts are reducing the Forest Service's ability to build and maintain logging roads and offer timber sales.[34]

Moreover, with federal timber harvesting enmeshed in controversy, private lands may once again be sufficiently productive to render national forest timber economically unnecessary. By the early 1990s, reforestation efforts were bearing fruit, and private forests were more than compensating for declines in federal harvests that were due to logging restrictions, meaning that total U.S. timber production was increasing even as federal timber harvests dropped.[35]

Yet the management of private lands is itself not exempt from the forestry debate. During the 1980s, there were a series of corporate takeovers of private timberlands. Following such takeovers, the new owners, many of them financiers, looked upon uncut trees as an asset to be liquidated for short-term servicing of corporate debt. Thousands of acres were clear-cut. One of the most notorious of these operations concerned private redwood stands in northern California and generated a national controversy. There have also been debates over the future of the Northeast's largely private Northern Forest, as concern grows over not only logging but also the threat of commercial development.[36]

The forestry debate has seesawed in recent years as successive White House administrations have put their contrasting ideological stamps on federal forest policies. The issue may be finding its own solution by default because a return to massive timber harvesting seems less likely. However, it is certainly too early to tell, and the continuing conflict has prevented the emergence of a guiding vision that might offer anything beyond muddling through.

Forest Politics in the Pacific Northwest

In the coastal region of the Pacific Northwest, environmentalists have fought the timber industry and timber-dependent communities to prevent the logging of some of the last remnants of North America's pre-Columbian forests. The battle concerns the "Westside," a 34.7-million-acre area lying between the Cascades and the Pacific Ocean, in Washington, Oregon, and northern California. Although the Westside includes metropolitan areas like Puget Sound and Portland, it is 75 percent forested.[37]

In the Westside, many of the legal battles have centered on the fate of the Northern spotted owl and, to a lesser degree, that of its cousin, the California spotted owl. The Northern spotted owl is an indicator species of the health of the old-growth ecosystem. Many scientists consider both the Northern and California spotted owls as threatened by continued logging in the region. Concern about the owls therefore sparked moves to protect forests in the Northwest. However, the Northern spotted owl has been thrust into the center of the debate partly because its imperiled status has enabled activists to use the Endangered Species Act as a legal weapon against logging.[38] Underlying much of the concern about the owl is a broader interest in the preservation and ecological health of the Northwest forests, particularly the region's older forests, and especially what scientists term old growth.

The Old-Growth Forest Ecosystem

The phrase *old growth* applies to forests that contain large numbers of "dead trees, snags, and decaying logs, and [having] multiple canopy layers, young saplings, and larger stands that are at least 200 years old."[39] Besides old-growth, there are other types of so-called mature forests in the region. These are forests beginning to develop an old-growth structure. Forests generally enter the mature stage when they are about eighty years old. Scientists sometimes refer to both mature and old-growth forests as late successional.[40]

Environmentalists and timber interests in the Pacific Northwest disagree over how much old-growth forest actually exists and where it is located.[41] According to one estimate, before logging began in the nineteenth century, old growth may have covered approximately 70 percent of the forested area in the Westside. By the early 1990s, this share was 14 to 18 percent and much of it was fragmented, reducing the health of the ecosystem.[42] Virtually all the old growth was gone from private and state-owned lands;[43] the remainder was almost entirely on federal land, mostly under the jurisdiction of the Forest Service and the BLM.

The Northwest's old-growth ecosystem has some distinctive hallmarks. It includes some of the world's only temperate rain forests. Moreover, the complex structure and considerable numbers of fallen and dead trees in old-growth forests make a remarkable biodiversity possible. These forests also provide a range of important ecological benefits, or ecosystem services, including erosion control, maintenance of watersheds, and protection of riparian breeding grounds for salmon and other anadromous fish that are born in fresh water but eventually make their way to the sea. They also boast the world's largest and most extensive stands of giant conifers, and one Westside forest, the Klamath, contains the most species of conifers anywhere on earth. Indigenous conifers include the redwood, which can grow to over 330 feet, and the Douglas fir, which can attain the same height, as well as a 10-foot diameter and a life span of more than 1,000 years.[44]

The Northwest Timber Economy and its Decline

This distinctive forest has also provided an important resource for the timber industry and society as a whole,[45] although this changed somewhat with the imposition of judicial and regulatory limits on logging and with restructuring in the timber industry.

Writing in 1992, journalist William Dietrich described the Westside forests of Washington and Oregon as being the most profitable and productive of the U.S. national forests: "The federal forests in the two states make up only 13 percent of the total [national forest] system but until the spotted owl restrictions they produced more than 40 percent of the wood cut and more than half the timber revenue."[46]

The region's forests have also supported thousands of timber workers.[47] Until the 1980s, some 135,000 workers in Washington and Oregon were employed in the timber industry.[48] A 1988 Forest Service report estimated that 44 percent of Oregon's economy and 28 percent of Washington's economy were directly or indirectly dependent on national forest timber.[49] Beuter noted that as recently as 1994, timber and wood products industries made up about a quarter of Oregon's economic base, and as much as a third of the economic base for rural Oregon.[50] In Washington and Oregon as of 1992, in about seventy communities the local sawmill was the largest single private taxpayer and employer.[51] Consequently, many small rural Northwest communities like Forks, Washington, with a population of about 2,500 in the late 1980s, have historically been based on timber. Coincident with Judge Dwyer's imposition of restrictions on Northwest logging, unemployment in Forks rose from 7 percent in 1989 to 20 percent in 1992. The town experienced a pervasive sense of identity loss and social breakdown, including a rise in domestic violence.[52]

Estimates of the economic impacts of logging restrictions have certainly varied, often according to one's perspective in the debate. In 1993, for example, President Clinton claimed that his Northwest Forest Plan would immediately cost 6,000 timber jobs but would generate

15,000 jobs to clean up debris and damage in logging roads and streams,[53] while industry and labor envisioned job losses totaling 85,000.[54] The Northwest did lose 21,000 timber-related jobs between 1989 and 1996.[55]

Nevertheless, despite declines in the Northwest forest industry, there is still significant employment in timber work and therefore much at stake in the continued loss of timber revenue, at least according to the industry. One industry estimate, from the year 2000, suggests that roughly 56,000 workers in Oregon are in some way economically dependent on timber harvesting, whether through direct employment in forestry or in related, support industries.[56] Interestingly, much of the timber economy involves harvesting from nonfederal lands. In Oregon, state and private timberlands have generated an average of 3.6 bbf per year since 1975.[57] In 2005, the *Oregonian* reported that the strong U.S. housing market fueled an 11 percent increase in timber harvesting in Oregon in 2004, which was the most in more than a decade. Although harvests from national forests in Oregon increased 66 percent, from 203 million board feet in 2003 to 337 million in 2004 (in part owing to resolution of legal challenges to timber sales), national forests accounted for only 8 percent of the state's timber harvest in 2004. Sixty-eight percent came from large industrial tree farmers like Weyerhaeuser. Meanwhile, in western Oregon, harvests from small woodland owners, most of whom have only a few hundred acres or less in timber, increased from 298 million board feet in 2003 to 478 million in 2004.[58]

To the economic stakes of timber harvesting must be added the fact that timber sales have supported county budgets. Under the system in place until 2000, a quarter of the receipts from federal timber sales went to the local county or counties where the sales were held. In 1989, sales of national forest timber provided $211 million to Washington and Oregon for roads, schools, and local governments.[59] As of 1992, 25 to 66 percent of the total income for ten counties in Oregon came from such federal payments.[60] In southwest Oregon, the logging out of prime timber and the imposition of logging restrictions devastated county budgets.[61] In order to stabilize payments to counties in the face of declining timber sales, in 2000 Congress passed the Secure Rural Schools and Community Self-Determination Act. Under this law, which expires in

September 2006, counties' annual receipts each year are based on an average of the three years between 1986 and 1999 in which they received their highest payments. Oregon is the largest beneficiary of the Act, and received $273 million in 2005. However, as of this writing, the Act faced an uncertain future. The Bush Administration has sought to reduce or eliminate funding under the program. The Administration has also tried, unsuccessfully, to pay for the program by selling off up to 300,000 acres of federal forest lands, an unpopular move that would undermine national support for the Act.[62]

The Forest Service has also long subsidized local and regional economies through its highly controversial practice of below-cost timber sales. When the Forest Service undertakes a timber sale, it has traditionally assumed the cost of preparing timber contracts, determining the value of the timber to be sold, conducting the necessary environmental reviews, and building logging roads. The Forest Service also frequently sells timber at a discount. The United States General Accounting Office reported that in fiscal year 1990, the Forest Service paid out $35.6 million for expenses related to timber sales, a taxpayer transfer to timber companies. When payments to the states were added in, the costs rose to $112.2 million. The GAO reported that according to the Forest Service's own data for that year, timber sale costs exceeded revenues for 65 of the 122 national forests.[63] The actual costs of the timber sale program have been hard to determine because of unreliable accounting practices at the Forest Service, and cost projections have thus varied. For example, the Forest Service reported that its timber sale program lost $126 million in 1998, while the organization Taxpayers for Common Sense estimated the loss at more than $407 million, with 105 out of 111 national forests losing money. A report by the Southeast Alaska Conservation Council maintains that in 2002, timber subsidies provided by the Forest Service meant that every logging job created in Alaska's Tongass National Forest cost U.S. taxpayers over $170,000.[64] Critics have understandably branded these subsidies an ecologically destructive form of corporate welfare, though some public support for logging may be justified, as I discuss in chapter 7.

Logging restrictions have by no means been solely responsible for economic woes in Pacific Northwest timber communities. The loss of large trees that fed sawmills dependent on large diameter logs; the overseas export of raw, unprocessed logs; consolidation in the wood products industry; the shift of large private timber operations to more plentiful forests in the South; and significantly, automation, have since the 1960s caused significant unemployment among timber workers and reduced the number of small to mid-sized timber-processing firms in the Northwest.[65] While total regional harvest levels between 1980 and 1989 actually increased 23 percent, total forest-related employment declined 6.25 percent.[66]

The U.S. Forest Service is also to blame. Its mandate included protecting the stability of timber-dependent communities, but, as Dietrich recounts, the agency showed little foresight. In 1911, George Cecil, chief of the Forest Service's Pacific Northwest Region said, "Communities will depend upon the National Forests for a steady supply of timber and if we cannot meet this demand, we will have failed in our mission.... [It is] doubly important that we regulate national forest cuttings with the greatest consideration for the future welfare of the local communities." However, Dietrich notes that after World War II, the Forest Service's Northwest region calculated its harvest on the assumption that all its prime timberland would be available for logging for the foreseeable future; it completely failed to anticipate the demand for more wilderness and wilderness preserves. The agency had unduly ignored nontimber values. When, in response to the old-growth controversy, it had to drastically lower the annual cut, there were disappointed expectations and anger in timber-dependent communities. In fairness to the Forest Service, the agency was not only plagued by poor planning, notes Dietrich, but by mandates from Congress to maintain a high cut.[67]

Jonathan Kusel, director of Forest Community Research, argues that the Forest Service's approach to community stability was flawed from the outset. The agency, he argues, was primarily interested in getting wood to the timber industry, and it narrowly defined community stability in terms of employment levels and timber harvest. Even then, Kusel says, it took a short-term approach, particularly since it drastically increased the cut after World War II. The agency rejected a broader definition of community stability, such as that advocated in the early twentieth century by Benton MacKaye. MacKaye argued that the federal government should bring timber communities and workers into resource management, create worker-run logging and milling enterprises, and foster integrated planning of public and private forestlands.[68] Instead, as Kusel points out, by substituting the logging of national forests for the already depleted industrial timber lands, the Forest Service was able to temporarily maintain rural timber employment while neglecting the broader meanings of community stability and community well-being. This meant that reduced timber harvests would one day devastate communities. Because community stability had long been identified only with timber employment and high harvest levels rather than broader notions of community capacity, rural communities dependent on the forest sector lacked sufficient resources to deal with drastic reductions in employment. This was true despite Forest Service subsidies to the timber industry and timber communities. The ensuing increases in poverty and other types of social breakdown revealed the hollowness of the Forest Service's previous commitments to community stability, says Kusel.[69]

A Regional Shift Away from Timber

Given the impact of environmental restrictions, industry restructuring, and the long-term policies of the Forest Service, it is not surprising that timber is becoming less significant as an economic force in the Northwest. Even as timber employment declined, the 1990s saw an overall boom in income and jobs in the Pacific Northwest, much of it driven by the new information economy and a growth in tourism and other service-sector employment. In Oregon, for example, high technology has surpassed timber as the leading employer.[70] Partly because of economic diversification, many timber areas in the state experienced healthy recoveries, including rising incomes and low unemployment.[71]

Indeed, the economy, demographics, and culture of the American West are radically changing. The portion of the region's population living in urban areas grew from less than half in the 1930s to 86 percent in 1996.[72] Urbanization reduces the region's economic dependence on exploitation of natural resources, and a more urbanized population is interested in wilderness recreation.[73] This also generates more jobs in tourism and therefore new occupational alternatives for loggers and timber communities.[74] Some timber-dependent communities may have come out of the transition stronger than before.[75]

These trends are not entirely positive. Affluent residents, seeking environmental amenities, have also moved into timber country. This has frequently led to friction with old-timers and interference with rural ways of life. Newcomers tend to support logging restrictions. Moreover, when acquiring land, they often abrogate long-standing customs that had allowed neighbors access to private property for recreation, hunting, fishing, and wood fuel. Such changes have undermined an important aspect of local community life and the local informal economy. Increased affluence and the resulting rise in property values and property taxes have also made booming rural areas less affordable for poor and working class residents.[76]

The influx of well-to-do residents also generates sprawl, which may be more ecologically destructive than logging.[77] As the timber industry has declined, urban and suburban sprawl has encroached on private timberlands. For example, in 2004, the Washington State Department of Natural Resources reported that the state is experiencing a net loss of about 17,500 acres of forestland each year, mainly to development.[78] This is especially troubling because private timberlands are an essential part of any solution to the Northwest forest crisis.

Many rural areas have simply been bypassed by the new Northwest economy, and poverty there has gotten worse.[79] Despite the Northwest Forest Plan, rural communities throughout the Northwest have remained dependent on forest industries, and either are finding it difficult or are unwilling to diversify. Moreover, there are insufficient financial resources to assist with these communities' transition from the timber economy.[80]

The overall economic outlook for displaced timber workers may not be so sanguine after all. A 2003 study by Oregon State University and the Oregon Employment Department says that more than half the 60,000 workers in Oregon's wood products industry at the beginning of the 1990s had left the industry by 1998, and almost half of these left the Oregon work rolls entirely. Of those who found work in Oregon outside the wood products industry, their median income had dropped 0.9 percent by 1998. This is a seemingly modest drop, although one must also consider that median annual wages for all Oregon workers *increased* by 23.3 percent during the same period.[81] Tourism jobs in the region are often seasonal and low paying, in some cases paying less than half as much as timber-related work.[82]

History of the Conflict

Logging in the Pacific Northwest began in the late nineteenth century. Yet, as with the rest of the country, it was only after World War II that harvesting of federal lands in the region really took off.

The 1970s and 1980s: The Battle Is Joined

By 1969, a Forest Service study was already warning of the rapid depletion of old growth in the region. During the 1970s and 1980s, it became clear that intensive timber harvesting—particularly clear-cutting and short logging rotations—and the associated construction of logging roads were generating other environmental impacts. Timber operations were defacing the landscape, fragmenting habitat, reducing soil fertility, causing soil erosion and mudslides, damaging watersheds and other riparian areas, depleting fisheries, and threatening various species, including the northern spotted owl. Environmentalists also criticized the Forest Service and the timber industry for replanting with even-aged monocultures. Such a practice, they charged, was replacing diverse forests with biologically impoverished tree farms that lacked genetic resilience against pest outbreaks, fire, and other environmental disturbances.[83] Management also suppressed natural events like fire that are necessary for maintaining the forest ecosystem.[84] Clear-cutting, although it was a disturbance, did not provide the same benefits as fire, windthrow, and other natural events that left deadwood and residual living trees, creating a complex mosaic of vegetation types.[85]

Controversy over the region's national forests heated up during the 1970s, sparked by the aerial spraying of herbicides, the construction of logging roads in previously untouched areas, and threats to the Northern spotted owl.[86] By the late 1980s, the region, especially its old-growth forests, was the focus of legal and legislative battles, demonstrations by loggers and forest activists, acts of civil disobedience, and even "eco-sabotage" of logging equipment and spiking of trees by radical environmentalists like members of the group Earth First![87]

As environmentalists organized to save the owl and the old-growth forest, the timber industry counterattacked. Timber workers formed groups like the Oregon Lands Coalition and organized demonstrations.

Despite a long history of labor unrest, the workers were supported by the industry, including giant timber concerns like Weyerhaeuser.

Both sides took the issue to a national audience, environmentalists playing on public concern for scenic wilderness and endangered species, and the industry trying to mobilize homebuilders, carpenters, and consumers. Nationalization of the issue created a public perception of conflict between spotted owls and timber workers.[88] Congress was awash in competing legislative and lobbying efforts concerning timber harvesting and endangered species, although with little net result.

There were also legal battles to compel federal agencies to desist from logging old growth. Environmentalists initiated lawsuits under the Endangered Species Act or on the grounds that timber sales had not been properly subject to environmental impact statements mandated by the NFMA and the National Environmental Policy Act. In 1991, U.S. District Court Judge William L. Dwyer ruled that the George H. W. Bush administration's timber practices in the region violated federal endangered species law. Dwyer suspended some 80 percent of federal timber sales in Washington and Oregon west of the Cascades until a suitable spotted owl protection plan had been established.[89]

Swings of the Pendulum: The Bill Clinton and George W. Bush Administrations

In April 1993, President Clinton held a conference in the Northwest to bring the various constituencies together and achieve a compromise. Out of these discussions emerged the administration's Northwest Forest Plan in 1994. The plan focused on both an ecosystem-oriented management approach (see chapter 7) and economic assistance to affected communities.[90] Covering 24.4 million acres of national forest in the Westside, the plan made 4.9 million acres available for timber harvesting, set aside 1.3 million acres for ten adaptive management areas (AMAs)—ranging in size from 83,900 to 399,500 acres—to be managed through experimental techniques, including bringing in local stakeholders, and provided varying levels of protection for the roughly 18.2 million remaining acres. The plan also provided for ecosystem restoration, the decommissioning of some roads, and improvements to other roads to reduce erosion. The plan set an annual harvest of 1.2 bbf from old-growth trees, compared with 5 bbf annually in 1987 and 1988. It provided for the protection of 47 percent of the federal lands under its jurisdiction.[91] Meanwhile, under the Northwest Economic Adjustment Initiative, $1.2 billion over five years would be provided by various federal and state agencies to assist timber workers and their families and communities through a number of programs, including job retraining, employment in ecosystem restoration, and payments to timber-dependent counties.[92] In response to the plan, Judge Dwyer lifted his injunction against timber harvesting in the region.

The Northwest Forest Plan was in many ways a hopeful initiative, and it signaled a decisive shift away from the commodity orientation of the Forest Service. Not only was a significant amount of land, and especially old-growth acreage, protected from logging, but the plan also established a "survey-and-manage" approach under which even old growth theoretically open to logging would be checked for the presence of so-called sensitive species.[93] Furthermore, the plan provided for a general policy of adaptive management that allowed flexible approaches in the light of improved or changing ecological information,[94] and it pursued experiments in community-based forest management. (The plan is discussed further in chapter 7.)

Legal battles nevertheless continued. Timber interests were unhappy with the plan's restrictions on logging; they claimed continued job losses and charged the administration with failing to meet targeted harvests from old-growth areas. The survey-and-manage requirements and the government's reluctance to log even in areas where logging would be allowed had indeed greatly lowered timber harvests below targeted levels. The AMAs were also managed conservatively with respect to logging,[95] and funding for the AMAs was drastically cut over time.[96] On 1997 the harvest from areas under the plan peaked, at 880 million board feet and declined to 308 million board feet in 2001.[97]

For their part, environmentalists were unhappy with provisions for salvage logging in protected areas and other supposed loopholes in the plan, and, despite the much-reduced old-growth harvest, with the Clinton administration's alleged failure to actually adhere to logging restrictions under the plan.[98] They were also concerned by the continued decline of the Northern spotted owl under the plan; a federal study in the 1990s found an annual decrease of 3.9 percent in the owl's population.[99]

The debate over Clinton's road-building ban, coupled with mounting efforts on the part of activists and wildlife officials to protect not only the spotted owl but salmon populations and other threatened or endangered animals and plants, yielded more tensions in the Northwest, including more court injunctions against logging.

President George W. Bush worked to undo some aspects of the Northwest Forest Plan, including eliminating the survey-and-manage requirements, and his administration has sought to limit the ability of citizens to file legal appeals against timber sales.[100] Bush also abandoned Dombeck's old-growth logging ban and sought to increase old-growth harvesting to levels that had been promised under the Northwest Forest Plan. As noted earlier, Bush has resisted Clinton's road-building ban and used the rationale of forest health to push for more logging. Kitzhaber charges that Bush's healthy forests gambit has substituted the goal of addressing a symptom of poor forest health—wildfires—for improving the ecosystem itself and has used fire suppression as an excuse for suspending environmental laws and judicial oversight. Bush, he says, has repolarized the Northwest debate, threatening what he sees as fragile elements of cooperation and trust between antagonists that had developed during the Clinton years.[101]

However, logging in the Northwest reflected the general decline in federal timber harvesting since the 1990s. For example, in Oregon, the total harvest from all timber lands, public and private, went from about 8 bbf per year before 1990 to about 3.5 bbf in 1998.[102] Figures for Oregon's national forests, cited by John H. Beuter, president of the Society of American Foresters, shows that despite a projected harvest of 1.3 bbf per year under the Northwest Forest Plan and an ecosystem management plan for eastern Oregon, the actual harvest averaged 400 million board feet for the years 1997–2001 and dropped to 173 million board feet in 2001.[103] According to former Forest Service chief Jack Ward Thomas, the implementation of the Northwest Forest Plan, the Endangered Species Act, court decisions favoring preservation, environmentalists' refusal to compromise, and perhaps the balance of prevailing national opinion all suggest that the era of significant old-growth logging may be over.[104] Yet, as on the national stage, years of policy efforts and court litigation have failed to resolve the fundamental disagreement over the nature, value or worth, and purpose of old-growth forests and forests in general.

Timber Interests and Forest Activists

Multiple interests are involved in the Northwest forest debate, yet the debate has created roughly two camps: timber interests and forest activists. This alignment has brought together even traditionally antagonistic groups, most notably within the timber industry.

Timber interests, who oppose logging restrictions, include several constituencies: loggers and other timber workers concerned about jobs; mill owners dependent on national forest timber, especially old growth; timber-dependent communities worried about economic and social survival; and private timberland owners, both large industrial forestry and wood products enterprises and owners of smaller timber parcels.

There are indeed differences within this camp. As Judith Lazyer notes, it is the small sawmills that are primarily dependent on wood from federal lands. The six large timber companies in the Northwest have their own large land base of about 7 million acres. This has been largely cleared of old growth; the large firms are now oriented toward the cultivation and logging of smaller trees. However, private timberland owners, large and small, fear that logging restrictions on public lands will eventually lead to regulation of their own landholdings.[105]

There is a major difference in outlook between timber workers on the one hand and what I call timber managers—professional foresters in and out of government and timber industry executives—on the other. Timber workers are concerned with the preservation of jobs and timber communities, which often conflicts with the efforts of timber managers to maximize profits and productive efficiency. Unsurprisingly, over the years the timber industry has been the scene of considerable labor unrest and working-class radicalism. There has been conflict among timber workers, small mill owners, and giant wood products firms on issues such as industry restructuring, mechanization, unsustainable logging, and overseas exports of raw logs. Nevertheless, the various parties have made common cause against forest activists. Timber interests share certain views of old growth and other forests, and of human beings' proper relationship with forests as places. As we will see, this view falls into line with an emphasis on founding.

Those favoring logging restrictions I call forest activists. They include forest ecologists and wildlife biologists (although some scientists work for the timber industry);[106] fishermen concerned about the impacts of logging on anadromous fish; hikers, backpackers, and other outdoor enthusiasts; rural residents enamored of the wilderness; the region's growing tourism industry; and, of course, environmental activists.[107] The environmental community is itself divided over whether or how much to compromise with industry or government. There are also tensions between primarily local organizations and those with a more regional or national constituency. Nevertheless, like the timber camp, environmentalists, along with many other forest activists, share some key fundamental views.

On both sides of the Northwest timber debate are federal, state, and local elected officials, as well as public agencies and the courts. Of the federal agencies, the Forest Service is of course at the center of the controversy, although the BLM and the Fish and Wildlife Service are also involved. The Forest Service's traditional hostility to strong wilderness preservation policies has long aligned the agency with timber interests. As I noted, this orientation was somewhat moderated during the Clinton years.

The Timber Perspective

The Forest as Timber Resource

How do timber interests view old growth and other forests? Most commonly, they see forests as having instrumental value, i.e., as means to a further end. Forests are resources for timber and wood products, great tree farms providing the nation with essential goods.[108] This view goes back to Pinchot, who said, "Forestry is tree farming.... Trees may be grown as a crop just as corn may be grown as a crop.... The forester gets crop after crop of logs, cordwood, shingles, poles, or railroad ties from his forest."[109] A 1992 article in the *Wall Street Journal* thus described as "the common local view" remarks by Matt Anderson, a former logger in Forks, Washington: "This whole area is just a big old tree farm.... We cut down the trees, they grow back."[110] Timber interests criticize forest activists for ignoring their own dependence on the goods yielded by such a "farm."[111]

Nature Needs Management

However, timber interests see more to logging than the harvesting of resources. Logging enables the orderly, efficient, productive, and even moral management of nature. Timber interests have traditionally ignored the complexity and diversity of old growth and paid insufficient attention to the ecosystem services that natural forests provide. Instead, in their view, the unmanaged forest is chaotic, precariously subject to death, change, and catastrophe. "Bugs, fire or man are going to harvest the trees; they don't live forever," remarks an Oregon mill owner.[112] Old-growth trees, which have stopped growing and have begun succumbing to death and decay, are objects of special opprobrium. In fact, old growth has historically been termed decadent.[113] Larry Mason, a Forks mill owner and logger, criticizes those who would protect old growth from logging: "People don't understand the dynamic nature of the forest. It's decadent—it's in the dying phase of its cycle. This concept of groves of eternal sentinels is just not true."[114] Similarly, the reframing of the national timber debate into an issue of forest health was motivated by the argument that unless they are intensively managed and harvested for timber, forests will ultimately destroy themselves.[115] An Idaho timber worker remarked, "If you can't log it and you don't maintain it, it's going to be destroyed."[116]

According to this view, says Steven Yaffee, old growth is the antithesis of good long-term forest management.[117] It has passed its point of efficient wood fiber production, and the large amount of fallen and dead timber provides an entry point for fires and insect infestations.[118] Furthermore, because it was once believed that old growth does not support big game animals, it was long called a biological desert by foresters and biologists.[119]

Founding a New Forest

If we focus on the Forest Service, we can see how this notion of management reflects a founding orientation toward place. The Forest Service was historically a leading proponent of the management of nature and showed an especial antipathy toward old growth. "Fundamentally,"

Yaffee says, "the Forest Service is about control"[120] and "landscape manipulation."[121]

This domineering ethos goes back to the origins of the Forest Service in the Progressive Era. Pinchot, who had studied scientific forestry in Germany and also subscribed to Progressive Era views about reform through "good government" elites, saw forestry as a top-down enterprise in which experts rationally administered resources on behalf of the public good, although without the interference of public participation.[122]

The Forest Service's managerial approach, coupled with its desire to maximize timber yields, led to an emphasis on founding. Experts at the Forest Service could sweepingly transform the landscape into a more productive, rationally organized forest that would serve the public need for timber. According this view, the problematic old-growth forests were a blank slate that allowed the creation of ideal multiple-use, maximum sustained-yield forests.[123] Yaffee, writing in 1994, noted that to many Forest Service employees, "forest management is a process of creating a new landscape on a broad canvas of forest resources that is exciting and motivating, similar perhaps to the process of creating a new piece of art."[124] Through most of its history, the Forest Service policy was to clear-cut old growth, harvest the timber, and substitute even-aged stands consisting mostly of Douglas fir. These would be managed scientifically and efficiently on a sixty-to-eighty year rotation to maximize the long-term yield of wood fiber, and along the way produce "deer and recreation user-days."[125]

Dietrich describes a new kind of forest that had taken the place of old growth in the vicinity of Forks, Washington:

The monstrous gloom of old-growth had been replaced with plantations of cone-like conifers, the same age, the same height, the same species. Clearcuts were burned clean for this progeny, planted so densely that competing vegetation would be squeezed out, and sprayed, thinned, and fertilized for maximum growth. To those who raised doubts about this transformation of the forest, the foresters and economists had charts and studies defending the utility of their practice. By the 1980s estimates varied on when the last of the original forest would be converted to this improved variety—some said thirty years, some fifty—but there was no question conversion would occur. Most foresters considered it an improvement.[126]

This effort to found a radically new forest in place of the old took on a moral fervor. "The unregulated forest was [regarded as] something to be altered for moral reasons," says environmental historian Nancy Langston. "The problem was not just with old growth or dying timber; the problem was with a forest that did not produce precisely what people wanted." It seemed to represent a "recalcitrant, complex nature marked by disorder and riot."[127] From this standpoint, nature needed the transformative hand of humans to secure a plentiful, predictable supply of useful resources.

The Forest Service compared its own work to the destructive, now-notorious "slum"-clearing enterprise of urban renewal, which I discuss later, and even acknowledged a violent aspect to its founding project. In 1965, Forest Service Chief Edward Cliff approvingly described clear-cutting as "something like an urban renewal project, a necessary violent prelude to a new housing project." Though it might cause a "temporary loss of natural beauty ... there is also the promise of what is to come: a thrifty new forest replacing the old."[128]

The timber industry has had an orientation similar to that of the Forest Service. Dietrich describes the future envisioned by major timber enterprises:

The old-growth forest is a matter of only historical interest to the big corporations, as interesting and irrelevant as the mastodon. They are well on their way to creating their own future: plantations of genetically improved "super trees," big-tired feller-buncher machines that snip trees mechanically and thus partially replace hand cutting with chainsaws, modern mills that require a minimum of labor to saw second-growth sticks into product, and a market driven by global supply and demand.[129]

It is interesting, that absent from this picture are not only old-growth trees, but also traditional loggers, who are largely replaced by machinery.[130] Whatever the "gee-whiz" quality of such futuristic forests, their architects in the Forest Service and the timber industry have more or less overlooked the long-term implications for timber communities and natural ecosystems. Timber managers in the Forest Service and the industry certainly did not intend to create something socially or ecologically unsustainable. They were conscious founders of a new forest, but did not aim, to borrow from Machiavelli, to simply "spoil things." However, in their fervor to found a new forest, they paid little real attention to the long-term preservation of socially functional communities and ecologically healthy and diverse forests. They did not even live up to Pinchot's longer-term perspective. They focused on their own founding ingenuity with insufficient attention to what was already there, and as a result they turned out to be clumsy, short-sighted, single-minded, and destructive founders. The idea that an existing landscape can be wiped away and replaced wholesale is the antithesis of a cultivation-and-care approach that combines founding and preservation.

Antidemocratic Implications of Timber Management

Such an emphasis on intensive management and landscape transformation also leads in a fundamentally antidemocratic direction, as noted earlier. The example of the Forest Service is again instructive. Various federal environmental laws have mandated public participation in agency planning. Nevertheless, public involvement has generally been resented, resisted, and kept to a minimum by the agency, in part by allowing the least effective forms of public participation. Kusel remarks that the Forest Service and other federal agencies dealing with resources have "insulated their decision-making authority and monopolistic claims to management expertise from the public participation mechanisms mandated in environmental legislation." He notes that resource agencies tend to limit participation to the agency-controlled public hearing and the formal comment periods required by regulations. "Once public input has been gathered, 'neutrally' competent technical experts within the agency make the final determination as to which plan option will be pursued."[131] Similarly, Yaffee says that the Forest Service

tended to view public involvement as a linear process, not a dynamic, interactive one. The agency's approach contained four steps: let the public express their concerns, go back to the office and figure out what is best for them, given the agency's understanding of its responsibilities and the capabilities of the resource base; produce a draft plan and provide a period for public comment; and make a decision. This approach reflected the agency's view of itself as the repository of technical expertise, its understanding of its statutory obligations, and its interest in controlling the flow of the decision at hand. What it did not provide was an opportunity for interchange between affected interests, a chance for creative solutions to emerge (that were not within the normal vision of agency personnel) or much ownership of the resulting decision on the part of affected interests.[132]

Dietrich puts it more bluntly: "[T]he agency seemed to view the general public as a bothersome blob to be kept at bay while the important work of old-growth liquidation and replanting went on."[133]

The timber industry, and not just the Forest Service, has been guilty of trying to shut out the public. The forest health policies pushed by pro-timber forces and their supporters in Congress and the Bush administration have limited public legal challenges to timber sales.

Recall how place founders must pursue their projects in the context of human plurality. To the degree that others get a voice in the place founding and planning process, the founder's original plan is subject to debate and uncertainty. Those who want to remake a forest into a tree plantation can come up against an environmentally conscious public that raises aesthetic, ecological, moral, and recreational questions, or even timber communities concerned about their own long-term viability. The solution for the single-minded founder is to control the process by excluding the public, mollifying it with the illusion of participation, and so legitimizing a fundamentally antidemocratic process.

The Forest as (Work) Place

The effort to gain control over the forest is perhaps experienced most immediately and tangibly by loggers, yet a logger's experience is not simply one of conquest and control. The rhetoric and attitudes of timber workers reveal a complex and interesting perspective on the forest. One gets the impression that timber work is a satisfying and valued vocation in and of itself, a fundamental constituent of a prized way of life, and a basis for place attachment to forests.

In national forests, contractors who employ loggers are hired by timber companies to do the harvesting. The work of cutting down trees is extremely strenuous and hazardous. Despite mechanization in recent decades, logging still remains one of the most physical trades.[134] This is especially true in the old-growth stands of the Pacific Northwest, where steep terrain and large trees limit mechanization and loggers still often use chain saws rather than large machines like feller-bunchers.[135]

The physical demands and the sense of danger provide an attractive challenge. Huge old-growth trees are especially challenging; felling them requires an especially high level of mental concentration. Loggers accordingly take pride in their technique and skill. Dietrich observes: "A good cutter likes to boast he can fall a tree so accurately that it will hit precisely enough to drive a stake into the ground," although "every tree is a bit of a mystery until it's cut."[136]

Tied in with this demanding, skilled work is a sense of independence, self-direction, and accomplishment. One logger thus explains to Dietrich that someone who cuts trees "is his own boss.... A cutter makes his own decisions at each tree, earning more [in terms of harvested timber] if he calls it right, risking his life if he guesses wrong. Most of the time a cutter works alone, at his own pace, one man at one tree."[137] There is a tangible sense of accomplishment, the pleasure of doing a good day's work. Alternatives are unappealing, says logger Russ Poppe: "I don't know if another job would be as satisfying. Not one that would have the physical and mental stimulation."[138]

Timber work also involves a deep sense of individual and collective identity. Tom Hirons, an Oregon logger, says in regard to job retraining, "You're not asking me to find a new job. You're asking me to re-identify myself, and that's a painful process."[139] Loggers, mill employees, and other forest workers see themselves as part of a storied vocation going back generations. Many are also embedded in long-standing communities built around the timber economy, although a large number of forest workers are migrants: Kusel notes that tree planters in the United States are mostly mobile Latinos, and Cassandra Moseley and Stacey Shankle report that contractors on national forest jobs in the Pacific Northwest may travel hundreds of miles to their work.[140]

Timber work generates a sense of community and local pride and independence. It may even foster political mobilization. This was perhaps evidenced by political activism and solidarity within timber communities in response to both logging restrictions and stigmatization by environmentalists. Although communities lacked sufficient social and economic resilience in the face of declining timber harvests, they did become somewhat politically assertive. Nearly every business in Forks closed down on May 23, 1991 for a protest rally in Olympia; almost a third of the town's inhabitants attended.[141] Theresa Satterfield says that a "swelling of pride in self as logger, mill worker, or simply member of timber-dependent community" was critical in such mobilization.[142]

However, one should not exaggerate loggers' activism or political efficacy; in many ways they have been profoundly disempowered by the timber conflict, as I discuss later. Moreover, Mark Baker and Jonathan Kusel argue that decades of exclusion from natural resource decision-making processes and direct and indirect retaliation by employers when workers tried to speak out may have made many timber workers averse to political participation.[143] Beverly Brown maintains that much of the mobilization in response to the threat of logging restrictions involved an industry-sponsored "yellow ribbon" campaign that tried to create a blue-collar counterweight to environmentalist successes. She argues that timber workers' distrust of the industry—the legacy of a long history of labor unrest—ultimately doomed this campaign and that timber communities failed to achieve a significant degree of organization.[144]

Beyond the attractions of a challenging, dangerous job, timber work also forges a place connection with the forest. Despite talk of decadent forests needing intensive management, timber workers express admiration for old-growth trees. Dietrich observes that old growth captures the imagination of loggers. The trees' "age and girth and the crash of their fall adds drama to a cutter's work.... Above all, their value and unpredictability calls for skill." He quotes logger Joe Helvey, who says, "I'd rather cut in old-growth," adding, "It's a lot more of a challenge. It's an accomplishment when you can lay it out and save it out to the berries at the end."[145]

Old growth is more than a resource; it provides for intrinsically satisfying work. Admittedly this is still an instrumental value; the trees are a means to a good work experience. In fact, though, for loggers, the value of old growth may be even more than instrumental. Old-growth trees seem to elicit wonder and appreciation by their inherent qualities, particularly their age and size. Old growth has value for more than its timber and the challenge of harvesting it.

Loggers and timber communities claim a deep knowledge of and attachment to the forests around them. They often regard the woods as a cherished place, and not only because of the challenging, spectacular trees. Bob Tuttle, the owner of a small woodlot, describes his work and his land: "It's not necessarily a way of life, so much—it's a place of life. These are roots that most people never get to know. If we sold it, we'd be rich on paper. But the truth is, we'd be poor. How could I come back here and know someone else had it?"[146] Timber workers have indeed built histories and communities in close relationship with the forest, sometimes over the course of generations. Cheri Jacobson, director of United Forest Families, says, "We have members who are third generation wood workers whose proud heritage comes from the forest."[147]

She claims, "We are the true environmentalists who work and care for the land."[148] During the early 1990s, a popular bumper sticker in Douglas County, Oregon, thus declared, FOR A FORESTER, EVERY DAY IS EARTH DAY.[149] Such remarks are partly strategic; they seek to sway public opinion by adopting environmentalist rhetoric. However, they also suggest a deep place attachment.

The future vision of the intensively managed forest, harvested through automated logging, may not provide much room for timber workers. Nevertheless, the managed forest that has emerged so far still evokes pride among timber communities. Communities like Forks take pride in the worked aspect of the landscape, in the legacy of past cuts. For the residents of Forks, "[t]he cut patches...underline the point that this is working town."[150] Dietrich notes that "in the center of town ... there is a graying slice from the trunk of a spruce, its diameter higher than any head, and a sign noting proudly that the tree sprouted before the arrival of Columbus. Above is a sign reflecting Forks' claim of the 1970s: LOGGING CAPITAL OF THE WORLD."[151]

Yet loggers and timber communities also express attachment to the more natural aspects of the landscape, i.e., to the forested landscape as a whole, including its wildlife. Commenting on timber workers' lack of enthusiasm for job retraining, a case manager for a retraining program in Forks remarked, "The woods are a lot more appealing than some place with fluorescent light bulbs. I have yet to see a bear or a deer or an eagle wander through this office."[152] At a 1989 public hearing, Jim Standard, an Oregon timber worker, proclaimed a profound connection with and respect for the landscape:

I was born and raised in Oregon from pioneer stock. For generations my family has been involved in the timber industry in one aspect or another. We have always depended on timber for our livelihood, and because of this dependence, we have probably gained a respect for the forest and the land that few people will ever know.... As long as I can remember, loggers have been accused of ruining wildlife habitat. From past experience, I would disagree. Unless a person has actually sat quietly at a logging site and watched and listened, they cannot appreciate the amount of wildlife that is around.... Ask any logger who shares his lunch with a raccoon, a chipmunk, a raven, or even a doe and her fawn if he is destroying habitat or enhancing it.[153]

This identification with vocation, community, and landscape involves the extension of self and identification with place discussed in chapter 1.

Although the forest is treated as a resource and commodity and even something to be tamed, is also integral to timber workers' and communities' sense of self or identity. In fact, the forest is a foundation of this identity, for without it, a way of life vanishes.

The forest becomes something larger with which one is affiliated. One inhabits the forested landscape, works in the woods, and is dependent on the forest for one's livelihood. This "something larger" transcends commodity value. The forest overshadows human beings and elicits wonder. More than that, it demands a level of esteem that becomes a kind of respect. Thus Jim Standard is able to talk about having "gained a respect for the forest." In their view of the forest, timber workers thus show commonalties with forest activists. Indeed, Dietrich notes that a person may see the woods as both a place of commodity production *and* a source of transcendent values.[154] Nevertheless, this combination of views is highly conflicted.

The Logger's Conflicted Perspective

The timber industry and the Forest Service have generally shown little regard for the attachments of timber workers and communities to the forest, to their work, and to their rural way of life. As I remarked earlier, the industry has been marked by labor conflict, and the Forest Service ultimately undermined community stability. Over the course of the twentieth century old growth was liquidated, timber harvesting became mechanized and more efficient, logging rotations were shortened, harvesting operations were relocated, and forests were clear-cut to service corporate debt. The forest was treated like a blank slate, to recall Yaffee's comment, a slate upon which the Forest Service and the timber industry could execute projects of founding and refounding. In the Pacific Northwest, the logging out of private lands and the subsequent drive to wipe out old growth and cut ever-higher levels of timber on public lands in the post-World War II era caused significant ecological damage and ultimately endangered the long-term prospects of the regional timber economy. An excess of founding, of trying to radically transform forests into maximally productive tree plantations, was pursued without regard to ecological and social impacts and so ended up undermining preservation of place. To paraphrase Machiavelli, the timber industry and the Forest Service used their founding activities to spoil things, not to mend them.

Yet at the same time, despite their appreciation for old growth and their place attachments, loggers have also viewed forests and trees as commodities. In the end, this commodifying perspective has won out in determining timber workers' political allegiance. Dietrich, citing sociologist Robert Lee, says that despite feeling caught between environmentalists and the timber industry, "loggers feel more closely allied to [wood products firms like] ITT-Rayonier or Plum Creek or Weyerhaeuser.... They see in industry more shared values." He quotes Lee: "Loggers focus on the fact that society needs products." Also, Lee says, "They are enamored of the free market."[155] However, a market-oriented perspective makes timber workers, timber communities, and the forest as a place potentially or actually expendable. The sympathies of loggers and timber communities are torn between the founding orientation of transforming the forest into an efficient timber-producing machine without sufficient regard for the stability of the local landscape and local ways of life, and an opposing desire to maintain their communities and the forest they work in and have grown attached to. In this ambivalence there may be some promise; there may be the basis for a balanced reintegration of founding and preservation.

Forest Activists

In arguing for old-growth protection, forest activists employ a variety of arguments. Sometimes they point to instrumental values, including resource considerations, such as pharmaceuticals to be obtained from old-growth's genetic library. However, the instrumental values most often cited by activists do not involve commodities, or at least not directly. Forest activists instead focus on recreation, tourism, scientific value, and ecosystem services, such as the role of old growth in maintaining watersheds and fisheries. Old growth is most valuable when it is left intact. Activists generally reject a primary reliance on instrumental values. Much more so than timber workers and timber communities, forest activists emphasize the forests' intrinsic value.

"Something Greater than Ourselves"

Forest activists first of all celebrate the aesthetic value of old growth. They see old growth as magnificently beautiful, a judgment that is hard to deny. Yet for forest activists that beauty goes beyond visual attributes. For one thing, activists emphasize the antiquity of old growth. "[O]ne of the aspects about old-growth trees that made them so fascinating" for forest activists, Dietrich says, was "the considerable age of these living things, routinely older than the republic and sometimes as old as the Norman Conquest."[156]

Journalist Catherine Caulfield, writing in the *New Yorker*, expresses this reverence for old growth's antiquity. She begins her account of the old-growth controversy with the line, "Ours was once a forested planet."[157] Telling of now-extirpated forests in the Middle East and Europe, she carries the saga of destruction to the settlers' logging of North America. "In the West," she says, "the loggers came up against their last frontier—the most magnificent forest on the continent and the greatest conifer forest on earth." In this forest, "[f]ive-hundred-year-old trees are not uncommon...and some of the trees are more than two thousand years old. These are the largest and oldest trees in the world, and their age and size imbue this forest with a solemnity so deep it seems to many visitors spiritual."[158] For Caulfield, the forest is a relic of a once-green, primeval Earth.

Christopher Manes, a former Earth First! activist, offers a similar picture in his description of Oregon's Kalmiopsis Forest: "Undisturbed by the icy assaults and retreats of glaciers, these stands of Douglas fir, cedar, and sugar pine are thought to have held their peaceful vigil over the area since the Pliocene Epoch some five million years ago."[159]

In a stark contrast to the proud display of a pre-Columbian trunk by her fellow Washingtonians in Forks, U.S. Senator Patty Murray (D-Washington) also invoked antiquity during a 1996 floor debate on logging. Exhibiting a photograph, she said, "My friends, this picture is of a tree that was cut down.... This tree is well over 250 years old. This tree is older than the Constitution of the United States of America."[160]

The invocation of antiquity suggests two possible rationales for forest preservation. First of all, antiquity can involve aesthetic appeal. The grandeur of old growth, often enhanced by shafts of light filtering through the trees, and the beautiful visual complexity of the forest, with its multistoried canopy, fallen logs, and standing dead trees, requires centuries to develop. Moreover, the sheer knowledge that something is very old can add directly to our perception of its beauty.

Beyond aesthetics, antiquity tangibly connects us to our own history. The idea that a tree may be hundreds or thousands of years old gives us the sense that the deep past still exists for us in an actual living organism. Antiquity can also imply merit. Old-growth trees have achieved something by virtue of their sheer endurance over the centuries.

Antiquity also suggests that the forest represents something even greater. Unlike their antagonists in the timber camp, forest activists do not see old growth as teetering on the brink of fire, pestilence, or other catastrophe. For activists, the antiquity of old growth reflects the strength and stability of a larger natural order with a good of its own. A focus on antiquity and long-term stability is evident in the term popularly favored in lieu of old-growth: *ancient forest*. An environmental group, the Oregon Natural Resources Council (ONRC), coined the label in 1988 and it stuck. The phrase, says geographer James Proctor, "stressed a long-standing, pre-existent nature that fascinated people and compelled them to help protect it."[161] Dietrich makes a similar point: "The trees themselves suggested the columns of an ancient ruin. Besides, environmentalists wanted to draw a contrast between the ecosystem that preceded humans and the more sterile industrial tree farms that were replacing it."[162]

Far from being decadent or expendable, the ancient forest is a venerable manifestation of a vast and timeless natural order predating human history and dwarfing human affairs, even the venerated Constitution. Such a natural order overshadows human interests and values and demands a deep measure of respect, not simply because it is beautiful or because it has survived all this time, but also because it is a lot more significant than humanity on a cosmic scale. To borrow from Lawrence Buell, an ancient forest renders human history "accountable to natural history as a higher authority than its own parochial institutions."[163]

In addition to highlighting antiquity, forest activists also emphasize the internal complexity and interdependence of old-growth forests. Activists speak of the ecosystem's biological diversity and myriad interactions among plants, birds, mammals, fungi, and other organisms. These accounts evoke a complex, interdependent, self-sustaining community, even a superorganism unto itself. Manes thus describes the Kalmiopsis:

Remote and rugged, the Kalmiopsis is not often visited by people, and only now are ecologists beginning to piece together the forest's complex and often mysterious relationship with the biosphere as a whole: through its ability to assimilate greenhouse gases, stabilize the runoff from rainstorms, and provide habitat for anadromous fish, like salmon, that live in the ocean but spawn in the clean, cool streams associated with virgin forest.[164]

Manes pictures the Kalmiopsis as bewilderingly complex, as having an almost purposeful character. It seems to be a vast, mysterious, quasi-sentient superorganism.

In his otherwise nonpartisan account, Dietrich conveys a similar image: the Northwest's old growth is "America's final great forest: one of the last in which the design of something greater than ourselves can clearly be seen." Regarding the giant conifers, he says, "The idea that something that big is alive, pumping water more than twenty stories high, grasping the sun with seventy million needles, and showering the ground with up to eight million seeds per acre each year is to remind us how unbelievable the planet is." He adds, "To ramble across the mossy mat of a big old-growth log ... is to walk across the breast of a giant, sleeping mother."[165]

This conception of the forest as an ancient, magnificent, complex, and mysterious superorganism suggests a commanding presence.[166] To see an entity as a commanding presence is to see it as having scale, power, and independence because it reflects or embodies great natural or historical forces that are not easily subject to human whim or control.[167] A commanding presence elicits the psychological experience of awe; the aesthetic sensibility of the sublime;[168] and the moral responses of reverence, respect, and care for an entity and its independent good. A commanding presence is not a quality that actually inheres in forests, giant conifers, etc. Rather, the perception of a commanding presence is our response to qualities that give the natural world or natural entities a kind of larger scale in comparison with human beings. The perception of a commanding presence in nature can arise through aesthetic, scientific, or spiritual experiences. It can come about through outdoor recreation. It can also arise through physical work: loggers who admire old growth see a commanding presence in the forest.

The experience of a commanding presence in the natural, as opposed to the built, environment may be uniquely powerful, for here the sense of something beyond our control is most compelling. Nevertheless, the notion of a commanding presence can also apply to built places. As products of long histories, many cities, neighborhoods, buildings, and agricultural landscapes are not the creatures of particular individuals or even particular generations. We consequently feel a reverence for historic places, places that have been shaped by or were the setting for significant social events, or places whose character reflects or helps to sustain a society's cultural practices. Like a mountain or an ancient forest or, for that matter, a long-standing timber community, such places are an embodiment of forces—in this case, social forces—larger than one individual and/or the present generation.

Of course, just because a place is a commanding presence in that it *reflects* forces beyond human control does not mean that that place is itself invulnerable to human beings. Certainly, it is difficult (though not impossible, as the highly destructive coal-mining practice of mountaintop removal demonstrates) to level a mountain. However, not all commanding presences are so resistant, as the cases in this book demonstrate. Commanding presence or not, a forest can be cleared or a historic neighborhood razed. For many environmentalists, the failure to recognize and respect the old-growth forest as a commanding presence involves a profound lack of respect, even a kind of desecration.

From characterizations of old growth's profound antiquity and complexity, it is a relatively small step to its sanctification. For many activists, old-growth forests provide a contemplative escape from society and the sense of participating in a vast creation. Thus Caulfield talks of "a solemnity so deep it seems to many visitors spiritual."[169] Activist Lou Gold, who camped for years atop Bald Mountain in the Kalmiopsis, called his spot a holy place.[170] Dietrich says Gold "felt as if he were walking back into some kind of Eden."[171] In the eyes of at least some activists, old growth is a sacred, mysterious, purposeful whole that demands respect and even reverence and obedience. Human beings have a profound, overriding moral duty to protect and preserve this ecosystem.

"Their Patch of Forest"

Forest activists are also moved by a more intimate, daily connection with old growth. Although timber interests characterize activists as urbanites and outsiders or meddlesome newcomers, many are from the rural Northwest.[172] Remarking on the local roots of forest activism, Caulfield says "The battle to preserve what remains of our ancient forests is … driven primarily by passion for a place. Across the Pacific region, people have fought to save their patch of forest—the one they live near, the one they know, the one they walk in or camp in, the one that overlooks their town, the one they see every day."[173]

She emphasizes that the campaign to save the ancient forest was not started by professional environmentalists in Washington, D.C., but by scores of local groups, who are carrying it on.[174]

These remarks suggest that forest activists, and especially those who are locally based, do not view the forest simply in reverential terms. They are also motivated by a more intimate identification with "their patch of forest," a passion for a familiar place. They have conceptualized a portion of it as their own "patch." They see this patch as integral to their daily lives, landscapes, and communities, as part of their identities. In a similar vein are many frequent visitors who have spent time in the forest and have grown personally attached to particular places there.

Like the more reverential image of the forest, this image of the forest as a familiar patch also gives preservation moral force. Local and other personal ties with the forest inspire deep loyalty and generate moral responsibilities that involve not only reverence but also fidelity and care.[175] The forest is like a community, neighbor, friend, or loved one toward which or whom one has built up a set of obligations through a shared history and set of relationships. As discussed in chapter 1, an individual can develop such a moral, respectful attitude toward a deeply familiar place. One's relationship with such a place may help shape one's identity and conception of one's own good and thus foster a set of preservationist moral obligations. It is important to note that this is not dissimilar to timber communities' fight on behalf of their own communities and "patch of forest."

Hostility to Logging

Despite some analogies between their own perspective and that of timber interests, forest activists see little cause to celebrate logging. Activists have put great hope in the Northwest's continuing economic transition away from timber and they seem to want the Northwest timber industry to just fade into history.[176] They emphasize how timber harvesting, especially clear-cutting, has disrupted and threatened an irreplaceable, ancient ecosystem. The forest, they argue, is not decadent and in need of management, but flourishes best without human interference. The ancient forest might be a place human beings live near and visit but one they should also leave be.[177] We should not regard the old-growth forest as a place for physical labor; work is conspicuously absent from Caulfield's description of how activists interact with their patch of forest. Armed with their chain saws, human beings become agents of destruction, degradation, disequilibrium, and desecration. Our monocultural tree plantations are poor replicas of nature's order, monuments to ham-fisted management. Indeed, forest activists see logging as a moral transgression against the old-growth forest and nature as a whole. At best, logging involves crude insensitivity to the natural world. Victor Rozek of the Native Forest Council says: "These trees are living museums. I find myself wondering whenever one of these trees goes down, what was going through the mind of the guy who cut it? Was it sadness? Or elation? Or was it just a job? Did he just go home, pop a beer, and watch 'Roseanne'?"[178]

For some forest activists, logging amounts to a kind of military invasion, and peace should be made even at the cost of timber jobs. Lou Gold remarks:

When you have a war between nations, you don't refuse peace just because it might cause unemployment among soldiers. And that's what we've got. We've been waging war on nature for a long time. It's time to declare peace with nature. We're going to have problems making the transition, but it's ridiculous not to end a bad practice because doing so would cause unemployment.[179]

The hostility of activists to logging can take on a hard-line character. This can be seen in opposition to thinning operations.

The Bush administration has used fire prevention and forest health as excuses for rolling back logging restrictions. Moreover, thinning operations can be poorly conceived. Because they involve cutting of small-diameter trees and brush, thinning is often unprofitable. Consequently, the Forest Service pursues an ill-advised policy of subsidizing thinning by cutting down large trees. Critics of the Healthy Forests Restoration Act and the Bush Administration's timber policies thus often regard thinning operations as little more than an excuse to log old-growth and other healthy, mature forests. They rightly point out that such logging can actually increase fire danger, by eliminating the larger, more fire-resistant trees and leaving debris, or slash, which is flammable.[180]

In addition, thinning and prescribed burns, which also help to prevent major fires, are mainly appropriate in forests subject to frequent (i.e., roughly every three years to every two or three decades), lower-intensity natural fires. Though useful in many parts of the Northwest and elsewhere, these measures may not be advisable in the Northwest's coastal Douglas-fir-western-hemlock forests, where the natural fire cycle consists of major stand-replacement fires that occur only every 250 to 500 years. Changing the fire behavior in these forests would require such intensive fuel treatments—thinning and removal of brush and other flammable debris—as to create "a fundamentally different and unnatural ecosystem," one that could no longer support the Northern spotted owl and many other species.

However, as Jerry Franklin and James Agee also point out, "Variability in forest fire patterns can be very local as well as regional, and fire policies must recognize that." In many areas, including parts of the Northwest, reduction of fuel loads through thinning and selective cutting, and use of prescribed burns, is thus necessary.[181] Environmentalists, though, have largely opposed such measures, not only because they are ecologically inappropriate in some areas, but because of the aforementioned mismanagement and because of an understandable fear of the timber industry's camel getting its nose under the tent.[182] Yet environmentalists' often reflexive opposition to fuel management measures goes to an extreme. Environmentalists' debate with timber interests on the thinning issue has become highly adversarial, so that both sides unproductively "take oversimplified positions fitting traditional stereotypes, such as commodity interests versus the environmental community."[183]

Furthermore, forest activists in the Northwest have also sought to impose what may be unreasonably stringent regulations on private timberlands, even where old growth is more or less gone. For example, a 1998 Oregon ballot measure that would have, among other restrictions, prohibited harvesting large trees on private land, would have also devalued many forest properties.[184]

All human activities alter the natural world. However, to environmentalists, logging seems a particularly offensive interference with nature. Describing the environmentalist view, Brian Donahue says, "The forest ... is the natural part of the landscape. Any human 'management' would seem to be in fundamental conflict with allowing ecosystems to function freely in ways that have evolved over eons to support the full diversity of indigenous species."[185] The forest is thus symbolic of wilderness, which is popularly regarded as the domain of nature outside the bounds of civilization. Indeed, according to cultural historian Simon Schama, forests have traditionally been seen in Western culture as places outside the bounds of civilization and its laws, which is why the term *forest* derives from *foris*, the Latin word for "outside."[186] Recall from the introduction how the Wilderness Act defines "wilderness" as a place "untrammeled by man" and "affected primarily by the forces of nature." It is in the wilderness that one can truly experience nature's sacred order. Logging and timber management violate the integrity of that quintessence of wilderness, the forest.

Selective Democratic Sympathies

Forest activists have frequently championed public input into national forest management. They have pushed for public review of timber sales and regulatory changes and have encouraged citizen use of the courts to challenge the legality of particular timber sales. The activists' ancient forest campaign has sparked a flowering of grassroots political participation. However, forest activists have turned out to be rather selective in their democratic sympathies. At times they have shown much the same aversion to democratic processes as that displayed by the Forest Service in the heyday of its timber orientation.

Forest activists have not been open to compromise or dialogue with timber interests. In 1993, they rejected a promising overture from organized labor. Labor offered a plan that would have protected old growth if a way could be found to quickly move some younger timber out of the woods and so employ loggers who were idled by court injunctions against timber harvesting.[187] A reluctance to work with timber interests is also evident in the opposition of many national environmental groups to the emerging phenomenon of collaborative conservation, in which local environmentalists and resource interests, including timber interests, organize partnerships and forums in which they try to work out disputes and develop local or regional management plans to preserve forests and other natural ecosystems while also sustaining the rural economy. (Collaborative conservation is discussed in more detail in chapter 7.)

Environmentalists' concerns about collaborative conservation stem in part from what they see as the excessive localization of the process. They charge that local groups do not involve outsiders and thus assume disproportionate decision-making power over public assets such as the national forests, and that industry can more easily dominate local processes.[188] Environmentalists also "worry that many of the hard-won battles at the national level against overexploitation of public lands resources by commodity interests may be lost if decision-making authority is shared with rural communities and groups through community-based collaborative processes that, they fear, might weaken the enforcement of important national environmental legislation."[189] Moreover, environmentalists believe that their perspective can get a better hearing on a national political stage.[190] Michael Hibbard and Jeremy Madsen remark, "Given the environmental community's record of success using the centralized regulatory framework, it is not surprising that environmentalists favor it."[191]

To some degree, forest activists and environmentalists cannot be blamed for their general reluctance to engage timber interests. The environmental movement has never had the political leverage of the timber industry; it has never captured the machinery of the state in the way that timber and other resource interests have. Moreover, environmentalists have been fighting what they rightly see as an urgent battle against the very ideologies of modernity: the domination of nature, unquestioned technological progress, and an obsession with economic growth. It goes without saying that environmentalists have been outmatched, and they understandably believe that it is their opponents who should compromise, especially on their economic self-interest. Hibbard and Madsen note that prominent forest activist Andy Kerr in fact regards participation in collaborations by interests with a financial stake as unethical.[192] More cynically, one could argue that such opposition to dialogue with timber interests is a matter of political power, particularly in view of larger organizations' fears of being eclipsed, whether by the timber industry or local green groups.[193]

However, there is even more to the environmentalist opposition to dialogue. In an interesting parallel with the attitudes of the Forest Service and the timber industry, some environmentalists express the idea that ecosystems should not be entrusted to the uncertainties and disorder of local democratic deliberation, a view reinforced by notions of the purity of wilderness. Some activists even opt for expert control, although in this case it should be guided by the need to minimize human interference and ensure the integrity of ecological processes. The Wilderness Society, for example, "questions the wisdom of legislating local control schemes on any scale. Our great public land systems ... are just that: systems. They are meant to be managed systematically, with baseline standards common to all—standards sufficient to guarantee the Integrity [sic] of each system and all of its component units."[194] A conception of the forest as a complex system to be governed entirely on the basis of pre-given ecological principles would seem to preclude public participation, especially by those not sharing a preservationist agenda.

We are back to a familiar issue. The pursuit of a strongly preservationist approach to the forest as a place is challenged by those with a different approach to the forest, including those who have more of a founding orientation. As with the Forest Service and the timber industry, preservationists' opposition to a more open, democratic approach to forest management seems to flow from a desire to enact their own vision of a place with minimal opposition. The result is an antidemocratic, even authoritarian approach.

Debating Forests as Places

The Northwest forest debate seems to have coalesced around two camps—notwithstanding the emergence of collaborative conservation—each with its own view of the character, value, and proper treatment of forests, particularly old growth. On one side are timber interests and their view of forests, and nature itself, as something to be radically reorganized and managed for maximum resource production, with relatively little attention paid to preserving natural ecosystems, ensuring the stability of timber-dependent communities, or even securing the long-term prospect of sustaining high timber yields. This approach radically emphasizes place founding—clearing away old growth and founding an efficient new forest, harvested as much as possible with automated machinery—over long-term preservation.

The nineteenth-century timber industry had pursued a short-sighted cut-and-run strategy, but the Forest Service and the forestry profession, led by Pinchot, had intended something longer lasting, guided by rational, expert management. The Forest Service initially set out to create enduring, sustainable timber plantations and stabilize timber communities. Founding was to be followed by preservation. However, this mission was misguided from the outset because it ignored the ecological characteristics and significance of old-growth forests, and because the Forest Service took an overly narrow view of community stability.

Whatever good intentions the Forest Service had, though, were ultimately betrayed in the decades after World War II. The Forest Service, Congress, and the timber industry ratcheted up logging on the national forests, paid inexcusably little attention to growing ecological problems and environmental consciousness, and eschewed any effective long-term planning for the continued viability of timber communities. In a kind of ecological and social violence, the Forest Service and the timber industry swept away most of the old growth, undermined the long-term livelihood of timber communities, and thus violated Machiavelli's dictum against using violence to spoil things. Founding had degenerated into a crude form, a wanton, short-term, destructive mining of the landscape and indeed of the labor of timber workers, with little attention to the long-term impacts.

Environmental activism has attempted to save the natural world from the ravages of this sort of crude, short-term perspective. Thus, on the other side of the timber debate are activists aiming to protect forests, especially old growth, as much as possible from human interference, management, and manipulation. Many activists see a moral obligation to preserve old-growth forests as valued places. They either see old growth as a commanding presence that also represents an ancient, transcendent, even sacred natural order or they see old-growth forests as places to which they have developed close personal attachments and obligations of care and protection. In either case, forest activists take an uncompromisingly preservationist position, morally condemning logging and often refusing any real dialogue with timber interests. Depending on which side one is on, as James Proctor has pointed out so effectively, the forest looks very different, functions differently, and has different uses and value.[195] This contrast is strikingly illustrated by the competing descriptions we have seen of old growth—as decadent or ancient.

Viewed from this standpoint, it is not surprising that the debate has grown so polarized. Places are sites of diverse, contending perspectives. However, when one side wants to completely transform a place and the other side wants to protect it against any human manipulation, one would expect the resulting conflict to be especially bitter and intractable. One might argue that this polarization of founding and preservation has also characterized U.S. forest politics in general over the past few decades.

However, a closer look at the Northwest debate reveals a much more complex, and perhaps promising, conceptual terrain. While there are two main camps in this debate, one can actually discern a spectrum of views concerning old-growth and other forests. The existence of a spectrum rather than simply a dualism of founding and preservation suggests possible common ground.

This spectrum has two endpoints. At one end are traditional forestry professionals in the Forest Service and the timber industry. For them, the forest is a blank slate on which to execute ambitious projects of landscape manipulation and founding, to found a new and better forest in place of the old, even at the expense of both ecological and communitarian values. At the other end are environmentalists who see the old-growth forest in terms of a transcendent order. For them, human alteration of the natural landscape amounts to moral transgression. The forest is a place, but not one that has been founded by human beings; rather, it has been discovered.

Between these two extremes is an interesting combination of attitudes toward the Northwest forests as places, a preservationist view coupled with a conception of the forest as a founded, humanized landscape. This combination is most evident among timber workers and their communities. Many are enamored of the logging profession and the challenging work of trying to conquer giant trees. They also have an attachment to their towns, to the worked landscape, and to the wild forest itself. One might say that timber workers and communities see the worked and natural landscapes as meaningful, coherent terrain in which they not only pursue a livelihood, but also feel grounded, even at home. Some of their remarks even suggest a respect for a larger natural order that preceded the arrival of axes and chain saws.

Some forest activists, particularly those who have lived in or frequently visited the rural Northwest, express a similar combination of attitudes.

They want to preserve their patch of forest, a cherished place that they regard as part of their own geographic community or an object of personal attachment. However, this local attachment to place involves a human creation. For a forest to be an individual's or a community's own special "patch" is for it to be somewhat domesticated, to be refounded as a familiar place on a very human scale.

In both these cases there is simultaneously an attempt to found a familiar, humanized place and to preserve that very same place as something already existent, already given by nature or by society. Thus for many timber workers and forest activists, particularly those local to the region, both founding and preservation are essential components of their relation to forests as places. It may be because locals on both sides of the debate pursue both founding and preservation in a sort of equal measure that locals have in some cases been able to come together in collaborative conservation groups and indeed recognize a shared sense of community and place.

This is not to say that the perspectives of groups on the extreme ends of the founding–preservation spectrum are illegitimate. Old-growth and other forests do have commodity value and they do have qualities that can legitimately inspire awe, respect, and reverence. Moreover, even forestry professionals who have attempted to transform and intensively manage forests have arguably intended to create a stable commodity source, and so have had something of a preservationist approach. And those environmentalists who see the forest as an embodiment of a preexisting natural order have nevertheless undertaken a founding project by conceptualizing old-growth forests as sacred spaces. Yet both of these groups have pursued either founding or preservation to an extreme. Timber managers need to pay much more attention to a preservationism that sustains community and ecological values, and the Forest Service, at least until George W. Bush, was possibly moving in this direction. Environmentalists need to recognize the legitimacy of founding activities, specifically timber harvesting, even if, as I later argue, cutting of old growth should still be sharply limited.

Nevertheless the meeting between founding and preservation is precarious because the old-growth debate, and indeed the more general U.S. forest debate, is marked by a seemingly hopeless polarization. Speaking in 1990 of a scientific plan to protect the spotted owl, Mark Rey, then director of the timber industry's American Forest Resource Alliance and now President Bush's Undersecretary of Agriculture for Natural Resources and Environment, said that it "offers a stark choice between people and owls."[196] Such stunningly simplistic characterizations as this[197] defeat any understanding of how both founding and preservation are fundamental aspects of our relationship with forests and other places around us. They cannot be pursued separately. Yet the old-growth debate has taken on the character of a nonsensical choice between founding and preservation. Framing the issue in terms of such an impossible, wrenching choice rules out constructive options. At best it leads to a partition of the landscape into single-use areas, what Baker and Kusel call "a zoning that reflects more the existing interest group divisions and groups' respective power than ecological imperatives and human and community well-being."[198] At worst, it leads to paralyzing deadlock.

In turning from the Northwest forest debate to two other issues, the problem of sprawl and the rebuilding of Ground Zero in Lower Manhattan, we will see similar problems.

3

Sprawl

The popular 1990s television comedy *Seinfeld* constructed plot lines around the absurdity of seemingly trivial and mundane aspects of daily life. In one episode,[1] the characters leave their car in a shopping mall parking garage and cannot find it when they return. They spend most of the episode searching for their car and asking for help from uncooperative strangers. The car has not moved; it is the characters that are lost. All they have to go on are their vague, conflicting recollections of the color and number code used to identify their parking spot: "blue-one," "pink-eleven," etc. They are having an all-too-familiar experience in a parking garage or parking lot: the inability to find one's way in a highly simplified, impersonal space laid out in identical, repetitive units, with few distinctive markers. The characters' amusing odyssey through the parking garage is a microcosm of the placelessness, disorientation, and alienation many people experience in the context of suburban sprawl.

In this chapter I look at the contemporary problem of sprawl and how it represents an emphasis of founding over preservation that involves socially and ecologically harmful and unsustainable land-use practices and an overall sense of placelessness. In a parallel with the old-growth forest debate, I also consider how certain responses to sprawl have gone the other way and overemphasized preservation.

What Is Sprawl?

What is sprawl? The term *sprawl* is frequently used to describe the uncontrolled spread of development into rural areas. However, it also refers to a particular land-use pattern, what Reid Ewing describes as one end of a spectrum of relative density or compactness.[2] Sprawl is a low-density, automobile-dependent, centerless approach to development. It is generally characterized by a separation of land uses—residential, commercial, and industrial—that are often mandated by local single-use zoning laws.

Construction is highly dispersed. Homes are typically detached, single-family units surrounded by lawns and located in subdivisions off major arteries. Roads are generally at least 36 feet wide, with large radii for turning, so that emergency vehicles can get through and cars can go at least 30 to 50 miles per hour,[3] and there are generally no sidewalks.[4] Commercial development is dispersed along roadways in the form of office parks, shopping malls, big-box stores, or smaller establishments ringed by parking lots. Traditional downtowns or town centers are absent.

Sprawl consequently involves heavy reliance on automobiles. Not only are structures too dispersed for pedestrian traffic, single-use zoning means that work, shopping, or recreation is only accessible by car; Ewing says that sprawl is marked by poor accessibility.[5] The overall landscape seems repetitive, monotonous, and lacking in distinctive, coherent locales.

Sprawl also tends to have little public space. Land is more or less thoroughly privatized: "Strip development presents a solid wall of commercial uses. Low-density suburban development subdivides land until every developable acre is spoken for." At the extreme lies "the walled and gated subdivision, where no land at all (not even street rights-of-way) is public."[6]

Impacts of Sprawl

The term *sprawl* is frequently pejorative and the less judgmental *exurb* is increasingly coming into use. For many people, sprawl signifies a sterile, uninspiring, arid, impersonal, forbidding, and depressing landscape.[7] Unsurprisingly, sprawl is a significant policy issue in contemporary America, but there is little agreement on how it ought to be addressed. Moreover, although many people do not like sprawl, there is indeed some debate as to whether it is a problem at all. One thing that is certain is that sprawl is rapidly transforming the American landscape. It is consuming large quantities of open space, i.e., farmland, woods, and wilderness areas. At the same time, it is draining economic activity and social vitality from inner cities, older suburbs, and downtowns. In other words, sprawl presents an expansion of development coupled with a hollowing-out of older population centers.

In a recent Natural Resources Inventory,[8] the U.S. Department of Agriculture (USDA) estimated that between 1992 and 1997, 2.2 million acres of land were developed each year in the United States, a rate 2.5 times that of the period from 1982 to 1992. Of the acreage developed from 1992 to 1997, 3.2 million acres were considered "prime farmland" by the USDA, amounting to an annual average loss of 645,000 acres of prime farmland per year. About 49,500 acres of wetlands were developed each year during this same period, contributing to an annual net loss of 32,600 acres of wetlands. The total U.S. acreage of developed land increased by about one-third from 1982 to 1997, and development accounted for the greatest increase in acreage by land-use category during this period.

Encroaching development disrupts rural economies, making further sprawl more likely. Farmers and private timberland owners face rising property taxes, reduced availability of additional lands, the loss of key suppliers, and even restrictive ordinances passed by newcomers who want pastoral scenery but discover that agriculture can be smelly and noisy and even involve chopping down trees.[9]

A 1998 report by the Sierra Club estimated that in the Atlanta, Georgia, area alone, about 500 acres of farmland, forest, and other green space were being developed *each week*.[10] The Atlanta metropolitan area's population and developed acreage doubled between 1980 and 2000.[11] Scenic, historic areas like Massachusetts' Cape Cod, which saw 10,000 acres developed from 1990 to 1997, Civil War battlefields, Pennsylvania's Lancaster County, and rural states like Maine have also been hit with sprawl. So have western metropolitan areas like Denver, Salt Lake City, and Seattle, places that had sold themselves on open space and livability. These cities now face overdevelopment, air pollution, traffic congestion, and/or looming water shortages.[12]

Indeed, sprawl brings a host of ecological, economic, and other social problems. These include loss or fragmentation of agricultural land, natural habitat and other green space; biodiversity loss; groundwater depletion; traffic congestion and increased commuting times; increased traffic accidents and fatalities; air pollution; increased fossil-fuel consumption and greenhouse gas emissions; increased levels of polluted runoff (from streets, parking lots, chemically treated lawns, and septic systems); flooding (pavement does not absorb water as easily as unpaved ground); rising infrastructure costs and property taxes; overextended municipal services; visual blight and monotony; loss of human scale; social isolation and loss of community; the economic and social marginalization of main streets, older suburbs, and inner cities; and increased racial and class segregation.[13] Sprawl has even been connected to the rise in obesity among Americans because dispersed development and less access to open space reduce opportunities for walking.[14] Sprawl also undermines national food production and makes it increasingly less efficient. Timothy Luke notes:

> The farm belts around U.S. cities are increasingly paved over for suburbia, shopping malls, and new service industries.... Meanwhile, billions of gallons of fuel are expended shipping fruit and vegetables from heavily irrigated, semiarid California fields to temperate zone cities in the North and East, which have lost their agricultural support networks to overdevelopment of land for housing or industry.[15]

Measures have been undertaken to stem sprawl. In November 1998, for example, voters across the country approved more than 100 anti-sprawl measures, including approval of funds for public land acquisition and protection of acquisition of open space.[16] In one such measure, New Jersey voters approved spending $1 billion over ten years to purchase half the state's remaining open space, or about one million acres. Communities and nonprofits, including private land trusts, have organized to protect open space, while groups of citizens have organized to keep out big-box stores, especially Wal-Mart, and other threats to local character and way of life.[17]

Despite many local victories, these and other efforts have enjoyed only limited success in fundamentally challenging the problem of sprawl. Henry Richmond of the National Growth Management Leadership Project says that despite a great deal of concern, little has been done over the past thirty years to effectively arrest sprawl, particularly because local power over zoning has not been widely challenged.[18] Moreover, as I will argue here and in chapter 6, the problem of sprawl ultimately requires a comprehensive regional approach that embraces land-use, environmental, agricultural, transportation, housing, economic development, and social justice policies. Such an approach balances and integrates founding and preservation. It is important to keep in mind, though, that the battle against sprawl is partly hampered by an over-emphasis on preservation.

Defending Sprawl

Not everyone is alarmed by sprawl.[19] Some defenders of sprawl, taking up the argument I discussed in chapter 1, see increasing dispersion of the built landscape as an inevitable and not entirely unwelcome concomitant of technology's supposed conquest of distance. Others focus on the detached suburban home, as opposed to the apartment or townhouse, and the automobile, as opposed to mass transit, as key means to personal freedom.[20] Such defenses of sprawl, often by libertarians, tend to mistakenly equate sprawl with lower density or suburbia per se. Given the popular appeal of the suburbs, it is then a short step for the apologists of sprawl to maintain that it reflects consumer choice, i.e., the natural operation of the market.

Sprawl makes economic sense, its defenders also argue. It creates affordable housing and the "furiously efficient means of retailing" provided by the shopping mall.[21]

Apologists often brand criticism of sprawl as selfish or as having disdain for popular preferences. One commentator is quite blunt: "Sprawl is an upper-class, elitist word that closes out the aspirations of lower-income and minority Americans for a safer and more spacious place to live and raise their kids."[22] Journalist Gregg Easterbrook talks of self-centered, even racist or classist suburbanites who want suburbia's amenities but employ growth controls to close the door on others who want to get in. He says that as an issue, "sprawl can also sound awfully similar to exclusionary zoning and other pull-up-the-ladder ideas that comfortable communities have used in the past to keep out unwanted arrivistes—often minorities and immigrants. One person's greenspace preservation is another's denied housing permit."[23]

Some accuse opponents of sprawl of a snobbish dislike of suburban culture. Joel Kotkin says, "Clearly the preference of millions, suburbs nonetheless won few admirers among sophisticated social critics," the harshest of whom "tended to be impassioned city-dwellers."[24]

Gordon and Richardson describe efforts to revitalize central cities in the face of sprawl as anti-market. They are rent-seeking efforts of those who would resist the natural operation of the market and "the 'creative destruction' of buoyant economic growth."[25]

Finally, defenders of sprawl claim that it affects only a small percentage of land in the United States. For example, Gordon and Richardson maintain that if the entire U.S. population lived at "suburban sprawl" densities of 1 acre per four-person household, only 3 percent of the total land area of the forty-eight contiguous states would be utilized.[26]

As I argue later, sprawl is not simply the result of consumer choice, but is also very much the result of public policy. Nor is sprawl all that desirable; it represents a fundamentally dysfunctional relationship with the places around us. Even if people do actually prefer sprawl, such preferences are not necessarily the result of reasoned reflection, nor are they necessarily sustainable, given the impacts of sprawl. As for the amount of space that sprawl consumes, this argument misses a key point. Saying that sprawl consumes only a small portion of the land area in the United States overlooks how sprawl affects particular places and those living there. Moreover, as we will see, the local and regional impacts of sprawl go beyond the land that is actually built on.

Causes of Sprawl

The causes of sprawl are related to the development of the American suburb through both market factors and government policy. American suburbs predate the twentieth century. The nineteenth and early twentieth-century suburbs, like Bronxville, New York; Riverside, Illinois; and Brookline, Massachusetts, were relatively high density by today's standards because they required easy access to railroad lines or to electric streetcars or trolleys, giving rise to the name "streetcar suburbs."[27]

The dramatic spread of sprawling, low-density suburbs and the transformation of the United States into a suburban nation was a phenomenon of the twentieth century and especially the post-World War II era. Several factors precipitated a massive population shift into suburban areas and created the problem of sprawl.[28] I present these factors in approximately chronological, although not necessarily causal, sequence.

Changes in Agriculture

The increased use of costly chemical and mechanical inputs in agriculture, together with federal and state subsidies and extension programs favoring large, corporate-style farms, made farming less labor intensive and marginalized small farmers.[29] Small farmers became more vulnerable to disruptions in the rural economy, including those arising from encroaching sprawl, and more likely to sell their land to developers. As of 1986, agriculture accounted for a mere 3 percent of the U.S. labor force, compared with 40 percent in 1900.[30]

Zoning Laws

Local zoning laws have generally mandated suburban-style planning in areas outside city centers. In the 1920s, state governments around the country delegated zoning powers to localities.[31] Local zoning has typically required separation of residential, commercial, and industrial land uses into single-use zones. It has also frequently mandated single-family suburban-style homes with minimum lot size and setback requirements. In other words, zoning has made compact, mixed-use development illegal in many places.[32]

Zoning was partly motivated by an interest in public health and quality of life—the desire to isolate noxious land uses such as factories and to keep residences away from noise and congestion. There was also a rationalist impulse to address urban chaos and create order through separation.[33] Zoning requirements that dictated detached single-family homes and minimum lot sizes (large-lot zoning) were ostensibly developed to prevent overcrowding and even control sprawl, but have ended up promoting low-density sprawl. Such requirements have frequently been motivated by exclusionary impulses: to keep housing expensive and keep out lower-income and minority residents.[34]

Single-use zoning tends to functionalize the landscape, reducing each place to one purpose and eliminating much of its complexity.[35] Zoning also fosters homogeneity: "Zoning codes devised by engineering firms have been 'packaged' and sold to municipalities for decades, eliminating the need for local officials to think about local design issues."[36] The role of zoning in shaping our built environment cannot be overestimated; in localities throughout the country, zoning has virtually mandated sprawl.[37]

Municipal Fragmentation

The political fragmentation of metropolitan areas through a proliferation of autonomous municipalities enabled exclusionary zoning, encouraged competition for development in order to increase local property tax revenues, and prevented regional approaches to land-use problems.[38] The number of local governments significantly increased during the twentieth century.[39] Ronald Hayduk notes that there are more than 90,000 governments across the United States today and most of them are new suburban political jurisdictions that came into being only in the past fifty years.[40] Many of these localities were organized to avoid paying taxes to cities and to protect their own tax base and local amenities, such as good school systems.[41] Consequently, such fragmentation has drained resources from cities.

Although it is seemingly democratic, municipal fragmentation actually disempowers local governments. Local jurisdictions, eager for economic growth and tax revenues, have courted sprawling development—especially malls, big-box stores, and high-end housing—through generous subsidies, whether in the form of tax breaks or funding for new infrastructure. Such subsidies lead to additional public expenditures because more inhabitants bring a greater demand for services. In an addictive cycle, localities address these expenses through even more development in the hope that tax revenues will outpace expenditures.[42]

The Rise of the Car Culture

The explosive popularity of the automobile encouraged more dispersed, ultra-low-density land uses.[43] The automobile has also been subsidized to a much greater extent than mass transit. Gasoline and car prices do not reflect the environmental and social costs of fossil fuel and automobile use. Moreover, between 1965 and the mid-1990s, the federal government spent roughly seven times more on highways than it did on public buses and subways.[44]

Federal Mortgage Insurance

The Federal Housing Administration (FHA), created in 1934, established federal mortgage insurance, which protected lending institutions that awarded mortgages to home buyers. Under the Servicemen's Readjustment Act of 1944, also known as the GI Bill, the system was expanded to aid veterans. The FHA and the GI Bill revolutionized the home finance industry, according to Kenneth T. Jackson.[45] With the federal government assuming much of the risk on loans, lenders could lower interest rates and make mortgages and homes significantly more affordable.

There was an anti-urban bias in federal mortgage insurance. The FHA targeted insurance where it was believed loans were least risky: new, single-family, detached homes in low-density areas outside central cities.[46] The FHA also favored racially segregated areas and discriminated against black home buyers and communities, a practice outlawed by the Fair Housing Act of 1968.[47]

The Postwar Baby Boom

The post-World War II baby boom, together with the influx of returning GIs, led to a housing shortage and demand for new development. However, sprawl increasingly became detached from population growth. The amount of urbanized land in the United States grew by 47 percent between 1982 and 1997, while the nation's population grew by only 17 percent.[48] Henry Richmond notes that even metropolitan areas like Cleveland and Pittsburgh that lost population from 1970 to 1990 experienced the same patterns of sprawl as areas with population growth.[49]

Mass Production in Housing

The rise of mass production and more mechanized technologies in housing and construction enabled the creation of vast suburban tracts and large retail centers as well as homogeneity in architecture irrespective of location.[50] Builders employed new power tools to increase worker productivity, brought in prefabricated components, and even adopted assembly-line techniques.[51] According to Jackson, before 1945 a typical contractor built fewer than 5 houses a year, but by 1959 the median single-family builder was putting up 22 structures.[52] Todd Bressi notes that today developers typically submit more than 100 acres to the approval process at a time and give sections to different builders who rarely take on projects with less than 150 houses or 100 apartments.[53] The prototypical postwar production project was the Long Island, New York, community of Levittown, established in 1947. Built by the family firm of Levitt and Sons, Levittown came to include more than 17,400 houses and 82,000 residents. At the peak of production, according to

Jackson, the Levitts were putting up more than 30 houses per day through assembly-line techniques.[54]

White Flight

White flight, i.e., the desire of white residents to leave multiracial cities, may have also promoted suburbanization. Racial and class exclusivity in the suburbs was historically encouraged by zoning laws and FHA guidelines, as well as by discrimination in the lending and real estate industries. For example, Jackson says that the Levitts publicly and officially refused to sell to blacks for two decades after the war.[55] Although the exodus from urban areas came to include considerable numbers of minority residents, Ronald Hayduk reports that in the nation's seventy-four largest metropolitan areas, "only 40 percent of blacks and Hispanics lived outside [the] central cities in 1990 compared to 67 percent of whites and Asians. Even more telling, only 16 percent of blacks and Hispanics lived in the suburbs."[56]

It remains an open question, though, as to whether white flight contributed significantly to sprawl. For example, sprawl exists across American metropolitan areas independently of significant differences in racial composition.[57]

The Interstate Highway System

The construction of the interstate highway system, a federal project, provided the transportation infrastructure to carry development far beyond cities and also shunted travelers away from urban and small town centers. The Interstate Highway Act of 1956 provided for 41,000 miles of road to be built, with the federal government picking up 90 percent of the tab.[58] Sprawl has itself created demand for even more road, highway, and rail construction, to provide transportation access for far-flung homes and businesses or to relieve traffic congestion, an approach that encourages more sprawl and has been compared to loosening one's belt in response to weight gain.

Urban Renewal

Urban renewal, a postwar federal program that provided assistance to state and local governments to use eminent domain to condemn and redevelop land, contributed to sprawl by making cities less desirable.[59]

Urban renewal destroyed thriving urban neighborhoods and replaced them with often bleak, paved-over landscapes of high rises, concrete plazas, parking lots, and highways. In most cities, the era of urban renewal ended in the 1970s. Unfortunately, the physical legacy of urban renewal is still very much with us. I will discuss urban renewal in more detail in chapter 4.

Growth of Sprawl-Dependent Businesses

Sprawl spurred the growth of business enterprises that were significantly geared toward serving suburban, automobile-dependent consumers. These included gas stations, auto dealerships and service centers, fast-food restaurants, hotels, motels, shopping malls, big-box stores, and the various honky-tonk establishments associated with strip development. Such businesses not only provide for life at the suburban frontier but also become advance guards for further development. For example, the fast-food giant McDonald's deliberately sites restaurants in areas where future sprawl is anticipated.[60]

Employers Relocate to the Suburbs

Major employers—offices and factories—also relocated to the suburbs. The dispersal of employers across metropolitan areas drained center cities of investment and tax revenues and led many residents to follow the job opportunities.[61]

Deindustrialization

Deindustrialization—often as a result of globalization—and the proliferation of abandoned hazardous waste sites in old industrial areas also sapped the economic vitality and quality of life of older cities.[62] The overall decline of urban town centers as a result of sprawl in turn reduced the local tax base and undermined key services like public schools. This led to further outmigration and increased poverty.[63]

Misunderstood Aspects of Sprawl

Market Driven versus Policy

One can see that despite arguments that sprawl is consumer driven, many of the above factors were supply side rather than demand side.

Government policies played a key role in setting mandates or standards for suburban development, undermining urban life, and providing the infrastructure and subsidies that made suburban sprawl viable. Without this array of public policies, a commercially viable market for sprawling development might never have arisen. Moreover, suburban sprawl, independently of direct consumer choice, has created the conditions for its own perpetuation and expansion. As noted earlier, the location of commercial establishments, employers, and homes in the suburban fringe necessitates building more roads, which means more sprawl and still more roads.

Of course, given the legacy and context created by these policies, and given cheap, available land, sprawl becomes much more profitable for builders, real estate firms, and retailers. As I will discuss, sprawl is now driven to a significant degree by the private sector, although with the active complicity of governments.

High versus Low Density

In claiming a market basis for sprawl, Gordon and Richardson note that many consumer surveys have indicated strong preferences for suburban living, meaning the single-family detached home.[64] Responding to Gordon and Richardson, Ewing acknowledges that while most people may favor suburban land-use patterns, this does not mean that they favor sprawl.[65] There is a vast difference between a compact, suburban neighborhood of detached homes on relatively small lots—say, six to seven houses per acre[66]—and a low-density development of widely separated homes on larger lots. Furthermore, a suburban neighborhood can be within walking distance of a town center or it can be located off of a highway.[67] Ewing says survey data suggest that given a choice between low and medium-to-high densities, home buyers are evenly split, that "residents are as satisfied with housing at six or seven units per acre as they are at three or four units per acre," and that "[p]eople are especially taken with the idea of neighborhoods clustered around a town or village center."[68]

One must also keep in mind that consumer preference is not a self-evident argument for the correctness of a particular choice. Such a choice may be unsustainable and indeed destructive of the very values that individuals hope to secure through that choice. As I hope to show, the promise of a clean, green, bucolic environment and the prospect of enhanced personal freedom cited by sprawl's defenders are belied by sprawl's profoundly destructive effects.

Sprawl and Placelessness

Consumption of the Landscape

One aspect of sprawl's metastasis is the cycle of abandonment it creates. Not only are central cities left behind, but suburban areas experience traffic congestion, overcrowding, visual blight, air and water pollution, and lack of green space. Their residents begin to leave, only to recreate these problems farther out in a cycle of sprawl.[69] Consequently, inner, working- and middle-class suburbs also face disinvestment as well as failing schools, increasing poverty, and declining social services.[70]

As the environmental, social, and public health costs of sprawl mount, there is a serial destruction of place that degrades and then abandons landscapes and leaves behind less affluent or mobile populations, chiefly minorities and the elderly. This lends a character of evanescence and disposability to the landscape.

Many of the built structures associated with sprawl age poorly, further encouraging abandonment.[71] Construction is often shoddy, employing inferior building materials. Says architect Douglas Kelbaugh, "copper has given way to aluminum, brass to brass plate, slate to asphalt, marble to plastic laminate, wood to particle board, tongue and groove siding to Texture-One-Eleven plywood, and plaster to Sheetrock."[72]

Kelbaugh describes a prevalence of short-term thinking in the contemporary real estate industry. In part this means that obsolescence is often intentional. He notes that "arterial strip stores [are not] constructed very well or very permanently, because their owners see them as quick investments. Wal-Mart expects and sometimes gets a payback period of less than two years for some of its big-box stores. The expectation renders buildings more like office equipment and supplies than a capital investment."[73] Wal-Mart will build "a new 60,000-square-foot store that has an expected life span of five years. After the local market has been primed, they build a 110,000-square-foot building a little further out and abandon the first building, whose cheap roof and mechanical system are beginning to wear out."[74] A February 2005 article in *Retail Traffic* reported, "At last count, there were more than 380 dark Wal-Marts nationwide."[75] Kelbaugh concludes, "No wonder the architecture is trash, literally."[76]

In the competition for market share, national retail chains also produce redundant stores or shopping centers. Many of the structures are ultimately abandoned. In 1997, Richard Moe and Carter Wilkie wrote, "With nearly 5 billion square feet of retail space, the United States has more than 19 square feet for every American.... Half a billion of that sits empty, the equivalent of more than four thousand abandoned shopping centers or 'dead malls'."[77]

The rapid transformation and degradation of the landscape amounts to a voracious consumption of places. Our surroundings seem to change overnight. Journalist David Brooks, noting the explosive growth of places like Atlanta, remarks in somewhat overheated prose: "It's as if Zeus came down and started plopping vast developments in the middle of farmland and the desert overnight.... How many times in American history have 300,000-person communities materialized practically out of nothing?"[78]

The past, if not abandoned or erased, is often commodified into the superficial architectural or natural trappings that adorn housing developments, shopping malls, and theme parks[79] while providing little genuine sense of place. This is especially the case with commercial architecture: "The design of retail architecture is usually formulaic, superficial, and divorced from place, however sophisticated its imagery and packaging may be."[80]

Privatization

With sprawl, land use is also increasingly functionalized and specialized for efficient distribution and consumption of products, often according to the model of single-use districts. Calthorpe and other critics of sprawl see a landscape of "ever larger and more remote distribution centers," in which human scale and neighborhood orientation have been relinquished to enable access by automobile and ease of national distribution. In such a landscape, even incidental shopping is removed from neighborhood and town and from the social interactions that animate and define a community.[81] Robert Fishman thus says that the land-use pattern that has emerged with sprawl most obviously departs from older urban design in terms of its scale. "The basic unit of the new city is not the street measured in blocks but the 'growth corridor' stretching 50 to 100 miles."[82]

In a relatively compact, mixed-use neighborhood, shopping is not just consumption. Rather, shopping helps foster social interaction between neighbors, especially because the close placement of downtown buildings encourages walking rather than quick forays out of the car. In a mixed-use setting, like the city block discussed in chapter 1, shopping intersects with other activities, such as recreation, gardening, commuting, and perhaps even work itself. Individuals—and particularly in urban areas, individuals with different backgrounds—encounter one another in multiple, unplanned situations. They begin to build multifaceted relationships and develop a sense of habitation in, identification with, and responsibility for, a shared place; in some cases, a shared sense of community might arise.[83] Meanwhile, the neighborhood itself is enriched and enlivened with a variety of meanings.

Certainly, more than the design of an area goes into building neighborly bonds and enriching a place, but land-use patterns have a major influence on the social dynamics and character of a place. Sprawling development disperses and segregates social activity and undermines neighborhood and community. Single-use zoning and reliance on the automobile encourage dispersal of development and a decline in accessible public spaces and pedestrian-friendly routes. Existing public spaces are abandoned and deemed unsafe, and new public spaces simply do not get built. Pedestrian activity declines. Transportation, and indeed the landscape as a whole, becomes more mechanized,[84] while streets become depopulated except by people in cars.

As public spaces decline, the landscape becomes characterized by "an exaggerated private domain: shopping malls, private clubs, and gated communities. Our basic public space, the street, is given over to the car and its accommodation, while our private world becomes more and more isolated behind garage doors and walled compounds."[85] Even public playgrounds, an ideal meeting place for both children and parents, give way to backyard play structures.[86] These factors have "clearly exacerbated social, class, and racial segregation and diminished the importance of common ground on which people of different backgrounds and outlooks might encounter each other."[87]

Sprawl not only corrodes public space, it also reduces the unplanned, diverse, and often repeated encounters that lend texture and richness to a locality. Instead, each place serves a specific function and as such limits the range of interactions that can occur within it. In a mall, for example, shopping takes place in a venue far removed from one's home, neighborhood, and workplace; one is entirely focused on consumption and there is little basis for interaction with the other consumers. In fact, shopping mall owners have sought to sterilize these places of public or civic-oriented activities. They have variously banned or discouraged petition gathering, leafleting, demonstrating, hanging out (here the targets are usually teenagers and the elderly), and in one case, even wearing an antiwar tee-shirt that had just been purchased at the mall.[88]

The loss of public and shared space also makes the public realm seem less familiar and more threatening. Individuals are more likely to exclude difference and novelty in favor of security and the protection of property values. There is an increasing proliferation of what Margaret Kohn calls "private communities"; these are "large developments such as condos, gated communities, co-ops, and apartment complexes where residents' units are not accessible to public streets."[89] Such developments often provide their own services. They tend to have homogeneous populations and exclude prospective residents on the basis of income and, de facto, race; this further heightens suspicion, hostility, and contempt toward outsiders.[90]

These developments offer little more than the illusion of community or public life. Their inhabitants are linked by common residence and perhaps leisure activities like golf, but then disperse into the far-flung world of malls and office parks when they go about their daily business. Residents thus avoid the hard work of building a multifaceted neighborhood or community with a diverse population.[91]

Moreover, many private communities are governed by residential community associations (RCAs), which are essentially private governments. These associations provide only the illusions of local, collective self-governance and of a lively, place-based public life.[92] According to Kohn, some 231,000 neighborhoods, composed of about 47 million Americans, are governed by residential community associations. She says that approximately 50 percent of all new homes built in major metropolitan areas fall under the jurisdiction of RCAs.[93] Residential community associations are created and controlled by real estate developers. They are often quite despotic and hostile to the vibrant, unplanned life that enriches places. Generally, RCAs prohibit a variety of activities that might lower property values: hanging laundry outside, parking a boat in front of one's house, leaving the garage door open. Often they also restrict political signs, display of the American flag, and in at least one case, the distribution of leaflets.[94] Key aspects of RCAs are insulated from the democratic process, says Kohn: "The majority of property owners cannot dissolve the association because it usually exists in perpetuity.... Even changing the rules is often difficult because of provisions that require super-majoritarian voting or mandate the approval of all residents, even when only a small minority attend meetings."[95]

Mobility Over Accessibility

Even for those not living in private communities, sprawl limits personal autonomy in a more direct, daily way: to go anywhere, one increasingly has to get into the car. The need to drive in order to leave a suburban subdivision or an office park is a serious obstacle to freedom of movement, especially for those who are too young, too old, or too poor to have a car. Those living in sprawling areas and unable to afford the annual $7,650 cost of operating a motor vehicle—estimated in 2001 by the American Automobile Association[96]—"are at the mercy of underfunded public transportation systems (primarily employing buses) that were introduced as an afterthought and hence ill-equipped for providing efficient and safe service."[97]

Sprawl thus favors mobility over accessibility.[98] Planners, builders, and public agencies sink inordinate amounts of money, resources, and political capital into facilitating mobility, mainly through motor vehicle transportation. A 1993 study by the Natural Resources Defense Council said that motor vehicle transportation costs society about one quarter of the gross domestic product.[99]

Assuming one has a car, it is easy to travel long distances. However, given the need to drive everywhere and given the long distances needed to reach specific places, one's destinations are more inaccessible in a sprawling built environment. Forty years ago, Lewis Mumford was already noting that driving a private motor vehicle had become "a compulsory and inescapable condition of suburban existence."[100] He used the phrase "compulsory mobility."[101]

Imposed Homogeneity

Contemporary development demonstrates little visual or spatial connection with its surroundings, whether built or natural.[102] Instead, there is mass production and repetition of the same kinds of structures, architectural styles, landscaping, and land uses from place to place, with little or no connection to local culture, history, or natural environment. Residential developers plan massive subdivisions according to prevailing architectural styles and land-use patterns. Commercial developers favor national and international chain stores and franchises because these businesses have greater economic reliability for long-term leases and are better able to afford high rents at shopping malls.[103] National and international chains put up their own free-standing structures, including the now-ubiquitous big-box stores. One thus sees throughout the United States the same sorts of suburban subdivisions, chain stores, franchises, and shopping malls—what Byers describes as "pieces of 'ageographical cities'."[104] A housing subdivision in Anchorage, Alaska, can look very much like one in Williamsburg, Virginia. A conference hotel is pretty much the same whether it is in Boston, Seattle, Denver, Las Vegas, or Atlanta.

Even the revitalization of urban historical districts has fallen victim to mass-produced homogeneity. Logan and Molotch note that development firms "apply 'cookie cutter' designs and tenants to diverse settings: old factories in San Francisco (Ghirardelli Square), a historic market in Boston (Faneuil Hall), new waterfront buildings in downtown Baltimore (Harbor Place). The same or similar tenants, known for their reliability and merchandising skills, reappear in project after project."[105]

From Meaningful Place to Abstract Space

Sprawl radically simplifies the actual locations it occupies. A low-density, single-use, functionalized, and homogenized landscape empties out rich, meaningful places and substitutes something a bit closer to abstract space.[106] The built environment also loses its distinctive locales and its defining centers and boundaries. The landscape becomes defined by little more than the repetition of businesses, like abstract coordinates on a grid. Communities also lose their coherent centers and boundaries as they merge in a matrix of highways and low-density development. In a recent book, novelist Tom Wolfe effectively captured this landscape:

He had driven through that whole area, from Vine Hill, where he lived, on east to Pittsburg and beyond, and it was now one vast goulash of condominiums and other new, cheap housing. The only way you could tell you were leaving one community and entering another was when the franchises started repeating and you spotted another 7-Eleven, another Wendy's, another Costco, another Home Depot.[107]

Peter Calthorpe thus speaks of "a growing sense of frustration and placelessness in our suburban landscape; a homogeneous quality which overlays the unique nature of each place with chain-store architecture, scaleless office parks, and monotonous subdivisions."[108] Fishman says, "The new city … lacks what gave shape and meaning to every urban form of the past: a dominant single core and definable boundaries. At most, it contains a multitude of partial centers, or 'edge cities,' more-or-less unified clusters of malls, office developments, and entertainment complexes that rise where major highways cross or converge."[109] The landscape is increasingly a macrocosm of *Seinfeld*'s parking garage, a placeless grid of emptied-out sameness in which it is ever more difficult to get one's bearings.

In "thinning out" the meanings of particular places, sprawl attenuates the individual's connection to these locales.[110] There is simply less to interact with, appreciate, reflect upon, or identify with. The landscape becomes alienating. Rapid traversal of the landscape by the automobile makes these surroundings seem even more emptied out and abstract.[111] Sprawl, says Ewing, results in a kind of environmental deprivation, characterized by "the absence of elements that provide activity and stimulation."[112]

Placeless Places

Overall, sprawl presents a disorienting, illegible experience of placelessness. Localities lose their center, definition, distinctiveness, and richness. The placelessness of sprawl was evident in an anecdote involving the New Jersey Devils professional hockey team and recounted by Moe and Wilkie. When the team won the Stanley Cup in 1995, "the franchise had no obvious location for a victory parade, so the team celebrated with fans outside the stadium in a parking lot." One fan told a reporter,

"It's too bad to have a rally in a parking lot, but there's no town to go to."[113]

To call sprawl placeless is not to say that there are no locations. Rather, sprawl offers relatively little in the way of meaningful, distinctive places with which one can identify, that communities can call home, that visitors will appreciate; i.e., places with which people can truly engage.

Powerlessness in the Face of Sprawl

Sprawl is in many ways the result of government policies, as I discussed earlier. However, it also reflects the enormous economic and political power of developers and retailers. These firms increasingly operate on a global scale, so that their land-use decisions are made in distant places (see chapter 5). Such firms exploit competition between localities eager for the tax revenue and jobs associated with development. They force concessions from local governments on issues from property tax relief to public underwriting of the infrastructure—roads, utility lines, sewers, water mains, etc.—needed to support development.[114] Matthew Lindstrom and Hugh Bartling note that as "suburban retail development became driven by the demands of large corporate chains, retailers often demanded large parking lots, wide access roads, and a homogeneous architecture to accommodate their centrally planned stores and restaurants."[115] An Oregon group advocating growth control once estimated that developers in the state pay only $2,000–6,000 of the $25,000 cost per home to supply infrastructure and other services to new subdivisions.[116]

Private developers and landowners eager to sell to them have used property rights to limit the public's ability to regulate land use. In sprawling southeastern Wisconsin, which includes the Milwaukee Metropolitan Area, officials in the town of Lisbon rejected farmland conservation partly on the grounds that it would interfere with farmers' private property rights.[117] In Oregon, a 2004 state ballot initiative established property rights protections aimed at undoing the state's vigorous land-use regulations (see chapters 6 and 7). In the United States, says Patricia Salkin, the "widespread belief by individual property owners that title to the land (or a deed) is tantamount to a right to do whatever the owner desires with the property" has created political and legal barriers to vigorous land-use regulation.[118]

Given these factors, localities are to a considerable degree powerless in the face of sprawl. Such powerlessness is often articulated through the defeatist mantra, "you can't stop progress," which appears countless times in newspaper articles quoting residents who are resigned to the transformation of their communities through sprawl.[119]

Yet what is ironic about such powerlessness is that it derives in part from localities' own powers over land use. Local zoning laws, as we have seen, directly encourage and even mandate sprawl. Local autonomy on land-use issues presents an enormous obstacle to fighting sprawl. Local communities are too often unable or unwilling to work together on regional planning. Except for very affluent bedroom communities, localities compete for business investment, jobs, and tax revenues and are afraid to lose out on the next office park, subdivision, or shopping mall. Moreover, within a metropolitan area, the more affluent local governments refuse to assist center cities and inner suburbs in bringing investment back to areas marginalized by sprawl. The resulting inability to obtain collective action means that even well-intentioned local governments feel themselves to be at a disadvantage if they try to stem sprawl. Suburban decentralization, or fragmentation, may seem more democratic, more responsive to local needs. However, suburban fragmentation actually puts local governments at the mercy of large retailers, developers, and manufacturers, who can do business elsewhere if one community's regulations are too onerous. As I will argue in chapter 6, regionalism may be the best approach to combating sprawl.

A Battle Between Founding and Preservation

There are similarities between sprawl and the unsustainable timber management discussed in chapter 2. Both involve an emphasis on founding over preservation; sprawl, like the timber harvesting practices in chapter 2, represents a kind of crude degeneration of founding. Like the Forest Service, the various levels of government that laid the groundwork for sprawl during the twentieth century were probably trying to found something enduring, i.e., to found and then preserve. Here, the analogue of the well-managed forest was the ideal of the low-density, clean, green suburb, based on the high-tech freedom provided by the automobile, removed from the pollution, congestion, and encumbrances of the city, and rationally governed according to single-use zoning. This modern suburban ideal was in many ways inspired by architect Frank Lloyd Wright, who envisioned an anti-urban, low-density landscape he termed "Broadacre City."[120] (Unfortunately, in the hands of government and the private sector, the suburban ideal was also racist because African-Americans were long excluded.)

Again, in a parallel with forestry politics, the phenomenon of sprawl involves a degeneration of the original vision. Under the impetus of private developers, retailers, and local governments seeking tax revenue and job creation, the founding project no longer aims at something enduring and thus the preservationist element is entirely lost. This is founding in its narrowest, most crude, debased form. The existing landscape is swept away and something new is put there without any real attention to its ultimate viability—it is consumed and allowed to degrade. Here, the founder spoils things rather than mending them.

This short-term, narrow, and crude approach to founding turns places into commodities. A commodity is something valued primarily as an object for economic exchange. When viewed as actual or potential commodities, places are regarded in terms of exchange value rather than their intrinsic value.[121] Places become real estate. When commodified as real estate, a place is always, to borrow from Martin Heidegger, "on call" for further transformations according to what the market deems most profitable.[122] Commodified places are refounded as the market dictates. The treatment of land according to market dictates pays little attention to a place's ecological, historic, community, cultural, or sentimental value, except to the degree that such value can be priced in the marketplace. Any attempt to sustain these noncommodity values becomes a barrier to further market exchange. Consequently, places must be founded and refounded in way that leaves them open to continual rearrangement and resale. In short, they must be disposable.

Any meaningful opposition to sprawl would therefore have to re-emphasize preservationist values. However, any such opposition must not go to the other extreme and advocate an intransigent preservationism that either shuts down economic development or prevents the natural evolution of communities as inhabited places. In other words, there must be a balance between founding and preservation. As I discuss in chapters 6 and 7, some approaches to sprawl show considerable promise in achieving this balance. However, some aspects of the antisprawl movement, while well intentioned, flirt with an extreme preservationism. To the degree that preservationism is carried to an extreme, land-use politics, like forestry politics, offers an unreasonable, unworkable, and unrealistic either/or choice between founding and preservation.

Antigrowth Movements: Trying to Stop Sprawl Dead in Its Tracks

The most frequent opposition to sprawl has been in the form of local antigrowth movements. Antigrowth activists generally aim to shut the door on development in their own communities. This is done through direct limits on development, through purchases of open space, or through private land trusts. Sometimes minimum lot sizes—often an acre—are employed. This limits local population growth, but it actually encourages sprawl by preventing higher-density development.

Antigrowth movements are frequently criticized as NIMBYism: development must be "not in my backyard," but in someone else's, an attitude that can be both exclusionary and elitist.[123] Critics charge that antigrowth movements aim to exclude outsiders, usually lower-income or minority residents or, in some cases, yuppies.[124] Often antigrowth activists are branded as privileged folk who have gotten their dream house out in the country and now want to shut the door on anyone else. These charges are in some cases valid. For example, in California in the 1980s, the impulse to manage development became intermixed with localism and exclusivism.[125]

Yet antigrowth activism, although it is often maligned as NIMBYism, also represents a more well-intentioned, preservationist impulse that, as is often pointed out, really says, "not in *anyone's* backyard." Activists try to preserve whatever has not yet been tainted by sprawl. It is hard to argue with the basic idea of stopping sprawl, and the rapidity and destructiveness with which sprawl occurs makes uncompromising opposition seem eminently reasonable. Moreover, antigrowth activism is correct in a larger sense: global and regional ecological constraints make unlimited development, which uses resources and land and produces waste, impossible.[126]

However, the idea of simply stopping development dead in its tracks at a local level is problematic. Activists and policy makers need to alter the actual behaviors, regulations, planning policies, land-use patterns, and governing structures that encourage sprawl. Most important, perhaps, land-use coordination and planning authority need to be lodged at an extralocal, regional level, at the scale of a metropolitan area, where the problem of sprawl really unfolds. A simple preservationist solution within individual communities will only divert sprawl to other areas.[127] Those communities that can afford to limit sprawl will also take advantage of their neighbors' willingness to put up big-box stores and shopping malls or inability to keep out undesirable land uses like toxic waste facilities. Furthermore, even if a community acts unilaterally to limit growth, its residents will still have to deal with existing sprawl and congested roads within and outside the community. Local growth controls will not address the regional impacts of sprawl or the decline of cities and older suburbs in a metropolitan region. Nor will they channel development and preservation to where they are most needed from a social and ecological viewpoint.

Furthermore, as Donahue points out, any viable strategy must recognize that development and suburbanization are bound to continue for the foreseeable future and that it is more realistic to decide how to channel them in minimally damaging, nonsprawling ways than to try to stop them outright: "The suburbs are coming.... Americans are going to continue moving to rural places and small towns. Unless we adopt better ideas about land ownership and care, Americans are going to continue ruining these places and bankrupting the future."[128] For better or worse, the question facing our landscape today is not so much whether to develop but how to develop, and the right sort of development is necessary to stem sprawl. Antigrowth preservationism is not adequate to address this issue. For example, targeted development policies such as the infill of low-density sprawl with more compact planning help bring economic vitality back to urban areas and divert development from the suburban fringe.[129] Unfortunately, antigrowth activists often oppose infill projects.[130]

Even well-intentioned local efforts to control development can lead to development policy being driven by "ad hoc reactions to specific, unwanted projects or the strident protests of special interest groups."[131] Such ad hoc efforts often create "patterns of disconnected, randomly dispersed and poorly utilized open spaces in a jurisdiction, a kind of archipelago of fields and forest adding up to no more than the sum of its parts."[132] Henry Richmond notes that land purchased by private trusts often ends up simply being isolated in a sea of sprawl and benefits adjacent property owners rather than the public.[133] Also, limitations on development by themselves run the risk of pushing up housing prices and punishing people with lower incomes.

New Urbanism

Another influential and more recent approach to sprawl is the architectural and planning movement known as New Urbanism. New Urbanism offers a mixed-use development model that is antithetical to sprawl. New Urbanists like Andres Duany, Elizabeth Plater-Zyberk, and Peter Calthorpe advocate compact, mixed-use, and mixed-income development; commercial activities restored to town or neighborhood centers; pedestrian-friendly streets, green spaces, public squares, and other public spaces; civic architecture prominently placed in town and neighborhood centers; and planning around coherent neighborhood and town centers.[134] New Urbanism is certainly a promising alternative to the dysfunctional development associated with sprawl.

However, New Urbanism often falls short in practice. It has mainly been employed in new developments, such as Seaside in Florida, Kentlands in Maryland, Laguna West in California, and, most famously and controversially, the Disney creation of Celebration, Florida. A key problem here is that New Urbanism becomes a prettified approach to sprawl.[135] These communities may have the compactness and pedestrian-friendly environment that sprawl lacks, but their construction is another part of the development wave consuming open space. Furthermore, these New Urbanist developments lack the commercial resources and employment opportunities to be much more than bedroom communities. Alex Marshall, a critic of New Urbanism, remarks that many New Urbanist developments are really not much different from traditional subdivisions.[136] Moreover, although New Urbanism champions mixed-income planning, which can produce a more diverse, vibrant community, actual New Urbanist developments tend to be very expensive and hence highly exclusive.

Moe and Wilkie argue that New Urbanism needs to shift its emphasis from designing new developments to rehabilitating older communities.[137] In fact, New Urbanist principles have been applied to the revitalization

of some cities. Providence and West Palm Beach, as well as neighborhoods in St. Louis, Trenton, and Cleveland, have successfully adopted
such planning principles.

New Urbanism faces a deeper theoretical problem, one involving the
issue of founding versus preservation. New Urbanism offers a combination of founding and preservation, but in a manner that does not integrate the two. Rather, it offers an extreme version of each, almost like
Rousseau's conception of the Great Legislator and his unchanging political community discussed in chapter 1.[138] New Urbanists, particularly
Duany, Plater-Zyberk, and Kunstler, draw upon 1920s urban and neighborhood design as a model for contemporary development. While this
model offers much in terms of improved pedestrian life, more compact
density, and appealing aesthetics, New Urbanism adopts it as an overly
rigid architectural and planning code. The New Urbanist development
of Seaside, Florida, has very stringent design criteria, down to small mi-
nutiae: "Rules mandate roof pitches, types of fencing, [and] porch
dimensions."[139] Some, like Kunstler, have posited a rigid dichotomy
between "good" pre-World War II development and "bad" postwar
development.[140] Such thinking invites charges of nostalgia and conservatism.[141]

New Urbanism shows an excessive faith that given the right physical
design, a sense of place and community can emerge.[142] Amanda Rees
calls this view architectural determinism.[143] To the degree that they are
indeed architectural determinists, New Urbanists try to create communities ex nihilo and freeze them in one configuration. Their creations,
including Seaside, can be quite lovely. However, that does not negate
the problems with this approach. Kunstler says that the aim of Seaside
"is to demonstrate how good relationships between public and private
space may be achieved by changing a few rules of building." Seaside
"makes the important point that if you change the rules of building,
you can reproduce these good relationships anywhere."[144] Kunstler also
quotes Plater-Zyberk: "In general, most zoning codes are *pro*scriptive.
They just try to prevent things from happening without offering a vision
of how things should be. Our codes are *pre*scriptive. We want the streets
to feel and act in a certain way."[145]

However, that is much too simple a view. In the rigidity and determinism of their design prescriptions, New Urbanists overlook how commu-

nities arise and evolve over time. Certainly, the relations between public and private space and between public and private life are partly a function of design, as I noted earlier, but they are also political relations. As such, these relations are an outgrowth of cultural and political norms and policies; of economic structures and practices; and of class, gender, and other power relations.

Such excessive focus on design and inattention to social dynamics is also reflected in a retail concept inspired by New Urbanism. Dissatisfaction with contemporary land-use patterns is causing some shift in the design of commercial developments. In affluent areas, developers are increasingly moving away from big-box stores and enclosed shopping malls and embracing the concept of "lifestyle centers." These are shopping malls (and often old ones that have been retooled), but with design elements of an urban or town center: open-air plazas and walkways, outdoor cafés and seating, cultural events, higher building density, and more traditional street frontage, including sidewalks and improved pedestrian access. In some cases, these developments even include office space and housing units. Lifestyle centers also tend to be smaller than other malls and are thus more likely to fit into an existing community.[146]

In terms of design, the lifestyle center is certainly an improvement over existing commercial developments. However, as Andrew Blum points out, there may be little here beyond the mere design trappings of a traditional downtown. A key problem is that the lifestyle center is still a private space—though made up to look like a public one—and it accordingly restricts the kinds of activities that one would normally associate with public spaces. For example, Blum notes that Desert Ridge Marketplace in Phoenix, Arizona, posts beneath its store directory a list of prohibited activities that includes "non-commercial expressive activity" and "taking photos, video or audio recording of any store, product, employee, customer or officer," though unsurprisingly the mall does allow taking "[p]hotos of shopping party with shopping center décor, as a backdrop."[147] Michael Southworth finds a similarly impressive list of verboten behaviors at the Bayfair Mall in San Leandro, California: "sitting in areas other than areas designated for that purpose," "standing or gathering in groups in such a way as to cause an inconvenience to others," "running," "horseplay," "the playing of radios or musical instruments," "literature distribution of any kind (without permission of the management)," and "taking unauthorized photographs of the centre property."[148]

Such lifestyle centers thus lack the spontaneity, freedom, and diverse activity of true public space. Moreover, with the possible exception of those lifestyle centers providing affordable housing, these developments still represent havens for the affluent, cut off from interaction with the rest of society. They also feature the familiar mix of national chain stores and thus fail to adequately support local businesses. In many cases, the design itself is also lacking: design elements are frequently downright fake—empty towers, new facades tacked on to old malls, false second stories, etc.—and, more important, lifestyle centers are often cut off from transit or pedestrian routes and only accessible by automobile.[149]

Though lifestyle centers show a New Urbanist influence, they are not necessarily embraced by New Urbanists themselves. Because most lifestyle centers are retail-only, New Urbanists have rightly criticized them as largely a marketing strategy.[150] However, the singular focus on design—though it is to the point of fakery and caricature—reflects a key pitfall of New Urbanism. Relatedly, New Urbanism fails to recognize that relations between public and private must evolve. It is unrealistic and undesirable that they be frozen in an architectural blueprint. A relationship between public and private that favors a strong sense of place and community is as much the precursor of good, functional urban forms as it is their product. Although planning is important in developing a functional city or region, design should also emerge from and reflect social dynamics, and the evolution of a community must allow some fluidity of spatial forms to reflect changing and inevitably contested perspectives and practices. To preempt such evolution and to prescribe an unchanging design is excessively preservationist. People seek to alter places over time; no place should be forever unchanging or beyond debate or challenge. In Harvey's words, "The effect [of the New Urbanist approach] is to destroy the possibility of history and ensure social stability by containing all processes within a spatial frame."[151]

What New Urbanism instead does, as I mentioned earlier, is combine fairly extreme forms of founding and preservation in a way that recalls Rousseau's Great Legislator. The Legislator does not actually rule, but molds a people and drafts their laws so that they pursue the general will, their "authentic" common good: "One who dares undertake the founding of a people should feel that he is capable of changing human nature, so to speak, of transforming each individual, who by himself is a perfect and solitary whole, into a part of a larger whole."[152] Once the people have been properly remade and educated, they ratify the Legislator's constitution and are then free to govern themselves. However, Rousseau shows hostility to any meaningful political self-governance because he inveighs against the sort of collective disagreement and debate that, as we saw, animates and enriches the life of a place: "The more harmony there is in the assemblies, that is, the closer opinions come to obtaining unanimous support, the more dominant as well is the general will. But long debates, dissensions, and tumult indicate the ascendance of private interests and the decline of the State."[153] There is thus an almost authoritarian founding moment followed by an extreme preservationism.

In essence, the New Urbanist architect or planner seeks to emulate Rousseau's Legislator. A community is founded complete with a design to ensure civic virtue. The resulting community must faithfully live out and preserve the plan lest the people become corrupted.

This approach was manifested in Celebration, a New Urbanist community designed by Duany and Plater-Zyberk, among others, and run by the Disney Corporation. In its promotional literature for Celebration, Disney promised an instant return to an idealized community of the past, a "place where the biggest decision is whether to play Kick the Can or King of the Hill. A place of caramel apples and cotton candy, secret forts, and hopscotch on the streets.... A new American town of block parties and Fourth of July parades."[154] Celebration was a brand-new development in what had a few years earlier been a wetland. However, the design and the promotional material tried to will a whole new community and its traditions into being. Given the governing role of the design, it was not surprising that the developers were reluctant to allow any deviation from it. Thus, even though residents found that alleyways were too short to accommodate garbage and recycling trucks, and garages were too close to the back of the lot to successfully park one's car, the builders continued to use the same design as the community expanded.[155] Kohn says that places like Celebration are planned to resist change.[156]

Another example of this problematic approach to combining founding and preservation took place in the working-class, urban neighborhood of

East Ocean View, in Norfolk, Virginia.[157] East Ocean View was plagued by crime and abandoned buildings, but it was also one of Norfolk's most integrated neighborhoods and one of the few areas in Norfolk with affordable housing near the beach. During the 1990s, Duany worked with city officials to design a New Urbanist development for the area. This meant that much of East Ocean View had to be bulldozed and the population evicted, to make way for a designed community.[158]

Certainly, New Urbanist designs have a lot to offer. However, a mixed-use, public-spirited community of the kind envisioned by New Urbanism requires not only a spatial design friendly to civic life but also economic opportunity; nearby social, cultural, and economic amenities; greater attention to social justice; and broad political participation, deliberation, and debate across lines of race and class. In a quest for community, New Urbanism's rigid design recipe tries to preempt such complex, messy social and political dynamics.[159] The result is a moment of radical founding followed by an imposed, rigid, and oppressive preservationism, something that falls far short of the New Urbanists' own admirable goals. New Urbanism needs to better integrate preservation and founding.

Antigrowth activists and New Urbanists are right to oppose sprawl, and their prescriptions are not without promise, but their approaches are often inadequate. Sprawl represents an excessive orientation toward founding. However, the alternatives examined here tend to rely too heavily on the preservation of places in some existing arrangement. Antigrowth activism pursues a reactive, ad hoc preservationism. New Urbanism pursues an architectural determinism in which the imposition of a rigid planning and architectural design becomes the solution to the loss of community and other social pathologies associated with sprawl. This approach leads to an unpalatable combination of extreme founding and extreme preservation. In later chapters I will turn to a conception of place that not only combines but balances and integrates founding and preservation. First, though, we must turn to our final case.

4

Rebuilding Ground Zero

Of the many pictures taken during and after the tragedy of September 11, 2001, several are especially memorable. One is reprinted in *City in the Sky*, James Glanz and Eric Lipton's history of the World Trade Center. The photo, taken in July 2002, shows three elderly men in business attire standing amid the rubble of Ground Zero, the site of the former World Trade Center. The three men are, as the caption reads, "David Rockefeller, who first proposed the World Trade Center; Les Robertson, a structural engineer who helped create the design that held them [i.e., the Twin Towers] up; and Guy Tozzoli, the Port Authority official who supervised the development and startup."[1] The picture captures a meeting of two very different eras, the era of big government, technological optimism, and urban renewal in which the World Trade Center was conceived and begun; and the era of uncertainty, fear, and international terrorism in which the Twin Towers came down in a blizzard of smoke, dust, paper, rubble, and human remains. Yet in this meeting of two eras, there are parallels as well as contrasts. Today, as in the late 1950s and early 1960s, new buildings are being planned for the site. Today, as then, there is considerable and often bitter debate about what should be built there. And today, as then, the public development agencies and corporate enterprises that individuals like these worked for may once again have the final say over what gets built.

The events of September 11, 2001 constituted a major turning point in U.S. history, and their significance is far beyond the scope of this book. However, the story of the World Trade Center's building and destruction and the subsequent debate on how to redevelop "Ground Zero," are as germane to the politics of place as are the Northwest forest debate and suburban sprawl. September 11, 2001 marked the demise of one of the best-known construction projects in the world, a group of buildings whose three-decade existence was preceded and followed by intense public controversy. The construction of the World Trade Center, popularly known as the Twin Towers, came at a time when the practice of urban renewal, which had razed urban neighborhoods and contributed to the decline of cities in the face of the suburban exodus, was becoming increasingly unpopular. Completed in 1973, the World Trade Center managed to get through just as the door on urban renewal slammed shut. Although controversial, the Twin Towers became a signature part of the Manhattan skyline and a symbol of American capitalism—characteristics that made them a terrorist target. In fact, the South Tower had already been bombed by terrorists in 1993.

When terrorism had destroyed the buildings and the World Trade Center became Ground Zero, political controversy returned to the site as public officials, developers, architects, planners, New York City residents, and the families of the 9/11 victims bitterly argued over what would replace the Twin Towers. That argument continues today.

The controversy over Ground Zero has challenged many of the values that originally brought the World Trade Center into being, especially the commodification of place and the antidemocratic, top-down governance of land use by public authorities like the Port Authority of New York and New Jersey.[2] The attacks of 9/11 did not just take lives and destroy buildings, they opened the gates to a host of new constituencies that lay claim to the former World Trade Center site: victims' families, survivors of the attack, local residents, and uniformed civil servants. These constituencies contested, often unwittingly, the ideological foundations of the Twin Towers.

Sharon Zukin says that 9/11 made "Lower Manhattan ... a site of conflict between two hostile regimes: the regimes of memory and of money."[3] Her characterization is partly correct, but underlying the conflict between memory and money is a deeper struggle between preservation and founding. Like the issues of the old-growth forest and sprawl, this is in many ways also a debate over the kinds of values and ends that should guide our construction and treatment of places. Like the other two cases, the debate over Ground Zero also reveals how founding and preservation conflict and interact in our relationships with our spatial surroundings and how we too often make the mistake of setting founding and preservation against one another.

Violent disruptions can create opportunities for founding when the landscape of the past is largely swept away. The brutal events on 9/11 provided such an opportunity. These events might themselves be considered an act of founding (an irony considering that Mohamed Atta, the leader of the hijackers, previously studied architecture and urban planning) because they helped set the future tone for the rebuilding debate. The existing landscape was demolished. It was never an option to simply leave a pile of debris to crumble away into a distant memory. Something had to be put at Ground Zero. As it so often does, tragedy created an opportunity to do things differently. There was now an opportunity to found, or refound, while also looking toward preservation. The new constituencies that gathered at Ground Zero have contested the overemphasis on founding over preservation that had been embodied in the World Trade Center from its beginnings. Unfortunately, it now looks as if that opportunity is already being squandered, perhaps irrevocably. The redevelopment of Ground Zero, as it is proceeding, has not balanced and integrated founding and preservation, but has favored extreme views of both while failing to dislodge founding from its dominant role.[4]

Building the World Trade Center

A Modern Ozymandias?

The World Trade Center and the Twin Towers may be enjoying more popularity in their afterlife than ever before. Marshall Berman says, "The earliest epitaphs for the towers were of the don't-speak-ill-of-the-dead variety." In fact, he says, "they were the most hated buildings in town. They were brutal and overbearing, designed on the scale of monuments to some modern Ozymandias. They were expressions of an urbanism that disdained the city and its people. They loomed over Downtown and blotted out the sky."[5]

The Twin Towers never had the elegance of the Empire State, Chrysler, or Woolworth buildings or other Manhattan skyscrapers. Writing in 1990, Tony Hiss said, "the towers are more tolerated than admired by New Yorkers, and the large plaza at the base of the towers is generally avoided in any weather."[6] Imposing, boxlike affairs[7] looming above a windswept, 5-acre plaza, the Twin Towers were examples of architectural modernism, a style often noted for its visual brutality. Architect Minoru Yamasaki did depart from modernism's prevailing, minimalist international style by including exterior columns that began and ended in arches. However, Yamasaki did not entirely reject mainstream modernism.[8] Much of the long façade on each tower was characterized by arid monotony, "a striped surface of aluminum and glass."[9]

Other features also evoked international-style development projects— the simple rectangular shapes of the buildings; the vast, paved plaza; the disconnection between the buildings' design and the surrounding neighborhood; and the Trade Center's literal detachment from the surrounding streetscape in a superblock cut off from the rest of the city.[10] The superblock lacked the diverse, vital street life that characterized other areas of the city and was largely dead after 6 p.m.[11] The plaza was rather uninviting at first, although efforts were later made to "humanize the space, to make it playful and accessible" through food carts, vending kiosks (much of them tourist related), lawn furniture, and free lunchtime concerts.[12]

Gillespie notes that many architectural critics dismissed the World Trade Center in part because the Twin Towers' simplicity did not allow a multiplicity of readings. With "a pair of simple geometric shapes... [w]hat you see is what you get." This simplicity enabled the towers to become icons, he says, but not to sustain interest.[13] They were significant as symbols, but as places they were resistant to any richness of meaning. Like the simplified landscapes of sprawl, the World Trade Center and other urban renewal projects evoked abstract, emptied-out space because they lacked much of the detail, intricacy, varied life, and competing interpretations that create a rich, meaningful place.

These negative assessments are by no means universal. On the whole, Gillespie actually offers a favorable account of the World Trade Center. Using language that might have been applied to the great conifers of the Pacific Northwest, he says that the Twin Towers, "because of their height, are regarded as sublime—as noble, grand, and majestic."[14] Indeed, from close up, the Towers were admittedly more impressive and interesting. Standing at the base and looking straight up the face of one of the towers offered the exhilarating experience of launching oneself into the sky.[15]

The Towers' enormous height and imposing, brutal simplicity actually made them landmarks that dominated the Lower Manhattan skyline. As architecture critic Paul Goldberger notes, the World Trade Center was visible from almost everywhere in and around the city and became an orienting device for many people, including me, I might add.[16] Visits to the observation deck were a major stop for tourists and residents. Gillespie says that the towers came to "symbolize American exceptionalism, or capitalism, or even America itself."[17] The World Trade Center was also symbolic of New York City. Glanz and Lipton describe the Twin Towers as "the biggest and brashest icons that New York has ever produced."[18]

Goldberger maintains that the Twin Towers were humanized by the opening of the restaurant Windows on the World, the conquest of the buildings by two daredevils (one walked a tightrope between the Towers; the other climbed one of the them), and the visual reintegration of the Towers into the Manhattan skyline after the development of adjacent Battery Park City.[19] Moreover, the minimalist modern style of the World Trade Center started to come back into fashion in the 1980s.[20]

Meanwhile residents of the surrounding neighborhood came to depend on the World Trade Center and its facilities. For local residents, the plaza was one of the largest nearby open spaces, and they had made regular use of the shopping mall and were eager to see it restored after 9/11.[21]

The loss of the World Trade Center created a gaping hole in New York's geography and skyline. A key part of the landscape and a major cultural symbol, whether intrinsically appealing or not, had been obliterated.

Urban Renewal

Whether or not the World Trade Center itself was unattractive and alienating, its creation was a rather brutal endeavor. It was a top-down, authoritarian project,[22] a part of the urban renewal era. Urban renewal was a notorious, mid-twentieth-century program under which cities and public authorities used the power of eminent domain to seize and purchase older, "slum" areas and redevelop and/or sell them to private developers.[23] The rationale was the elimination of urban disorder, decay, and poverty; the creation of modern commercial and residential units; the building of new high-speed roads and parking for greater automobility; and the attraction of new business investment and tax revenues. The federal government underwrote urban renewal. The Housing Act of 1949 provided federal funds for localities and other public agencies to undertake urban renewal projects.

Recall Forest Service Chief Cliff's 1965 comparison of clear-cutting with urban renewal. In both cases, a sweeping founding action obliterated an existing landscape deemed "decadent" or "blighted" and replaced it with something ostensibly more rationally organized and productive. Just as Forest Service professionals denigrated old growth, many planners, public officials, and architects saw old urban neighborhoods and business districts as crowded, decaying, chaotic, and dirty—in short, as slums.

Although the wholesale transformation of cities was presented as progress, urban renewal created empty, depopulated cityscapes. The so-called slums targeted by urban renewal often turned out to be vibrant minority or working-class neighborhoods like Boston's West End.[24] From the 1950s to the early 1970s, federally funded projects erased a number of neighborhoods and historic downtowns around the nation. "The older districts near downtown—whose historic structures and eclectic enterprises gave a sense of character and history to the whole city—were usually the first to be declared 'blighted' and ruthlessly leveled, especially if their residents were black."[25] Neighborhoods were replaced by highways; parking lots; enormous, poorly designed housing projects; useless strips of greenery; indoor malls; and high-rise buildings that presented blank, often windowless, facades to the street. It was believed that only "the complete leveling of whole neighborhoods and their rebuilding in the new superblock 'tower-in-the-park' could create a viable modern central city."[26] The resulting landscapes were sterile and placeless, neither distinctively urban nor suburban. They also lacked diversity, fine-grained spatial interactions, or connection to local history or culture. Moreover, in most cases, say Moe and Wilkie, residents were displaced without being provided with alternative housing.[27] When residents were rehoused, it was often in de facto segregated public housing projects.[28]

Urban renewal sought to erase the urban past, something I discuss further in chapter 5. Modernist architects like the Swiss-born Le Corbusier were influential in this devaluation of existing cities. One of Corbusier's American disciples was Robert Moses. Moses held a number of powerful state and local positions in the New York Metropolitan Area and oversaw numerous redevelopment and highway-building efforts in the region. In language strikingly reminiscent of clearing old growth, Moses remarked, "You can draw any kind of picture you want on a clean slate, but when you're operating in an overbuilt metropolis, you have to hack your way with a meat axe."[29] Moses was said to have evicted more than 250,000 people through his highway construction efforts.[30]

Urban renewal had run out of steam by the 1970s. It faced mounting opposition from urban neighborhoods, both poor and affluent, as well as from historic preservationists, environmentalists, and architects and planners like Jane Jacobs, who was a major critic of the World Trade Center.[31] As a creature of so-called big government, urban renewal also fell out of favor as fiscal constraints, political conservatism, and privatization of government functions sapped the ability of localities and public agencies to undertake major redevelopment efforts on their own. The construction of the World Trade Center came at the end of the urban renewal era and was accordingly quite controversial and bitterly fought.

The clearing of urban neighborhoods for business-friendly, revenue-enhancing projects has not entirely ceased, although such projects face a great deal more opposition and regulatory hurdles today. The use of eminent domain to force out residents to make way for private development was in fact the subject of one of the most notorious U.S. Supreme Court rulings in recent years. In a 5-4 decision on June 23, 2005, the Court, in *Kelo v. New London*, upheld an action by the city of New London, Connecticut, to use eminent domain to seize private homes and turn the land over to private developers.[32] The top-down, authoritarian urban renewal mentality also survives in plans for the redevelopment of Ground Zero, as I will discuss.

The Port Authority's "Public Purpose"

Urban renewal projects were often carried out by powerful unelected public authorities, one of which was the agency that built, owned, and until just six weeks before 9/11, managed the World Trade Center: the

Port of New York Authority, renamed the Port Authority of New York and New Jersey in 1972.

Public authorities operate like quasi-private firms, unable to tax but able to raise money through bond sales and user fees.[33] The Port Authority, the creature of the New York and New Jersey state governments, operates independently of the New York City government. It does not have to pay taxes to the city; it is exempt from city fire codes and has its own police force. The agency is also able to take land by eminent domain, and its holdings include airports, tunnels, railways, and bridges throughout the New York City metropolitan area. The Port Authority owns the World Trade Center site, but leased it to developer Larry Silverstein, who paid $3.2 billion for a 99-year lease just six weeks before 9/11. The Twin Towers and their superblock were built under the watch of the agency's long-time executive director, Austin Tobin, who was fond of quoting architect Daniel Burnham: "Make no small plans. For they have no power to stir the blood."[34]

The origins of the World Trade Center go back to the mid-1950s with David Rockefeller, scion of one of the nation's wealthiest families, a vice president of Chase Manhattan Bank, and brother of the future governor of New York. Rockefeller, who sought an economic revival for Lower Manhattan, wanted a new headquarters for Chase in the area.[35] After consulting with Robert Moses, he came up with the idea of a massive building project. He then turned to the Port Authority because of its ability to raise funds and use eminent domain.[36] The concept evolved into a world trade center that would house all of the Port of New York's import-export activities in one location.[37] The proximity of various functions and personnel would supposedly enhance all of these operations.

The project ultimately faced a number of criticisms. However, the builders of the World Trade Center were determined place founders. Glanz and Lipton write that they "were possessed of a determination that sometimes crossed the line into hubris: they refused to admit defeat before any problem that natural forces, economics, or politics could throw in their way." The "talisman that the builders brandished, again and again, to counter their opponents was the technological optimism of the early space age."[38] One of the project's selling points—or flaws, depending on one's perspective at the time—was its massive scale. The Port Authority set out to build 10 million square feet of new office space, a figure that the agency made non-negotiable.[39] The Port Authority also undertook to erect the world's tallest buildings. And they would expand Manhattan Island itself, another selling point for the project. Battery Park City, a residential and financial area, would be built on fill excavated from the World Trade Center site and poured into the adjacent Hudson River.

The Battle of Radio Row

Despite these grandiose selling points and strong backing from New York Governor Nelson Rockefeller, the project attracted considerable opposition. Real estate interests feared a glut of office space and a collapse of real estate prices. Opponents of urban renewal, like Jacobs, as well as many architectural critics, attacked the project for its planning or stylistic features.[40] The New York City government created obstacles in return for being excluded from the planning of the project. According to Glanz and Lipton, secrecy was standard operating procedure for the Port Authority, especially when dealing with the city.[41] The Port Authority's initial planning, including the trade center's location and ever-growing footprint, the amount of office space, and the technical approaches to dealing with issues such as the towers swaying in the wind, was done in secret.

Opposition also came from local business owners. The area to be condemned for the towers included a bustling, renowned district of small businesses, including a knot of electronics shops known as Radio Row. According to Glanz and Lipton, this was one of Manhattan's most vibrant shopping areas.[42] Goldberger notes that by the time the World Trade Center opened in the early 1970s, historic preservationism had taken hold in New York. He remarks that Radio Row, had it been spared, might have eventually been considered a historic district by the city's Landmarks Preservation Commission.[43]

However, historic preservationism came too late to save Radio Row. World Trade Center architect Yamasaki, who believed that Radio Row's businesses could be easily relocated, saw the area as blighted, without any buildings worth saving from demolition.[44]

The Radio Row merchants, some of whom had been there since the 1920s, organized against the project. They held street demonstrations and went to court, charging that building office space did not constitute enough of a public purpose for the Port Authority to exercise eminent domain.[45] On February 28, 1963, after victories in the lower state courts, the Radio Row merchants lost in the New York State Court of Appeals, the state's highest court, which validated the Port Authority's public purpose argument. In his majority opinion, Judge Adrian P. Burke affirmed the philosophy behind urban renewal. He said that "the indirect benefits deriving from slum clearance and from a 'plan to turn a predominantly vacant, poorly developed and organized area into a site for new industrial buildings'," as well as the aesthetic improvements that would result, all justified eminent domain.[46] The U.S. Supreme Court refused to hear the case on appeal; Radio Row was finished. Some of the displaced merchants successfully relocated, keeping their old businesses or starting new ones; others never recovered. In the end, the construction of the World Trade Center not only razed Radio Row, but also erased the streets that had run through the 16-acre site.

After the Twin Towers were completed, they long seemed a failure because tenants were slow to move in, partly because of the economic downturn during the 1970s. The buildings initially relied heavily on government tenants paying discounted rates.[47] However, they eventually had success in attracting private tenants, although ultimately in banking, insurance, and investment rather than in import-export. This reflected New York City's reliance on the so-called FIRE industries: financial services, insurance, and real estate. During the 1980s and 1990s, the World Trade Center became an epicenter of globalization and a symbol of American economic and political might, although it did not turn a profit until the late 1990s.[48] In July 2001, developer Larry Silverstein leased the World Trade Center from the Port Authority for $3.2 billion.

As a center of the FIRE industries, the World Trade Center became, ironically perhaps, a physical embodiment of the seemingly invisible, ethereal, electronic networks constituting Castells' networked space of flows. Eric Darton remarks that construction of the World Trade Center "literally buried the piers at the southern edge of Manhattan and ended three hundred years of maritime culture there."[49] There is an irresistible symbolism in how a tangible, physical doorway to the outside world—a seaport—was replaced by a center for the exchange of numbers and computer bytes.

Lessons from the Construction of the World Trade Center

The construction of the World Trade Center was emblematic of New York City's traditional approach to land use as well as its approach to urban renewal. The city has gone through constant rebuilding, erasing the past and the present, in the form of existing neighborhoods, to make way for more commercially valuable land uses and accommodate the ambitions of business elites and public development agencies.[50] Commodity values, those that would yield the highest short-term returns for real-estate developers and investors, have traditionally taken precedence over either neighborhoods or historic preservation.[51] The erasure of Radio Row thus completed the destruction of the Lower West Side, once a thriving immigrant neighborhood that until 1956 had had a great public market, the Washington Market.[52]

Darton describes the World Trade Center as created through a kind of brutal abstraction from lived human realities. In the wake of 9/11, he says that we must "contemplate the building of the World Trade Center itself as a destructive act."[53] The attempt of quasi-authoritarian development projects like the World Trade Center to reorganize urban life for order, efficiency, and profit meant the sacrifice of neighborhoods and livelihoods. "By the mid-1980s," says Clay Risen, the World Trade Center "had become a symbol for the hollowing out of America's urban environment."[54]

The aggressive, destructive determination to complete the World Trade Center project was such that the builders were even willing to risk fire safety. As mentioned earlier, Port Authority holdings were not covered under New York City fire codes. A recent report by the National Institute of Standards and Technology, partly in response to the question of whether building design contributed to the tragedy on September 11, says that the Twin Towers' design was in fact generally consistent with New York City codes at the time.[55] However, fire safety was not adequately determined at the time of construction. Malcolm Levy, head of the planning division in the Port Authority's World Trade Department, decided not to test the fire safety of the buildings' unorthodox, thin steel trusses for fear of having to completely redesign the project.[56] "As incredible as it sounds," Glanz and Lipton write, "the Port Authority had built what were then the tallest buildings in the world without knowing how their components would hold up in a fire."[57]

Throughout the design and construction of the World Trade Center, the Port Authority was driven by the single-minded goal of creating the tallest buildings in the world with an astounding amount of office space. Like the U.S. Forest Service and the timber industry, the builders of the World Trade Center were founders on a grand scale, focused on a radical transformation or refounding of land conceived as a blank space. They aimed to build something lasting but really gave little genuine heed to preservationist values, instead emphasizing newness, innovation, audacity, and glory—worthy goals but taken to an extreme that trumped all competing values. They showed little respect for the existing landscape or for the social and political values that governed it. Says Goldberger: "Sweeping away the old and providing a clean slate for the new was the highest and best calling of city planning, or so the Port Authority seemed to believe."[58]

Nothing could hold back the ambition to build the World Trade Center, not the preservation of an existing business district nor democratic deference to the elected government of New York City nor the public's right to know the emerging details of a massive building project nor fundamental considerations of building safety. Risen remarks:

Had the Port Authority been accountable to the city, had the local community possessed some element of control over the planning process, the center might never have been built, or it would have been made to heed and to enhance the public weal, instead of merely enhancing the egos and pockets of Tobin, Rockefeller, and the Port Authority.[59]

However, on September 11, 2001, an act of mass murder and destruction created the opportunity to rebuild the site according to a different set of values and processes.

Ground Zero

With the World Trade Center reduced to rubble by two hijacked jetliners, the 16-acre site became popularly known as Ground Zero, the epicenter of a cataclysm.[60] The site could not remain a smoking rubble-filled ruin, the handiwork of terrorism. Nor could the old structures be recreated or made even taller, despite the demands of many New Yorkers and other Americans, including flamboyant developer and self-promoter Donald Trump. Such a restoration was seen by the survivors of the 9/11 victims as, in Goldberger's words, "tasteless, even grotesque." Moreover, replicating the Twin Towers, he argues, would have effaced one of the most momentous events in the history of New York City and the nation as a whole.[61] In addition, the site could not simply revert to its earlier status as a symbol and node of global capitalism. It was now too significant to be a mere piece of profit-making commercial real estate;[62] or at least many people thought so. Thus, even as the towers burned, new constituencies and values claimed the site.

New Possibilities in the Wake of an Atrocity

In some ways the destruction of a nexus of global finance was a very local event. It was a tragedy for New York City and in particular the neighborhoods of Lower Manhattan, as well as for the surrounding suburbs, to which many of the victims would have returned home on any other September 11th evening. On the other hand, 9/11 was also a national and global event. Although the World Trade Center had been built in quasi-isolation from the rest of the city, its boundaries were, like any place, porous. They were of course porous enough to interweave the World Trade Center in the flows of globalized capitalism. After 9/11, the boundaries were further dissolved. The surrounding neighborhood wanted to reclaim Ground Zero as a mixed-use area rather than a commercially oriented superblock. Moreover, as the site of an attack on the United States as a whole, Ground Zero was now claimed by the entire nation. The construction of a viewing station turned the area into a strange combination of disaster site, crime scene, holy place, and tourist attraction.

Unsurprisingly, many now saw new possibilities at Ground Zero. Not only was this a founding opportunity for the site, but also perhaps for Lower Manhattan and for the entire city.[63] Would-be founders could have focused on memorializing the disaster and thus creating the perpetual preservationism of a standing museum piece. Or the founders could have looked at rebuilding from a much more short-term perspective, as a chance for lucrative redevelopment, and paid little attention to the long-term character and significance of the place. In such a case, the focus would have been on founding something profitable, but not on how the place might sustain noncommodity values and how it might affect the character and vitality of the places around it. Finally, the founders, even if they were to make a great gesture, could have worked to integrate economic and cultural vitality with memory and so tried to combine founding and preservation.

This third approach would have been the most appropriate for the site and the most attentive to both founding and preservation. The opportunities for founding were dramatic, and yet a grand vision could have also considered long-term preservation and the requirements of the surrounding area. Accordingly, in one scenario, architect Michael Sorkin combined founding with environmental values: "In New York, we have the opportunity for a dramatic pedestrianization downtown, with Ground Zero as its center. This local greening might be accompanied by a large-scale reduction in private vehicles in the city as a whole and the replacement of no-longer-required road space with parks, bikeways, and other public amenities."[64] City University professor Setha Low called for a civic-oriented locale for both remembrance and citizenship: "[T]he World Trade Center site provides an opportunity to reimagine the postindustrial plaza as a space of reflection and recovery as well as a place of civic action and discussion rather than a privatized space driven by global capital. This site of trauma can be transformed into a communal center for people to meet, mix, mourn, and remember."[65] The past would be remembered, and a humane reconstitution of Ground Zero would proceed through the democratic participation of city residents, recovery workers, and mourners. If only it had been so.

Conflict Over Rebuilding

Whatever the new character of Ground Zero, its founding—and now I return mainly to the present tense because the process is still very much under way—cannot be smooth or tidy. *New York Times* architecture critic Herbert Muschamp called it "a heavily contested site."[66] That is an understatement, if anything; Ground Zero bears none of the monolithic simplicity of the old World Trade Center. A large number of people and interests have been affected by 9/11; Ground Zero is freighted with tremendous symbolism and the future of the site initially seemed up for grabs. This has produced an explosive brew of concerns, hopes, fears, perspectives, debates, resentments, and controversies. Concerned parties include the families of the civilian victims; the families and comrades of the fallen police officers and firefighters; the residents and small and large businesses of Lower Manhattan, who were physically and economically affected by 9/11; the residents of the city as a whole; Silverstein (who, having leased the site from the Port Authority, has had considerable power over what would be built there); the city's artists, planners, and architects; and the various public officials and agencies and authorities, including the governments of New York City and New York State and the Port Authority.

Goldberger says that the months after 9/11 revealed "that the greatest conflict was not between those who wanted to build and those who wanted the site to remain empty but between those who saw the priority of new construction on the site as primarily commercial and those who saw it as primarily symbolic and cultural."[67] However, I would argue that three main groups have ultimately emerged: the family, friends, and comrades of the fallen (I call them the 9/11 families for short); state-level public agencies—the New York State governor's office, the Port Authority, and the Lower Manhattan Development Corporation, together with Silverstein; and the local community, often allied with the city's artists, planners, and architects and with City Hall. Although each of these three groups has had serious internal divisions, this tripartite schema highlights the main perspectives in the debate: preservation, founding, and an integration of both—a third position that showed the way out of the founding versus preservation debate.

Three Perspectives

Preservation In his farewell address, outgoing New York Mayor Rudolph Giuliani declared that Ground Zero should become a memorial to the fallen and not a site for economic development. These sentiments reflected the views of many of the victims' families, friends, co-workers, and fellow uniformed civil servants that Ground Zero was now a sacred burial site or even a battlefield. A number of the dead, their bodies lost and destroyed, were permanently entombed there.

The 9/11 families have become a local and national constituency urging that Ground Zero be devoted to a memorial. Although the creation of a memorial is itself an act of founding, the families are primarily focused on preservation. They are quite understandably concerned with preserving the tragedy and heroism of 9/11 and believe that at least a significant portion of Ground Zero should be saved for memory, mourning, and inspiration rather than commerce.

The group as a whole has not been in full agreement over how much space should be devoted to a memorial. A number of family members, but not all, have been willing to see a memorial on just part of the site rather than on all 16 acres. Also, the families, friends, and comrades of the fallen firefighters sought a special rescuers' memorial, separate from the memorial to the civilian dead.[68]

Among the families, though, there is widespread agreement that the footprints of the Twin Towers should be set aside for a memorial, especially after their more expansive requests for the site were denied. New York Governor George Pataki supported this position, and he and the victims' families have been criticized for constraining the planning process from the start. Architecture critic Philip Nobel writes, "The designation of the footprints as holy ground had a devastating effect on the planning possibilities at Ground Zero, but the two enormous squares also made a very awkward site for the memorial they were fated to contain."[69]

Nobel argues that in declaring the footprints off limits for anything other than a memorial, Pataki was motivated by his own desire for reelection in 2002.[70] In fact, the sanctity of the tower footprints is quite arbitrary, Nobel maintains: "There was nothing inevitable about regarding those two offset squares as sacred. The families' justification was that concentrations of remains had been found there, but there were other areas of similar density, and if a sacrosanct zone were to be delimited by the places where people came to rest, it would have to extend many blocks beyond the spots where the towers had stood."[71]

Whatever the configuration of the memorial, the bereavement and desire for commemoration on the part of the friends and families and coworkers of almost three thousand dead cannot be dismissed. Moreover, 9/11 was a loss for the entire nation and indeed the entire world; many of those working at the World Trade Center were foreign nationals.[72]

The families' vision for Ground Zero is strongly preservationist, and it is a preservationist perspective that has to be in some measure respected.

However, Ground Zero is also in the midst of a neighborhood that grew up around the old World Trade Center and came to rely on its facilities. The residents of Lower Manhattan now want Ground Zero reintegrated into the neighborhood as a mixed-use area, not just a memorial. Consequently, while a memorial has to built, it should not dominate the entire site.

Founding The Port Authority and Silverstein have sought to restore the lost 10 million square feet of office space, though the final amount could be 12 percent less. They want to rebuild rapidly and use the site to generate revenue, all the while ignoring some important implications of this endeavor. Their view in many ways represents the sort of narrow, debased approach to founding exhibited in the case of sprawl. Unfortunately, Governor Pataki acceded to their wishes and did so privately, without consulting the public.[73] As of this writing, the most recent plan opens the way for a slight scaling back of the total square footage, to 8.8 million, on the grounds that one of the planned towers might be residential. However, the plan also accelerates the completion of the Ground Zero redevelopment by three years, to 2012.[74]

One might call restoration of the lost office space a preservationist move, but it is motivated less by an attachment to the particular character of the site and the site's long-term viability than the revenue the site can generate in the short term. Ground Zero is, in Heideggerian terms, on call and pressed into service as a money-making resource.

Michael Goodwin, writing in the *New York Daily News*, says that the aim to restore the lost office space was heavily pushed by the Port Authority and by Silverstein. The Port Authority sought to maximize Silverstein's rental payments, while Silverstein sought to maximize the amount his insurers would pay him for the destruction of the World Trade Center. Both monetary figures were proportional to the amount of office space to be restored.[75]

Claiming that his lease legally obligated him to recreate all 10 million square feet, although the language of the lease seemed to give him an out,[76] Silverstein quickly announced that he wanted to rebuild and rebuild fast. Goldberger recounts, "He issued a statement not long after the buildings came down proclaiming his right and his intention to reconstruct the World Trade Center.... He was not insisting on reconstructing the towers as they were," but on restoring the lost office space as quickly as possible.[77] Nobel quotes Silverstein, just months after 9/11: "For a developer, nothing can move fast enough."[78] In what Silverstein thought was a display of civic pride but was perceived as greed, the developer even asked his architect David Childs to begin planning a new World Trade Center, an initiative quickly squashed by public outcry.[79]

The idea of replacing almost all the lost office space is narrow-minded. First of all, a heavy emphasis on commerce is insulting to the 9/11 families. Monica Iken, the founder of September's Mission Foundation, which is dedicated to creating a memorial, lamented, "How can we build on top of their souls that are crying? We have to send a strong message that this is not about money."[80]

Moreover, there simply isn't the demand among commercial tenants to move back into the site. One factor may be continuing fear that the city and its skyscrapers are terrorist targets. Such concerns have helped fuel an exodus of employers from the city. Many people no longer feel as safe working in very tall buildings, and especially in any building that is an icon, like the heavily symbolic Freedom Tower that will anchor the project.[81] Perhaps more important, the local real estate market may not support a restoration of even 8.8 million square feet of the lost office space. Silverstein has had difficulty attracting tenants for 7 World Trade Center, which was adjacent to the original World Trade Center site and which he has already rebuilt.[82] There is concern that a rebuilt World Trade Center with even 8.8 million, rather than 10 million, square feet of office space will replicate the initial woes of the original towers. Though commercial rents in Manhattan are rising as vacancies shrink, critics continue to worry that the new development will have trouble filling up, that it will end up depressing real estate prices in the area, and that it will have to be sustained by government tenants rather than the marketplace. They point to a controversial commitment by Governor Pataki to fill 1 million of the Freedom Tower's planned 2.6 million square feet of office space with public agencies, at an inflated rent of $59 per square foot. Critics of Pataki's pledge, made partly through an agreement with Silverstein to reduce the latter's role in the redevelopment process (see below), call it a taxpayer subsidy for a misguided construction project.[83]

The *New York Times* at one point editorialized that Silverstein, in demanding restoration of the lost office space, was "serving his own needs more than the community's or even ... the market's." The *Times* went on to argue, "The World Trade Center site must be a treasured public space and a critical piece of a renewed community, not just another huge commercial development looming over a few public amenities."[84] In the end, as we will see, Silverstein lost his preeminent position, but as of this writing, this has not appreciably changed the character of the rebuilding plan aside from the small possible decrease in office space noted earlier.

What was most needed at the site, argues Goldberger, is not office space, but mixed-use development, particularly more housing, as well as hotels and retail. The residential population around the World Trade Center has long been growing, and it resumed its growth after 9/11.[85] Yet, just as with the designation of the tower footprints as memorial space, the restoration of all, or almost all, the office space became a non-negotiable premise that has constrained the rebuilding process: "The need to fill all that space ... proscribed the future of the site in a way that nothing else would; all the democracy in the world was not going to change those numbers or the conditions they dictated."[86] The result is a short-sighted founding project: build 8.8 to 10 million square feet of office space to secure insurance money or rental payments and don't pay attention to the long-term needs of the surrounding community for more housing or even to the lack of demand for commercial space in Lower Manhattan. Silverstein and the Port Authority have thus treated Ground Zero as a commodity for short-term gain.

A longer-term view with more preservationist sensibilities has emerged in one aspect of the rebuilding plans: attention to a greener building process and design. Calling for greater ecological awareness in the rebuilding of Ground Zero, frequent critic Sorkin said, "Building safety must also encompass the effects of architecture on climate, the health-related effects of 'sick building syndrome,' the damage to workers and resources in remote locations, the flat-out toxicity of many of the materials with which we build, the dangers of the building process, and the insecurities engendered by the massive consumption of energy by buildings."[87] As with any part of the built environment, Ground Zero is also part of the natural world, embedded in physical, chemical, and biological processes and having impacts on ecological systems. These impacts should not be ignored in the rebuilding.[88]

A green design approach has in fact been partly adopted at Ground Zero. Anthony DePalma wrote in the *New York Times* that the Port Authority, the Lower Manhattan Development Corporation, and Silverstein will be building "an environmentally sensitive city within a city that is attuned to nature as well as the real estate market." Under guidelines established for Ground Zero, "[t]he roofs of buildings will be designed to catch rainwater for flushing toilets and boosting cooling systems. Developers will be encouraged to reuse pilings and other materials already on site and to specify that recycled material and products made from renewable resources, like fast-growing trees and sunflower seed husks, be used for interior and insulating materials." Environmental standards will also apply to the construction process. Green guidelines will "requir[e] all large diesel engines on the building site to use ultra-low-sulfur fuel to reduce emissions. Half of all the waste wood, cardboard and metal generated during construction will be recycled, and construction crews will be encouraged to substitute corn oil or other natural substances for petroleum-based oils to keep concrete from sticking to wooden forms." DePalma noted that "such 'green' goals have never been applied to anything as large as the trade center site, which when complete will contain about as much commercial space as the city of Indianapolis."[89]

Environmental standards have been applied to the rebuilding of 7 World Trade Center, which began in November 2002. The standards, which added over $10 million to the cost of rebuilding, include more reliance on sunlight through large windows that are also treated to keep out heat, computer control of heating and lighting, energy metering of commercial tenants, co-generation of power through steam produced by the heating system, use of stored rainwater for toilets and for watering an adjacent park, and greater filtering of indoor air. Construction vehicles at the site have been using emissions filters and fuel that is lower in sulfur content, which has led to the adoption of a city law mandating low-sulfur fuel and high-efficiency filters at all public construction sites. Regarding the higher cost of greener building methods, Janno Lieber, a

Silverstein official, says, "This was a down payment on the broader commitment that Larry has made to having the trade center redevelopment be state of the art from an environmental standpoint."[90]

The developers have also responded to concerns about the site's air-conditioning and water-chilling system, which will use water drawn from the Hudson River through intake pipes. The previous plan was to reuse surviving infrastructure from the old World Trade Center. The old cooling system drew as much as 90 million gallons a day from the Hudson, pulling in lots of marine life and resulting in large fish kills. Plans for the cooling system have been revised. Water intake from the Hudson will drop to about 15 million gallons per day. Compared to the original plan, this will reduce by 82 percent the number of organisms sucked in through the pipes.[91]

Though the new World Trade Center might be a showpiece for green building, a key point is obscured by all the attention given to the environmentally friendly features. In building as much commercial space as that contained in the city of Indianapolis when public demand is for housing, not commercial space, the developers are engaged in a massive waste of energy and resources. From this standpoint, the use of green building processes and design starts to look like public relations and superficial preservationism.

Integrating Founding and Preservation?   Civic groups and local residents and businesses agree on the need for a memorial. However, they are, as I noted, concerned to bring the World Trade Center site back into the surrounding community and erase some of the damage caused by the original development.

The population of Lower Manhattan has grown considerably since the Twin Towers were completed. In Community District 1, which consists of the Wall Street area and the Civic Center, and the neighborhoods of Tribeca and Battery Park City, the population more than doubled between 1980 and 2000, increasing from 15,918 to 34,420.[92] That growth has resumed since 9/11, so that about 50,000 people live in the area today.[93]

Could one credit the World Trade Center for having stimulated growth in the area? Goldberger, citing the design features of the World Trade Center, which, as I described, involved an austere superblock physically cut off from the rest of the neighborhood, basically says no. He maintains that "in some ways the towers were a regressive force, not enabling the urban regeneration that later took place in Lower Manhattan … but acting as a brake on it."[94] Moreover, it was not just employment in the FIRE industries associated with the World Trade Center that drew residents to Lower Manhattan. Before 9/11, only about 31 percent of employed residents in the portion of Community District 1 below Chambers Street, the area that includes the World Trade Center site, actually worked there. In 2004, only 27 percent of employed residents living below Chambers worked in the FIRE sector.[95] In addition, Lower Manhattan has attracted residents because of various amenities beyond employment. The Alliance for Downtown New York noted in 2004, "Several aspects of the community that residents rated highly include convenience to work, waterfront and open spaces, neighborhood feel, and safety." The Alliance also reported that Lower Manhattan residents are generally happy with the area's quality of life, although they cite the absence of grocery stores and other shopping options as drawbacks to living downtown.[96]

The World Trade Center did positively affect the growth of Lower Manhattan in an indirect way. As noted earlier, in building the World Trade Center the Port Authority used fill from the excavation to begin the creation of Battery Park City. Battery Park City had been included as a "deal sweetener" to get New York City Mayor John Lindsay on board.[97] Today, it is a mixed-use, affluent ("exclusive" would also be apt) neighborhood with about 9,000 residents. It will have between 12,000 and 14,000 inhabitants when residential development is complete in 2009.[98]

Given the growth of Lower Manhattan as a residential area and the need for increased amenities like shopping, it is not surprising that many of the residents, as well as Mayor Michael R. Bloomberg and a group of architects called New York New Visions, have wanted to create a mixed-use, 24-hour neighborhood with cultural and entertainment venues and attractive green spaces, in part by restoring the streets that had been obliterated decades earlier.[99] Local residents and civic groups have regarded the disaster, not as an opportunity to restore the conditions predating the World Trade Center, but as I noted earlier, a chance for improved urban planning. They envision the redeveloped site as a place that would fit into and sustain a growing residential neighborhood. "We have a blank slate," said one resident at a public forum. "Why not make it better?"[100]

At the same time, the locals have tried to temper proposals for a memorial. They fear that a large chunk of Lower Manhattan might be turned more or less into a graveyard or mausoleum. This concern was voiced by Madelyn Wils during her tenure as chair of Community District 1: "It is very difficult to live and work in an area that other people consider a cemetery. I can understand how the families of victims feel that way. But this isn't Gettysburg; it isn't Normandy Beach. This is a place that is vital and one that wants to be vital again."[101] For example, Wils argued that the Twin Towers' footprints should not be off limits for construction.[102] Moreover, according to Nobel, Wils almost single-handedly prevented the 9/11 families from using the only park in Tribeca to house *The Sphere*, a huge Fritz Koenig sculpture. The *Sphere* had been at the World Trade Center and the families wanted it put up again as a 9/11 memorial.[103] It is not surprising that Wils incurred the resentment, indeed the hatred, of many of the 9/11 families. She even received death threats.[104]

As Nobel puts it, "Wils wanted Ground Zero to belong again to Manhattan—a place for work and shopping and sidewalk life, as well as for an appropriate yet modestly scaled commemoration."[105] One of the most revealing episodes in Wils's effort occurred at an April 10, 2003 meeting of the Lower Manhattan Development Corporation (LMDC), the state-level agency nominally in charge of rebuilding Ground Zero (see the following section). Wils was on the LMDC board of directors. As Nobel recounts,[106] Wils was concerned about wording in the mission statement for the World Trade Center memorial: "Respect this place made sacred through tragic loss."[107] Wils wanted "sacred" to mean "entitled to respect and reverence" so as to admit secular interpretations of the term.[108] She was concerned that the term *sacred* could be interpreted to mean that Ground Zero "could *only be* used for one holy purpose *only*,"[109] namely, a memorial. An argument ensued with another director, Paul Crotty, over the meaning of the word *sacred*. Wils's stipulation was not adopted.

As the argument reveals, Wils wanted a meaning that would allow a dynamic character for Ground Zero, even as the site was respected. Her definition of sacred would have promoted the creation of a memorial on part of the site, but would have also admitted other interpretations and uses of Ground Zero, including those emphasizing a role for everyday living, recreation, and commerce.

In essence, the local residents and civic groups have gone beyond the simple dichotomy of commerce and commemoration and have sought a dynamic balance between founding and preservation. They want to found a new mixed-use area and through the founding action sustain the surrounding neighborhood. At the same time they are also prepared to provide space for remembrance. Residents' concerns about the prominence of the memorial have been supported by Mayor Bloomberg. Bloomberg also put forth a redevelopment proposal for Lower Manhattan as a whole. The plan featured a transition away from dependence on the financial sector to a mixed-use area with new public parks.[110]

Also thinking along lines similar to the residents has been the Civic Alliance to Rebuild Downtown New York, formed by Regional Plan Association President Robert Yaro. The Civic Alliance has pushed for, in Goldberger's words, "an open planning process with significant public participation—in effect the opposite of the process by which the original World Trade Center was planned—and for the effort to encompass all of Lower Manhattan.... The alliance [has] also called for sustainable, environmentally friendly development and for attention to the needs of a wide range of economic groups, not just the financial community that had traditionally been Lower Manhattan's primary business."[111]

In July and August 2002, the Civic Alliance sponsored Listening to the City, a series of in-person and on-line public forums. The first of these events, Goldberger says, generated a set of vague but influential recommendations: "[A] new transportation hub for Lower Manhattan, greater pedestrian amenity in the area, improved local services, more public open space, more cultural facilities, distinguished architecture, and a memorial that honored all of the dead and would speak clearly to the living as well."[112]

However, the efforts of local residents and civic groups have not been very successful. In the end, the planning process has failed to truly integrate founding and preservation. In part this is because Bloomberg became distracted from Ground Zero. By mid-2004, he became preoccupied with efforts to build a football stadium for the New York Jets on the west side of midtown Manhattan and to try to bring the 2012 Olympics to New York City. With Bloomberg's attention elsewhere, Governor Pataki could exert enormous power over the planning process.[113] More fundamentally, though, what was billed as a democratic process has been unduly limited by the excessively preservationist objectives of the 9/11 families and the narrow-minded founding approach of Silverstein and the Port Authority.

Selecting a Plan: Democracy at Ground Zero?
To oversee planning for the Ground Zero rebuilding, New York Governor George Pataki created the Lower Manhattan Development Corporation. The LMDC has pursued a public–private partnership; it has worked with private developers at the site.

The management of the LMDC was appointed by both Pataki and the mayor of New York. However, Pataki, who appointed the LMDC's chair and president, held the balance of power.[114] It is widely acknowledged that Pataki and lame-duck Mayor Giuliani arranged things this way when they thought the next mayor of New York would be a Democrat, Mark Green. When Bloomberg, a Republican, was elected, the new mayor was given more power over the LMDC, but he let Pataki take the lead as long as Pataki supported his proposals for the West Side.[115] In creating the LMDC, Pataki also seemed to bypass the Port Authority, which is also answerable to the governor of New Jersey, but the Port Authority's interests have often held sway. The LMDC is scheduled to be phased out, as its mission of planning a rebuilt Ground Zero is supposedly complete. Despite the continuing power of the Port Authority, the departure of the LMDC could create an opening for the city government to take on more of a leadership role.[116]

Indeed, despite the creation of the LMDC, the jurisdictional picture is confusing. The LMDC has had to compete with the Port Authority, the site's owner, as well as with Silverstein. The power of the Port Authority and Silverstein underscores how the future of the World Trade Center site could be much like its past.

The LMDC tried to take charge of the redevelopment process early on. At the time of its creation, the new agency was heavily criticized as being tilted toward business and political insiders and unrepresentative of the local community.[117] "Heavy with financial types," the LMDC's board "had but one representative of the downtown residents, small businesses and cultural institutions that were hardest hit by the attack's economic fallout."[118] The 9/11 families were not represented.

However, John Whitehead, the chair of the LMDC, made it his business to listen to all the various stakeholders, and he established a number of stakeholder advisory groups.[119] Moreover, the LMDC presented two sets of rebuilding proposals to the public and in the process seemed to democratize decision making about the site and admit the concerns of a variety of constituencies. In opening up the process, the agency increased its own profile.

The LMDC offered its first set of proposals in July 2002. There were six proposals, developed in cooperation with the Port Authority and presented by the architecture firm Beyer Blinder Belle. All six were roughly similar. They restored the lost office space and featured a crowd of large buildings surrounding a park. The six proposals were presented at a July 20, 2002 Listening to the City forum attended by more than 4,000 people.

The attendees and public at large roundly vilified the proposals. They saw the designs as unimaginative and too oriented to commercial space. In the eyes of many critics, the LMDC was simply catering to developers and others in the business community and reproducing what was formerly at the site.[120] This loud, public rejection forced the LMDC to solicit a whole new set of proposals and further open up the planning process.

The LMDC reported on the public's concerns: "Chief among them was creating a fitting memorial to those who were killed at the World Trade Center site. Others included restoring the skyline, increased connectivity with the World Trade Center site and adjacent neighborhoods, preserving the footprints of the Twin Towers, additional parks and open spaces, and others." In democratic fashion, the LMDC then translated these concerns into design requirements for a second round of proposals.[121]

Yet, "Port Authority officials," says the *New York Times'* Edward Wyatt, "were livid at the development corporation's attempt to establish its own design for what the authority saw as its site." The LMDC mollified the Port Authority by presenting the competition as one of ideas rather than final plans, a key qualification that got lost in the general excitement over the competition.[122]

Nine new proposals were unveiled in December 2002. This time the
LMDC went for more innovative, avant-garde architectural designs,
and the public response was more positive. With the exception of a virtual holdover from the earlier designs offered in July, each proposal
imagined a striking, fairly unusual building design and layout to replace
the original World Trade Center. The review process for the proposals
was further democratized. Public hearings, simulcast in other locations
and/or on the web, were held in Lower Manhattan and New Jersey in
January 2003. The nine proposals were displayed at the World Financial
Center from December 19, 2002 through February 2, 2003. More than
100,000 people visited the display and more than 8,000 comment cards
were completed. The LMDC also met with Community Board 1 and sent
mailings to the victims' families. Videos of the architects' proposals,
along with public comment brochures, were distributed to all public library branches in New York City. Informational mailings were sent to
every city, state, and federal elected official in New York City. The proposals, as well as opportunities for comment, were provided on the
LMDC's website.[123]

The new proposals were narrowed down to two, one by a group of
architects called the THINK Team, the other by Berlin-based architect
Daniel Libeskind. Although the LMDC was prepared to award the commission to THINK, the intercession of Pataki, who was influenced by the
victims' families and their preference for Libeskind's design,[124] and
Bloomberg ensured selection of the other proposal. With its jagged building designs, Libeskind's proposal captured the moment of the Towers'
destruction, although the buildings were also given a distinctive crystal-
line look. In his buildings, Libeskind also provided for commercial, residential, and cultural space.

The plan, which was not big on subtlety, also maintained and highlighted, as a symbol of democracy's strength, the World Trade Center's
underground "slurry wall," which had kept the Hudson from flooding
in beneath the site. Libeskind saw the wall as symbolic of the strength
of democracy and the U.S. Constitution. Libeskind also designated space
for a memorial 70 feet below ground, at bedrock level. The aim was to
provide a memorial in the pit into which the Towers and the thousands
who perished there fell. Reaching in the other direction as well, Libeskind included the Freedom Tower, which, at a patriotic 1,776 feet,

would be the world's tallest building. Libeskind's design was selected for these and other distinctive features, as well as for the architect's attention to restoring part of the pre-World Trade Center streetscape, specifically Greenwich and Fulton streets.

To the degree that the LMDC could be seen as having come to represent the public's wishes, the intercession of Pataki disrupted the democratic process. However, Libeskind was at least the second choice, and he got there through what the *Times'* Wyatt described as an unprecedented public dialogue and involvement in architectural design.[125] The public had reclaimed Ground Zero in a way that starkly contrasted with the process by which the World Trade Center had been built. Or so it seemed.

Libeskind's Plan Unravels
Various pressures, particularly from Silverstein and the Port Authority, led Libeskind to revise his original plan. Silverstein, who wanted more space for lucrative tenants, did not like Libeskind's design and in fact ridiculed it.[126] He hired Childs, his own architect, to come up with alterations.[127] Childs and Libeskind had an antagonistic working relationship and frequently clashed.[128]

Silverstein wielded considerable power not just because of his lease. His command of several billion dollars, including anticipated insurance payments, gave him the resources to undertake the rebuilding, whereas the city and state governments faced budget shortfalls.[129] Because of Silverstein's resources, Pataki, the Port Authority, and the LMDC gave him the major responsibility for rebuilding Ground Zero[130] (although Silverstein's fortunes would eventually change) and the actual design of Libeskind's Freedom Tower was turned over to Childs. Libeskind became a kind of junior partner in executing his own master plan. Moreover, Pataki, a Republican, was eager to break ground on the Freedom Tower before the Republican National Convention came to New York on August 2004, and he thought Silverstein had the resources to meet this deadline.[131] In setting the deadlines, Pataki acted with little involvement from the city.[132]

As the new design evolved, Libeskind's entire plan was virtually modified out of existence, bringing it closer and closer to the character of the original six designs presented by the LMDC and Beyer Blinder Belle. Port

Authority Director Joseph Seymour said, with surprising candor and even arrogance: "When we roll it out, the land-use plan is going to be almost exactly what Beyer Blinder Belle proposed."[133]

Almost all of the distinctive features of Libeskind's design vanished.[134] For example, to accommodate more office and retail space, the buildings became boxier and more conventional, residential buildings were eliminated, and parks and other open spaces were shrunk, in some places to little more than flower beds.[135]

The plans for the memorial were also altered. The depth of the memorial was raised from 70 to 30 feet to accommodate pedestrian concourses and a train station beneath.[136] The idea of raising the memorial up from the bedrock and building anything else on the tower footprints infuriated many of the victims' families, who saw the cheapening of a sacred site.[137] They also felt betrayed by Pataki.[138] Former Mayor Giuliani echoed the families' concerns: "The first thing that should emerge from [the] design is the importance of the place—historically, patriotically, spiritually." He criticized the rebuilding process: "What has happened is the office buildings have become the dominant theme, and the memorial has been the footnote. We have no choice but to accept ... that it's a burial ground."[139] In fact, the families still exercised considerable power over the shape of the site in that nothing but a memorial would be at the footprints' *ground level*.

The *Times'* Wyatt sharply criticized the whole evolution of the process. The master plan had changed considerably and without public input since Libeskind's selection, and Wyatt lamented the abandonment of the democratic process: "The secretive evolution of the plan contrasts sharply with the continuing portrayal of the rebuilding process as one of the most open and inclusive civic building projects in memory." Wyatt cited Pataki's control over the process, the Port Authority's interest in maintaining its revenues, and Silverstein's financial clout and willingness to "push for his own priorities." He also cited the constraint imposed by the families' demand for a memorial on the footprints.[140]

Perhaps the final blow to the Libeskind plan came in April 2005. The New York City Police Department expressed concern that the Freedom Tower was vulnerable to a terrorist truck bomb and argued that it would have to be redesigned and made more impregnable. Such measures would include moving the tower away from the street, to a distance of as much as 100 feet. The police department claimed that it had been airing these concerns for a year and a half but had been ignored.[141]

Childs again redesigned the tower, and the result was disturbingly fortresslike. *New York Times* architecture critic Nicolai Ouroussoff remarked, "Somber, oppressive and clumsily conceived, the project suggests a monument to a society that has turned its back on any notion of cultural openness. It is exactly the kind of nightmare that government officials repeatedly asserted would never happen here: an impregnable tower braced against the outside world." A tower was placed atop a twenty-story concrete base. The base was windowless but for thin slots, with a skinny spire added so that the tower would reach its mandated 1,776 feet. Ouroussoff said, "The new obelisk-shaped tower ... evokes a gigantic glass paperweight with a toothpick stuck on top." He concluded, "The [new] Freedom Tower embodies, in its way, a world shaped by fear."[142] By May 2005, there was increasing public frustration with the process, and not only because of the changes and the nullification of the public's will; pointless delay and conflict seemed to plague the whole effort. Of all the major projects at Ground Zero, only a transit hub, designed by famed Spanish architect Santiago Calatrava and under the tight reins of the Port Authority, was proceeding relatively smoothly (demonstrating perhaps that authoritarian planning could at times be efficient even if on the whole undesirable). Ouroussoff wrote, "The master plan for ground zero is unraveling."[143]

As noted earlier, the LMDC meant for the winning plan to provide general guidelines and ideas, a rough master plan that would later be filled in, as opposed to a set of detailed instructions. However, the agency had failed to make sure that this important qualification was publicly understood.[144] This fundamental misunderstanding reflected the sad truth that the LMDC's supposedly democratic process was really a sham.

A postscript to the process, but one that did not change the basic plan, was the ultimate elimination of Silverstein's dominating role. A protracted struggle ensued when it became apparent that Silverstein, far from having the most resources to rebuild Ground Zero, might run out of money before the expensive redevelopment was complete. This was the conclusion of a study done by the City of New York. Mayor Bloomberg, concerned about the lack of housing in the plans for Ground Zero, had by late 2005 begun taking a much more active role in the rebuilding debate. According to the *New York Times*, "Bloomberg repeatedly said that Mr. Silverstein did not have enough money to complete the $7 billion project. He raised the possibility that the developer would run out of money in 2009 after building only two towers, default on his lease and walk away with tens of millions in profits, while the project was left unfinished."[145] Lack of progress on the rebuilding was also creating doubts about Silverstein.

Over the first four months of 2006, the Port Authority, Governor Pataki, New Jersey Governor John Corzine, and Mayor Bloomberg engaged in acrimonious negotiations with Silverstein so that he might relinquish his controlling position in the project. Silverstein's financial demands and hard bargaining led public officials to charge him with greed. In April 2006, however, the parties reached an agreement. "The deal," according to a *Times* article the next day, "calls for Mr. Silverstein to surrender control of the $2 billion Freedom Tower, along with more than one third of the ground zero site, to the Port Authority of New York and New Jersey. But he would retain the right to build three office towers on the most valuable parcels there."[146] Silverstein would share rebuilding money from insurance proceeds and from the sale of Liberty Bonds with the Port Authority, and he received "promises to fill more than 1 million square feet of office space towers under [his] control with state and city leases."[147] Governor Pataki crowed that the deal "recognizes the unique public nature of this project and will ensure that the rebuilding moves forward expeditiously and with certainty."[148] Certainly, public authorities had, rather belatedly, reined in an individual property owner who was hijacking the rebuilding process. Construction of the Freedom Tower finally began on April 27, 2006 (ironically, a cornerstone placed in a pointless rebuilding ceremony staged by Pataki almost two years earlier, on July 4, 2004, had to be temporarily moved out of the way). However, the public nature of the project had never been recognized through a truly democratic process.

"Shirley Temples and Candy Cigarettes"

The process was actually undemocratic from the outset. First of all, as Sorkin notes, the decision on the future of Ground Zero had been unnecessarily hurried; the initial attitude should have been to approach the site with "reverence and deliberation, not to solve the 'problem' of Ground Zero."[149] The rush, as Nobel argues, was in part due to Pataki and his political considerations, including winning reelection in 2002, hosting the Republican National Convention in 2004, and nurturing presidential ambitions. The governor thus imposed unreasonable deadlines at various stages[150] and held the aforementioned July 2004 groundbreaking, which preceded real construction by two years. The consequent rush undermined any thoughtful public consideration of redevelopment options and precluded serious consideration of fundamental planning alternatives rather than of competing architectural designs for buildings and grounds.

The *New Republic*'s Clay Risen argues that haste was driven not only by Pataki's political concerns, but also by Silverstein's—and, I would add, the Port Authority's—short-term economic interests, resulting in serious oversights regarding how rebuilding would affect the surrounding community. In my own terms, Pataki, Silverstein, and the Port Authority pursued a narrow-minded, quick-fix approach to founding. Risen charges that "Pataki and Silverstein failed to consider a variety of rebuilding strategies, and instead pushed through a plan geared more toward meeting immediate political and financial goals than the long-term needs of the city. Claiming an obligation to rebuild as quickly as possible, the two resisted calls by civic leaders to put together a master plan." Libeskind's so-called master plan "was anything but." Silverstein and Pataki "failed to take into account how changing demographic patterns or economic development (in recent decades, financial firms have been moving further uptown or across the Hudson to New Jersey) would affect Lower Manhattan and how the site would fit within it."[151]

Second, the LMDC had much less power over the process than Silverstein, the Port Authority, and Pataki, all of whom determined the main parameters of the redevelopment plan. A number of alternatives were never seriously entertained by the LMDC and others in the supposedly democratic planning process. The LMDC, Sorkin says, acted undemocratically as a gatekeeper, filtering out and shaping the ideas that were presented to the public.[152] The public could only choose among a narrow set of predetermined options. Choices were limited to a matter of architectural design and pretty models and computer-generated images by architecture firms rather than any serious consideration of the fundamental character of the site and the surrounding neighborhoods. Sorkin argues that the confusion of architecture and planning enabled the LMDC to bury the more fundamental planning questions about the site under a competition over building design.[153]

"What is excluded [from the process]," said Sorkin, listing some of the omissions, was "the idea that the plan must be driven by the memorial, the idea that commercial activity is not the invariable default, the idea that designs might come from people other than those carefully filtered by the uninspiring leadership of the LMDC or produced in secrecy by the Port Authority or the lessor."[154] Sorkin says that the process should have considered not just rebuilding Ground Zero, but also looked more broadly at the residential, commercial, and ecological requirements of New York City as a whole (see chapter 7).

There were other possibilities that were never considered. Many of these came out during the brief period of possibility after 9/11. They included Setha Low's vision, discussed earlier, as well as architect Denise Scott Brown's proposal for an incremental building process beginning with small buildings and parks,[155] Michael Abelman's proposal for an urban farm to symbolize life and reconnect the site with the Earth,[156] and various proposals presented in the collection *After the World Trade Center*, edited by Michael Sorkin and Sharon Zukin, for the creation of public parks and mixed-use residential neighborhoods at and around Ground Zero.[157]

Sorkin maintains that no one "seriously entertained any idea save the construction of millions of square feet of office space on the site," and what was chosen did not fundamentally depart, in terms of its "arrangement of buildings, streets, and open spaces," from the designs rejected earlier by the public. The whole process, he says, wasted what had been an unprecedented outpouring of public interest in architecture, planning, and development.[158]

Citing the lack of true democracy, Noble quotes a participant in one of the Listening to the City forums: "This is the story of a thousand people drinking Shirley Temples and smoking candy cigarettes, and they all think they're in a back room with their Scotch and cigars."[159]

Secrecy: Choosing a Memorial Design

As the master plan evolved, or mutated, another contest, again organized by the LMDC, was held for the design of the 9/11 memorial, to be situated within the overall master plan. Again, the LMDC would be choosing general ideas, not finalized, detailed plans. As with the selection committee for the redevelopment proposals, only one downtown resident was on the thirteen-member committee that selected the memorial design. The victims' families also had but one representative. There was not even the appearance of openness that had characterized selection of the redevelopment plan. The contest, which drew 5,200 entries, was held in secrecy, with anonymous entries and the jury meeting at an undisclosed location.[160] Jurors were also kept away from the media. The rationale was that secrecy would shield the process from undue outside pressure.[161]

On November 19, 2003, the LMDC publicly unveiled eight finalists and put the proposals on public display. The nonprofit Municipal Art Society organized public meetings on the proposals, but the LMDC itself made no provision for a formal public comment period.[162] Finalists were kept from speaking to the media.[163] LMDC staff also made alterations to the finalists' submissions before they were made public. The *Engineering News-Record* editorialized that the public had been locked out of a process that was supposed to be open and inclusive from the beginning.[164]

In January 2004, the jury chose "Reflecting Absence," by Michael Arad and Peter Walker, as the winning design. In another step away from Libeskind's plan, the memorial was brought up to ground level. The footprints of the towers were to be filled with reflecting pools. A survey by the Municipal Art Society discovered that many found the design to be excessively cold, bleak, and angular.[165] In the end, though, there was some response to public criticism. For example, the harshness of the design was softened through greater attention to landscaping.[166] To mollify criticisms of the plan from the Coalition of 9/11 Families, the designers also added a vast underground space to display ruins and artifacts from the World Trade Center, and provided that unidentified victims' remains would be housed in a stone container placed at bedrock level.[167] However, controversy over the memorial and changes in its design were to continue.

The Battle Over Cultural Institutions

In addition to the so-called master plan and the memorial, there was another aspect to the planned redevelopment: the siting of cultural facilities. This provided the occasion for another contentious and revealing debate, one that displayed the excessively preservationist program of some of the 9/11 families.

Newsday's Justin Davidson expressed a fairly common sentiment in justifying cultural, including artistic, institutions at Ground Zero: "The memorial will be a vast, solemn expanse framed by the fabric of forgetfulness: offices, shops and apartments full of worker bees, all focused on today's labor and tomorrow's check. We need a portal between these two worlds." Culture, particularly art, would supply this portal: "Art exists in the vague terrain between mammon and memory. Art can negotiate between an oblivious downtown rededicated to business and a grim downtown devoted to emptiness."[168]

Artistic and cultural institutions—dance, visual arts, opera, historical exhibits—participate in the everyday, dynamic present and entertain us, but they also sustain more transcendent values, such as aesthetics, reflection, and collective identity. At Ground Zero, culture could thus bridge preservationist remembrance with the more founding-oriented, forgetful vitality of daily life.

The LMDC chose the cultural institutions for Ground Zero. Two of these institutions, the International Freedom Center (IFC) and the Drawing Center, generated an uproar. In June 2005, Debra Burlingame, an influential 9/11 family member whose brother, Charles Burlingame, was the pilot of the plane that crashed into the Pentagon, launched a successful movement to bar the IFC and the Drawing Center from Ground Zero.[169] To publicize and accomplish their mission, she and like-minded family members formed a group called Take Back the Memorial.

The IFC and the Drawing Center were to be housed in a building right next to Arad's memorial. The IFC was being created specifically for Ground Zero. It was conceived as a museum to celebrate struggles for freedom around the world, including in the United States. Burlingame, along with other—though by no means all—members of the 9/11 families, as well as the New York City firefighters' union, the *New York Daily News*, the *New York Post*, and a number of elected officials, bitterly attacked the IFC on the grounds that it was not specifically about 9/11 and that its planned coverage of freedom struggles within the United States, as well as international reaction to 9/11, invited anti-American messages on hallowed ground.[170] The Drawing Center, a SoHo arts facility that planned to relocate to Ground Zero, was also targeted because it had exhibited politically controversial artwork, including material sharply critical of George Bush. Pataki said, "I view that memorial site as sacred grounds, akin to the beaches of Normandy or Pearl Harbor, and we will not tolerate anything on that site that denigrates America, denigrates New York or freedom, or denigrates the sacrifice or courage that the heroes showed on Sept. 11." He threatened to bar both institutions.[171]

Opponents of the IFC and the Drawing Center were in essence declaring that there was only one 9/11 story to tell at Ground Zero, and any attempt to tell a different one should not be permitted at the site. Burlingame warned, "Any museum that goes beyond the story of what happened on that day is inappropriate and an insult to people who died."[172]

Yet Paula Berry, who lost her husband on 9/11 and who was not only on the World Trade Center Memorial Foundation but also vice chair of the Freedom Center, disagreed: "There is a larger story that needs to be told here. We need to explore the historical message of 9/11, the meaning of what happened on that day." She argued, "The museum can't just be something that looks backward. It has to give us a sense of the future, something that's alive and relevant to us now."[173]

Rather than submit to censorship, the Drawing Center decided not to move to Ground Zero. But Freedom Center Chair Tom Bernstein was cowed: "We will not invite or permit debates on the World Trade Center site or anywhere under the auspices of the International Freedom Center about possible rationalizations for the Sept. 11 attacks."[174] In essence, he was saying that he would not allow the facility to engage in any reinterpretation of 9/11. The *Daily News* was barely mollified. An editorial warned ominously: "Close scrutiny will be in order, because the IFC is only starting a likely five-year effort to create a major cultural institution. Particular attention must be given to the center's plan for evening, university-sponsored programs and discussions, lest they violate the sanctity of the site. At some point, the IFC may have to jettison the talkfests."[175] In the end, Pataki, who was not satisfied with the IFC's assurances, rejected the museum.

Opposition to the IFC and the Drawing Center was not representative of all the 9/11 families, as Berry's views indicated. Robert Kolker wrote in *New York Magazine*,

The untold story of Take Back the Memorial may be that a silent majority of family members disagreed with the decision to oppose the IFC, yet were shouted down by Burlingame and the other members of her group. "I thought what happened with the Freedom Center last summer reeked of McCarthyism," says Chris Burke, founder of Tuesday's Children, which provides social services to 1,100 9/11 families; his brother worked at Cantor Fitzgerald. "Look, we all know how these things work. When you throw a couple 9/11 families on a soapbox talking about justifying terrorism and blaming America, the New York *Post* is going to print that. These are 9/11 family members who are actively doing a disservice to 9/11 families. There is this fatigue about 9/11 now, thanks to these families who continually complain, *We were promised this, we were promised that*. You know what? Nine-eleven is not just about the families."[176]

Meanwhile, the conflict over the IFC and the Drawing Center set off a larger debate over how to treat the World Trade Center site as a whole. Steve Cassidy, president of the city firefighters' union, inveighed against cultural facilities on the entire site, not just the memorial area: "I think people around the world would be outraged to find out that there were proposals for dance theaters and a freedom center on the graves of 2,800 Americans."[177] *Times* reporter David Dunlap wondered, "If certain cultural uses denigrate hallowed ground, why would a shopping arcade be more appropriate?" Dunlap also mused: And what about returning Borders bookstore to the site? Could it sell left-wing material like DVDs of "Fahrenheit 9/11"? 9/11 family member Iken acknowledged that that might be a problem.[178]

The cultural debate represents a victory for at least one faction of the 9/11 families. It upholds the view that there is only one interpretation of what happened on 9/11, only one story to tell. The opponents of the IFC and the Drawing Center have sought to close off all evolution in the meaning of Ground Zero and to freeze one conception of the place for all time. This is in many ways what Wils feared when she raised questions about the definition of sacred—a narrow meaning that would turn Ground Zero into a frozen memorial. Yet in the view of some of the family members, the meaning of Ground Zero as a place does not need to be debated or developed; it is simply there, to be discovered by visitors. In essence, the real founding of the place was on 9/11, not only in the act of mass murder and destruction, but also in the heroism that followed, and from then on the story of that founding, and one version of it only, is what should be told. This view is not unlike that of the forest activists in chapter 2 who saw the old-growth forest as a place to be discovered and preserved, not founded, and regarded any human use of the forest for resources as violating the sanctity of the landscape. Although Ground Zero was in essence founded as a new place on 9/11 itself, and although a memorial will be built, preservation would now be the guiding principle. Cultural institutions, particularly those involving entertainment, and attempts to make sense of 9/11 through discussions and presentations that raised potentially uncomfortable questions like the United States' foreign policy and image abroad, would violate the sanctity of hallowed ground and go against the place's one legitimate story.

Newsday columnist Sheryl McCarthy angrily expressed her disagreement with the foes of the IFC and the Drawing Center and at the same time underscored the power of the 9/11 families in shaping the site: "A small group of 9/11 victims' relatives and first responders were allowed to wrest control of the site from the rest of us, even though they're a tiny fraction of those who will use it." She declared: "A certain egotism characterizes the families of some 9/11 victims. They have exploited the international outpouring of sympathy for their loss in every possible way. But while they have the right to grieve and memorialize their dead, they don't have the right to force the rest of us, in our public spaces, into an endless orgy of grief. Frankly, a museum whose exhibits will always focus on a single day sounds boring."[179] British journalist Nicholas Wapshott, writing in the *New Statesman*, was even more critical of the families, saying that they had "a stranglehold on the future of the site." Citing their demands that all or much of Ground Zero be reserved for a memorial, he noted, "Had the relatives of the 3,000 people killed each month in the Blitz demanded a similar concession, the East End of London would be one huge park."[180]

While some family members have decried threats to the memorial, the *Times'* Ouroussoff has seen the memorial as coming to dominate Ground Zero and cast a permanent pall over it. He has criticized additions to the memorial: "Bit by bit, the scheme gradually ballooned to include an underground memorial center occupying more than 100,000 square feet, a memorial hall, a family room and a room for remains of the dead." The memorial threatens to make Ground Zero entirely a place of remembrance and preservation, not life: "[T]he constant revisions continue to gobble up space for the living, threatening to transform the site into a theme park haunted by death." Meanwhile, the families have continued to be unhappy with the memorial design and have forced further changes in it. The cost of the memorial has also soared, partly because of the expense of support infrastructure and the need to secure the site against terrorism. The memorial has thus had problems getting past the planning stage.[181]

September's Snowfall and the EPA Controversy

Parallel to the redevelopment debate was another controversy—over the environmental impacts of 9/11. "The destruction of the World Trade Center (WTC) on 11 September 2001" remarked the authors of one study, "caused the largest acute environmental disaster that ever has befallen New York City."[182] The World Trade Center's collapse threw up an enormous amount of material, including human ashes and remains. The shock waves shattered windows and blew huge quantities of dust and debris into homes and offices. The pulverized and incinerated remains of the World Trade Center, two jetliners, and the human dead blanketed Lower Manhattan in an eerie, unnatural "snowfall" that coated buildings, streets, cars, and people. In Lower Manhattan, 250,000 to 400,000 people were exposed to dust from the World Trade Center.[183] An enormous plume of smoke also drifted for about thirty hours over heavily populated Long Island, Staten Island, and New Jersey, with the greatest impact on the New York City borough of Brooklyn, on the western end of Long Island.[184] The air had "an acrid dusty stench."[185] After the collapse, fires smoldered at Ground Zero until December 20, 2001 and continued to release debris into the air.

People were alarmed about what the debris might contain and their concern was understandable. A study co-authored by Philip J. Landrigan, an environmental health specialist at the Mount Sinai School of Medicine in New York City, and more than a dozen other researchers enumerated an astounding list of pollutants released by the destruction of the World Trade Center:

The combustion of more than 90,000 L of jet fuel at temperatures above 1,000°C released a dense and intensely toxic atmospheric plume containing soot, metals, volatile organic compounds (VOCs), and hydrochloric acid. The collapse of the towers pulverized cement, glass, and building contents and generated thousands of tons of particulate matter (PM) composed of cement dust, glass fibers, asbestos, lead, polycyclic aromatic hydrocarbons (PAHs), polychlorinated biphenyls (PCBs), organochlorine pesticides, and polychlorinated furans and dioxins. . . . These materials dispersed over lower Manhattan, Brooklyn, and for miles beyond. They entered nearby office, school, and residential buildings. Much remained at the site to form Ground Zero, a six-story pile of smoking rubble that burned intermittently for more than 3 months.[186]

According to environmental scientist Marjorie Clarke, the dust from the World Trade Center represented an entirely new combination of harmful substances. "Forget that each has its own carcinogenic properties," she remarked. "When you mix them up, what happens?"[187]

Landrigan and his colleagues said that those

at greatest risk of exposure [from these pollutants] included firefighters, police, paramedics, other first responders . . ., and construction workers and volunteers who worked initially in rescue and recovery and then for many months cleared rubble at Ground Zero. Others at potentially elevated risk included workers who cleaned WTC dust from nearby buildings, women who were pregnant on 11 September and succeeding weeks in lower Manhattan and adjacent areas of Brooklyn, and community residents, especially the 3,000 children who resided within 1 km of the towers and the 5,500 who attended school there.[188]

Individuals involved in rescue or recovery at the World Trade Center site were thus at the greatest risk.[189] Many of them, it turns out, either had inadequate protective masks or simply wore none at all.[190]

Optimism and Disinformation

Writing in early 2002, journalist Alyssa Katz echoed a view held by many health professionals: "No one can yet claim to know the extent of the environmental fallout." However, the federal Environmental Protection Agency (EPA), which had been testing for asbestos and other regulated pollutants, did see fit to claim knowledge very early on, and in so doing acted with unwarranted, dangerous haste.[191] On September 16, 2001, EPA Administrator Christie Todd Whitman declared, "There's no need for the general public to be concerned."[192] On September 18, she announced that she was "glad to reassure the people of New York that . . . their air is safe to breathe, and their water is safe to drink."[193]

Environmental groups, members of New York's congressional delegation, community activists, and some journalists accused public officials of minimizing the problem. In fact, in the months after 9/11, a number of people, particularly workers at Ground Zero, developed respiratory symptoms, including a new condition named "World Trade Center

Cough." Symptoms of the ailment included "severe sinus infections, asthma attacks, nausea, headaches, rashes, beet-red eyes, and coughing that can bring a person to his knees."[194] Laurie Garrett reported that the condition "appears to be caused by a combination of pollutants not previously known to produce human disease and thus not covered by Clean Air Act standards or subject to EPA monitoring."[195] What people were inhaling was also highly alkaline—in some cases as alkaline as drain cleaner—and caustic to the lungs.[196]

In addition to its excessively optimistic statements, the EPA failed to fully acknowledge both what it knew and the limitations of its own monitoring. The agency in fact knew about the high alkalinity of the World Trade Center dust, but did not initially release its findings.[197] Meanwhile, in its asbestos testing, the EPA had been using dated technology. More sophisticated tests showed significantly higher levels of asbestos than previously thought.[198] The EPA's reassurances about air quality were also challenged by researchers at the University of California, Davis, who reported extremely high, dangerous levels of pollution from tiny, damaging metallic particles.[199]

People were also given inaccurate, misleading information on clean-up precautions, such as whether to wear masks, and what sort of masks to wear.[200] The EPA and the city simply advised people cleaning indoors to use wet mops so as not to stir up lots of dust. Indoor cleanup was often done by residents without protective gear or by poorly paid, trained, and equipped immigrant workers.[201] "The nightmare facing many New Yorkers now," Britain's *Guardian* newspaper reported in June 2002, "is that their apartments and offices may still be contaminated and whole buildings may have to be professionally cleaned."[202]

In February 2002, EPA ombudsman Robert J. Martin, who later resigned from the agency over what he saw as efforts to silence him, charged that the EPA had provided erroneous information to the public and had not used the best available technology to measure asbestos levels.[203] A 2003 report by the office of EPA Inspector General Nikki Tinsley concluded that "when EPA made a September 18 announcement that the air was 'safe' to breathe, it did not have sufficient data and analyses to make such a blanket statement." Moreover, the report said, "The White House Council on Environmental Quality influenced ... the information that EPA communicated to the public through its early press releases when it convinced EPA to add reassuring statements and delete cautionary ones."[204] Press releases left out "guidance for cleaning indoor spaces and information about the potential health effects from WTC debris."[205]

As for the reasons behind the White House effort, the authors of the report noted, "[EPA Chief of Staff Eileen McGinnis] told us that other considerations, such as the desire to reopen Wall Street and national security concerns, were considered when preparing EPA's early press releases."[206] Joel Shufro, executive director of the New York Committee for Occupational Safety and Health remarked, "The agencies have made it a priority to get the lower Manhattan financial and stock markets up and running at any cost."[207]

An August 2004 Sierra Club report similarly charged that the federal government put economic objectives ahead of human health and safety. The Sierra Club cited Tinsley's report as well as memoirs by former White House antiterrorism czar Richard Clarke and former Treasury Secretary Paul O'Neill in which President Bush was quoted as saying that he wanted to reopen Wall Street within two days.[208]

The *Daily News'* Gonzalez accused the EPA of being irresponsible, even deceptive, in reassuring the public. "There are no federal safety levels for most of these contaminants," he said. "The EPA tried to portray that they had the situation under control, when the reality was, they didn't." The agency, he argued, should have been more honest about the potential hazards and then let people "make up their own minds. When you tell people there's nothing to worry about and [that] everything is OK, you're lying to them."[209]

The people of Lower Manhattan, Andrew Schneider says, felt betrayed by the government: "[M]any of the 340,000 or so people who live in the lower part of that island feel they were abandoned and, at the least, fed conflicting information by federal, state and city officials on how to avoid asbestos exposure."[210]

The EPA's reassurances may have encouraged downtown employers to prematurely order employees back to work and misled Ground Zero recovery workers into thinking they didn't have to wear respirators.[211] The *New York Times'* Kirk Johnson and Jennifer 8. Lee suggest that "what will ultimately emerge as the real scandal of 9/11" is "the fact that wearing a respirator at ground zero was voluntary."[212]

The federal government was not alone in its haste to minimize environmental concerns in the wake of 9/11. The local authorities and media did the same. When, in the weeks after 9/11, the *Daily News'* Juan Gonzalez wrote a series of articles raising serious concerns about pollution, there were complaints from the mayor and from the EPA, and his editors began to apply closer scrutiny to his work.[213] The *New York Times* also tried to downplay concerns. The paper, Katz noted in February 2002, "has run at least 13 stories emphasizing the safety of the site."[214]

As with the federal government, economic considerations seem to have loomed large in the minimization of pollution concerns. According to Susan Stranahan, attempts to reassure the public may have been "rooted in a desire by government and media bosses to get life, and the city's battered economy, back to normal." This included getting people back to their homes as soon as possible.[215] Meanwhile, newspapers were also losing advertising revenue.[216] However, Stranahan cites a more basic human motive for the optimism of local reporters: there was a "hunger for life pre-9/11."[217]

Health Impacts of 9/11 Pollution

The ultimate health impacts of exposure to the 9/11 pollutants are not known for certain, but there is evidence of harm.[218] Respiratory maladies like World Trade Center cough have been well documented. Moreover, two studies suggested that pregnant women at or within ten blocks of the World Trade Center on 9/11 were more likely to have shorter gestational periods or to deliver babies with lower birth weights or smaller head circumferences.[219] Another study suggested a 1.6 percent increase in cancer risk over normal rates for residents of Lower Manhattan, owing to exposure to certain harmful organic compounds during the six weeks after 9/11.[220] Those who worked at the World Trade Center site on 9/11 or in the following weeks face long-term risks, including the risk of mesothelioma, a form of cancer, as a result of exposure to asbestos. Landrigan said, "We remain concerned that there now exists a risk for mesothelioma caused by occupational exposure to asbestos for the brave men and women who worked and volunteered at Ground Zero." He remarks, "The greatest future risk of mesothelioma would appear to exist among first responders who were covered by the cloud of dust on 11 September 2001 as well as in other workers employed directly at Ground

Zero and workers employed in cleaning asbestos-laden dust from contaminated buildings." He notes, though, that "the number of mesothelioma cases will probably not be great."[221] Some health impacts from
9/11 may ultimately be more serious for children exposed to the World
Trade Center pollutants. Children are still developing and can thus be
more vulnerable to chemical contaminants.[222] Moreover, there were
indications of increased severity in pediatric asthma cases in the vicinity
of the World Trade Center after 9/11.[223] Given the unprecedented nature
of the pollution associated with 9/11, researchers as yet can only speculate on future impacts on health. As of this writing, litigation on the
health impacts of 9/11 is under way. Ground Zero workers have sued
the EPA, Whitman, the City of New York, the Port Authority, and
others in charge of cleanup or worker safety at the site.

Parallels with the Rebuilding Process
The management of the environmental impacts of 9/11 shows disturbing
parallels with the rebuilding process. In both cases economic considerations have led policy makers to put a place into service as quickly as
possible. In the case of rebuilding Ground Zero, the financial interests
of Silverstein and the Port Authority have rushed the planning process
and short-circuited careful deliberation. These financial interests have
also significantly determined the character of the redevelopment plan,
namely, that at least 88 percent of the lost office space would be restored,
whether or not this actually made sense. Similarly, the type of information about environmental quality disseminated after 9/11 was initially
determined in part by the desire to reopen Wall Street.[224]

Certainly the desire to reopen the financial district and, more generally, to approach the entire 9/11 disaster with some measure of optimism
was also probably motivated by the need to restore national morale and
return to normalcy, as mentioned earlier. This yearning for normalcy
could be seen as a preservationist sentiment, a desire to return to homes
and neighborhoods and restore a familiar life as much as possible. At the
same time, though, this sentiment fueled an unthinking preservationism:
the long-run viability of Lower Manhattan depends on the area's environmental quality and the health of its residents.

To the degree that financial considerations played a role in distorting
information about pollution hazards, Lower Manhattan was treated as a

resource to be harnessed for economic returns, again without concern for environmental quality or the health of its citizens. Unlike the desire to return to normalcy, which involves resuming the lived experience of inhabiting a place, the financial motive reduces a place and its inhabitants to an instrument or a commodity, not unlike the treatment of the old-growth forest and loggers or of locales cleared for sprawling development. This commodification is more in the realm of founding, but a short-sighted founding that disregards ecological and community sustainability.

Evaluating the Redevelopment Process

Architecture critic Herbert Muschamp remarked, "Throughout the ground zero design process, many New Yorkers have felt 'powerful and powerless at the same time'."[225] As I discussed, the rebuilding process appeared democratic, particularly during the selection of the master plan, but has in fact not been so. The *New Republic*'s Risen is quite damning:

[C]ontrary to the assertions of the parties to the rebuilding that the process has been a model of democratic participation, they have repeatedly denied the public a meaningful role in the decision-making. As a result, what is emerging at Ground Zero ... is not only an insult to those who hoped that the process would itself be an American memorial to the attacks, but also an almost comic repetition of the planning mistakes that went into building the World Trade Center itself.[226]

Risen argues that private real estate and bureaucratic power trumped the interests of the surrounding community and New York City. In fact, he believes that the supposedly democratic process associated with the selection of the original redevelopment plan was a ploy by the LMDC, the Port Authority, and Silverstein to distract the public from a substantive debate about the principles underlying the site's future. The plan that emerged, he says, ignored the public desires for a more prominent memorial, less office space, and greater connectivity to the surrounding neighborhood. Pataki, the LMDC and the Port Authority, and Silverstein all rushed the planning of the site, when slower, more careful deliberation of a wide variety of alternatives was necessary.[227] The resulting process and the plan emerging from it, Risen notes, fit squarely into the authoritarian social engineering ethos of urban renewal.[228] Ouroussoff similarly laments, "[T]he city, and those of us who care about it, will have to live with the consequences of these decisions for decades."[229]

What Went Wrong?: Founding and Preservation at Ground Zero
Goldberger says that after 9/11, there was momentarily the hope that development in New York City would depart from its old principle of maximizing the short-term return for real-estate developers and investors. He argues that there was a reversion to the old mentality in part because Pataki did not exercise eminent domain at the beginning and take over the site from the Port Authority and Larry Silverstein.[230] Perhaps, Goldberger speculates, Pataki thought that trying to seize the site would have delayed the rebuilding and thus hurt him politically.[231] Goldberger also speaks of a "fallacy of speed": just as the building of the World Trade Center "demonstrated a great fallacy of America in the 1960s—the fallacy of size, the beliefs that bigger was always better and that American might and power could solve any problem—the planning process since September 11 demonstrates the fallacy of America in the 1990s and beyond, which is the fallacy of speed, the belief that faster is always better."[232]

Criticism of the process and its outcome is perhaps premature given that the rebuilding has only just begun. But why have things already gone awry? The history of the World Trade Center and Ground Zero has been dominated by actors exercising top-down, authoritarian control over the area. These actors have included the Port Authority, the LMDC, the New York State governor, and Larry Silverstein. They have treated the area, not as a place embedded in a larger history, community, and geography, but as a blank slate on which to work their will. Consequently, the Radio Row merchants were dispossessed, the World Trade Center was built in isolation from the surrounding neighborhood, many of the public's desires regarding the future of Ground Zero were ultimately ignored, and the site was treated primarily as a place of commerce. Like the foresters who cleared out old growth in the Pacific Northwest and like the builders of sprawl, these actors have been driven by the desire to found, but in a narrow way that overlooks preservationist dimensions. They have sought to arrange space as they see fit and use it as their instrument.

As Goldberger says, with the building of the World Trade Center, the founders' exercise of power was displayed in an excessive scale that required eliminating a significant chunk of Lower Manhattan. In the rebuilding at Ground Zero, the founders have similarly pursued unnecessary scale in the form of millions of square feet of unneeded office space.

However, Goldberger is correct that the fallacy shifted from one of size to one of speed. Ground Zero has been treated as an instrument for maximum and rapid generation of revenue, as well as a stepstool for short-term political objectives. The founders at Ground Zero have displayed an unjustified haste in pushing the rebuilding plans along. Their haste was echoed in the heedless rush by government and the media to declare Lower Manhattan environmentally safe after the area had been inundated with noxious debris. Indeed, the handling of pollution concerns by the White House and the EPA after 9/11 showed not only haste but serious moral failure. In essence, the federal government sought to get the economic machinery up and running as quickly as possible, even if that meant endangering public health through exposure to hazardous substances.

The founders of the original World Trade Center, including the now-elderly men in the picture described at the beginning of this chapter, were thinking of a great, lasting public works project. To that degree their founding had a preservationist element. However, the founding at Ground Zero has been decidedly more short-term: Silverstein's insurance money, the Port Authority's rental receipts, Pataki's political ambitions, and the release of misinformation on environmental hazards all precluded any careful and truly democratic discussion about both the future of the site and the clean-up of the surrounding area; they also hindered long-term planning for all of Lower Manhattan.

At the opposite extreme are the 9/11 families. Their concern has been entirely with remembrance, with preserving the memory of lost loved ones or comrades and turning as much of Ground Zero as possible into a memorial. The victims' families want to keep Ground Zero focused on 9/11, to create a place where the casualties and heroes and struggles of that harrowing day are kept alive and honored. Even though remembering 9/11 involves building a memorial, the main impulse here is not so much founding anew as preserving the past.

The 9/11 families have constrained the rebuilding plans by establishing the tower footprints as a memorial site from the start. This has been anti-democratic in that one constituency has gained perhaps disproportionate influence on the process and used its influence to promote an overly preservationist agenda. However, given the enormous loss and significance of 9/11, it is unsurprising, understandable, and indeed fitting that the 9/11 families have wielded considerable influence over the process. The need for a memorial is undeniable and has been recognized by the larger public. Even the families' insistence on devoting the tower footprints to a memorial, while limiting the possibilities for the site, provides a tangible spatial connection with 9/11 and the site's past.

Where the families, or at least some of them, have more clearly gone to excess is in their veto of the IFC and the Drawing Center and their increasing hostility to cultural institutions at Ground Zero. Here the families have confirmed the fears of Madelyn Wils and other local residents. That part of Ground Zero that is not taken up by office space may end up being dominated by remembrance, to the virtual exclusion of living connections with the surrounding area, and Ground Zero may be subject to a single interpretation and tell only a single story.

The power struggle between the builders and the families has created an odd combination of founding and preservation. The founders have dominated in that they control more than half the space. The large buildings with their restored office space reflect commodity values and a short-term, narrow founding orientation. Meanwhile, the rest of the site increasingly focuses on a single-minded remembrance and preservation. These two elements—founding and preservation—occur alongside one another in a seeming tension, the tension of compromise rather than integration. Goldberger thus suggests that the rebuilding process has split the site into a memorial sector and a business sector.[233] In other words, the site has been partitioned between founding and preservation. There will still be other land uses, such as cultural institutions and perhaps some housing, but these components have been reduced or seriously compromised.

The third major set of actors in this debate, the local residents and businesses, often allied with City Hall and with local artists, planners, and architects, has sought to limit both memorializing and large commercial development. These groups want the neighborhood to be neither a cemetery or museum nor a reincarnation of the old World Trade Center. Instead, they aim at a revival of the streetscape, cultural and entertainment institutions, and a 24-hour, mixed-use neighborhood with residences, more open space, and significantly less office space. This would not be a return to Radio Row and the past, but it would be a revival of the human-scaled urban landscape that existed before the World

Trade Center. This would be a place once more connected to the surrounding neighborhood. It would include a significant memorial but would be as much about affirming neighborhood, life, and new possibilities as it would be about maintaining a connection with the immediate and more distant past. Such a mixed-use development, including residences, might in fact do a better job of honoring the memory of 9/11 and integrating the memorial into its surroundings than would a set of office buildings. Unfortunately, the planning under way for Ground Zero has fallen far short of what the local community wants. The residents of Lower Manhattan have not come up empty-handed; for example, Greenwich and Fulton streets will be restored and, as mentioned earlier, there will be cultural venues, some open space, and perhaps housing, but the overall result reflects a tug-of-war between the two most influential groups in the debate: Silverstein and the public officials and agencies on the one hand, and the 9/11 families on the other. The site has been divided between them.

The battle at Ground Zero is a battle between founding and preservation, much like the battles that have been fought over the old-growth forest and suburban sprawl. However, to choose either founding or preservation is to make a false and impossible choice because both are integral to our relationship with the spatial environment and to the places around us. In the next chapter I move beyond the case studies and investigate why the practice of place has become so needlessly polarized and is now in crisis.

5

The Crisis of Place

A constant vogue of triumphs dislocate[s] man.
—Yes, "Close to the Edge" (1972)

Each of the three case studies shows a problematic approach to place, specifically a short-sighted approach to founding that disregards preservationist considerations and destroys important ecological, social, cultural, and historical features of the landscape. The opposition often makes the mistake of going to the other extreme and overemphasizing preservation. This zero-sum contest prevents the balance and integration of founding and preservation. Although the resulting landscape has places in a literal sense, it lacks an integrated balance of founding and preservation and is therefore not faithful to the activity of place. In this chapter, I more fully consider the nature and origins of this crisis of place.

This crisis has had four phases, the first of which began in the early modern era. Although these phases arose at different times, elements of each remain with us. The four have therefore become "moments" of the crisis of place rather than delimited historical periods.

The first phase, or moment, involves the exercise of top-down, governmental power to rationalize and simplify complex natural and built landscapes that had arisen organically and replace them with highly planned and controlled environments. I refer to this phase as modernism.[1] Here, I mean an ideological approach to land-use management, rather than modernist-style architecture in particular. However, the latter, with its highly simplified approach to building and urban design, fits in with modernist land-use approaches. The term *modernism* should also be distinguished from modernity as an era in human history, even though modernism has flourished and been a significant ideology or worldview during this period.

The second moment of the crisis involves an increasing emphasis on the power of international corporate entities to reshape and commodify places around the world. This phase is part of the phenomenon of contemporary globalization (although globalization in general dates back to the Age of Exploration), but in many ways it also carries on the themes of modernism.

The third moment involves the seeming marginalization of place itself, through a postmodern shift to global, electronically mediated flows of political and economic power. This postmodern phase is associated with the so-called Information Age.

Each of these three moments reflects an overemphasis on founding or, one might say, an approach to founding that pays insufficient attention to preservation. Throughout these three phases, there is also an implicit view that places can and should be rapidly and radically transformed to meet the demands of power structures, structures that are often external to those places.

The fourth moment of the crisis is a response to the first three. Here the overemphasis on founding is met with a reaction, most clearly articulated by some portions of the environmental movement, which overemphasizes preservation without integrating it with founding.

The Modern State and Radical Founding

Getting Lost in Space

A key historical development of the modern era is the reduction of complex places to simplified spaces. This story has unfolded on both a philosophical and practical level. In his massive history of philosophical conceptualizations of place and space, Edward Casey sees an "assimilation" of place to space in early modern thought and on up to the eighteenth century, and the dethronement of place as an important conceptual category.[2]

In chapter 1 I distinguished place from space. Place is particular, concrete, sensory, qualitative, and distinctive; it is thick with meaning. Space is abstract, quantitative, and universal. A quantity of space or a positional point in space is, in terms of its intrinsic qualities, the same everywhere. It has no particular characteristics that tie it to a specific location. Whether or not it is filled with matter, space is pure extension and dimension, to be described mathematically and through the use of coordinates. While place partakes of spatial dimensions, it is not properly reducible to space.

However, as Casey argues, place became conceptualized as an instance or modification of space. In the works of seventeenth- and eighteenth-century philosophers Pierre Gassendi, Isaac Newton, René Descartes, John Locke, and Gottfried Wilhelm Leibniz, the focus on space disregarded, even denigrated, the intrinsic nature of things occupying a place and the distinctive qualities of places themselves. Place was increasingly supposed to be comprehensible through measurement alone.[3] With the particularities of place erased, all locations could be subject to uniform physical, mechanical laws and to mathematical description and measurement.[4]

The philosophical and scientific reconceptualization of place as space influenced more practical endeavors. Casey discusses the rise of the notion of a site.[5] A site is place imagined as space, as an empty parcel open for new use or occupancy. Its contents are readily swept away and replaced to accommodate new buildings or other projects.[6] "Site is the very undoing of place."[7]

The notion of a site favors founding. Sites are locations of both demolition and building, but not of preservation. The site is land conceived of as a blank slate for the exercise of a place founder's power. The site presents an unencumbered space for the founder to create a new landscape. To view an area as a site is to ignore the significance, and sanction the destruction, of what is already there. The American frontier was thus a site for nation building, achieved through the destruction of natural ecosystems and the ethnic cleansing and genocide of the original inhabitants. Designation of the frontier as wasteland by European and American governments, colonists, and philosophers like Locke legitimated this destruction.[8] In a plan adopted with some modifications by Congress, Thomas Jefferson was able, without any recognition of the absurdity of the undertaking, to map the frontier into a grid with no regard for natural topography. The individual rectangular parcels, abstracted from their constituent elements, could be easily delineated, titled, bought and sold, settled, and taxed.[9]

Places have been similarly transformed into sites by managers in the U.S. Forest Service who clear-cut forests, by developers who bulldoze woods and farmlands, and by state and local governments and highway builders who clear neighborhoods to make way for urban renewal. In all cases, there is the exercise of destructive power as a "necessary violent prelude"—to recall Forest Service Chief Edward Cliff's unfortunate phrase—to a brand-new landscape. The "blank" slate or site is a canvas for the founder's scene of demolition and reconstruction.

Seeking to exercise control over the landscape, a founder will often replace a complex terrain with a simpler one that can be more easily surveyed, monitored, and maintained to conform to the founder's own ends. Industrial forestry, sprawl, and urban renewal have all involved a radical simplification of the landscape. The simplified landscape, regarded as a site and emptied of much of its distinction and richness, is itself a step or two closer to abstract space. The site is in effect never entirely filled in. It remains a site and is theoretically on call for further reorganization and refounding.

The State as Place Founder

The treatment of places as sites and the associated destruction, refounding, and simplification of the landscape were central to the development of the modern state from the seventeenth to the twentieth century. David Harvey notes, "The process of state formation was, and still is, dependent upon the creation of certain kinds of geographical understandings (everything from the mapping of boundaries to the cultivation of some sense of national identity within those boundaries)."[10]

James Scott details how the modern state reshaped its landscape.[11] Wielding the modernist value repertoire of scientific progress, reason, administration by experts, consumer satisfaction, accumulation of material goods, and maximization of efficiency, the state worked to centralize power, consolidate and exploit markets, rationalize the social order, and control its terrain. In order to make its terrain legible and controllable, the state had to reorganize both nature and society to eliminate complexity and unpredictability and substitute simplicity and order. State authorities used their expertise to eradicate both local societal particularities and unmanaged, wild nature. Such actions were often justified in terms of "progress." John Barry says, "The identification of the Western model of development with progress signifies an inevitability and desirability which is used to silence any criticism. Progress is good, and after all, you can't stop progress."[12]

One of the means by which the modern state imposed itself on the landscape was by simplifying land tenure arrangements and creating clear, consolidated parcels of private property that could be easily surveyed and taxed,[13] just as Jefferson sought in planning the frontier. As I noted earlier, determination of neat property boundaries also enabled subdivision of land into salable, commodified parcels. Here the extension of state power went hand-in-hand with the opening of new areas to the market. Such an approach to planning, Scott emphasizes, served both administration and commodification.[14] State and market were intertwined in a common enterprise.

Scientific Agriculture

Scott sees commonalities between modernist, scientific agriculture, including industrial forestry, and the creation of the modern built environment. Scientific agriculture, whether as farming or forestry, simplified and rationalized the landscape. As Wendell Berry has also noted,[15] scientific agriculture subordinates all aspects of agriculture or forestry, and the land itself, to the imperative of maximal yield. This results in larger fields, uniform farming practices across geographic locales, increased reliance on managerial expertise (both governmental and corporate), heavy use of mechanized and chemical inputs, monocropping and standardization of crops for easy mechanized harvesting and supermarket sale, and the use of genetically modified and patented crop varieties.[16] Scientific forestry, which arose in late eighteenth-century Germany[17] and later influenced Gifford Pinchot, biologically simplified the forest by removing nonproductive tree types, competing vegetation, and dead trees. Scientific forestry also spatially simplified the forest, as trees were planted in highly regimented ranks, like spatial grids.

"The Plan: Dictator"

A similar ruthless transformation and simplification was applied to urban areas. European cities that had arisen organically over time, their streets a complex and dizzying warren inherited from the Middle Ages, were an administrative nightmare for the state and offended modern sensibilities.[18] A city laid out in a grid, like an industrial forest, and with land uses rigorously separated into districts[19]—an idea that eventually bore fruit with a vengeance in contemporary single-use zoning[20]—would be much more orderly, efficient, and congenial to a modern, centralized state.[21] Overall, the modernist city—realized, for example, in Baron Haussmann's design for mid-nineteenth-century Paris or in twentieth-century urban renewal projects in the United States—is more legible to bureaucrats. It provides an easier terrain for the provision of infrastructure, the delivery of services, or the use of police or military power. It allows easier monitoring of inhabitants and their physical environs and enables the exercise of standardizing, normalizing, disciplinary authority.[22]

Charles Édouard Jeanneret, also known as Le Corbusier, was the leading twentieth-century theorist of the rationalized modernist city and a major inspiration for urban renewal. Le Corbusier saw the city as a machine[23] to be fashioned by a dictatorial planner as radical founder. He remarked that city planning was "too important to be left to the citizens,"[24] and, according to Scott, the first of his principles of urbanism was "The Plan: Dictator."[25] The authoritarian planner was to completely sweep away the messy, disorganized city inherited from the past. Dictatorship of the planner of course went hand-in-hand with the expanding power of the state.[26]

Le Corbusier's second principle of urbanism was "the death of the street."[27] Modernists like Le Corbusier sought to eliminate unplanned and hence uncontrollable street life. Significantly, in this approach to urban planning, "Corbusier preferred revolution to evolution. He was eager to wipe the surface of the city clean, obliterating its history, variety, and human scale to realize the promise of new technology that made possible an environment of high-speed travel and high-rise towers open to sunlight and fresh air."[28]

Le Corbusier's new city, whose plan he called the Radiant City, would be standardized and assembled from mass-produced parts. It would be built for efficient operation and ease of administration through single-use districts. The terrain would consist of regularly spaced towers and open plazas and parks, all crisscrossed at regular intervals by highways. This model was ultimately echoed, albeit at a much smaller scale, in the World Trade Center.

Impoverishing Life on the Ground

What is problematic in both modernist agriculture and city planning is not so much the idea of planning per se. Many complex human endeavors require some degree of governance and planning; otherwise they eventually break down. For example, a well-run city and its environs require water, sewer, transport, electric utility, trash disposal, and recycling systems; ecologically sound coordination of development and preservation of open space; coordination of locally unwanted land uses (LULUs),[29] such as trash facilities, heavy industry, and prisons; and the optimal siting of regional facilities like airports. Every farm requires careful management. Even wilderness requires management because the area must be protected from illegal logging or hunting, external sources of pollution, invasive species, excessive human visitors, etc. In chapter 6 I discuss the need for regional planning as part of the practice of place.

What is problematic about modernist planning is first of all its authoritarian mindset; the expert or bureaucrat presumes full knowledge of what is needed for a place to flourish. Related to this is the tendency of the forester or planner or agronomist to freely act as a radical and heedless founder, sweeping away the existing landscape without regard for ecological and social dynamics on the ground or the input or needs of those inhabiting, working in, or otherwise dependent on existing places. As we saw in the cases of forestry, sprawl, and urban renewal, such sweeping efforts at founding often proceed without any real provision for the long-term health or stability of what is created.

Moreover, in its quest for manageable simplicity, modernist founding also eradicates existing complexity. Scott, drawing on Jacobs, thus criticizes the modernist approach to city planning: "Although certain state services may be more easily provided ..., these apparent advantages may be negated by such perceived disadvantages as the absence of a dense street life, the intrusion of hostile authorities, the loss of the spatial irregularities that foster coziness, gathering places for informal recreation, and neighborhood feeling."[30]

The vantage point of the modernist forester, agronomist, planner, or developer is from above, as Scott observes. The modernist founder imposes a coherent, macrolevel pattern that maximizes a given set of usually quantifiable performance objectives and realizes an aesthetic of order, regularity, or cleanliness. This founding process cannot be anything but authoritarian,[31] even if it happens in the context of an ostensibly democratic state. Planning is conceived of as the work of experts who must shut out the troublesome noise of politics and the public as much as possible.

However, order viewed from a distance may not be functional on the ground. An old-growth forest, a diverse agricultural landscape, or a fine-grained, multipurpose cityscape looks chaotic from above but actually contains an ordered pattern generated through interactions on the ground.[32] Certainly such spontaneous order does not necessarily negate the need for some measure of top-down management. However, one must also recognize that key aspects of social and ecological order emerge from the ground up rather than through deliberate planning.

Consequently, founding as an ambitious, top-down project that tries to erase the past in the name of a rationalist future ironically often ends up impoverishing or even destroying life on the ground. For example, the residents of Brasília, a city wholly designed and created by modernist planners and architects, complain of spatial monotony and social isolation.[33] The more or less total imposition of order from above leads to dysfunction on the ground.

At issue is a misperception of complexity. The modernist founder, as Jacobs argued, sees the existing landscape as embodying disorganized complexity, or problematic chaos.[34] Recall how foresters dismissed old growth as decadent and Yamasaki condemned Radio Row as blighted. For the modernist land-use manager or planner, such chaos requires top-down reorganization and management. Cities, forests, and farms, along with their human or nonhuman inhabitants, are treated as statistical assemblages to be rearranged and administered through quantitative formulas. The components of these systems are reimagined as standardized units that can be subject to predictive laws and reorganized at will. Urban planning becomes a matter of laying out so many structures and housing units or so much office space, securing a certain amount of business investment, relocating some number of people, and moving a targeted number of persons and vehicles per unit of time. The builders of the World Trade Center thus "package[d] 50,000 people in a 10-million-square-foot office block."[35] Forestry becomes a science of producing so many board feet of timber per year, grown in geometrically regularized, monocultural tree plantations. Agriculture becomes an enterprise solely for maximizing annual crop yields on large, mechanized farms.

Yet, as Jacobs observed, cities, farms, and natural ecosystems are organic wholes of interrelated elements possessing organized complexity (see chapter 1). These elements are numerous enough to generate a complex structure, but they are neither so numerous nor so random as to be successfully predicted and managed through abstract formulas or a focus on a few easily quantifiable variables or outputs. Organized complexity is not amenable to external manipulation; attempts to manipulate a few variables can throw the system into disequilibrium and decline. Truly good management of such a system requires respect for and coordination with on-the-ground elements and dynamics.

Given the resistance posed by systems of organized complexity, the founding of a modernist landscape must become brutal and disruptive. The founder, to simplify and rationalize the landscape and achieve the goals associated with modernist ideology, has little choice but to sweep away the existing terrain; thus the need to "hack [one's] way with a meat ax," whether through a city or, for that matter, an ancient forest or a traditional rural landscape. Modernism makes no concessions to preservation, but consciously rejects what is old.[36] Although often well-intentioned and motivated by visions of human improvement,[37] the modernist founder acts with arrogance, recklessness, and destructive zeal. Eric Darton thus draws similarities between the building of the World Trade Center and the destruction wrought by the 9/11 hijackers. The building of the World Trade Center did not, of course, cause almost 3,000 deaths, numerous injuries, massive psychological and social trauma, or major physical devastation and chaos. Nevertheless, in both the building and destruction of the World Trade Center, there was the inhumane, brutal exercise of an abstract plan from above with little regard for the people below. "Whether a master plan entails casting away stones or gathering stones together, the project rests upon the creation of an abstract, quantitative logic that supposes itself to operate on a higher plane than that inhabited by the human material beneath it."[38]

Commodification and Globalization

Scott's focus on state power leads him to neglect what is perhaps the apotheosis of modernism and its project of treating the world as a blank slate for rational reorganization. This is the phenomenon of commodification, by which places are transformed into commodities (i.e., as investment or disinvestment sites for business) and managed according to the universal, simplifying, reductive measurement of monetary value.

Here the engine of change is not so much the state as it is domestic and international capital. One should keep in mind, though, that public and private forces work may hand-in-hand here, as noted in the previous section and previous chapters. Historically, government action enabled the commodification of the landscape in the United States. Reorganization of the frontier for settlement, scientific forestry and agriculture, mining, and urban renewal all proceeded under the aegis of government agencies, specialists, and funding. Government provision of infrastructure, such as railroads and interstate highways, opened up land for resource extraction or real estate development.

Government action has at least the pretense of serving the common good. Whether disingenuously or not, the New York State Court of Appeals upheld the condemnation of Radio Row on the grounds that construction of the World Trade Center served a public purpose. By contrast, the private sector is more directly and openly driven by profit and pursuit of exchange value. Market forces unabashedly reorganize the spatial environment into easily exchangeable, detachable commodities.

Commodification Through Property Rights

This commodification of place is strikingly revealed by the arguments of property-rights advocates who oppose most government regulations, especially land-use regulations, as violating the "takings" clause of the Fifth Amendment to the U.S. Constitution. The takings clause states, "nor shall private property be taken for public use, without just compensation." Property-rights advocates consider government regulation without reimbursement a taking because the government supposedly seizes control of the land even though it does not actually gain title.

Many property rights cases admittedly involve land takings or regulations that threaten attachments to places. In many such situations, citizens oppose the sort of authoritarian planning discussed in the previous section. In eminent domain cases, such as the Radio Row controversy or *Kelo v. New London*, businesses, homeowners, or tenants were being forced to vacate valued or even cherished places. At issue was more than the commercial value of the land and whether or not the government was paying adequate compensation. The debate over Radio Row involved merchants who had been in business for decades and had created a famed, distinctive commercial area. The Kelo case involved residents trying to hold on to their homes and neighborhood.

While not involving the outright seizure of property, regulation can itself significantly restrict the use and management of one's own home, business, or farm. Property-rights advocates are fond of citing cases where environmental regulations have prevented homeowners from pursuing even routine maintenance activities on their land. The passage of Oregon's radical property rights initiative, Measure 37, in 2004, was in part spurred by the story of Portland resident Rebecca Muntean, who was fined $15,000 by the city for taking out the blackberry bushes covering her backyard. The city regarded the yard and its vegetation as wildlife habitat.[39]

Although some property rights cases may involve interference with attachments to places, many cases in fact involve developers attempting to build on large parcels of land and acting as heavy-handed planners themselves. More fundamentally, the property rights theory that has influenced courts and policy makers in recent decades is less concerned with place as a value than with protecting the employment of land as a commodity.

In arguing against uncompensated regulation, property-rights advocates like influential legal theorist Richard Epstein view ownership as entailing exclusive discretion over an indivisible bundle of rights, including the possession, use, and disposition of one's holdings. Property owners are limited only in that they may not use their holdings to exercise force or fraud or commit harm against others.[40] Use can include abuse, which is purely at the individual's discretion.[41] Furthermore, such discretion applies without differentiation to all forms of property. There is nothing special about owning places. Places or not, all holdings are mere things at the owner's disposal, whether they are jogging shoes, wheat futures, Ford Explorers, home entertainment centers, McDonald's Happy Meals, redwood forests, 200-year-old farms, or skyscrapers. A parcel of land, i.e., a place, may be regarded in detachment from its social and ecological context and developed, redeveloped, subdivided, and sold at will, unconstrained by most ecological or social considerations. To say that one may possess something while being responsible to the larger community for its use would, according to this view, negate ownership itself.[42]

In considerably freeing a landowner from broader social and ecological concerns, the property rights perspective ultimately regards places like any other exchangeable commodity. As with detachable, movable goods on a rack, the use and disposition of places can be utterly subordinated to the will of an individual making rational investment or consumption decisions in the marketplace.[43]

Many property-rights advocates also go beyond a libertarian emphasis on the freedom of the individual owner and maintain that land *should* be employed in its economically most productive use. Private ownership and market discipline promote the most economically efficient and productive use of land,[44] which generally means resource extraction or real estate development.[45]

With the development of market relationships around land and the philosophical justification of these relationships in terms of both individualized private property rights and social utility, a fundamental change occurs in the connection between people and place. Land is turned from an integral part of human existence into an economic commodity for exchange.[46]

Commodification thus distances us from places. Places become things we perceive only through their monetary value. As Plumwood critically characterizes this view, "Pieces of land are real estate, readily interchangeable as equivalent means to the end of human satisfaction."[47] We have no moral responsibility toward these places, nor any real identification with them. Places are entirely instrumentalized and monetized. They are always on call for monetary exchange.[48]

The Market as Radical Founder

The market's ability to subdivide and reorganize the landscape according to monetary relations enables a radical pursuit of founding, perhaps surpassing the transformative role of the state. For the market to be able to free up land for exchange, restrictions on land use, whether legal or social, must be eliminated as much as possible. Land must be detached from any contextual considerations other than those that can be captured in the marketplace and influence real estate values.[49] In this way, individual parcels of land may be isolated for sale and investment.

Preservationist values would conflict with this commodification of land. Commodification only promotes preservation when a place's age or historic significance can be priced and marketed. Moreover, whatever the economic benefits of preservation—and there are many—the market, in its demand that land and places serve as money-making resources, requires that the character of places be subject to transformation when uses other than preservation promise greater returns. For example, privately owned forests in areas like the Adirondacks or northern Maine were long kept from real estate development because of their timber value. Although they were subject to logging and not always managed well, these lands at least remained free of subdivisions, second and vacation homes, and resorts, and were often publicly available for hunting, fishing, hiking, and camping. However, recent changes in the timber industry have led forest products firms to put these lands up for sale, raising fears that they will be purchased by developers, or even to propose development plans themselves.[50] The landowners' commitment to preservation lasted only as long as such a policy was economically viable.

In erasing existing landscapes and exploiting the land for greater economic returns, the market carries out what economist Joseph Schumpeter called "creative destruction."[51] The market, like the modernist state, is thus primarily an agent of founding, transforming the existing landscape. However, once the state has subdued and reworked the landscape, it tries to consolidate its power and structure by maintaining the new status quo. The state, or its leadership, thus often tries to create something lasting, such as a structure like the World Trade Center. By contrast, to provide for changing consumption needs and new investment opportunities, the market must continually revolutionize existing arrangements.

The market's transformation of places and of place-based cultural and economic activities is enormous. As Harvey points out,

the landscape shaped in relation to a certain phase of development (capitalist or pre-capitalist) becomes a barrier to further accumulation. The geographical configuration of places must then be reshaped around new transport and communications systems and physical infrastructures, new centers and styles of production and consumption, new agglomerations of labor power, and modified social infrastructures.[52]

The implications are sweeping, and often devastating:

Old places ... have to be devalued, destroyed, and redeveloped while new places are created. The cathedral city becomes a heritage center, the mining community becomes a ghost town, the old industrial center is deindustrialized, speculative boom towns or gentrified neighborhoods arise on the frontiers of capitalist development or out of the ashes of deindustrialized communities. The history of capitalism is, then, punctuated by intense phases of spatial reorganization.[53]

Similarly, as Timothy Luke recounts, "megamachines" of "finance capital, professional organizations, interventionist bureaucracy, and applied sciences"[54] have thoroughly transformed and commodified places and lives:

Small-holding agriculture gave way to corporate farming, little shops were displaced by big factories, local economies imploded under global trade, and skilled trades were restructured as professional technical science or unskilled wage labor. The ecology of human communities was totally transformed as these megamachines infiltrated the structures of everyday life in the name of efficiency, progress, or development to fabricate urban-industrial hyperecologies. What once was homemade now could be store bought. Items that once came from local fields, streams, forests, and soils arrived from faraway.[55]

Now, "[e]very product increasingly depends on matter, energy, and information outsourced from everywhere to operate anywhere. Consequently, almost no one can act truly autonomously as an authentically independent producer, and no place is capable of sustaining its economy or society without considerable dependencies on outside sources of supply."[56] The economic and cultural elements of a place-based life have been turned into commodities produced elsewhere and sold back to the people who had once produced or created them. The production and consumption of goods have become geographically decoupled and, as we will see, increasingly mediated through intangible processes that neither producers nor consumers can easily understand.[57] The connections between work and place are thus attenuated, and work moves from being a social and cultural activity to a purely economic one.[58]

Global Disruption and Homogenization of Place

The forces generating land-use changes operate on an increasingly global scale. Contemplating the reshaping of the landscape through global capitalism, Harvey speaks of "the destruction, invasion, and restructuring of socially constituted places on an unprecedented scale." The viability of actual places has been seriously undermined. He says, "There has been a powerful surge of such reorganization since around 1970, creating considerable insecurity within and between places."[59] Since roughly that year, telecommunications; cargo transport by jets; containerization of shipping; the development of futures markets; and electronic banking and computerized production systems have led to "time-space compression," in which the world feels much smaller and time horizons have become much shorter. This compression has not only disrupted places; it has also disrupted human identities, which are significantly based on one's location in space and time. It has thus created a widespread sense of insecurity.[60]

The increasing mobility of capital associated with globalization opens up more and more areas to transformation.[61] Global chains like Starbucks or McDonald's or Blockbuster Video establish operations in virtually any corner of the world where there are potential customers. Energy-prospecting and forest products firms readily open up new areas for resource exploitation, particularly in developing countries. Agribusinesses and food conglomerates supplant local crops and agricultural practices and traditions around the world.

The real estate industry is itself increasingly globalized. Housing prices reflect global factors, such as deregulated, linked financial markets; decisions by major central banks; and the overseas purchases and investments of affluent professionals. This sensitivity to global forces makes areas vulnerable to swings in the housing market.[62] Moreover, the real estate industry has become more and more concentrated. A report by the University of Southern California's Lusk Center for Real Estate notes that over the past fifty years, ownership and management in real estate has gradually shifted from individuals or small partnerships that developed or owned a few properties to large corporate entities that control portfolios of hundreds or thousands of assets.[63]

Meanwhile, the breakdown of international trade barriers has enabled and even compelled businesses to abandon their existing locales and set up shop—often across the United States or overseas—where labor and other costs, regulatory burdens, and distance from resource and transportation networks are lower. We saw this with the exodus of the timber industry from the Pacific Northwest. The abandonment of a community by a long-time employer can be economically and socially devastating to a place. The threat of such a flight of capital or the desire to court investment has made states and localities very compliant in offering tax breaks and other subsidies.[64]

Harvey observes that as local jurisdictions compete for investment by corporations and investors who are able to shift their assets around the globe, a somewhat paradoxical development sets in.[65] Places attempt to market their individual distinctiveness. However, such marketing by places leads to their homogenization because localities all end up participating in an increasingly globalized commodity culture and trying to appeal to the same investors or the same sort of investment. For example, a favorite strategy of localities today is to market themselves to tourists and to the mobile professional class by building convention centers, hotels, and other visitor-oriented amenities. The uniform rush of municipalities to embrace this kind of development means that convention center space in the United States increased 51 percent between 1990 and 2003 and greatly outstripped demand. The resulting oversupply has only led to more competition among localities for shrinking shares of the hospitality industry and the expansion of already existing convention centers.[66]

As localities homogenize themselves, corporate investors remake places according to whatever prevailing model maximizes market returns. Places lose their distinctive meaning or character and become sites for the same establishments. Places and localities become more like standardized commodities for investors to "purchase."

As Luke points out, this homogenization is often carried out in total disregard of local environmental conditions. Thus, "virtually identical houses [are] built in frigid Buffalo, New York, and torrid Brownsville, Texas,"[67] and lush lawns sprout in suburban developments in the arid American West.

Even the seeming revival of older cities and towns fits into this pattern of commodification. The era of urban renewal is past, and there is a revived interest in preserving the historic architecture of cities and towns. However, the kind of radical founding associated with the state and the market does not rise or fall with modern architectural styles; it can assume more traditional appearances. In older urban areas, local, independent businesses give way to large chain stores that are much the same as establishments in the suburbs. Thus, economically successful revivals of old urban districts or buildings like Boston's Faneuil Hall sacrifice local character by devoting considerable space to national chains. A listing of businesses in Faneuil Hall is saturated with national names like Ann Taylor, Nine West, the Discovery Channel Store, Victoria's Secret, Crate &

Barrel, and Crabtree & Evelyn. New York's Times Square was rescued from its dangerous, seedy condition at the cost of being "Disneyfied" (see chapter 6). The redeveloped Times Square prominently features the New Amsterdam Theater, renovated and taken over by Disney, and a Disney Store.

A similar fate befell another famed Manhattan neighborhood, SoHo, which has become one of New York City's most affluent areas. In the 1960s, Robert Moses wanted to demolish much of SoHo and its cast-iron buildings to make way for an expressway. Preservation activists, led by Jane Jacobs, defeated Moses' plan. Unfortunately, as *New York Times* architecture critic Nicolai Ouroussoff noted a few days after Jacobs' death in April 2006, "[t]he activists of Ms. Jacobs' generation may have saved SoHo from Mr. Moses' bulldozers, but they could not stop it from becoming an open-air mall. The old buildings are still there, the streets are once again paved in cobblestone, but the rich mix of manufacturers, artists and gallery owners has been replaced by homogenous [sic] crowds of lemming-like shoppers. Nothing is produced there any more. It is a corner of the city that is nearly as soulless, in its way, as the superblocks that Ms. Jacobs so reviled."[68]

Cities are even selling off the naming rights to their locales. Developers of municipal institutions like stadiums have sold naming rights to private corporations, yielding such inspiring monikers as SBC Park, the Staples Center, and the former Enron Field. Cities like New York are considering selling naming rights to subway stops, parks, and bridges.[69]

An Illegible Geography

Globalization and commodification render the landscape increasingly illegible. The globalized marketplace actually increases the connections of places to one another as individual places become less culturally and economically self-sufficient.[70] Even as places are fragmented according to economic use or value and considered as commodities in isolation from their surroundings, they are progressively integrated into a broader fabric of global networks.

Individuals find such far-flung networks difficult to decipher.[71] Ordinary persons often have little or no idea where or by whom the products they purchase are made or, for example, who runs Home Depot, let alone the environmental and social impacts of these businesses.

Placeless Architecture

Indeed, even structures themselves become indecipherable. Mark Wigley notes that the World Trade Center, as an example of the modern corporate building, presented a blank external face that revealed little of what went on inside, thus serving as a symbol for the "dematerialized, invisible, placeless market."[72] The sterile modern architecture that furnishes much of the suburban landscape has had a similar inscrutability, says Douglas Kelbaugh: "A Modernist glass box on a suburban street could be a gas station, an insurance office, a church, or a house."[73]

Postmodern architecture, the successor to the modern style, is visually more engaging and pleasing and pays superficial homage to local context. However, postmodern architecture is also indecipherable in its own way. It borrows indiscriminately from past architectural details and styles for ornamental purposes, creating a playful but also decontextualized, placeless potpourri of images that reveal neither physical depth nor history, but convey only surface. Castells sees postmodern architecture as fitting for a networked society: "Because the spatial manifestation of the dominant interests takes place around the world, and across cultures, the uprooting of experience, history, and specific culture as the background of meaning is leading to the generalization of ahistorical, acultural architecture." Postmodern architecture ironically mixes stylistic elements from different historical periods. "Yet, in fact what postmodernism does is to express, in almost direct terms, the new dominant ideology: the end of history and the supersession of places in the space of flows."[74]

The successor to postmodern architecture, deconstructivism, also rejects history and context, but through idiosyncratic, bizarre buildings that seem like jumbles of off-kilter shapes and even heaps of sheet metal, as exhibited, for example, in the buildings of Frank Gehry. Like modernist architecture and its strident minimalism, deconstructivist buildings seem to express disdain for their surroundings. However, deconstructivism does not embrace statist, modernist order but explicitly "celebrates the fragmentation, dislocation, acuteness, and impermanence of contemporary life."[75] Kelbaugh remarks that "[d]econstructivism has given up hope of urban clarity, coherence, and civility."[76]

The combination of inscrutable, placeless architecture and increasingly complex and electronically mediated global relations makes it harder and harder to understand the spatial environment and how one fits into it.

"We often find it impossible to know how things are interrelated," observes Sack. "[O]ur sense is as though we live through many lives that seem disconnected from each other and from the rest of the world."[77] We feel as floating nodes in a network of incoherent, shifting social forces and relations.[78]

Detachment from Place

Accompanying the indecipherability of our landscape is the "thinning out" of places and their meaning that I discussed in chapter 3. This thinning out does not make places easier to understand as much as it disconnects us from them. We are less committed to thinned-out places, less willing to understand them, and less willing to try to shape their destinies. The landscape, as I discussed in chapter 3, begins to seem more like abstract space. As Casey remarks, place can never actually become pure space because the latter is an abstraction.[79] However, this "does not prevent thinned-out places from becoming something similar to space, thanks to taking on certain of the predicates of space, such as planiformity, isotropism, isometrism, homogeneity and so on."[80] In other words, places can take on the some of the uniformity, emptiness, and geometric abstraction that we have associated with space. Here we have another instance of the transformation of place into site. Places are emptied of meaning and made more readily available for use as commodities.

Increasingly, we superficially go from one thinned-out place to another, always distracted and never making deep connections along the way.[81] This thinning out, Casey maintains, impoverishes the very selfhood that grows out of interaction with places.[82] Selves become less robust, less committed, more nomadic.[83]

In a concession to postmodern notions of nomadism and mobility, Casey does allow the possibility that the self may be enriched through contact with a variety of places and by being able to move between the realm of virtual space and actual places.[84] However, he also points out that we ultimately lose the density of habitudes that can develop through close interaction with richly constituted places. Our bodies are less engaged with places, our interactions with places are more routinized, and places are regarded more as entertaining or instrumental rather than being of intrinsic value and fundamental concern.[85] "The consequence can only be a desiccation of both self and place."[86] This detachment from place is heightened by the increasing loss of place-based economic and cultural life and activities discussed earlier. We have less tangible, material involvement and interaction with our geographic environs.

Atemporality

Geographic existence and experience are only further impoverished as commodification erases the temporal context of places. To be available for exchange, a commodity must be unencumbered by considerations of past or future. The commodity must be on call at a moment's notice to be transferred to new owners or uses or discarded. Consequently, the landscape must be detached from any historical and associated cultural importance it may have originally had, except to the degree that history and culture can themselves be marketed.

Atemporality concretely manifests itself in the tendency to literally consume the landscape: to demolish or neglect cities and downtowns rather than renovate and revitalize them; to pursue sweeping, large-scale development projects rather than incremental improvements; to use shoddy, short-lived building materials; and to abandon commercial developments after only a few years. Such approaches to planning and building give the landscape the evanescent, disposable character discussed in chapter 3. These approaches also lead to rapid changes in the built or natural landscape that can render homes, jobs, or communities insecure, and can thus hinder life projects like cultivating kin and friendship networks, planning a family or a home, or pursuing a career.[87]

Atemporality need not require the physical degradation or destruction of the existing landscape. Even where historical structures are reused or older communities are revived, there can be a detachment from temporal context. The tendency to bring in national or global commercial establishments or to revitalize cities with placeless architecture obscures the history of particular places.

Moe and Wilkie warn that atemporality threatens the role of our physical environment as a repository of collective memory. "Like individuals," they note, "a community can fall victim to amnesia, can lose the memory of what it was, and thereby lose touch with what it is and what it was meant to be. The loss of community memory happens most frequently and most dramatically in the destruction of landmarks that are reminders of who we were, what we believed, and where we were headed." Without due consideration for and connection to our history, "existence leaves us adrift, rootless, and disoriented." We lose the sense of belonging to something larger than our self.[88] Over forty years ago, Arendt similarly remarked that "if ... we were truly nothing but members of a consumers' society, we would no longer live in a world at all but simply be driven by a process in whose ever-recurring cycles things appear and disappear, manifest themselves and vanish."[89] As we will now see, the ultimate outcome of commodification and globalization may be the utter disappearance of place in any meaningful sense.

The Information Age and the Space of Flows

The "creative destruction" that capitalism and commodification visit on the landscape has traditionally had a self-limiting quality. Even though capitalism in its pure form would have all places on call for exchange and transformation, there is inertia in the system. Capital investment in industrial facilities, infrastructure, office buildings, retail stores, and housing developments creates some interest in ensuring permanence on the part of the investors. "Those who have invested in the physical qualities of place have to ensure that activities arise which render their investments profitable by ensuring the permanence of place."[90] This is more than just a matter of money or business. The physical creations of investors, entrepreneurs, and developers can also become a source of local pride and identity.

Moreover, a mid-twentieth-century alliance among the state, capital, and to some degree labor, generated a social contract involving the welfare state, regulation of the private sector, and collective bargaining. A social safety net, regulatory constraints on the market, and relative job security provided some countervailing modicum of social and geographic stability in the face of disruptive economic development.

However, even the rather limited permanence created by capitalism and the welfare state is now threatened. The "regime of industrial production, capital accumulation, state intervention formed during the 1930s through the 1970s ... has been replaced by a new regime of flexible accumulation, productive specialization, and state deregulation in loosely coupled transnational alliances of market centers, factory concentrations, technology generators, capital suppliers, and public administrators."[91]

In this milieu, there is also, Harvey observes, a profound tension between speculative investment in the development of places and the geographic mobility of other forms of capital. In other words, the long-term nature of investment in physical infrastructure conflicts with the much greater mobility of financial capital.[92] Such mobility has been enhanced by deregulation and the development of new information and telecommunications technologies.

These trends all threaten to finally annihilate the geographic coherence of social, economic, and political relations. Recall that Castells sees an opposition between the space of flows and the space of places (see chapter 1).[93] The networks of services, capital, knowledge, organizational relationships, and information that constitute the space of flows are reshaping global society. Significantly, the nodes of these networks are not geographically proximate, but are physically disjointed.[94]

This global space of flows consists of three layers: (1) a physical circuit of electronic exchanges and high-speed transportation networks; (2) key network points, including both "milieux of innovation" and nodal centers that command and coordinate flows; and (3) the spatial arrangement of dominant, managerial elites. These elites tend to exist in socially cohesive, cosmopolitan groupings that separate themselves within a particular geographic area—through high housing prices, exclusive meeting and recreational venues, and gated communities—from the more place-bound, locally rooted public.[95] They form a homogeneous "international culture whose identity is not linked to any specific society but to membership of the managerial circles of the informational economy across a global cultural spectrum."[96]

Luke similarly describes a new class of "symbolic analysts, professional experts, technical planners, administrative specialists, and design consultants [who] have been empowered through their knowledge in both the private and public sectors to command and control the ecologies and economies first of advanced industrial societies and now of advanced informational societies."[97] These individuals are expert in managing and exchanging information. They are employed in large organizations such as important research universities, major corporations, professional or technical associations, and state bureaucracies.

Let us consider the key network points, the second layer in the space of flows. The network, or a globally intertwined set of networks, is governed by nodal "command-and-control centers" in a select group of metropolitan areas: New York, Tokyo, London, Chicago, Singapore, Hong Kong, Osaka, Zurich, Frankfurt, Paris, Los Angeles, San Francisco, Amsterdam, Milan, and on a lesser, more regional level, Madrid, São Paulo, Buenos Aires, Mexico City, Taipei, Moscow, Budapest, and others.[98] These nodes coordinate information flows and "advanced services, producer centers, and markets in a global network."[99] By coordinating networked flows of information, nodal centers control material production around the globe.

Key network points also include milieux of innovation, where spatially proximate individuals, often operating in businesses or research institutions, are able to generate new knowledge, processes, and products.[100] In the United States, such places are found in Boston, Seattle, Silicon Valley, Austin, North Carolina's research triangle, New York, Minneapolis, and the Los Angeles area. Research and development, innovation, and fabrication of prototypes are all located in command centers and milieux of innovation.[101]

Several factors maintain the status of the key metropolitan areas or cities in the network. In these places, Castells says, corporate headquarters and advanced financial firms can find needed suppliers and highly skilled, specialized labor. Sunk costs in real estate also keep corporate activities from dispersing too much,[102] a point I made earlier. Moreover, in an age of widespread eavesdropping, face-to-face contacts are still necessary for critical decisions. In addition, major metropolitan centers offer the greatest opportunities for the personal development, social status, and self-gratification of upper-level professionals—from good schools to sophisticated cultural amenities.[103] Finally, there is of course the physical proximity of skilled personnel, which enables the creation of social networks and organizational cultures that cultivate learning and the communication of ideas.[104] Thus, Elliott Sclar, an urban planner, remarks that while Citicorp can locate the management of its credit card accounts in Sioux City, South Dakota, it maintains its world headquarters in New

York City.[105] The World Trade Center itself became a physical site for the concentration of expertise in the FIRE industries.

These factors would all suggest the continuing importance of place. In fact, the qualities that make for good command or innovation centers have helped revive cities like New York, Boston, and San Francisco, even as other central cities have declined.

However, the global network society is in many ways antithetical to the value of place. First, the advantages that give particular localities a commanding role in global networks and foster the revitalization of urban centers also encourage sprawl in these same metropolitan areas, especially in the United States.[106] Housing costs soar in the center of the cities and corporate employees move outward to pursue "good" suburban public schools or more affordable housing. Boston has accordingly experienced massive suburban growth along its Route 495 beltway. Moreover, in an economy increasingly based on information flows, the production of physical goods or the execution of services like data processing do not need to be near command centers or sites of innovation,[107] and information technology enables individuals to live farther away from their jobs.[108]

Internally Fragmented Megacities
The network society also undermines place by internally fragmenting metropolitan areas. In contemporary cities in general, "urban space is increasingly differentiated in social terms, while being functionally interrelated beyond physical contiguity."[109] The extreme of this development characterizes those giant urban agglomerations of 10 million or more individuals called megacities. Examples include New York, Los Angeles, Mexico City, Rio de Janeiro, Buenos Aires, Lagos, Cairo, London, Paris, Moscow, Bombay, Calcutta, New Delhi, Hong Kong, Shanghai, Seoul, Tokyo, and Jakarta. Megacities embrace whole clusters of cities. For example, the megacity of Hong Kong is really an emerging agglomeration of "40–50 million people, connecting Hong Kong, Shenzhen, Guangzhou, Zhuhai, Macau, and small towns in the Pearl River Delta."[110]

These huge metropolitan areas are both population centers and nodes in the global network.[111] As these nodal centers become increasingly linked with one another, they are correspondingly more detached from their immediately surrounding territories. These centers are globally connected while locally disconnected. Within the megacity of Hong Kong are disconnected "rural settlements, agricultural land, and undeveloped areas separating urban centers, and industrial factories being scattered all over the region."[112] Thus, "what is most significant about megacities is that they are connected externally to global networks and to segments of their own countries, while internally disconnecting local populations that are either functionally unnecessary or socially disruptive.... *It is this distinctive feature of being globally connected and locally disconnected, physically and socially, that makes mega-cities a new urban form.*"[113]

Geographic regions thus develop internal discontinuities. Areas surrounding a node may be cut off from global networks and marginalized. This magnifies the fragmentation we saw with sprawl. Network connections and interdependencies leapfrog from one city to another and link up with the global network, even as elites see themselves as having little connection with other inhabitants and communities within their own region.

In a study of Internet activity in U.S. cities, Mitchell Moss thus noted a significant disparity within New York City:

New York City has the largest Internet presence of any city in the United States, and in all likelihood, the entire world. With 17,579 registered domains, New York City accounts for 4.2 percent of the U.S. total.... The borough of Manhattan dominates New York City's Internet activity. Since the introduction of the World Wide Web in 1993, the number of domains per capita in New York City has grown nearly 10 times more quickly than [in] the nation as a whole. Among the outer boroughs, Brooklyn has the largest number of domains, with 1,036. Queens is the second largest at 997, with the Bronx at 181 and Staten Island at 174. *The boroughs of Brooklyn, Queens, and Staten Island have less than a third of the national average of domains, while the Bronx has only one-tenth.*[114]

This study, which was published in 1997, may be somewhat dated now, but it underscores the degree to which links with global networks may be radically unequal even within one city. Manhattan led the nation in Internet domains, while its sister boroughs lagged behind the rest of the United States. An investor in downtown Manhattan may be much more connected through daily communications and business transactions to an entrepreneur in Shanghai than to a grocer or unemployed laborer across the East River in Brooklyn or, for that matter, to a farmer up the Hudson River.

This does not mean that intraregional connections cease to exist. Localities are still linked through important intraregional relationships. They are still bound together by ecological and social interdependencies, cultural ties, and transportation networks and other shared infrastructure. Land-use policies in one locality affect neighboring communities. Economic decay in one part of a region will ultimately affect the whole region.

However, it does seem that social, material, and ecological relationships within metropolitan areas are becoming less physically tangible or coherent. Thus, common problems are not as readily identified; localities engage in destructive competition or mutual neglect; elites retreat behind gates and affluence; and collective action problems arise on a regional scale. Acknowledging continued regional intradependence despite lack of cooperation, Castells envisions water shortages, epidemics, and breakdowns in social control even as megacities become increasingly important global actors.[115]

Flexible Capitalism

Within the network society, capitalism shifts to a more flexible mode. This increases the insecurity and disruption visited on places. The most competitive firms are able to use global networks and information technology to develop computerized production processes, decentralized organizational structures, and the ability to respond to global transfers of financial capital and rapid changes in demand, including new niche markets and consumer tastes.[116] Moreover, firms can break down production processes and shift individual operations around the world to exploit differences and changes in labor costs.[117] This means that despite the fact that the geographic arrangement of the major nodes in the network does not readily change, the relative fortunes of these and other localities and regions can shift rapidly. Castells cites the major swings in real estate prices in North American, European, and Asian cities during the 1990s: "This urban roller-coaster at different periods, across areas of the world, illustrates both the dependence and vulnerability of any locale, including major cities, to changing global flows."[118]

Globalized, flexible capitalism also further enhances the ability of large corporations to see the entire world as a resource bank and move operations to wherever goods or land are available for exploitation, especially as other areas are used up or otherwise despoiled.[119] The result is a global technosphere reliant on abstract production decisions based on measurements of "the density, velocity, intensity, and quantity of goods and services being exchanged in mass consumption" rather than on any consideration of local or regional interrelationships "among land, water, plants, animals, climate, and peoples."[120]

Such environmental destruction may involve complex global transactions among various firms. A case in point is illustrated in a recent Greenpeace investigation of soybean farming in Brazil's Amazon region.[121] In order to stimulate soybean production in the Amazon, the U.S.-based multinational agribusiness Cargill has built soybean storage and shipping facilities in the Amazon port of Santarém and provided farmers with seed and chemicals. Cargill ships the soybeans to Sun Valley, an affiliate in the United Kingdom that raises chickens and uses a soy-based feed. The chickens are then used to supply meat for the production of Chicken McNuggets for the European market by fast food giant McDonald's.

According to Greenpeace, the opening of the Cargill facilities in 2003 had a profound local effect and was not good news for the rain forest. The subsequent clearing of land by farmers led to a virtual doubling of the deforestation rate in the region around Santarém—from 15,000 hectares in 2002 to 28,000 hectares in 2004. Moreover, according to Greenpeace, Cargill's suppliers have used slave labor and seized land from indigenous tribes. The report quotes Ionaluka, an official with the Xingu Indigenous Land Association, on deforestation and agrochemical pollution in the vicinity of the Xingu Indigenous Park: "The soya is arriving very fast. Every time I leave the reserve I do not recognise anything because the forest keeps disappearing."[122] Soybean production can exhaust the soil, yet once an area is ecologically depleted, a company with global operations and assets like Cargill may simply move on and set up shop elsewhere.

Loss of Local Business Elites

An additional consequence of globalized, flexible capitalism for places is the loss of locally headquartered corporations through a series of relocations, mergers, and consolidations of firms. Local business elites have been justly criticized for exercising undue economic and political power, skewing local government policies to their own interest, and pursuing development projects at the expense of local residents and environmental quality.[123]

Nevertheless, locally headquartered firms have also had a strong interest in local prosperity and quality of life because local conditions affect their business.[124] Studies have also indicated that among the private-sector employers in a city, it is the locally headquartered companies that give the most to charities and have the largest numbers of executives involved in local civic and cultural organizations.[125]

Business analyst Rosabeth Moss Kanter notes that as corporations disperse their operations around the globe, their headquarters lose personnel as well as much of their decision-making power, including the allocation of funds to charitable or other civic causes.[126] Moreover, globalized companies are simply less interested in local affairs. Even when they are interested in public service, they are more likely to look to the global stage. For example, Kanter says that Reebok, which is located outside of Boston, is known for receiving international human rights awards, but not for making contributions in its headquarters area.[127]

The End of Place?

In sum, the space of flows works against the stability of places and threatens the role of physical contiguity in defining social relationships.[128] Castells accordingly says "The global city is not a place, but a process."[129]

Traditionally, even international trade depended on proximity to commercial routes, trading posts, and ports. However, as symbolized by the burying of Manhattan's piers through the construction of the World Trade Center, the electronic circuits of the space of flows connect widely separated areas while bypassing physically contiguous ones. The space of flows thus emphasizes physical discontinuity and emphemerality. By contrast, the concept of place emphasizes physical proximity and geographic stability. The space of flows is placeless.

Intellectually, this world is legitimated by techno-utopians on the right and postmodernists on the left, as I discussed in chapter 1. Both groups reject rootedness as outdated and limiting, and emphasize the virtues of mobility, dislocation, and the disruption of spatial attachments.

Postmodernists' embrace of placelessness involves a profound irony. Postmodernism tries to challenge oppressive, settled ways of thinking and the power structures behind them, yet it becomes a hegemonic discourse "naturalizing" the dislocation imposed by capitalism and the space of flows.[130] When authors like Honig or de Lauretis tell us to give up on the concept of home, there is a totalitarian tone of trying to forcibly remake society by disrupting all existing, coherent, social formations.[131] This is not much different from what Luke describes as elite efforts to oppose the "traditionalism" of strong, settled communities and impose "far more fluid, mobile, and variable forms of everyday life, such as those produced by new class experts."[132]

Postmodernity's placeless perspective may have something to do with the situation of elite symbolic analysts, a group that one might extend to include academics of all stripes, including those in the humanities. Luke describes symbolic analysts as "deterritorialized souls" lacking a sense of place.[133] Relatedly, Harvey argues that postmodernism, with its emphasis on disruption, difference, and ephemerality, is perfectly consistent with flexible capitalism and its emphasis on exploring rapidly changing niche markets for new products.[134]

However, the space of flows does not entirely describe the daily, lived, concrete experience of most people, even today. Despite intellectual rationalizations for placelessness and despite a good deal of hype about such things as telecommuting, distance learning, and medical examinations over the Internet, many facilities (e.g., workplaces, schools, hospitals, sports arenas, parks, and shopping areas) must still have central physical locations and still depend on physical proximity.[135] "Indeed," Castells notes, "the overwhelming majority of people, in advanced and traditional societies alike, live in places, and so they perceive their space as place-based."[136] Again, recall that the centers of global commerce are still physical centers, even if they are connected to one another through electronic networks.

At the same time, much of life is certainly transacted in what Luke describes as networked, global "technoregions" detached from particular places: "the banking world, the scientific world, the art world, the literary world, the financial world, the auto world, the fashion world, the business world, the music world, the advertising world, the military world, the medical world, the aerospace world, the computer world, or the professional world." Luke notes that these technoregional settings form our everyday lifescapes. Every household imports and exports life's necessities from these technoregions.[137]

The result is Castells' clash between the space of flows and the space of places. Because so much of what goes on now in individual places is determined by the space of flows or by what transpires in technoregions, people feel a dissonance between their conception of and experience of the world as structured around physical places and their increasing sense that placeless, global forces and relationships are shaping the landscape. An individual's local or regional connections are increasingly obscured, distorted, or undermined by more globalized, networked relationships and by the spatial and social fragmentation that characterizes the contemporary sprawling landscape.

Meanwhile, as Luke points out, the non-territorial technoregions, with their intensive and interdependent use of resources, still exploit and degrade concrete, physical nature and spoil local ecological conditions.[138] The biophysical environment around us deteriorates as a result of pollution, climate change, loss of open space, congestion, and sprawl even as consumption seems to promise ever-richer fulfillment in the fantasy worlds conjured up by advertising and the entertainment media.[139] Barry says that consumption "consumes the world even as it fails to recognize the dependence of consumption on the world."[140]

The overall effect of these dissonances is to throw our spatial perspective and the practice of place into chaos. Individuals can no longer conceptualize their surroundings to produce a coherent map because many of the forces shaping that map are deterritorialized and difficult to understand, while geographically based relationships and local ecological conditions are increasingly disrupted or destroyed. As Luke says, the work of symbolic analysts continues modernity's assault on the geographically embedded lifeworld of local or regional practices and traditions.[141] Average citizens experience a disempowering sense of incompetence,[142] as they are reduced to clients, customers, and consumers.[143] This is an issue not only of place, but also of democracy.

Globalization, Commodification, and Democracy

Symbolic analysts, major property owners, entrepreneurs, and businesses are radically and globally remaking landscapes, practices, communities, and lifeworlds without any political accountability to those whose lives are thus transformed. The radical founding inherent in commodification and globalization is antithetical to democratic control over places, although in ways less direct than state-sponsored, authoritarian modernism. Democracy is undermined in several ways.

Private property rights, particularly in the case of vast individual holdings, act as a fetter on the political will of the community. Large private landholders, operating under the aegis of property rights, can undertake major and often irrevocable planning decisions and fundamentally change a community and its natural environment with little or no public input. We saw this most dramatically with Larry Silverstein's enormous power over the rebuilding of Ground Zero. Although Silverstein does not actually own the World Trade Center, his leasehold constituted a property right until he was ultimately compelled, after a good deal of time and much negotiation, to accept a lesser but still significant role.

Less visibly, global networks constitute what Luke, in part drawing on Ulrich Beck, describes as a "subpolitics," or "subpolis," which is not apparent to most individuals.[144] Networks operate "underneath, above, and apart from the polis, but they are also structures of power, systems of exchange, and signs of culture constructed by authoritative experts to operate authoritatively beyond much popular control."[145] The workings of the subpolis are obscured by their categorization as apolitical matters of business, property rights, expert management, economics, science, and engineering. Technical discourses, professional "codes of performativity,"[146] and the mantle of expert authority also inhibit and even delegitimate public oversight and participation.

As I discussed earlier, globalized connections among places are invisible, incomprehensible, unaccountable, and disorienting for people who see a progressive destruction of tangible, meaningful, geographically based relations but don't quite know the reason. Since the subpolis and its actors are not territorially based, in contrast to both the nation-state and more local authorities, they operate outside a public attention that is focused on more traditional, geographic political structures:

Unlike the national-statal polis, which has been seen as a community of people situated in a specific geographic locality or particular nation-state, the subpolis is an ever-shifting assembly of ordinary people and extraordinary technics interoperating locally and globally with many other technical assemblies and people elsewhere along multi-, trans-, and supernational lines as well as within inter-, infra-, and intralocal spaces.[147]

The competition among communities, large or small, for business investment also undermines democracy. Driven by the need to capture elusive investment or face a collapse of their economy or tax base, communities lose the power to really choose how to govern their own places. Democracy gives way to politics as administration, taken up with attracting investment and pursuing economic growth.[148]

Democratic control over place is also eroded in even subtler ways. The fragmentation of the landscape into disconnected parcels of private property, the loss of local distinctiveness and the spread of corporate imagery, the increasing illegibility of the landscape, the incomprehensibility of globalized connections among places, the increasingly atemporal quality of the landscape, and the thinning out of meaning in places all undermine the possibility for individual and collective commitments to places. This in turn makes collective deliberation about places more difficult. Arendt's well-known observations about mass society are especially apt here. Individuals find themselves in a world that "has lost its power to gather [them] together, to relate and to separate them."[149] People are "deprived of an 'objective' relationship ... that comes from being related to and separated from [one another] through the intermediary of a common world of things."[150] The result is spatial and social incoherence and a collective powerless in the face of land-use decisions and changes.

Place is truly in crisis, not because it is obsolete or irrelevant, but because it remains essential but is nevertheless threatened. Globalized, networked, flexible capitalism makes places insecure and unstable and throws the practice of place into confusion. Given this insecurity and instability, preservationist values are completely marginalized. Furthermore, the disorientation, insecurity, and powerlessness of individuals and communities in the face of global networks seriously undermine any democratic control over place. In the next two chapters, I will consider how we might resolve this crisis. First, though, I want to turn to one prominent and promising, but inadequate, response.

The Preservationist Defense of Place

Environmentalism as Defender of Place
The environmental movement is one of the staunchest defenders of the value of place and of specific places. Sagoff, who is quoted in chapter 1,

suggests that much of environmental politics is fundamentally about place. When we consider not only logging and sprawl but also issues like loss of habitat and biodiversity, air and water pollution, hazardous waste disposal, environmental justice, acid rain, nuclear power, and climate change, it is evident that most if not all environmental issues are manifested through problems or impacts that bear on the security, flourishing, and character of individual places. Degradation of the environment is also degradation of places: familiar places, places people rely on, ecologically significant places, aesthetically pleasing places, sacred places, places with cultural or historical importance. Furthermore, the impacts of environmental problems fall as much on the built environment as on the natural one. Acid rain damages statues and building facades as well as forests. Hazardous waste sites ruin neighborhoods as well as aquifers.

Luke argues that many, although certainly not all, environmentalists have been co-opted by globalized power structures, so that activists and scientists often work to facilitate continued global capitalist activity by making the world more ecologically stable, predictable, and rational. Such "bureaucratic greens"[151] assist in the disempowerment of local or regional control over place.[152] Luke's critique is similar to critiques of Pinchot's top-down resource management and contemporary ecological modernization theory.[153]

A globalized, bureaucratic green mentality does not characterize the environmental movement as a whole. As we saw in the old-growth forest debate, many environmentalists speak in terms of moral responsibility to specific places. According to Leopold's land ethic and its ecocentric descendants, human beings have a responsibility to maintain both the larger biotic community and its specific places.[154] As discussed in chapter 1, greens often emphasize how human beings have, or ought to have, powerful ties to particular places they inhabit or visit. Such ties, based on appreciation, love, or even reverence, can shape individual identities and connect an individual's own good with the good of a particular place.

The environmental movement has been a formidable antagonist for ideologies and interests that seek to radically transform the place-world. It has been an influential force for preservation when powerful economic and political actors have pushed founding with little restraint. Notions of responsibility for the biotic community and for particular places have given environmentalism a powerful moral voice, especially when it confronts the instrumentalist values of capitalism.

However, many environmental activists, in their response to ruthless founding by governments and corporations, have gone to the other extreme and overemphasized preservation to the exclusion of founding. In part, this may be a political posture, an attempt to balance overzealous founding and create a compromise that falls in a moderate middle.[155] Even if hard-line preservationism is meant to be strategic—and I don't believe that it is *fundamentally* strategic—it is a problematic response to the forces of placelessness, as I will discuss.

The Wise Use Challenge to Environmentalism

As a strategy, radical preservation would actually backfire because it alienates rural communities that might otherwise work with environmentalists.

Since the 1990s, the environmental movement has been on the defensive. Instead of successfully launching new initiatives, greens have been preoccupied with halting or at least limiting efforts by resource industries, property-rights activists, libertarian and conservative organizations and think tanks, and congressional and White House Republicans to weaken or even roll back environmental laws and regulations.

Opposition to environmentalism has been boosted by the Wise Use movement. Located mainly in the West, the movement has attracted ranchers and other landowners, workers in resource industries, and off-road vehicle enthusiasts. Wise Use activists oppose restrictions on the use of federal lands for logging, mining, ranching, and offroad vehicles and also oppose environmental restrictions on the use of private property. Certainly, many Wise Use activists are motivated by economic interests. Yet as John Meyer rightly argues, they are committed to the places where they live and work. The antienvironmentalist anger of Wise Use activists may be "based less on economics than on the quality of life possible in [their] communities and the perceived threat posed to this life— not just their income—by environmental policies."[156] Philip Brick and Edward Weber note, "Nothing could be further from the truth" that "rural Westerners are not worried about the economic, social, and environmental changes that are transforming their communities."[157]

It is true that Wise Use activists have at times shown a knee-jerk or even violent and pathological opposition to environmentalism. Wise Use founder Ron Arnold has publicly declared "holy war against the new pagans who worship trees and sacrifice people" and says, "we have to pick up a sword and shield and kill the bastards," although he adds, "I mean politically not physically."[158] Environmental writer David Helvarg has documented various instances of violence or intimidation against environmentalists and employees of federal resource agencies.[159]

Moreover, the Wise Use movement espouses policies that would amount to a reversal of decades of protection for wilderness and endangered species. It has also received considerable backing from corporate interests,[160] particularly in mining, energy, timber, and real estate, who are not necessarily motivated by what is best for rural westerners.

However, the success of the Wise Use movement also reflects a failing on the part of environmentalists. Green groups have not done enough to reach out to rural westerners concerned about place.[161] In the old-growth forest debate, as we saw in chapter 2, environmentalists have missed key opportunities to join forces with timber workers against timber managers. Often hostile to collaborative conservation efforts, the larger, national environmental groups have been reluctant to engage in democratic deliberation with resource-dependent rural westerners. Donald Snow charges that "some environmentalists have been among those most deeply invested in the antidemocratic management regime exercised on the public lands. Any suggestions aimed at devolving power or land management authority to more local levels—even on a temporary, experimental basis—are met with howls of derision, especially from national environmental leaders."[162]

Discovery Is Not Founding: Radical Preservationism

A key reason, I would argue, for the reluctance of many environmentalists to sit down with their opponents is that many greens hold a concept of place that radically excludes founding. Again, one should be wary about categorizing environmentalism as a whole. An antifounding perspective is not universally held among environmentalists.[163] As we will see in chapter 7, there are promising strands of the environmental movement that offer a much more balanced and integrated view of place that embraces both founding and preservation. However, the popular rhetoric of the environmental movement often conveys an overly preservationist perspective. Implicit in such a perspective is the belief that human beings do not define places and create maps of the world so much as *discover* a preexisting map.

There is a profound difference between founding and discovery. Founding involves a new beginning, the creation of places and meanings, and the initiation of an open-ended process of developing a place. Properly tempered by preservation, founding need not be brutal, sudden, or destructive. It can involve careful building and cultivation and a willingness to leave much of the landscape physically unaltered. In fact, as we saw, founding can also involve the designation and management of land for preservationist purposes.

Discovery, on the other hand, is a matter of finding, not founding, a matter of finding what already exists.[164] If the world, governed by a preexisting cosmic order, is already organized into coherent, meaningful places by nature itself, then there is much less need for people to engage in founding places. From this standpoint, any act of founding a place is potentially problematic because it alters a world that is already formed and meaningful.

The emphasis on discovery rather founding is most unambiguously exemplified, perhaps almost to the level of caricature, in Kirkpatrick Sale's 1985 book, *Dwellers in the Land*. Though his book is perhaps a bit dated, Sale, a bioregionalist and ecocentric, forcefully expresses what is often implicit in the views of some of his fellow environmental activists.

Bioregionalism is a strain of radical environmentalism that focuses on reviving attachments between individuals and their local or regional ecological surroundings and reorienting human communities toward a greater focus on the possibilities and limits inherent in their own ecosystems, i.e., their own bioregions. Bioregionalism opposes the sort of roving, globalized plunder discussed earlier.

The bioregional program advocated by Sale aims at the complete reorganization of political, economic, and cultural institutions so that they conform to bioregional boundaries. A bioregion, says Sale, is "any part of the earth's surface whose rough boundaries are determined by natural characteristics rather than human dictates, distinguishable from other areas by particular attributes of flora, fauna, water, climate, soils, and landforms, and by the human settlements and cultures those attributes have given rise to."[165] A bioregion is "a place defined by its life-forms, its topography and its biota, rather than by human dictates; a region governed by nature, not legislature."[166] A bioregion is thus "defined by ... the *givens* of nature."[167]

To truly connect with one's place, one must cultivate "bioregional awareness."[168] This involves "knowing the land," i.e., its resident life-forms, natural features, land-use patterns, and ecological carrying capacity; "learning the lore," i.e., the history of a place, the "record of how the human and natural possibilities of the region have been explored," and in particular the "ways and wisdom" of "earlier cultures, particularly those well-rooted in the earth"; and "developing the potential." By developing the potential, Sale means employing all of a region's "funds, facilities, stocks, and talents to their fullest, limited only by the carrying capacity of the land and its ecological constraints." It entails "self-reliance ... at the regional level," accommodated to regional ecological processes and carrying capacities.[169] This is not development in the traditional sense, but a reorientation of human activities and material wants so that they fit into ecological processes and limits and do not depend on raiding or exploiting other places for their resources. "Self-reliance" thus means dependence on a place's local ecological amenities and conformity to that place's ecological constraints. It therefore entails decentralization of political and economic arrangements along bioregional or other eco-systemic lines.

Much of what Sale advocates is worthwhile; indeed, bioregionalism is in many ways a promising place-oriented green perspective. As Barry notes, bioregionalism attempts to rectify our sense of detachment from the landscape.[170] Moreover, in the next chapter I argue for a regional framework for governance as well as attention to regional ecological integrity. Throughout this book I have also argued that in the creation of places, human beings should take into account natural features and ecological relationships.

However, Sale's conception of place and society reflects what Meyer identifies as a derivative relationship between nature and politics[171] and what I would also consider a derivative relationship between nature and place. A derivative view holds that social and political values and ends are directly derived from some prior conception of a natural order. Barry, similarly, calls this the "reading-off hypothesis." According to this view, Barry says, we "can 'read off' how human society is and ought to be from looking at the nonhuman world."[172] Sale thus maintains,

Of course the entire moral structure of an ecologically conscious society would rest on Gaean principles [i.e., the organizing principles of the biosphere]. Oughts and Shoulds would not be based primarily on protecting private property or personal wealth or individual achievement, as in Western morality, but on securing bioregional stasis and environmental equilibrium.[173]

Derivative, or reading-off, views are fairly common among activists like Sale, but they also creep into more sophisticated and worthy attempts to work up environmental values into a systematic theoretical framework. In a passage that Meyer also cites for similar reasons, leading green political theorist Robyn Eckersley explains the relationship between ecocentrism and politics. Ecocentrism, she says, sees:

the question of our proper place in the rest of nature as logically prior to the question of what are the most appropriate social and political arrangements for human communities. That is, the determination of social and political questions *must proceed from*, or at least be consistent with, an adequate determination of this more fundamental question.[174]

According to this passage, ecocentrism tells us that in crafting their ends, communities ought to refer to their place, metaphorically and literally, in nature and discover their preexisting interests. Nature acts as a standard for politics; we ought to look to nature to see how political life should be ordered. This verges on what Barry critically calls "a complete submersion within, and total acceptance of, the order of nature."[175]

In Sale's view, nature, through its ecologically determined bioregions, acts as a template for all place founding. Human beings apply nature's pregiven map to the organization of their spatial world.

Yet, as we have seen, the whole activity of founding and preserving places is inherently political. It involves competing perspectives and power relationships. Direct application of what is supposedly nature's map to society would therefore require that competing perspectives on place be somehow overruled or silenced. Those who can claim to somehow have the "correct" interpretation of nature and who can invoke nature's own order or map, would have the final say in defining places and their character and bounds.[176] They would automatically prevail over those who conceive of place in terms of other parameters: human history, ethnicity, culture, religion, economic relationships, etc.

One should be mindful that those who try to read off nature's map are actually "reading into" nature, as Barry says. They are projecting their own social perspectives onto the natural world.[177] Instead of applying a real, pregiven natural map, they are mapping their world in line with their own image of how human communities ought to be organized with respect to the natural terrain, and they are in fact naturalizing their particular political perspective.

Given these considerations, it is not surprising that some environmentalists, although they might claim to be champions of democracy, actually have trouble with democratic deliberation and debate about place, especially when deliberation brings in those who are unlikely to share a strongly preservationist perspective. The derivative or reading-off approach to politics and place rules out Arendt's human plurality. We must all accept the "correct" map of the world. Fundamental social and political principles are pregiven by nature. This means that democratic politics is only reliable to the degree that it can discover and apply the right ecological principles, that humans can discover their proper place in nature. In reality, though, democratic deliberation, especially about places and other ecologically relevant topics, is too open-ended, too uncertain, and too messy to be trusted by such preservationists. Politics itself, as a deliberative enterprise, must disappear. In a critique of bioregionalism, Barry thus notes that in the hands of an author like Sale who tries to read off from nature, bioregionalism can be fundamentally hostile to political debate within a community.[178]

In a similar rejection of democracy on naturalistic grounds, the Wilderness Society a few years ago posted on its website an official commentary on collaborative conservation that "questions the wisdom of legislating local control schemes on any scale." The author goes on to say, "Our great public land systems ... are just that: systems. They are meant to be managed systematically, with baseline standards common to all—standards sufficient to guarantee the Integrity [sic] of each system and all of its component units."[179]

What this amounts to is radical preservationism. Human beings are to apply and preserve nature's pregiven map and do little or no real founding of their own. Of course, the determination of bioregions would itself be an instance of founding (recall Barry's point that we in fact "read into" rather than "read off" of nature), but greens like Sale would refuse to recognize this. Instead, they would see themselves as simply recognizing nature's terrain. Even if they were to recognize an element of founding in defining the exact boundaries of bioregions, they would still maintain that nature has supplied the basic map and they would follow any bioregional founding with a rigid preservation of the favored map. This is what Barry would describe as an attempt to "seek a *permanent* solution to human-nature relations, in the sense of finding the definitive, final, once-for-all answer to this aspect of the human condition."[180]

This view turns out to be as antidemocratic as the radical founding perspectives discussed earlier. Upholding extreme preservation requires the exclusion of more balanced or founding-oriented views and thus entails a top-down, even authoritarian, politics rather than democratic debate.

These criticisms are not meant to imply that we cannot have obligations to the preservation of undeveloped places shaped primarily by natural forces. However, such places must be understood from within the context of a practice that initially defines coherent places, whether wild or settled, through founding. Such a practice bases preservationist obligations on historical, cultural, communal, and personal identification with particular places, as well as on the importance of places, whether social or ecological, for the flourishing of the human and/or nonhuman life there. Such a practice makes the treatment of places a matter of political deliberation rather than simple discovery. This does not exclude ecological considerations. The treatment of places must absolutely consider how places are shaped by natural processes and embedded in natural ecosystems. One may go further and bring in ecocentric considerations through recognition that the founding and preservation of places affects the flourishing of nonhuman organisms and natural ecosystems, both of which may have independent moral standing.

Meyer points out that "politics allows us to develop answers to the multitude of questions and challenges posed by our condition as beings embedded in nature."[181] Under the rubric of politics is the collective endeavor of founding and preserving places. One of the key starting points of this endeavor is embeddedness in nature, although human history and culture are also important starting points here as well.

In mapping the world, in founding and preserving places, we try to make sense of and integrate all of these starting points into a coherent but never finalized picture that takes into account our relationships and obligations to nature and to one another and suggests to us further possibilities, conflicts, ends, and aspirations. The activities of founding and preservation reflect on and incorporate what is given by nature or history, but also enable us to advance from such givens. Founding and preservation should be reflective, integrative, creative, and open-ended. Their primary purpose is not discovery.

Avoiding the Question of Use: A World of Natural and Fallen Landscapes

It is not surprising that radical preservationists like Sale are most concerned about place foundings that involve extensive physical alteration of the environment. Such greens express a doubly preservationist view. They are procedurally preservationist in that they want to apply nature's preexisting map, whatever that map entails. They are also substantively preservationist in that they are opposed to particular sorts of land uses that would unacceptably alter natural conditions. We have been considering procedural preservationism. I now want to turn to substantive preservationism. First, however, I will relate two brief anecdotes.

In 1993, William Arthur, the Sierra Club's Northwest regional director, logged his own land in Washington State. Timber interests accused him of hypocrisy, claiming he had logged old growth and with minimal adherence to state environmental regulations.[182] However, as the *New York Times* reported, "Arthur's most vocal critics [were] Sierra Club members" who saw his action as symbolic of a national environmental leadership "gone soft."[183] Arthur claimed that he had logged second-growth timber and that the cut had not been ecologically damaging. He also offered a lesson: "Environmentalists do not oppose all timber cutting. The real issues are where you log and how you log. And how we protect and manage for sustainable functioning ecosystems." He argued, "It is not inconsistent to support responsible selective cutting of second-growth forests and at the same time argue for protecting our remaining wild areas and old-growth forests."[184] At issue in the debate was not just commitment to environmental laws but also the presumably shocking idea that an environmental activist would ever cut down a tree.

In a book on the Northern Forest in New England and New York State, David Dobbs and Richard Ober described a visit by a college environmental ethics class to a logging site in Maine. The students were shocked and angered to see live trees being cut down. The owner of the timber company—whom the authors describe as an ecologically responsible landowner—pointed out, to no avail, that such trees provide the materials for books and houses.[185]

These views are not universal to the environmental movement, and many greens recognize the importance of resource work in sustaining human life and cultivating human connections with the rest of nature. However, these stories, as well as my discussion of the Northwest forest debate in chapter 2, indicate the frequent hostility of environmentalists to the alteration of natural landscapes. Many greens, as environmental historian Richard White observes, "equate productive work in nature with destruction," and are especially hostile to "heavy bodily labor, blue-collar work."[186] They "imagine that when people who make things finish their day's work, nature is the poorer for it. Nature seems safest when shielded from human labor."[187] Although environmentalists often celebrate "certain kinds of archaic work, most typically the farming of peasants," many are uncomfortable with modern-day, technologically enhanced work.[188]

Such views on work and alteration of the landscape also emerge in Sale's view of the built environment. He acknowledges that bioregional awareness and place identification are available for city dwellers. However, urbanites must gain knowledge of and recover the "natural foundation" or "natural potential" that has been considerably obscured and degraded by urbanization: "[O]ur huge conurbations have largely displaced natural life by diverting rivers, cutting down forests, paving over soils, and confining most animal life to zoos and parks."[189] Sale goes further, branding the urban built environment as ecologically illegitimate. He describes the modern-day metropolis as "an ecological parasite as it extracts its lifeblood from elsewhere and an ecological pathogen as it sends back its wastes."[190] At the same time, he extols Paleolithic and hunter-gatherer cultures that saw the Earth as a great living entity and perceived no separation between themselves and the rest of nature. They supposedly experienced a now-lost harmony between humanity and the rest of nature and had "a liberating, psychically healthy sense of wholeness, of oneness, of *place*."[191]

Are urban dwellers then supposed to return to a hunter-gatherer or at least a rustic peasant way of life and abandon all the founding activities that have created built landscapes like cities? Aside from some Earth First! activists during the 1980s,[192] environmentalists have not, in spite of some of their detractors' claims, called on us to abandon modern civilization. Furthermore, many environmentalists have offered valuable insights on the sustainable use of resources, urban planning, green technologies, and so on. However, to the degree that activists sweepingly condemn work and other physical place-founding activities, they see built environments, and especially vast human creations like cities, as evils we must now contend with and make the best of. Indeed they see them as fallen landscapes that have lost the original meaning, wholeness, and purity of nature. In so doing, such environmentalists create a troubling dichotomy between founding and preservation.

At the same time, Sale, like many other environmentalists, calls on us to identify with nature by "reinhabiting" our natural environment; i.e., once again seeing our natural landscape as home and learning to care for it, rather than exploiting it. Recall that habitation can build attachments that motivate preservationist responsibilities, as was evident with activists' defense of their "patch of forest." Yet if individuals are to truly inhabit a place and obtain a reasonable livelihood, they must cultivate a fair amount of land, establish buildings and infrastructure, and extract minerals and other natural resources (unless of course they settle down in one place and exploit another). Even rustic living necessitates altering one's surroundings, as Luke points out: "[A]re not bioregionalists living in the woods 'industrialistic'? Rustic cabins, outdoor plumbing, and wood-burning stoves rest on human assumptions that nature can be controlled by fabricating shelter systems, latrine technics, and heating mechanisms to evade the weather, eliminate body waste, and warm homes."[193]

To resolve this dilemma, preservationists like Sale need to better address our proper relationship to nature, i.e., what Wendell Berry calls the issue of defining responsible use of nature.[194] By "use," Berry does not mean the complete instrumentalization of nature. What he means is our interaction with nature as we inevitably draw our sustenance and livelihoods from it. Defining responsible use means integrating founding and preservation. Barry, who similarly articulates what he calls an "ethic of use," takes pains to note that proper use must, and can, be distinguished from abuse.[195] Making this distinction means addressing questions like the one Brian Donahue faced in managing a town forest: "Good forest management ... somehow had to mean cutting living trees. The question was, Which trees to cut?"[196]

Unfortunately, environmentalists have too often failed to confront this question. Instead, they have traditionally focused on preserving the remaining places that are still truly natural, i.e., relatively "untainted" by human activity, such as wilderness areas like the ancient forest.[197] This approach informs much modern wilderness philosophy, as articulated in the Wilderness Act, which I discussed earlier. William Cronon says, "For many Americans wilderness stands as the last remaining place where civilization, that all too human disease, has not fully infected the earth. It is an island in the polluted sea of urban-industrial modernity."[198]

Preservation of wilderness is certainly an extremely important objective in any worthwhile politics of place. Wilderness areas have beauty and spiritual significance. They provide a welcome escape from civilization and a place for reflection or recreation. They are reservoirs of biological diversity and providers of important ecosystem services. Wild places can be objects of strong place attachment, and individuals can develop a sense of obligation toward them. Finally, if human beings have moral responsibilities toward the rest of nature, such responsibilities would certainly include protecting wilderness areas.

However, equating wilderness with purity and with nature's authentic map, and the corresponding equating of society with pollution, lead to a deeply problematic partition of the landscape. One part of the landscape is rigorously preserved while the other is abandoned to the ruthless founding activities of modern society and capitalism, as suggested by Pollan, who was quoted in the introduction. This partition mentality also encourages neglect of nonwild but ecologically stressed places, such as inner cities and poor rural communities faced with toxic pollution. Moreover, it encourages neglect of agricultural landscapes, which are not wild and are not always spectacular, but which are "often the environments that have the least protection and are disappearing the most rapidly."[199]

As we separate society from nature conceived of as wilderness, we also risk "condemn[ing] ourselves to spending most of our lives outside of nature, for there can be no permanent place for us inside."[200] We end up withdrawing from nature in order to save it. In the long run, this not only harms human beings by depriving them of much of their connection with the nonhuman world, but it also endangers the natural world itself by trivializing it. With "nature" far off in wilderness preserves, we might, like those aghast at the idea that someone would actually cut down a tree, forget our dependence on the rest of the biosphere and in the end regard ecological responsibility as a secondary concern.[201] We risk turning "nature" into a playground, pretty scenery, or entertainment, an inconsequential part of our lives.[202] This trivializing of nature actually encourages sprawl; people see nature as scenery and want to live close by it, but are unaware of the ecological costs.

The either-or approach to founding and preservation has also alienated resource communities from the environmental movement and hindered resolution of debates like the old-growth controversy. Caught between the imperatives of economic survival and the market on the one hand and the rigid preservationist demands of environmentalists on the other, individuals and communities involved in timber harvesting or other resource industries reject preservation entirely. Instead, they choose more immediate, tangible economic interests and see preservationist values as insensitive to local communities.

This either-or choice between unrestrained founding and uncompromising preservation also emerged in our other two case studies. Opponents of sprawl often articulated a hard-line preservationist approach. For New Urbanists, the 1920s planning model is itself a pregiven landscape that must be rediscovered. In the case of Ground Zero, the 9/11 families viewed the tragedy that occurred at the World Trade Center as a defining moment that shaped the area forever. The deaths of almost 3,000 people made Ground Zero a sacred burial spot, and any interference with the transformation of the spot into a memorial was an act of desecration. The 9/11 families relented somewhat and many of them accepted a memorial confined to the Twin Towers' footprints, but the

overall battle turned into one of commodity-minded development officials and real estate interests versus the preservation-minded families.
Too little scope was given to either the surrounding neighborhood's concerns or to a truly democratic determination of Ground Zero's future.
Ground Zero ended up being partitioned like the rest of the nation, into
separate zones for founding and preservation.

Many, although not all environmentalists, along with others who have
responded to the sweeping, destructive transformation of the world's
places, have abetted the crisis of place by rejecting a reintegration of
founding and preservation. They wield preservation as a defensive, counterproductive response to founding. This leaves no credible guidance for
individuals and communities on how they might pursue founding activities and properly balance founding and preservation.

Overcoming the crisis of place requires a reintegration of founding
and preservation. Such a reintegration would yield a broader framework
of how we ought to approach our relationships with our landscape, a
landscape that we inhabit and inevitably use but that we must also treat
with moral consideration and care. Such a reintegration would also
involve democratic deliberation about places and their proper care and
cultivation. I now turn to this framework, which I call *the working
landscape*.

6

The Working Landscape

In the previous chapters, we saw how the contemporary politics of place sets founding and preservation against one another. An overbalance of founding embodied in state building and capitalism is opposed by overly preservationist movements in defense of place. How do we resolve the crisis of place? Solutions to this crisis are partly beyond the scope of this book because they would involve transnational or supranational regulation of the global economy to curb the destabilizing aspects of globalization. Moreover, efforts to combat global environmental problems like climate change—which I discuss briefly at the end of this book—are also necessary to help prevent the degradation or outright loss of many places. However, there are land-use policies, especially at the subnational, regional level, that would go a long way toward addressing the crisis of place. This chapter accordingly provides the outlines for an approach to land use that balances and integrates founding and preservation and combats environmental degradation, sprawl, and authoritarian urban development. I do not provide a formula for combining founding and preservation in every place. These are two dimensions of place that are always necessary and yet always in tension, and it may at times be necessary to lean toward one or the other, depending on the particular place and time. There is no clear a priori standard for determining when either founding or preservation is excessive.[1] Instead, one has to pursue a set of political structures and practices that would best balance and integrate founding and preservation. In my view, a democratic, regional political framework provides the most promise for embracing both founding and preservation and restoring the practice of place. This framework I call the working landscape.

Defining the Working Landscape

The term *working landscape* generally refers to agricultural lands characterized by a long-standing balance between human and natural forces. We are not talking about the monotonous, chemical-intensive, mechanized monoculture of industrial agriculture. Rather, a working landscape is exemplified by a historic countryside that displays an intricate combination of cultivation and natural habitat. Tony Hiss describes such a landscape as one "whose function and look, or character, or feel, have been shaped over time by sequential, ongoing human activities as much as by natural processes."[2]

Working landscapes emerge through generations of interplay between founding and preservation. A working landscape maintains a distinctive character over time but also attends to the changing needs of those living and laboring there. Such a landscape is an ongoing, collective project of many individuals and generations. As examples of working landscapes, one might think of New Mexico's Hispano pastoral lands, terraced landscapes in the Andes, Pennsylvania's Amish country, Virginia's Piedmont, Italy's Tuscany region, the farm country of central New York, or the English countryside.

The idea of a working landscape need not be limited to rural areas or rustic settings. I intend to use the concept in a much more general sense. The interplay of founding and preservation, of economic and cultural vitality on the one hand and ecological stability and historical character on the other, can be exhibited by urban, suburban, and small-town neighborhoods and downtowns. I present the working landscape model on a regional level as a tapestry of many different but interrelated types of places, often ranging from wilderness to urban centers.

My proposals draw upon existing policies, proposals, and political movements, as I discuss in chapter 7. However, the overall framework of the working landscape is directly inspired by several other authors. As noted earlier, the concepts of founding and preservation come from Iris Marion Young. She also presents the sketches of a regional politics in *Justice and the Politics of Difference*.[3] The regional land-use program I outline here is even more heavily indebted to three other authors: John Barry, William Shutkin, and Peter Calthorpe.

Writing at the most theoretical level is Barry. In *Rethinking Green Politics*, Barry, a political theorist, offers a framework called "collective ecological management." As with my attempt to balance founding and preservation, Barry attempts to navigate between dominating and passively accepting nature.[4] His ethic of use emphasizes symbiotic interactions between humanity and nature that can simultaneously promote human goods, aspirations, and even progress, while also showing moral consideration and care for nonhuman nature.

As mentioned in chapter 5, Barry draws an important distinction between the use and abuse of nature. Proper use entails a reflective attitude that limits the transformation or destruction of the natural environment to the fulfillment of serious, nontrivial human interests. It also involves consideration of the interests of nonhuman nature, a caring attitude toward nonhuman nature, and attention to the goods involved in particular human relationships with nonhuman organisms or parts of the natural world, including place-based relationships. With regard to agriculture, for example, following Barry's ethic of use means that while "the land and animals are used and consumed, the former is not 'mined' or 'exploited' for short-term profit, nor are the latter treated purely as 'food resources'."[5] To consider nonhuman nature as nothing other than an economic resource or commodity, as in factory farming,[6] is to cross over into abuse. "The 'ethic of use' is thus a particular way of acting in the world, which while being respectful of the non-human world, does not lapse into a submissive 'quietism'."[7]

This distinction between use and abuse is similar to my own position; namely, that we may change the landscape through founding and refounding but that we must also pay attention to the social and ecological character of places and temper founding with preservationist considerations. Founding without preservation is abusive in that it leads to the pure instrumentalization of places, i.e., their treatment as objects to be disposed of at will, just like animals in a factory farm. On the other hand, a preservationist injunction against any founding or other use leads to passive acquiescence to the given natural or built environment, which prevents the ongoing creation of a meaningful, habitable landscape.

An ethic of use yields what Barry, borrowing from ecologist Eugene Odum, calls an "anthropogenic subclimax," which is similar to a working landscape. An anthropogenic subclimax is a landscape "transformed by and in part the combined outcome of human intentional activity and natural processes."[8] There is no one anthropogenic subclimax or landscape, but a "range within which stewardship is operative."[9] While this niche certainly includes agricultural and urban landscapes,[10] Barry suggests that the range of landscapes subject to stewardship can also include wilderness, which requires human management for its protection.[11] The concept of anthropogenic subclimax highlights the complex and potentially symbiotic way in which human beings and the rest of nature interact in the creation of a landscape, and how those interactions generate a variety of landscapes covering a range from wild to intensively settled and urbanized.

There are historical, cultural, and moral dimensions to Barry's landscape. An anthropogenic subclimax is "not the work of the present generation alone, but … of many previous generations." Such a landscape can therefore be a basis for the formation of collective identity.[12] Interactions with the landscape can also generate local or regional cultural knowledge of place and involve strong moral commitments.[13] Such commitments can involve care for nonhuman nature, not just in the wilderness, but in more humanized places like gardens.[14]

Barry's ethic of use and his concept of the anthropogenic subclimax reflect his refusal to automatically favor either development—what I would term founding—or preservation:

[C]ollective ecological management requires that there be no presupposition in favour of either preservation or development. Rather such issues must be resolved politically, which can be understood that no form of environmental valuation or human interest in the world is exempt from public criticism and justification, particularly in the case of major land-use proposals, for example, road-building, mining, and dam-building. The onus of justification falls equally on all who propose particular social-environmental relations. From a democratic point of view, we simply cannot say in advance whether "use" or "non-use" will be the outcome.[15]

The proper mixture of development, or founding, and preservation must thus be determined democratically, through a deliberative process. While collective ecological management places a major share of political, economic, and ecological governance at the global and national levels, Barry also emphasizes decentralizing decision making, where it is appropriate, to the state or local level.[16] He warns that "a centralized, bureaucratic organization such as that associated with the contemporary nation-state may be ecologically rational across only a specific range of environmental problems."[17] Instead, the governance structure must be multilayered, flexible in dealing with changes in social-ecological systems, and reliant not just on top-down scientific expertise, but also on culturally and geographically embedded local knowledge.[18] This entails a significant role for bottom-up, participatory approaches to decision making.[19] We will see such principles in collaborative conservation, the Northwest Forest Plan, and the environmental justice movement.

Barry argues that inclusive, discursive, democratic institutions would be open to new information and hence would be flexible in the face of ecological change. Moreover, such institutions could cultivate citizens' collective knowledge and judgment of the relations through which society interacts with the natural environment.[20] He singles out land-use policy as especially appropriate for democratic deliberation.[21]

Barry provides a compelling theoretical perspective for balancing and integrating founding and preservation. However, despite a few examples, his discussion does not explore practical applications of the ethic of use or provide detailed illustrations of an anthropogenic subclimax. Shutkin and Calthorpe advance more practical programs for a politics of place that embraces both founding and preservation.

Shutkin's book *The Land That Could Be* offers the framework of *civic environmentalism*: "Civic environmentalism entails a set of core concepts that embraces civic action and community planning on the part of a diverse group of stakeholders aimed at promoting both environmental protection and democratic renewal: participatory process, community and regional planning, environmental education, industrial ecology, environmental justice, and place."[22] Although Shutkin does not match Barry's theoretical depth, he provides an excellent set of detailed case studies of a place-based politics aimed at both the ecological preservation and economic and social revitalization of localities and regions, ranging from rural to urban. Like Barry, Shutkin also favors participatory democracy.

One major difference between my own approach and Shutkin's concerns formal regional governance. Shutkin emphasizes building "the civic capacity of communities to engage in effective environmental problem-solving."[23] He also advocates a regional approach that links the common concerns of urban, suburban, and regional constituencies about public goods, such as protection of open space and environmental quality. He says, "The focus is on coordinating regional land use and development, and devising systems of governance bigger than local but smaller than state and federal governments that are matched to the scale of regional problems."[24] However, his overall approach to governance and his examples lean more to ad hoc coalition building and shifting and overlapping partnerships among public and private groups and jurisdictions. By contrast, I believe that formal, enduring regional political structures are necessary for good land-use planning.

Calthorpe is the least theoretical of the three authors, but he goes further than even Shutkin in developing a coherent regional framework for land-use planning. Calthorpe is a well-known New Urbanist; he favors the high-density, pedestrian-friendly planning that is central to this movement. However, he departs from other New Urbanists in being much less focused on design as a determining factor in urban life. This rescues him from some of the problems of New Urbanism discussed in chapter 3.

In *The Regional City*, Calthorpe and his collaborator William Fulton certainly put great emphasis on design. However, they also recognize that design is not sufficient to reverse the damaging effects of decades of sprawl, environmentally destructive development, and urban disinvestment. Design must be "married to a set of progressive regional policies."[25] These include tax sharing between localities, development assistance to inner-city communities, affordable housing, transportation networks serving the working poor, improvement of schools, and provision of other educational opportunities.[26] My major difference with Calthorpe and Fulton is that they disavow the need for new governmental forms to deal with regional problems, saying that the creation of a comprehensive set of policies does not necessarily require new levels of government, at either the regional or the neighborhood level. They argue, "Every metropolitan region already has a policy and institutional framework that can serve as the foundation for a consistent regional strategy."[27] However, jurisdictional fragmentation hinders sound regional policy making. The history of the World Trade Center and Ground Zero shows how the current institutional framework in metropolitan areas can generate unaccountable and confusing or invisible power structures. What is required instead is a coherent, democratically constituted regional government.

Founding, Preservation, and Democracy

As I have emphasized, places are sites of competing perspectives. Diverse individuals, communities, and constituencies negotiate the character of their shared geography. Common habitation requires ongoing, perpetual negotiation. Such negotiation inevitably involves power relations, including political and class structures. Negotiation may proceed democratically in that the contesting parties are fairly equal in power. Or, one or a few parties may impose an outcome, as the Port Authority has repeatedly done in the New York City area, abrogating meaningful deliberation and enforcing their own vision of a place. This group may act in an authoritarian, hierarchical, or exclusionary manner, bypassing collective deliberation about founding and/or preservation. We saw such undemocratic planning in each of our three cases. In each case, both those favoring founding and those favoring preservation acted in an antidemocratic manner by trying to shut out, constrain, or ignore input from those not sharing their particular view of a place.

Because the meaning and character of every place is inevitably contested, some parties will be more likely to see a place as in need of change, or refounding, while others will want to preserve what they see as a place's essential character. A fully inclusive and deliberative process would necessarily bring in both founding- and preservation-oriented perspectives. Such a democratic approach would therefore be more likely to balance founding and preservation. Conversely, when either founding or preservation are pursued to an extreme, political actors will try to exclude their opponents from meaningful democratic participation. They will try to delegitimize opposing voices, perhaps by branding them as enemies of progress or environmental despoilers, or as insensitive to a recent tragedy.

A democratic process that brings in a variety of voices is thus a key step toward balancing and integrating founding and preservation. Ideally, a democratic approach here means that all those in some way involved with a place ought to have direct input into its creation, shaping, interpretation, and care, even if that place is privately owned or is under the jurisdiction of a particular government entity. A democratic approach sees all inhabitants or users of an area as stakeholders with a prima facie right to a collective voice in the management even of private property.[28] Indeed, as discussed in chapter 1, one may question the degree to which property in land is ever really private, given the enormous ecological and social impacts of land use.[29] As I discuss later, democratic governance of place can best flourish through the creation of regional political structures.

Democratic Deliberation Need Not Entail Communal Harmony

Although it is intended to generate actual decisions, democratic deliberation about places does not require mutual agreement on the character of a place. Some measure of ongoing disagreement is not only inevitable, but it also enriches and enlivens places with a complexity of meanings and enables people to debate and respond to changing social and ecological conditions. The ideal is therefore not seamless communal harmony about a shared place, but an inclusive, ongoing conversation about that place, with enough points of resolution to make decision making possible. Although decisions are made, there is always the possibility of reconsideration or revision in the future. In such a context, it is evident that far from suppressing or denying politics or difference, place attachments can generate contestation and sustain plurality.

However, there must be some commonality surrounding a place. Some commonality is necessary for a conversation to be possible at all, i.e., if there is to be anything to discuss. "Deliberative speech," notes Dana Villa, "must be anchored in a shared world" that is the object of some minimum agreement. "Where such an agreement dissolves or is shattered, it is no longer possible to view the same thing from a variety of perspectives." For deliberation and even conflict about a place to be at all possible, there must be shared concern about that place and shared recognition that that place is in some way significant.[30]

When parties are able to deliberate rather than resort to violence, the conversation and argument about places can create varying levels of coexistence or community. The debate can generate shared cultural practices, a shared public life, shared patterns for dwelling together, and even a shared sense of community.[31] Ideally, a shared conversation can ease some of the deepest, most divisive conflicts about a place.[32] Barry says that "a virtue of responsible green citizenship is a willingness to accommodate the interests of others, within an expanded conception of the 'ecological common good'."[33] Again, this does not require an undifferentiated, homogeneous community. Rather, it can be described as what Villa calls a "shared enterprise," a "partnership, in argument and conversation."[34] Later, I discuss some institutional structures for deliberation.

Has the Governance of Places Become More Democratic?

One might ask whether land-use politics and the governance of places have become more or less inclusive and democratic in recent years, despite the trends discussed in chapter 5. In some ways there has been a move toward more democracy over the past half century, even as governments and globalized corporations have exerted enormous power over the creation of places. Environmental and neighborhood and historic preservation groups have organized against urban renewal, sprawl, and ecological degradation. Citizens' groups and the general public have demanded more accountability on the part of public and private development interests and sought more transparent, inclusive planning processes. Citizens participate in land-use planning through advisory boards, stakeholder committees, public hearings, public referenda, town meetings, and public review of design proposals or environmental impact statements. They also participate by taking on government and the private sector in the courts. These avenues of participation have been promoted through federal and state legislation, perhaps most notably the National Environmental Policy Act of 1970. Moreover, one need only compare the authoritarian, top-down building of the World Trade Center with the rebuilding of Ground Zero, which at least attempted a *semblance* of democratic participation, to see that the public now expects more of a voice in land use.

However, the Ground Zero redevelopment also shows how public participation is often little more than a showpiece. Indeed, the degree of public participation on land-use issues is still too limited to effectively challenge many development projects or significantly inhibit the current trend toward explosive, sprawling development. As we have seen, individuals and communities often assent to economic development out of a sense of powerlessness or resignation to the inevitability of "progress" rather than because of genuine agreement. Furthermore, as we have seen, there has been a decline in the public spaces and interactions necessary to nurture place-based democracy.

Entrenched power structures can perpetuate the dominance of particular groups with either founding or preservationist agendas.[35] Those in power will also use places to suppress, constrain, or discipline; here one might think of prisons, reformatories, schools, hospitals, workplaces, and the modern, "rationally" planned cityscapes or farms discussed in chapter 5.[36] Moreover, powerful groups will use places to inculcate certain ideologies.[37] Monuments, places of worship, public buildings, schools, officially designated historical sites, architectural designs, and even wilderness areas have all been used to uphold ideological systems.

Different political and economic systems will also operate through distinctive types of places.[38] Liberal democracy finds its expression through the voting booth and the parliamentary building. The successive modes of production of feudalism and industrial capitalism were realized, respectively, through the manor and the factory. Postindustrial capitalism has favored the office high-rise and, more recently, the office park. Modernity as a worldview has favored a built environment emphasizing, among other things, the highway as a means of rapid, personalized transportation.

Dominant class, cultural, or political forces often maintain power through hegemonic discourses about places or place in general. Hegemony is the dominance of a ruling class or faction through beliefs and values that naturalize such domination. Hegemonic discourses shape ideas about place so as to legitimate certain power structures.[39] Such discourses can operate even in the presence of ostensibly democratic political processes. As a result, certain conceptions of place are accepted, whether willingly or grudgingly, by the populace. For instance, the association of sprawl with inevitable "progress" plays into the hands of political and corporate powers seeking to commodify places. Massey describes a related hegemonic discourse in the ideological notion of the inevitability of globalization and its homogenization of the world's places.[40]

Hegemonic discourses will often favor certain concepts of place over lived experience. Timber workers in the Northwest are trapped by a hegemonic discourse about markets, progress, and nature's disorder that makes them accept the unrestrained exploitation of forests even though such unsustainable exploitation ultimately undermines their own livelihoods. For democratic control of places to be meaningful, hegemonic discourses must be challenged and demystified.[41]

These considerations suggest limits to any recent democratization of land-use politics, and also warn us that an increase in formal democratic participation is not sufficient to ensure substantive democracy. Moreover, as we have seen, even if there is genuine democratic debate, polarization between extreme versions of founding and preservation can prevent an effective integration of the two and result in a division of the landscape into an either/or pattern, with some areas entirely subject to founding and others set aside purely for preservation.

Place-Based Democracy by Default?

Democratic governance of place may perhaps emerge by default. Although the founding or preservation of a place might initially proceed undemocratically, public habitation or use may ultimately reshape that place and claim it for the populace as a whole. Harvey thus recounts the history of New York City's Times Square.[42] Formerly Longacre Square, Times Square was built as a speculative real-estate and business venture at the turn of the twentieth century. The crowds drawn by its advertising spectacle transformed this spot into a democratic meeting place in which all sectors of the city's population mingled. The Square "became the symbolic heart of New York city [*sic*] and, until its decline (largely under the impact of television) from the 1950s onwards, was the focus of a sense of togetherness and community for many New Yorkers and even, for a while, for many Americans. Times Square became the symbolic place where everyone congregated to celebrate, mourn, or express their collective anger, joy, or fear." With the growth of television and other mass media, Times Square declined in importance and became a center of sleaze, yet it remained famous for the throngs gathered there on New Years Eve to watch the "Ball" drop.

Unfortunately, democratization by default is gradual, limited, and precarious. First, Times Square was appropriated from the public by the sex industry, which brought crime and blight. Although some intellectuals and artists might now romanticize the area's culturally subversive sleaze,[43] Times Square had become depressing and dangerous. However, its revitalization in the 1990s did not really win the area back for the public. As Harvey notes, the recent redevelopment of Times Square has meant its "Disneyfication."[44] The area is now occupied by the establishments and imagery of global capitalism—Disney, Toys Я Us, The Gap, etc.—making it seem more like a recreation of a suburban shopping mall. Although it continues to be a gathering place, Times Square has thus lost much of its public character. It has been reappropriated by corporate interests, significantly reversing its prior democratization.

Moreover, the democratization of Times Square may be a less typical story today. Fewer places built in the past half century have been available for public appropriation the way Times Square was. The modernist architecture that characterized the World Trade Center and other urban renewal projects was so outwardly hostile to nature and history,[45] and so homogeneous, austere, and forbidding in design, as to be resistant to public reinterpretation and use. Recall Gillespie's observation that the simplicity of the World Trade Center did not lend itself to a richness or multiplicity of readings. The abstract austerity of the World Trade Center and other modernist structures in fact impoverished the lived experience of such places.[46] Also, the vast, windswept plazas of modern construction have created alienating spaces, even when public space was deliberately included (although poorly conceived).

The contemporary shopping mall, big-box store, or gated community is resistant to public reappropriation for its own set of reasons. As discussed in chapter 3, these icons of sprawl offer little in the way of actual public space, not even windswept plazas. The built environment is increasingly devoted to the automobile—roadways and parking lots—on the one hand and highly controlled, fenced-in corporate or other private space on the other. There is simply nowhere for large numbers of people to freely congregate and engage in a variety of social, political, and cultural activities, and numerous forms of public expression are forbidden.

A Regional Approach

To be truly meaningful and effective and avoid some of the problems outlined here, a democratic approach would require significant changes in land-use policy making and governance to actually secure democratic participation and also prevent such participation from being counterproductive.

As discussed in chapter 3, the current fragmentation of land-use powers among thousands of small municipalities leaves local governments too small to effectively control development, growth, and economic investment. Instead, localities within a metropolitan area or other region find themselves in mutual competition for jobs and property tax revenue. Localities offer incentives to developers, thus straining public budgets and encouraging sprawl, or affluent communities that do not need more development successfully refuse LULUs and pass them off on their neighbors. Local democracy would not solve the problems of municipal fragmentation, and can even exacerbade them.

The best approach for democratization is an elected regional or metropolitan government coupled with local governance on legitimately local issues. The dilution of formal local municipal autonomy would not result in a true loss of democracy, for localities would be much more empowered through collective control over their region. Furthermore, bringing a wider variety of perspectives, discourses, interests, and constituencies to the table in a regional forum would create a more inclusive debate and enhance democratic deliberation. Founding- and preservation-oriented perspectives are more likely to both be included, and there is more likelihood that hegemonic discourses might be diluted or countered as many voices gain a forum.

The need for regionalism also arises from the impossibility of finding a precise formula for combining founding and preservation. Not even democratic deliberation can define such a formula. Founding and preservation exist in a kind of dialectic or creative contradiction.[47] Places embody both flux and permanence. They are defined or founded by processes, and out of those processes emerge relative permanences, which eventually break down to enable new processes of formation or new foundings.[48] Maintaining these two dimensions of place entails ongoing negotiation and a navigation of conflicts between the two, and at times more of an emphasis on either founding or preservation as circumstances demand.

For example, when the survival of an ecosystem is at stake, it would make sense to limit physically transformative founding activities like real estate or resource development, although founding activities aimed at subsequent preservation, such as creating parks or wilderness areas, would be advisable. If, on the other hand, a rural region faces severe economic distress, wilderness preservation might have to more fully accommodate economic development.

Although place incorporates both founding and preservation, individual locations, whether conceived of as separate places or as locales within places, might distinguish themselves by reflecting either one of these dimensions of place somewhat more than the other, and the two sorts of places can play off each other. Locations that are more dynamic and subject to refounding can offer outlets for certain aspirations that would be more limited in heavily protected ecosystems, in historic areas, or in people's homes. By contrast, preserved places, as we saw when discussing the concept of home, can provide a stable anchor for individual or collective identity or a setting for reflecting on how identities have changed. Such places can also enable a critical perspective on society at large, particularly in times of disruptive social change, and can provide ecological and cultural sustenance for more dynamic places.

To address the danger of simply partitioning the landscape into commodified real estate and sealed-off preserves, citizens and policy makers should adopt a landscape, or regional, perspective, embracing an interrelated, coordinated mosaic of different kinds of places (and in most cases avoiding extremes of either founding or preservation even at the local level) and balancing founding and preservation across the region. In virtually all cases, critical social and physical aspects of a landscape, such as natural ecosystems, recreational areas, prime or historic agricultural land, long-established societal networks, prosperous businesses (especially those that are locally owned), aesthetically pleasing architecture, sidewalks and other provisions for pedestrian access, high-density urban centers, usable public spaces and parks, and cultural and historical landmarks, should be preserved.

At the same time, impoverished agricultural or urban areas should be revitalized or redeveloped so that local inhabitants can secure a viable, prosperous way of life and have access to basic amenities, such as jobs, health care, quality housing, and education. Such development must not be based solely on economic or other material considerations, as Barry notes. One must think of certain land uses, like farming, for example, as social practices having certain intrinsic goods and not simply erase them in the name of "progress." To continue the example, farming should be viewed not just as crop production but as "a way of life which expresses particular biocultural values and virtues."[49] Similarly, Barry says that work in crafts and local enterprises should also be seen as cultivating a way of life, and as involving "internal goods ... such as autonomy, solidarity, creativity, and innovation, education, self-esteem, and self-confidence."[50] Moving activities like work away from purely economic considerations and back toward the status of intrinsically valuable pursuits would reembed them into their social and ecological context,[51] and revive connections between people and place.

Regional Organizing Principles

A region would be organized around certain common ecological and social characteristics and would function as an interdependent system of people and nonhuman organisms, built and natural environments, and all the conflicting interests and forces embodied therein. Therefore, despite its shared, defining characteristics, a region would also be considerably pluralist, diverse, and fractious.

A Wide Range of Places and Functions

A regional working landscape would embody a wide range of places, in some cases all the way from wilderness to urban, and its government would have a variety of responsibilities or functions. A working landscape would incorporate protected wilderness areas and historic districts, as well as areas slated for economic development. Some areas might also be protected to provide a continuing land base for small-scale resource producers and rural ways of life that might otherwise be destroyed by the market. The whole continuum of land uses embodied in the working landscape would not only integrate founding and preservation, but would also provide a rich tapestry of places to visit or inhabit. Calthorpe and Fulton envision a region made up of mixed-use population and economic centers (village, town, and urban); special-use districts such as universities or airports; preserves for agriculture and natural habitat; greenbelts to define regional and community boundaries; and corridors for greenways, transportation, and infrastructure.[52] Shutkin similarly discusses how state officials in New Jersey have attempted to integrate the state's diverse landscapes into a plan for managing New Jersey's future population growth and economic development.[53]

Regional government would be charged with coordinating land-use policies, including planning for development, preservation, and transportation. Regional government should manage utilities like water and sewer systems and solid waste disposal. It should address regional sources of air and water pollution, although interregional pollution problems like acid rain would be a federal responsibility.

Regional government should also allocate public spending among communities to equalize significant disparities in services, education, infrastructure, housing, public amenities like parks, and LULUs like waste dumps or sewage treatment plants. To facilitate such equalization, a regional government should be able to redistribute resources among localities. Such redistribution could be achieved through regional taxation authority or regional sharing of federal, state, or local tax revenues. Wim Wiewel and Kimberly Schaffer suggest that localities could share property tax revenue, an approach pursued in Minneapolis-St. Paul.[54] Suburbs often object to revenue sharing out of fear that they will have to subsidize the city. However, the reverse can turn out to be true, especially as older suburbs are increasingly in need of resources.[55]

As Wiewel and Schaffer point out, localities need to reduce their reliance on their own property tax revenue. Dependence on property taxes to fund education and other services encourages localities to compete for business investment and development, leading to more sprawl. It also contributes to inequities among communities, most visibly in regard to education, because some places have a larger tax base than others.[56] Moreover, as communities try to keep tax revenues ahead of school expenditures, they encourage large houses on large lots, which produce high tax revenues but fewer children per developed acre.[57] This means more exclusionary, sprawling development.

What Is a "Region"?

What is a region? A region is itself a place with unifying characteristics.[58] A region, however, is on the spatial scale of a metropolitan area[59] or a watershed and thus embraces many smaller localities.

Regions, like other places, are human constructs.[60] Although regions often reflect natural relations or characteristics, their boundaries are not predetermined by nature, contrary to the claims of bioregionalists like Sale. First, the boundaries of a region, even of a natural ecosystem, need to be specified by human beings. Natural regions and ecosystems blend into one another, overlap, or are nested one inside another. Ultimately, human beings must decide what natural characteristics and geographic features are most relevant in defining a particular region. Second, regions are often delineated in social terms, including formal jurisdictional boundaries, infrastructure and other built structures, demographics, economic activities and relations, and less tangible qualities, such as "ideas, loyalties, a sense of belonging, structures of feeling, ways of life, memories and history, imagined community, and the like."[61] Young, focusing on mainly social characteristics, says that a region ought to be defined as "both an economic unit and a territory that people identify as their living space. A region is the space across which people commonly travel to work, shop, play, visit their friends, and take the children on errands, the span of a day trip. It is the range of television and radio transmission." It is also the territory within which major distribution of goods occurs.[62]

Regions are generally defined in terms of *both* natural and social characteristics. We can think of the New York metropolitan area in terms of its topography and its location at the nexus of the Hudson River, Long Island Sound, and Atlantic Ocean. We also define the area in terms of political jurisdictions, including the five boroughs and the adjacent counties in New York, New Jersey, and Connecticut, as well as in terms of settlement patterns and concentrations of people and buildings, transportation networks and other physical infrastructure, regional industries, and regional demographic profile. There are also the less tangible but no less important characteristics: the region's maritime history, its cultural diversity, its moderate-to-liberal politics, its cosmopolitanism, brashness, and pretensions to sophistication, its fast-paced life, and its focus on Manhattan as a de facto regional capital.

A region must have boundaries to be coherent. However, if there is a mismatch between natural and social boundaries, which sort of boundary should take precedence? Once again, there is no formula. It depends. A region should be defined in a way that best facilitates the livelihoods and mutual flourishing of both its human and nonhuman constituents. In urbanized parts of the country the bounds of the region would more closely reflect social qualities, while in rural areas the bounds would more likely conform to ecological or other natural features.

In terms of the sheer practicality of creating a new political jurisdiction like a region, and in the interests of tempering the founding of a regional entity with some preservationist sensibilities, one possible guideline would be to build on existing, familiar boundaries, particularly political boundaries. Thus a regional government for the New York City metropolitan area would necessarily transcend state boundaries but its outer bounds might be defined by existing county lines.

Metropolitan Regions as Polycentric

The U.S. Census Bureau defines metropolitan areas in terms of a population nucleus and its surrounding communities,[63] yet metropolitan regions can no longer be considered monocentric. The model of a central city surrounded by suburbs is increasingly outmoded. As Calthorpe and Fulton recognize in their own regional planning model, partly because of sprawl metropolitan areas have become polycentric and crisscrossed by transportation and communication networks connecting large and small cities and suburbs.[64] For example, despite the continued prominence of Manhattan, the population centers in the New York metropolitan area include not only Manhattan and the other boroughs of New York City but also New York's Nassau County and the cities of Newark, White Plains, New Haven, and Stamford, to name just a few.

Polycentric does not mean acentric, however. Many regions are also still economically and culturally defined by one or more urban centers, even with Castells' space of flows. As Castells reminds us, by providing concentrations of skilled labor, face-to-face business interactions, and cultural and consumer resources, such cities remain epicenters of economic activity, even if much activity has dispersed to the suburbs.

While centers still matter, metropolitan regions are not neatly divided between cities and suburbs. The physical distinction between the two is often blurred by sprawl and by older suburbs' increasing commonality, in terms of demographics and density, with cities. Moreover, the notion that cities are declining as suburbs flourish is not always accurate because some central cities, like New York, San Francisco, and Boston, are doing well, while many American suburbs, especially older ones, are declining.[65]

Regional Self-Reliance

Even with globalization, regions are still organized around unifying social factors, including economic and cultural characteristics, social and political outlook, home industries (such as automobile manufacturing, aerospace, information technology, or tourism) or distinctive agricultural or other resource-related activities. Even international commerce, migration, and investment, which tend to flatten distinctions among places, can in some cases help give a region its particular character, as global economic transactions have done with the New York City area. In fact, Castells' networked globalization may be particularly suited to regionalism as metropolitan areas play an increasingly important role in the global economy. Calthorpe and Fulton echo an increasingly common view in the geography literature when they say, "In today's global economy, it is regions, not nations, that vie for economic dominance throughout the world."[66]

Despite globalization, some measure of regional economic self-reliance is desirable. Barry rejects calls from some environmentalists for local or regional self-sufficiency. Self-sufficiency is too inward looking and unreasonably autarkic. He rightly prefers self-reliance: "Whereas self-sufficiency as a virtue implies a notion of detachment, and an inward-looking, almost contemplative disposition of inner contentment, self-reliance ... conveys a sense of autonomy, independence, and self-determination."[67] Unlike self-sufficiency, self-reliance does not entail total disengagement from global markets, but increased independence from them.

Self-reliant regions would promote the processing and/or consumption of their own resources, such as locally harvested timber and food. This would enhance democratic control over founding and preservation. Regions would have more power to set their own political and economic goals and policies because producers and businesses would be more insulated from fluctuations of the global marketplace. Self-reliance could also reduce environmental abuse, especially impacts between regions, in that producers and consumers would have to contend more directly with the environmental impacts of their behavior rather than raiding other parts of the world for profit. Moreover, self-reliance, in shortening the links between production and consumption, would once again make geographic relations more tangible, strengthen regional identities and place attachments, and create easily accessible markets for nearby producers. Self-reliance would also improve the quality of perishable products, which would not have to be shipped long distances, and save money and energy through reduced transportation needs.[68]

Self-reliance at the right regional scale would also limit externalities between local communities or regions. Oran Young maintains that a political unit ought to be sufficiently large to capture, or internalize, major externalities.[69] In other words, communities should not simply foist the impacts of environmentally destructive behavior onto another jurisdiction or free-ride on their neighbors' efforts to maintain environmental quality. Similarly, communities should not routinely draw investment and public spending away from one another or pass along LULUs or wastes. Jurisdictions must be sufficiently large to encompass relations of ecological and economic interdependence and their associated spillovers.

However, in a globalized economy, many externalities simply cannot be captured within a region. These include impacts on the Earth's atmosphere; on global climate; on the health of the oceans; and on migratory organisms such as birds, fish, or certain insects. Furthermore, much international trade cannot be replaced by regionally based commerce for the simple reason that not all areas are equally endowed with food crops and natural resources. In all these cases, the appropriate level of regulation is national or global, although implementation may sometimes be at the regional level. Governing institutions need to be organized at various scales, as they already are in federal systems. The regional level is but one such scale, albeit an important one.

Regional Democracy

I call for democratic processes to combine founding and preservation, yet I also advocate regionalism. Can regionalism be democratic? Yes.[70]

Although creating a regional government would mean curbing or eliminating the autonomy of small suburban municipalities, an elected regional government would actually empower citizens and localities. First of all, a single, elected regional government would be more democratic and accountable than a confusing tangle of special-purpose regional agencies. A regional government would replace unaccountable public authorities, like the Port Authority. Such special jurisdictions, while having a broader geographic purview than many local governments, have an excessively narrow policy scope, and as the story of the World Trade Center makes clear, are often not publicly accountable, are excessively friendly with special economic interests, and are barely understood by the public, who view government in terms of elected officials. With an elected regional government, development policies, like those pursued at Ground Zero, would be more directly subject to public input and review.

Second, a single, elected regional government would also replace the current jurisdictional fragmentation in each metropolis or at least establish significant cooperation among localities. As noted earlier, municipal fragmentation is falsely democratic, as localities are too small to control economic forces and development and end up in mutual competition. Regionally coordinated governance can empower localities by collectively giving them more meaningful control over land use, economic investment and development, and environmental quality.

Third, specific institutional arrangements could combine regional government with meaningful participation at the local level. Many proposals revolve around what john a. powell calls "federated regionalism,"[71] in which local and regional institutions divide responsibilities based on the scope of particular issues. For example, in the area of transportation networks, localities could deal with speed limits, street repairs, snow removal, traffic signs and lights, and the siting of bus shelters.[72]

Some proposals for combining regional and local democracy would create direct institutional links between the two levels of government. Iris Young suggests neighborhood assemblies that would send representatives to a regional government.[73] Another approach is a federative structure arranged as a pyramid in which groups at each level have a certain measure of institutional competence and authority. Such groups federate, through several layers of consolidation, into organizations covering a broader part of the community, eventually culminating in an executive committee at the top. Elinor Ostrom points to such structures in the regional or local governance of common property resources in places throughout the world.[74] These pyramid structures have been created to govern irrigation systems, fisheries, and groundwater basins. On the other hand, instead of a vertical structure like a unified regional government or a federative pyramid, Gerald Frug envisions a more horizontal relationship among localities. Through the forum of a regional legislature, separate localities would negotiate with one another on zoning and development issues.[75] I would favor a directly elected regional executive, council, or legislature, because this would provide the clearest account-ability to individual citizens. An elected regional council governs the Portland, Oregon, metro area, as we will see.

Local democratic participation can also be organized on a more ad hoc basis through temporary citizens' advisory boards or through shift-ing coalitions of advocacy groups. Such ad hoc institutions can play a key role in addressing a temporary, unique, and pressing problem. The Ground Zero redevelopment is perhaps the epitome of such a problem. An unusual range of participants—from bereaved families to real estate developers—were brought together by 9/11 and then engaged in an ad hoc planning process, although one that turned out to be profoundly and fatally flawed. Ad hoc approaches to local participation and gover-nance have often been pushed by, for example, collaborative conser-vation and environmental justice groups, although in some cases the resulting ad hoc groups have taken on quasi-official governance roles. The ad hoc approach has also been adopted by architects and planners interested in public participation. An example is the charette, a demo-cratic professional design workshop held over several days to plan land development or redevelopment. It includes public meetings in which the stakeholders are brought together. Participants typically include developers, architects, citizens, public officials, traffic engineers, and envi-ronmentalists.[76] Charettes have often been organized by New Urbanist planners.

Though authors like David Schlosberg have powerfully advocated an ad hoc, coalitional approach to democratic environmental politics,[77] I believe that this approach is ultimately inadequate. For one thing, ad hoc approaches do not provide long-term institutional accountability. There is no guarantee that an ad hoc group formed around an issue to-day will still exist in the future to deal with a similar issue or follow up on the original one. Moreover, the absence of a formal, enduring structure means that those who lack the time or resources to actually participate in an ad hoc group during its lifetime will be excluded from the process. I further address this issue below.

Whatever the arrangement for combining democratic empowerment and regional or other large-scale coordination, a larger jurisdiction need not micromanage smaller ones. Larger units might set standards or draw up the broad outlines of regional land-use plans, build planning or regulatory capacity at the local level, and allow smaller units discretion in implementation. For example, under a regional plan for equitably sharing sewage treatment plants or other LULUs among localities, an individual municipality might have discretion over where to actually site its share of these facilities.

Democratic Architecture

Regional democracy also requires a built environment that is suited to an active civic life. Earlier, I criticized New Urbanists for their almost exclusive focus on urban design as a basis for community. New Urbanist practice has also fallen far short of the movement's own often admirable principles. However, New Urbanists are right in seeing some forms of urban planning as more conducive to a vibrant civic life than others,[78] and their design proposals have promise. New Urbanism owes a good deal to Jacobs' critique of urban renewal and her alternative model for cities. Vibrant urban life and a functional urban community, Jacobs tells us, require multipurpose districts, short blocks, close-grained mingling of old and new buildings, and dense concentrations of people.[79] New Urbanist design emphasizes a city or town rich in mixed-use districts and plenty of public gathering places. In such an urban landscape, individuals can have multifaceted, repeated, and informal interactions. While they often have no apparent direct purpose, such interactions build the relationships that create a functional social order. Public gathering places include town squares, sidewalks, streets, and parks, as well as schools, post offices, stores, cafes, community centers, restaurants, bars, laundromats, health clubs, and newsstands.[80] Such gathering places should be in close proximity to one another and to residential districts, so that people can walk from place to place and encounter one another along the way. New Urbanism also advocates a diversity of housing types within individual neighborhoods, so that people of different incomes and ages can be accommodated and brought together.

While insufficient on its own, in combination with other public policies New Urbanist design can *help* cultivate the informal networks that build social capital, neighborhood, and community; foster interaction among persons of diverse backgrounds; build a shared sense of place; and nurture a more active civic life.[81]

A Role for "Outsiders"?

Can a regional, democratic system of governance give voice to those who live outside a region but have a legitimate interest in what goes on there? For example, both the old-growth forests and Ground Zero are extremely significant places to many people living outside the Pacific Northwest or New York City. The problem of national constituencies and others outside a region can perhaps be addressed through the involvement of state or federal officials in local or regional bodies, as we will see with collaborative conservation. One might also give outsiders a voice through advisory bodies or direct representation. Another strategy that has been tried is to give local or regional bodies the power to craft and implement policies, but under federal or state supervision. One example, which I discuss later, was the provision for locally managed adaptive management areas in President Clinton's Northwest Forest Plan. Under this program, local citizens' groups like southwest Oregon's Applegate Partnership worked with and under the oversight of federal officials, with the latter presumably representing the views of outside, national constituencies. There is also the example of the Quincy Library Group (QLG), a citizens' group in northern California. Federal legislation in 1998 devolved management of three national forests, the Lassen, Plumas, and Tahoe, an area totaling 4,000 square miles, or 2.5 million acres, to the QLG, under the oversight of Congress.[82]

In some cases, a more temporary, ad hoc procedure might be the best means for engaging local or regional groups with external or national ties or constituencies. Again, this was halfheartedly tried with the rebuilding of Ground Zero. A much more successful example was the 1974–1977 Mackenzie Valley Pipeline Inquiry in Canada's Northwest Territories. The inquiry managed to combine local participation with decision making for a vast area of the country and also involve Canadians outside the affected region.[83] The inquiry investigated the impacts of a proposed project to construct pipelines in northern Canada to bring oil and gas to the southern part of the country and to the United States. Justice Thomas R. Berger, who directed the inquiry, held an exhaustive series of local, publicly broadcast hearings throughout Canada to determine the social, ecological, and economic impacts of the project and develop recommendations on whether it should go forward. Through the hearings, he created a dialogue among all concerned parties, both within the affected region and around the nation.

The existence of interested outsiders illustrates the fluid nature of the boundaries of places and regions and the difficulty of distinguishing what is internal from what is external. Harvey speaks of "a fluid but highly complex interaction between processes and institutions operating at a variety of quite different spatial scales (such as nation, regional, metropolitan and local)."[84] This might suggest that regional boundaries and institutions should themselves be temporary and ad hoc, perhaps based on coalitions organized around specific issues. Furthermore, Schlosberg suggests that shifting, decentralized, ad hoc coalitional networks may be a more appropriate political model for an age in which capital, the greatest contemporary threat to place, has itself become networked, decentralized, deterritorialized, and fluid in its structures. Traditional governmental institutions, especially at the national level, are simply unable to address environmental problems that emerge from business decisions made by shifting networks at a variety of geographic levels.[85] Ad hoc, shifting networks of activists are able to mobilize action across geographically disparate localities and on a global level. Such networks, says Schlosberg, "exemplify an attempt at an alternative political structure."[86] The Mackenzie Valley Inquiry may be the applicable model here.

However, an ad hoc regional coalitional network, or overlapping set of such networks, would be an inadequate substitute for more formalized regional institutions and boundaries. Regional concerns are made up of complex and enduring groups of issues situated in broad spatial and temporal contexts. They require considerable institutional capacity, complex coordination, deep historical memory, long time horizons, and proactive, forward-looking planning. Even though he does not endorse formal regional government, Shutkin discusses community and regional planning in terms of comprehensive, long-term solutions. Regional planning through democratic processes "allows stakeholders to envision their community five, ten, or twenty years down the road and to take stock of the resources necessary to achieve that vision."[87] Also, democratic governance requires clear and long-term institutional accountability; established, coherent communications and decision-making channels; and a citizenry with developed political and deliberative competence. Shutkin says that "civic environmental planning assumes that some measure of civic infrastructure is in place to carry out a meaningful, comprehensive planning process. Without a stable civic infrastructure, communities cannot engage in genuine planning projects, whether on a project or community-wide basis."[88] Over time, regional boundaries and institutions might be adjusted, but there is no way around the need for highly stable structures and borders, even if there are costs in terms of some measure of inflexibility and even exclusion. Indeed, on this issue, preservation should have some priority over founding.

Finally, ad hoc governance faces the problem of legitimacy. Without clear, established procedures for elections, channels for public input, and provisions for public accountability, there will always be the question of whether an ad hoc group actually speaks for the community. Unless the question of who speaks for the community is resolved, seemingly democratic procedures could even turn out to be fly-by-night hoaxes like the one perpetrated on the citizens of New York during the planning for Ground Zero.

At the same time, regional government need not rule out more ad hoc coalitions outside of formal political structures. Certainly, coalitional networks are likely to fare much better in the context of regionalism, as Channels of political communication and deliberation among regional constituencies would already be established. In addition, shifting coalitions could help provide the underlying social capital to support regionalism as well as the connective tissue that eases coordination among regions.

Reconciling the Particular and the Universal

Related to the problem of regional boundaries is the equally difficult issue of particular versus more universal identities and concerns.[89] Place attachments are particular and particularism can lead to parochialism. One advantage of regionalism here is that even though regions may develop their own identities, they are internally diverse enough to promote respect and tolerance for difference as well as enable coalition building among different kinds of communities and constituencies. As I discuss later, coalitional networks formed by the environmental justice and collaborative conservation movements offer positive lessons here because they are able to bring very different, even formerly antagonistic, parties together. Regionalism in almost any U.S. metropolitan area will necessarily bring together a variety of communities differentially defined by race, ethnicity, class, geography, culture, political orientation, and livelihood. Furthermore, given the size of a region, citizens and public officials will inevitably have to confront national or global-level issues. A regional megacity will be a significant player in the global space of flows; any region, whether a metropolitan area or a watershed, will have to confront climate change. In short, regional scale and diversity can be a bridge to a broader, more global engagement and perspective.

Of course, regions would have to yield much of their political autonomy on more universal concerns. Regions would be embedded within larger political units, so their sovereignty would be limited from the start. In addition, individual regions might have to cooperate directly with one another, for example, to avoid mutually destructive economic competition[90] and to address larger-scale issues like those facing the Pacific Northwest, an area that embraces a number of regions. Regional governments will also need to deal with new global authorities, for example, those that will likely emerge in response to climate change. In some cases, as in climate change, regions might implement mandates from above, deciding for themselves, for example, how to best meet targets for the reduction of greenhouse gas emissions.

Creating Regional Government

Regional institutions would most likely develop incrementally.[91] There are many obstacles to new regional structures, particularly the immediate self-interest of existing municipalities and constituencies. Creating regional institutions requires coalition building.

Given the large number of interests embraced in a region, any regionalization process would face widespread resistance. A 1991 attempt at regional planning in southeastern Michigan collapsed when no intergovernmental consensus could be formed between new communities eager for development and older cities that were desperate to stop the competition.[92] Yet regional governance is not utopian. According to David Rusk, regional planning and governance are becoming increasingly prominent in the United States, and "in coming decades, directly elected metropolitan governments are likely to evolve in a growing number of regions."[93]

The Portland Example

The best-known, most forward-looking, and most successful regional entity is the one that governs the Portland, Oregon, metropolitan area. powell says that Portland comes close to the ideal of federated regionalism.[94]

Portland has had a directly elected metropolitan government, "Metro," since 1978. Metro arose gradually through Oregon's statewide growth management plan, developed under the leadership of Republican Governor Tom McCall in the early 1970s and through a combination of two agencies, a council of local governments in the metropolitan area and the Metropolitan Services District, which had various responsibilities, including solid waste disposal and management of a zoo.[95] Metro is not a single municipality, but oversees twenty-five cities in three counties. More than 1.3 million people live within Metro's boundaries. The Metro Council consists of seven members, including one regionally elected president and one councilor elected from each of six districts.

Metro addresses issues of land use, development, transportation, water supply, and solid waste management.[96] It has worked to directly manage development and limit sprawl within Portland's urban growth boundary (UGB) (see later discussion) by mandating higher-density, mixed-use, neighborhood-oriented development that features mass transit and parks and other public space.[97] Limits on sprawl have thus kept middle- and upper-income residents in the center city and moderated geographic economic and racial divisions across the region.[98]

In keeping with federated regionalism, Metro also sets affordable housing requirements for municipalities within the UGB, but it is up to each locality to decide how to meet these requirements. This has allowed a measure of local autonomy, although this arrangement has not addressed problems like local gentrification and the concentration of affordable housing, both of which tend to exacerbate racial divisions. However, Portland is seeking to address these issues through a fair-share housing plan that includes protecting low-income areas from gentrification.[99]

Metro is also democratic and accountable. It is an elected, known, transparent governing body. Rusk says, "Portland area citizens know where the crucial decisions affecting the future of their region are made: Metro. They know when and how such decisions will be made:

in well-advertised public meetings after extensive public hearings.... And citizens know who will make the decisions": their directly elected councilors and president.[100] In drawing up a long-range plan, called Region 2040, during the 1990s, Metro also emphasized public participation by holding six public workshops for local stakeholders to create their own proposals, as well as other public meetings.[101]

Portland's policy has been controversial with property owners, builders, and developers. Steven Hayward, writing in 1998, indicated that the plan was becoming unpopular with the general public.[102] For a long time, Hayward's contention was not borne out. Voters repeatedly turned down initiatives intended to weaken or eliminate Metro. This is not surprising, given that regional land-use planning has helped make Portland a beautiful, prosperous, and extremely desirable place to live. The area's natural and rural amenities have been preserved, and investment has been channeled back into the city rather than being dispersed into sprawling suburbs.[103]

However, in 2000, a property rights measure, spearheaded by the group Oregonians in Action, passed in the state. It was struck down by the Oregon Supreme Court on constitutional grounds. In November 2004, Oregonians in Action and other opponents of land-use planning finally got the upper hand. Oregon voters approved Measure 37, a radical property rights initiative, with 61 percent support. The initiative survived legal challenges and an unfavorable ruling by an Oregon Circuit Court; it was upheld by Oregon's Supreme Court in February 2006.

Measure 37 was a stunning victory for property-rights advocates in a traditionally liberal state that has long supported ambitious land-use restrictions. The law is quite radical. It requires compensation for any state or local regulation that limits the use or market value of a piece of property, and it applies to existing regulations if they were not in force when the owner or his or her parents or grandparents acquired the property. Property owners who are not compensated for lost value are free to use the land as they see fit.[104]

Under Measure 37, property owners have filed thousands of claims. In July 2006, Ray Ring reported in *High Country News* that there were already about 2,700 claims, seeking to develop about 143,000 acres. The claimants were pursuing a range of development activities, from erecting billboards to building a few houses to putting up resort hotels or hundreds of homes to establishing mines. Compensation for all these claims would total almost $4 billion, and cash-strapped counties and cities have not come up with the money: "in almost every one of the 700 claims settled to date, governments have waived the regulations."[105]

Measure 37 could well mean the end of Oregon's visionary, regional land-use planning. However, the ultimate impacts of the law are as yet unclear. One major obstacle to effectively dismantling Oregon's land-use regulations has been an opinion by the state attorney general's office that Measure 37 does not apply to property once it has been transferred to a new owner. Many counties have gone along with the attorney general. As a result, attempts by landowners to actually sell off their property to developers, rather than going through the difficult process of developing the land themselves, have largely been stymied. Having one's development plans approved may be insufficient if one cannot actually sell the land to a developer.[106] State courts are starting to rule on the interpretation of the law; as of this writing, it is unclear how they will ultimately decide.

The law's surprising passage has been attributed in part to changes in Oregon since the 1970s. These are, ironically enough, the very same changes that have marginalized the state's timber industry and increased support for forest preservation. Oregon has become more economically diversified and less dependent on agriculture. This has helped fuel rapid population growth (more than 20 percent during the 1990s),[107] suburbanization, and increasing pressure on rural lands. Laura Oppenheimer writes in the *Oregonian* that "it's not 1970 anymore. Nursery stock and vineyards have eclipsed fields of berries and green beans. High-tech factories consume large swaths of land while creating robust employment. And suburban growth continually pulses outward into areas once considered far-flung."[108] Meanwhile, builders, the real estate industry, Oregonians in Action, and lower-density communities concerned about Metro's efforts to mandate higher density have all been organizing against land-use regulations.[109]

Judith Layzer suggests that Measure 37 indicates the public may simply not be supportive of antisprawl measures, saying that it is not clear how many people really dislike sprawl and that it is even less obvious whether the public will readily accept higher density as an alternative.[110] At the same time, Layzer also notes, "The puzzling fact remained that, when polled, Oregonians said they either supported or strongly supported land-use regulations in the same proportions by which voters passed Measure 37."[111] A number of critics of the new law called the language on the ballot misleadingly innocuous. Also, Jonathan Walters, writing in *Governing*, notes that there are "polls that indicate most Oregonians—apparently attuned to a world where government is active in land conservation—figured that government would come up with ways to blunt any of the worst potential consequences of Measure 37, including paying claims to preserve open space and farmland."[112]

Furthermore, it is alleged that voters who supported the law did so on grounds of fairness and populist antielitism. Oregon's land-use regulations may have indeed become overly burdensome. Some of the stories circulated by Measure 37 proponents involved ordinary citizens victimized by overly rigid, onerous regulations that had prevented them from building a home for themselves on their own property.[113] Other favorite stories were that of Rebecca Muntean and her blackberry bushes (see chapter 5) and that of 92-year-old Dorothy English, who had been prevented from carving up her 20 Portland-area acres into buildable lots.[114] Walters suggests that a key source of resentment, and a turning point in arousing public opposition to land-use rules, "was a 1994 [state] regulation that required landowners whose parcels had been designated high-value agriculture to show a certain gross revenue from farming before they would be allowed to build a house on their property—even parcels as large as 80 acres."[115] He also notes that supporters of land-use regulation showed little interest in compensating struggling farmers who were unable to sell their land because of antidevelopment restrictions.

The *Oregonian* thus editorialized that the voters, unlike the groups spearheading Measure 37, were only concerned about fairness and government overreaching and did not envision opening up the countryside to big developments.[116] In line with this view, one could argue that the authorities in Oregon had become overly preservationist and that the public was pushing, not for a radical property rights law, but for more moderate policies that would give increased allowance to founding activities when fairness to ordinary citizens was at stake.

Now many landowners are worried about the loss of their own property values as neighbors announce development plans. Ring interviewed Oregonians who had voted for Measure 37 but now regret it as neighbors have begun to go ahead with development plans, many involving hundreds of homes. Ted Schroeder, a resident of rural Grande Ronde Valley in northeast Oregon, says that he voted for Measure 37 because of ads presenting the initiative as a fairness issue for small property owners. "If you polled a lot of people who voted for Measure 37, none of them voted for these mega-projects that are going to create multimillionaires," he says ruefully. "People got bamboozled, they got suckered in.... I kick myself for being so naive." Bill Rose, who breeds grasses in the Willamette Valley near Portland, thought that Measure 37 would simply relax regulations enough to build houses in some spots where the land was not fit for farming. Now that a neighbor has decided to turn a 40-acre berry farm into a site for 280 houses, he says that Measure 37 "will destroy this valley—the best place to live and farm that I know of." He thinks that the "sewage, cars and people would be very detrimental to the livability here. I have a 40-acre lake I made, and all the drainage will come into it. I am sure my lake will be ruined." Molalla resident Renee Ross dreads the gravel mine that a neighbor is now going to dig: "Our atmosphere here now is totally peaceful—the birds, the creek rambling through our property. When they start up, it'll be within 200 feet of our house. They'll be doing blasting, and they'll run a rock-crushing machine. They can operate from 7 A.M. to 6 P.M., Monday through Saturday. It'll also be trucks backing up, the beep-beep-beep, all day long, because they have to back up to the gravel pile. We live in a little valley, so the sound will echo. We're just devastated.... It's happening all over Oregon." Despite having voted for Measure 37, she says, "I hope other states don't do this. We went from having a very strict land-use policy to having no policy." She underscores the fundamentally anti-democratic nature of allowing individual property owners virtually unlimited discretion to impose drastic changes on an entire landscape: "We don't have any rights at all. It leaves us no say in the types of surroundings we live in, the undesirable businesses that can be put in right next to our property."[117]

Unfortunately, the property rights victory in Oregon is being looked at as a model by activists in other states. In November 2006, measures similar to Oregon's were on the ballot in four Western states: Arizona, California, Idaho, and Washington. The initiatives, which were being heavily funded by out-of-state libertarian groups and New York City real-estate mogul Howard S. Rich, were presented to voters as measures against the use of eminent domain to secure land for private developers, which was at issue in the *Kelo* case. In fact, as in Oregon, the measures were really aimed at dismantling most land-use regulations by mandating compensation for affected property owners. Opponents charged that these measures were using the eminent domain issue as a cover for a stealth campaign to promote a radical property-rights agenda. Indeed, these measures would have significantly undermined the ability of state and local governments to curb explosive growth and protect place-related values.[118] In the end, voters defeated the initiatives in California, Idaho, and Washington, a hopeful sign that the electorate may have learned from Oregon's experience with Measure 37.

Other Regional Experiments

Despite the controversies surrounding Metro and land-use planning in Oregon and surrounding property rights more generally, metropolitan and other regional governance is being tried in other areas, although not to the degree found in Portland. Minnesota's Twin Cities area, i.e., Minneapolis-St.Paul, had a promising start with metropolitan government in the late 1960s and early 1970s. The area's Metropolitan Council was appointed by the governor and charged with overseeing sewers, solid waste disposal, parks, and a scheme for sharing tax revenue throughout the region.[119] The Metropolitan Council lost political support in the 1980s and became virtually moribund.[120] However, under the leadership of Minnesota state representative Myron Orfield, a regionalist movement was revived in the 1990s. Orfield and his allies have come close to transforming the Metropolitan Council into an elected one. In 1997, they were defeated only by the governor's veto.[121]

In the Atlanta metropolitan area, land-use decisions are controlled by the Georgia Regional Transportation Authority (GRTA), created in 1999. The agency consists of a fifteen-member board appointed by the governor. It has power over transportation projects in the Atlanta metro counties that have been found in violation of federal clean air standards. In these counties, it has the power to plan, coordinate, or directly operate transit systems.[122] It can influence local land-use decisions by determining which localities receive federal and state transportation funding, and it has used this power to push for more mass transit and higher-density development, principles embodied in its long-term Regional Transportation

Plan.[123] Surprisingly, GRTA arose in part through the efforts of Atlanta's business elite, which in the past had promoted the city's explosive sprawl. By the 1990s, the Atlanta metropolitan area was being hit with federal sanctions for air quality violations. National publicity about the area's overdevelopment, traffic congestion, and air pollution was threatening the prospect of future business investment and potentially dissuading people from moving to Atlanta.

However, despite, or perhaps because of, its considerable powers, GRTA's ability to control sprawl is still not certain.[124] The agency does not govern democratically. It has acted as a tool of the governor, even supporting former Governor Roy Barnes' bid for another major highway in the region, and has incurred resentment from some local governments. Ultimately, GRTA could evolve into a muscular, comprehensive regional government like Portland's,[125] or it could eventually be rendered powerless by local opposition.[126]

More tentative steps toward metropolitan or regional government are taking place in various parts of the nation. The collaborative conservation movement and Clinton's Northwest Forest Plan, which I discuss later, represent efforts of this sort. Under two federal laws—the 1991 Intermodal Surface Transportation Efficiency Act and the 1998 Transportation Efficiency Act for the 21st Century—in areas of 200,000 or more residents, the allocation of transportation funding among various projects is determined by metropolitan planning organizations (MPOs). These are not full-scale regional governments. Some are regional councils, or voluntary consortia of local governments that have a variety of interests beyond transportation planning. Other MPOs are regional economic development organizations, transportation planning agencies, and arms of state highway departments.[127] Calthorpe and Fulton see MPOs as a basis for eventual regional land-use coordination.[128] These organizations, however, have been "reluctant to propose radical actions or investments that might threaten the status quo of their powerful (and usually cautious) state or local leadership."[129]

Over the past century, states have also created entities to govern regions of special significance. New York State's Adirondack Park Agency (APA) is one well-known example. The governance of these agencies varies greatly.[130] To the degree they are top-down arms of the state government, they can be resented by local residents as undemocratic. The APA, which is appointed by the state, has been a lightning rod for local hostility.[131]

More voluntary regional planning efforts are also under way. Such efforts rely on incentives and guidance for local municipalities to improve land-use planning and fight sprawl,[132] although they may represent initial steps toward a more institutionalized regionalism. New York State, for example, provides financial incentives, legal protections, and technical assistance to communities who form land-use planning compacts with one another and/or with state or federal agencies. The best-known is the New York City Watershed Agreement, which created watershed protection programs that address land-use and economic issues for a mainly rural watershed of 2,000 square miles serving New York City's water needs. The compact was negotiated among the governor, New York City, upstate watershed communities, environmental groups, and the EPA.[133]

Coalitions for Regionalism

Given the diversity of communities and interests within a region, the establishment of a constituency for regional government requires coalition building. However, creating a successful regionalist coalition is tricky. Margaret Weir says that past successes depended on "at least one politically powerful interest that saw metropolitan regionalism as a way to address its concerns, bipartisan coalition building, and relatively weak opposing groups."[134] The creation of Portland's Metro, as well as Oregon's adoption of statewide land-use controls and UGBs in the 1970s, fit these conditions. Influential groups supporting regionalism and growth management included farmers, environmentalists, and political leaders in Portland. The concentration of Oregon's urban and agricultural land in the Willamette Valley meant that development was much more costly in terms of lost farmland and threats to rural life, which led farmers to support management of regional growth. Participation by moderate Republicans enabled bipartisan support. Moreover, "the groups most likely to oppose metropolitan initiatives—developers and suburban interests—were unusually weak or quiescent."[135] In Oregon, suburban growth had so far been moderate. Supporters of land-use controls and regionalism also blunted potential opposition from homebuilders by working to eliminate, within urban growth boundaries, minimum lot sizes and other zoning restrictions that had mandated low density. Furthermore, Oregon was relatively racially homogeneous, which meant that regionalism was not complicated by a racially charged urban-suburban conflict. Oregon also had no tradition of urban machine politics, which made the suburbs less distrustful of the city. As we saw, some of these conditions, particularly the importance of Oregon's rural economy and the position of developers and suburban interests, have changed radically, resulting in the fraying of support for land-use controls and the passage of Measure 37.

Oregon's long success in land-use planning need not be unique. As Weir points out,[136] there are a number of possible avenues for building coalitions to manage regional growth. These include a strategy, pursued by Orfield in Minnesota, of taking advantage of divisions among the suburbs and allying cities with the inner-ring suburbs. Regionalist coalitions can also bring in natural supporters like environmentalists and farmland preservationists, as well as other constituencies like churches concerned about urban disinvestment.

Nonprofits can also help push for regionalism. Shutkin describes a number of such efforts in New Jersey. In Morris County, a nonprofit group called Morris 2000 has provided a forum for citizens, elected officials, civic groups, and businesses to develop strategic plans for the county's social and environmental future. Morris 2000 has also campaigned for open space initiatives; developed watershed plans; promoted high-density, mass-transit-oriented development; and pushed for brownfields redevelopment and increases in affordable housing.[137] A statewide nonprofit, New Jersey Future, has issued a series of regional development recommendations and plans for the state and works to push the state government toward more vigorous, regionally coordinated, ecologically oriented planning.[138]

Support for regionalism can even be obtained from some developers by eliminating local growth restrictions, which interfere with regional growth management, and by offering opportunities for infill and for redevelopment of brownfields and other abandoned sites.[139] Also, as the Atlanta case showed, the business community can itself become worried about sprawl's effect on a region.

In their case study of GRTA, Ulf Zimmerman, Göktuğ Morçöl, and Bethany Stich speculate that metropolitan area business elites, in Atlanta and elsewhere, may be the most natural and effective constituency for regional governance.[140] They tend to think in terms of the economic vitality of a whole region and have the political and economic power to put their policy agendas into effect.[141]

However, not all business elites are interested in local or regional concerns, as we saw in chapter 5. Corporations that can easily shift their operations elsewhere or are not locally owned are less supportive of regional initiatives. Even in the case of civic-minded businesses, community leaders from the corporate sector tend to promote and rely on an increasingly hegemonic discourse that proclaims business to be entrepreneurial and innovative, and government inefficient, partisan, corrupt, and beholden to special interests.[142] Such views encourage public–private partnerships in which business groups have an increasingly official role in land-use and many other public policy decisions.[143] Although the business community's funding and expertise can be useful, and although business can be a force for regionalism, the increasing power of business, coupled with public disdain for politics and the public sector, can delegitimize democratic processes. Furthermore, business leaders are not directly accountable to the public and are not necessarily motivated by the public interest,[144] as is evident in the controversy over Ground Zero.

Another key variable in coalition building is racial politics. powell notes that distrust runs in both directions between whites and minorities, leading both to resist regionalism.[145] White communities have tended to be exclusionary, while minority communities, who have achieved considerable political power in many central cities, are concerned that regionalism would dilute such power. However, both groups end up suffering. Whites in small suburban communities have little control over larger political and economic forces, while minorities face continued discrimination, de facto segregation, and concentrated poverty.[146]

Given their power in urban areas, minorities are more likely to favor "in-place" over "mobility" strategies. In-place strategies aim at bringing jobs and development to urban neighborhoods, while mobility strategies emphasize giving urban residents access to jobs and housing throughout a region.[147] Minorities often perceive mobility strategies as too assimilationist, leading to the dilution and dispersal of political power.[148]

However, powell argues that in-place strategies by themselves cannot address economic disparities and demographic shifts across a region. He calls for a combination of mobility and in-place strategies (see later discussion) that would address the shortcomings of each and give residents a choice between staying put and moving. He also proposes proportional representation voting mechanisms that would enable the expression of minority interests without requiring racially segregated residential patterns.[149] As for bridging racial divisions, one way to do this, as we saw with Minnesota, is through alliances between inner-city minorities and poorer or ethnic whites, many of whom live in cities and inner-ring suburbs. Interracial alliances have also emerged around environmental justice issues where lower-income communities are unduly burdened with LULUs and pollution.

One may also bring outer suburbs, which tend to be white, on board. This may be done through conditional development assistance. Minneapolis-St.Paul's Metropolitan Council is trying to obtain affordable housing in the outer suburbs in exchange for funding for infrastructure and other development.[150] However, this policy tends to subsidize sprawl.

The bottom line, however, is that affluent, mostly white suburbs cannot run away from the problems affecting cities or inner suburbs, just as minority communities cannot run away from regionalism. In the short run, communities within a metropolitan area may be able to survive connected to global networks and disconnected from their struggling neighbors, or they may be able to hold onto political power and autonomy within inner cities. However, over time, disinvestment, urban decay, poverty, and related social problems create costs for a region as a whole. Such costs include increased poverty and suffering, deteriorating schools, a need for more policing and social services and a greater sense of insecurity for all residents of a region, the decline of urban cultural resources and urban synergies dependent on dense populations, and a decline in local and outside business investment.[151] In the long run, the health of a region as a whole matters, even in remaining globally competitive. Both Castells and Rosabeth Moss Kanter point out that global competition puts pressure on businesses to improve the economy and infrastructure where they operate so that they have access to skilled labor and research institutions, and so that their employees will have access to cultural amenities and good schools for their children.[152] It is unclear, though, whether this can outweigh the incentives for footloose corporations to simply move their operations to more desirable places when local conditions deteriorate.

Sustaining Regionalism, and Lessons of Measure 37

Weir also highlights the importance of grassroots mobilization in sustaining regionalism. Such mobilization took place in Oregon through citizens' groups like 1,000 Friends of Oregon and through provisions for public participation in land-use planning. Grassroots mobilization, says Weir, enabled land-use planning in Oregon to beat back challenges from property-rights groups, developers, and conservative Republicans during the 1990s. However, the importance of the grassroots was also negatively highlighted when Oregonians in Action and other antiregulatory activists pushed through Measure 37.

In Minnesota, the Metropolitan Council was more the product of technocrats and elite good-government groups. Without grassroots support, the Metropolitan Council declined.[153] Orfield's efforts to revitalize regionalism in the Twin Cities rely on a grassroots coalition uniting cities, inner-ring suburbs, environmentalists, social-justice groups, churches, and good-government organizations.[154]

Regionalists can also take away lessons from the Measure 37 debacle. Perhaps the central lesson is that state or regional land-use governance, given its ambitious control over private property and its broad geographic scope, can become excessive and unfair. Oregon's land-use regime was arguably guilty of overreaching and inequity, as we saw earlier. Land-use governance requires constant vigilance on issues of fairness and reasonability, especially when regulations threaten hardship for ordinary citizens. Unfairness, whether real or perceived, can seriously undermine the grassroots support needed for regional land-use planning.

The experience of Measure 37 may also offer lessons on regional democracy. Measure 37 was the second consecutive property-rights initiative approved by Oregon voters, and it passed in every county but one. Even if voters were misled on the nature of Measure 37, there was nevertheless a mismatch between public opinion on land-use policy and the ambitious regulations passed by state, regional, and local authorities. With regard to Portland's Metro, the serious efforts at democratic governance may not have been sufficient. Public hearings and workshops, which are attended only by those with the time and other resources to participate, and a seven-member council may not be sufficient to represent a diverse region of 1.3 million people. A regional legislature may be necessary to more fully represent the public and its range of perspectives on preservation and founding.

Having laid out the basic philosophical and political foundations of regionalism, I now offer a more specific set of policy proposals to realize proper land-use management within a broader regional context. A number of these proposals originate from political movements like collaborative conservation and environmental justice. These movements have articulated a conception of place that integrates founding and preservation. Other proposals come from planners like Calthorpe and Fulton. Still others, such as smart growth or the Northwest Forest Plan, have already been adopted by policy makers.

7

A Policy Agenda

My three case studies—Northwest forest politics, sprawl, and Ground Zero—involved three kinds of landscapes. To offer solutions to problems raised in each landscape, I turn to regional policies for integrating founding and preservation in three sets of landscapes: (1) wilderness and rural areas, (2) the urban/suburban/rural interface, and (3) cities. My discussion of cities in part addresses Ground Zero, but also looks at urban revitalization, a problem raised by the decline of cities and the problem of sprawl. Also keep in mind that a region can embrace all three sets of landscapes; in such cases, regional policies must coordinate land use among a full range of places.

As noted at the end of chapter 6, the proposals offered here have already been crafted elsewhere. The working landscape already exists in nascent, scattered form in various corners of contemporary land-use politics. Throughout this book I have tried to articulate a theoretical and political framework for a healthier politics of place that integrates founding and preservation. This framework can also unify the disparate proposals of the nascent working landscape, as catalogued here, into a coherent policy agenda to challenge today's dominant, dysfunctional approaches to land use.

Wilderness and Rural Areas

Regional Planning and Ecosystem Management in the Northwest
The Westside area of the Pacific Northwest may offer an excellent laboratory, not only for collaborative conservation, but also for an even more ambitious regionalism that embraces landscapes ranging from wilderness to urban. The Westside contains vast, magnificent forests as well as the

metropolitan regions of Portland and Seattle/Puget Sound. Portland already has a metropolitan government and Seattle is now undertaking its own experiment in regionalism.[1] The metropolitan areas face the task of managing and properly developing cities while preserving farms and forests.

A regional future for the Northwest presents some intriguing possibilities. A single regional government for the Westside is not workable, given the size of the area. It would in effect be a new state.[2] What would make sense, though, is a set of regions cutting across state lines and coordinating with one another on interrelated issues of forest and agricultural preservation, fisheries protection, hydroelectric power and riparian management, and urban and suburban planning.

The Westside and its constituent regions would need to adopt policies that simultaneously protect wilderness areas, including old-growth forests, and sustain rural timber communities as much as possible. A key principle here is *ecosystem management.* In the context of forestry, former Forest Service Chief Jack Ward Thomas describes ecosystem management as

moving beyond a compartmentalized approach focusing on the individual parts of the forest. It is an approach that steps back from the forest stand and focuses on the forest landscape and its position in the larger environment in order to integrate the human, biological, and physical dimensions of natural resource management. Its purpose is to achieve sustainability of all resources.[3]

Ecosystem management is thus a holistic approach to integrating human and ecological elements of a landscape so as to sustain both. Like a regionalism that balances founding and preservation, it coordinates the different parts of a diverse landscape, some preserved and some open to development, so that they function as a whole. Such integrated land-use management may take place on a variety of spatial scales. Dietrich describes what an ecosystem management scheme for the entire Westside would look like:

Its backbone would be the parks and wilderness areas along the region's mountain ranges. Its skeleton, or veins, would be riparian zones along rivers and streams that stretched from mountain to tidewater.... Urban areas would be given some geographic limit, and the surviving forest would be managed in a variety of ways: some of it set aside as permanent old-growth groves, some of it managed as tree farms for wood, and some of it harvested in much longer rotations, two centuries that allowed second-growth trees enough time to become habitat for owls and other species. Clear-cutting would fade.[4]

Lessons from the Northwest Forest Plan

Turning more specifically to the Westside's forests, ecosystem management was a guiding principle for the Northwest Forest Plan adopted by President Clinton. Former Oregon Governor John Kitzhaber calls the plan the largest ecosystem planning effort in the world.[5] As discussed in chapter 2, the plan reduced logging from the levels of the late 1980s and provided for a range of land uses, including timber harvesting, experimental management, and forest protection. According to Joe Bowersox, the plan was a radical step forward in forest policy, "a concerted attempt not simply to restore the previous policy landscape, but to create a much more complex and holistic policy landscape involving more actors, more numerous and more robust relationships, and interconnection with other substantive policy areas like regional economic development, education and retraining, and international trade."[6] Though I discussed the plan earlier, I want to highlight some aspects that were compelling from a regional standpoint and discuss how the plan ultimately failed to fully implement them.

First of all, the plan reflected the dynamism inherent in places and the need for flexible decision making by incorporating an experimental element that Margaret Shannon calls "reflexive learning," in which actions become opportunities for critical analysis and a possible change in approach.[7] The plan's use of AMAs and survey-and-manage provisions meant that timber harvesting would be contingent on the evaluation of ecological data from the field (see chapter 2). This experimental approach is well suited to a regional context. Experimental or adaptive areas can provide important information for managing the rest of the regional landscape. However, both Shannon and Bowersox argue that federal agencies did not work hard enough to put reflexive learning into practice. Agencies did not make a sufficient effort to learn from the AMAs or to experiment with changes in their own procedures and organizational structures.[8] One problem that should have been addressed was that the survey-and-manage provisions lowered harvesting below projected levels, thus disappointing the timber industry and timber communities (see also chapter 2).

The plan also sought more horizontal coordination between agencies and more of a local role in policy implementation, ideas that fit in with a more decentralized, federated approach to regionalism. Land management and resource agencies would work together and with local experts, managers, and communities to create place-specific management approaches, including AMAs. In fact, the plan set generic management guidelines with the idea that more place-specific policies would be developed. This overall approach would have involved more local, democratic participation. However, one major obstacle was the reluctance of agency personnel to experiment and depart from the plan's generic guidelines lest they face legal challenges. This helped prevent the development of participatory, locally based structures as a more common method of forest management. Consequently, the Northwest Forest Plan has ended up acting more like a traditional top-down management scheme.[9] Thus Kitzhaber maintains that the plan did not democratically involve stakeholders in the management process.[10]

In its approach to actually harvesting timber, the plan called for more ecologically benign approaches to logging, including in some old-growth forests. The plan pursued what forest ecologist Jerry Franklin terms "variable retention harvesting."[11] This harvesting method eschews clear-cutting in favor of the retention of some portion of a timber stand after logging. Retained portions often include key structural elements of the forests, including large-diameter living trees and dead standing trees and fallen logs. In old-growth ecosystems, variable retention harvesting attempts to log in a way that maintains old-growth characteristics. Unfortunately, in its implementation, the Northwest Forest Plan did not provide sufficient follow-through on development of experimental logging methods. Moreover, both forest preservationists and timber interests have often opposed such new approaches to timber harvesting. Depending on one's perspective, such approaches involve either too much or too little logging.[12]

Setting Aside Old Growth, Rejecting the Zero-Cut Option

Even at the plan's originally projected timber harvest, there would have been a very significant reduction in old-growth logging from earlier levels. A major reduction was necessary. Although loggers value working with old growth, there is simply too little of it left to replicate the enormous, unsustainable timber yields of the past, and what is left is too valuable, for ecological and other nontimber reasons. With almost all the old growth gone, "society has no other option but to make hard choices,"[13] although some selective harvesting in old growth forests may be feasible over the long term, as provided under the Northwest Forest Plan.

However, this should not doom logging in the Northwest. Extensive timber harvesting should continue in many younger stands on federal land. Contrary to the zero-cut argument, public forests should not be automatically closed to logging and other resource work. Public lands can continue to serve, although in a reduced capacity, as a resource for providing wood and sustaining timber communities and their connection to the landscape.

Admittedly, logging has been not only ecologically damaging but also financially costly for the Forest Service, and timber jobs have often required heavy subsidies, as noted in chapter 2. However, public funding is also used, for example, to maintain the 83.6 million acres of the National Park system and their recreational and preservationist land uses through a budgetary outlay of over $2 billion per year.[14] Arguably, some public funds and lands should be similarly set aside to support the work practices and place-attachments that have grown up around logging national forest lands, provided that timber harvesting is carried out in an ecologically sound manner.

In chapter 6 I noted that work can help cultivate attachment to place. In fact, resource work like timber harvesting may foster a distinctive connection with the landscape that is not available through leisure activities. In criticizing environmentalist attitudes toward work, White argues that work enables a much more intense connection than outdoor recreation, or play:

Work entails an embodiment, an interaction with the world that is far more intense than play. We work to live. We cannot stop. But play ... does not so fully submerge us in the world. At play we can stop and start. A game unfinished ultimately means nothing ... Work left unfinished has consequences.[15]

Moreover, there is a sensual understanding of nature that comes about through physically working with it. "A logger's tools," White remarks, "extend his body into trees so that he knows how the texture of their wood and bark differs and varies, how they smell and fall."[16] Just as parks and wilderness areas enable a spiritual, aesthetic, or recreational connection with natural places, some portion of public lands might be set aside for the connections that arise through resource work. However, we may not have to devote all that much public land to logging, as private lands offer another venue for timber harvesting.

The Importance of Private Timberlands

The Northwest Forest Plan created a fundamental paradox, as highlighted by Kitzhaber. It severely restricted logging on federal old-growth forests and yet still relied on such forests to provide 80 percent of its projected timber harvest.[17] This difficulty could have been avoided if the plan had more broadly embraced the region's landscape, including private timberlands.

As noted in chapter 2, nonfederal forests are supplying 3.6 bbf in Oregon. As I also noted, these are not just giant, corporate tree farms; small woodland owners in Oregon supply hundreds of millions of board feet of timber per year. In 2000, Nels Hanson, executive director of the Washington Farm Forestry Association, a group in Olympia representing small landowners, told me that out of a total timber harvest in Washington of about 4 bbf per year, about 1 bbf is from owners of 5,000 acres or less, with larger, industrial timber owners accounting for 1–1.5 bbf and the rest coming from federal, state, and tribal lands.[18]

When managed best, such small woodlands are logged on a long-term sustainable basis, kept as patchworks of different-aged trees, and maintained as wildlife habitat.[19] Ideally, these woodlands are not treated as a mere timber resource by their owners, but as valued places that allow individuals and families to identify with the land. Hanson described woodland ownership as an intergenerational investment because one's grandchildren will harvest the trees that one plants.[20]

The Northwest's patchwork of thousands of different timber holdings, each harvested at different times, could also contribute to biodiversity and ecological diversity in the region.[21] A more complete regional approach that went beyond the Northwest Forest Plan's focus on federal lands would thus take both public and private forests into account.

Unfortunately, the prospects for small woodland forestry are diminishing. As I mentioned in chapter 2, sprawl is threatening private timberlands. In the absence of sufficient tax and other financial incentives, small woodland owners are selling out to large timber companies and developers.

To help reverse these trends, assistance for timberland owners needs to be restored. The Oregon Small Woodlands Association urges changes in estate and inheritance taxes to promote intergenerational transfer of small woodlands as well as other tax policies, such as reform of property taxes, to support long-term investment in woodlands. The organization also urges expansion of extension programs geared toward forestry.[22] Rocky Barker suggests tax incentives to encourage owners to preserve wildlife habitat and cooperate in ecosystem management programs.[23] Land-use planning is also essential here, but planning is now threatened by Oregon's Measure 37 and its potential progeny in other states.

Forest Restoration

As provided for under the Northwest Forest Plan, displaced timber workers could also find alternative or supplemental employment in forest and watershed restoration projects. Restoration activities keep workers in the woods and engaged with the landscape. Such activities can include replanting native vegetation, removing logging roads, rehabilitating damaged streams, and reducing erosion. As noted in chapter 2, forest restoration work to reduce fuel loads, such as prescribed fire and thinning, is appropriate in parts of the Northwest whose natural fire regime consists of frequent, low-intensity fires, but not in areas subject to infrequent, stand-replacing fires.

Value-Added Processing of Regional Timber Harvests

Protecting the countryside requires directly preservationist strategies like land purchases and easements. However, there is also the need for more founding-oriented efforts, particularly revitalization of the rural economy so that farmers and timberland owners do not abandon their land and their communities and/or feel compelled to sell out to developers. Such efforts encourage protection of working forests and fields, promote regional self-reliance, sustain the local or regional economy, cultivate regional identity, and reduce external pressure for unsustainable harvesting. Value-added processing of timber harvested within a region is one promising approach. In the wood products sector, value-added production includes not just sawmilling operations, but also, for example, the manufacture of building components like flooring or moldings, and furniture making. Such activities tend to be good job producers. Says Ryan Temple, marketing manager of the Portland nonprofit group,

Sustainable Northwest's Healthy Forests, Healthy Communities Partnership (HFHC),[25] "Studies show that typical primary mills employ about 3–5 persons annually per mmbf [million board feet] of lumber produced. Compare that to manufacturers of moldings and millwork products that employ approximately 12 to 18 persons annually per mmbf or furniture manufacturers who employ 60 to 80 persons annually per mmbf of wood processed." In fact, between 1990 and 2000, as timber harvests, income, and jobs declined in Oregon, "the furniture and fixtures sector, considered to be value-added manufacturing, grew by 122%." Temple also notes, "Eighty percent of these businesses have less than 20 employees, indicating that the smaller businesses are the foundation of the value-added sector. Clearly, a value oriented approach shows promise as a means to sustain economies as harvest volumes decline." The jobs are also high-skilled and well paid.

The HFHC program is attempting to promote such value-added manufacturing in the Northwest and tie it to ecologically sustainable forestry. Ryan says, "The challenge is to promote furniture, flooring, and other value-added enterprises that can manufacture products with the small diameter Douglas Fir and, to a lesser extent, the mixed hardwoods which thrive in our region." Through such an effort, "artisans in local towns can begin to realize some of the benefits of the wood that is removed adjacent to their communities."

Yet, says Ryan, local manufacturers face "an unpredictable long-term source of raw materials, lack of capital for inventory and equipment, and difficulty accessing distant markets. Coordinated efforts are needed to assist communities in meeting these challenges." The HFHC Partnership operates as a business network helping manufacturers market goods made from timber that is locally obtained through responsible forestry practices. The "green" angle is one of the selling points used by the HFHC. A regional government could help here with marketing and the provision of capital. Such strategies could also help with urban revitalization if manufacturers are located in cities.

Collaborative Conservation

We saw in chapter 2 that the forest politics of the Pacific Northwest has been marked by a conflict between founding-oriented timber managers and workers on the one hand and preservation-oriented environmentalists and their allies on the other. The debate over the Westside's old growth has degenerated into a deadlock, yielding simplistic, nonsensical choices between timber jobs and forest protection, when in fact timber workers have an underlying interest in more sustainable forms of forestry and environmentalists have largely failed to recognize their common ground with timber workers. There are some efforts to get beyond this polarization, and one of the most promising has taken the form of a regional approach. This is the collaborative conservation movement.

Collaborative conservation dates back to the late 1980s. It is centered in rural areas in the United States, particularly in the West, although similar efforts have emerged in other parts of the nation, such as Chesapeake Bay. The movement aims at more cooperative, ecosystem-oriented, and local and regional approaches to divisive land-use issues. It brings together at the grassroots level environmental activists, resource workers and industries (i.e., logging, ranching, and farming), and government agencies. Native American tribes, fishermen, outdoor enthusiasts, hunters, elected officials, and scientists are also involved, depending on the issue. Participants form what are called consensus or stakeholder groups.

In bringing together former adversaries, the movement explicitly seeks to address deadlocked debates like that over the Northwest forests.[26] Collaborative conservation is oriented toward care or preservation of valued places and their environmental quality, yet it rejects the prioritization of wilderness over humanized landscapes and embraces founding activities that shape at least part of the landscape.

Collaborative conservation also tries to cultivate local democracy and build community. It responds to the impasse in land and resource issues as well as to the top-down, undemocratic land-use policy process imposed on the American West by the federal government—which owns enormous portions of the West—and by large national environmental groups, resource industries, and large corporations.[27] Participants are also motivated by a shared concern that surrounding ecosystems and rural ways of life are being threatened by bitter environmental conflicts, sprawling development, unsustainable resource extraction, and growth due to recreational activities and tourism.[28] Furthermore, participants want to get along with their neighbors and restore peace in communities polarized by sometimes violent clashes over resources and wilderness.

Attachment to shared place is a central organizing principle for these groups.[29] Although the geographic scale may vary, many groups are organized at the regional level of a watershed, which seems a natural scale for many ecological relationships and the resource activities that depend on them.[30] The movement tries to balance national environmental standards with attention to local and regional conditions; it uses place-based knowledge and experience in addition to scientific expertise, and offers flexibility in the face of local or regional ecological and social dynamics. It attempts to bring together all the local or regional interests concerned with land and resource management, and to cultivate horizontal cooperation among various public and private actors rather than top-down regulation.[31]

In crafting policies, collaborative conservation recognizes ecological connections, both between geographic areas and across political and property boundaries. It pursues a long-term perspective on ecosystem health rather than a short-term emphasis on commodity production.[32] Collaborative conservation thus "incorporates an understanding of ecological systems, considers extended time and spatial scales, and highlights interconnections between landscapes, ecological processes, and humans and other organisms."[33]

Collaborative conservation efforts are in some cases initiated by public agencies or even large nonprofits like the Nature Conservancy, but they frequently originate at the grassroots level. The groups thus range from formally structured, federally chartered advisory committees to unofficial, loose partnerships among stakeholders.[34] Snow says that these groups aim "not to erase or abdicate existing structures of government … but to make them more responsive, more attuned to public needs (especially local needs), more *democratic*."[35]

Collaborative conservation groups pursue a variety of activities. These include "research [including inventories of an area's ecological, social, and economic characteristics], stakeholder involvement, ecosystem restoration, promotion of compatible human land uses, education and outreach, and land protection through set-asides."[36]

I mentioned collaborative conservation in chapter 2 when I discussed national environmentalist opposition to the movement. Collaborative conservation has received support mainly from locally based environmentalists, who are more likely than their national counterparts to support limited forms of logging, including measures to reduce fire danger: "In an interesting divergence from the trend at the national level, environmentalists who live near forestlands often support limited forest restoration activity focused on fuel reduction and forest thinning. This support for local forms of collaborative resource management by local environmentalists has kicked off debates and resulted in tensions between them and national environmental groups that oppose such forms of resource management."[37]

Collaborative conservation has also faced opposition from resource and property-rights interests who were emboldened by the rhetoric of congressional Republicans after the 1994 elections.[38] Moreover, there has sometimes been opposition from federal agencies mired in organizational complexity, jealous of turf, or rooted in traditional imperatives like the Forest Service's mission to "get the cut out." Nevertheless, despite the antidemocratic history of public lands agencies, they have often been quite supportive, in part because of a desire to restore their own credibility after years of failing to resolve wilderness and resource disputes. Public officials have organized collaborative efforts or acted as facilitators; adopted local proposals; provided educational, technical, and financial assistance; and even held out the threat of regulation and enforcement if parties did not reach agreement.[39]

The Applegate Partnership

A prominent collaborative conservation group involved in Northwest forestry issues is the Applegate Partnership. The partnership is concerned with managing the 500,000-acre Applegate River watershed in southwest Oregon, an area of about 12,000 inhabitants that includes both public and private lands. The group started in 1992, driven by desire for change on the part of local timber interests, environmentalists, federal land managers, and plain citizens. Judge Dwyer's injunctions against timber harvesting in much of the Northwest had made the industry desperate for some timber sales to proceed. Local environmentalists were simultaneously concerned about old-growth preservation in the region, anger and suspicion from their neighbors, and even the hardships faced by timber-dependent families. Public lands agencies sought "to rebuild lost credibility as institutions able to mediate balanced use of public lands." The community as a whole saw the partnership as "a way to try

to take back a sense of control over its own destiny."⁴⁰ Also, participants
in the Applegate Partnership were concerned about the hazards created
by decades of fire suppression⁴¹ and about protecting traditional rural
lifestyles threatened by transformation of agricultural land into upscale
residential development.⁴²

In 1993, the partnership was seized upon by the Clinton administration as the sort of cooperation needed to resolve the Northwest forest
impasse and as a promising experiment in ecologically friendly forest
management. The Applegate watershed was accordingly established by
the administration as one of several experimental, partially stakeholder-
run AMAs under the Northwest Forest Plan.⁴³

Building on a Shared Sense of Place
Significantly, the partnership's founder, a local environmentalist named
Jack Shipley, pushed the idea that the Applegate watershed should be
managed as one integrated ecosystem rather than by the current patchwork of public agencies and private individuals.⁴⁴ He brought together
environmentalists, timber industry representatives, employees of public
lands agencies, farmers, ranchers, and other local residents, all of them
committed to the Applegate watershed as a place. Upon introducing
themselves, the attendees "were asked to not disclose which interest
they represented or organization they worked for, but to simply say
what was important to them about the watershed"⁴⁵ and how they envisioned its future.⁴⁶ The partnership was thus at its very origins based on
a shared place as a unifying factor and attempted to develop a broad vision that would embrace all concerned parties. The participants initially
"agreed on one basic set of principles: Resource management should be
ecologically creditable, aesthetically acceptable, and economically viable
and must be carried out in a coordinated manner across the landscape."⁴⁷ Victoria Sturtevant and Jonathan Lange say that over time,
"love of their place held [the participants] together, as members walked
forest trails, flew observation planes, and held community potlucks." A
group identity eventually developed.⁴⁸

Like other collaborative conservation efforts, the Applegate Partnership has also utilized local social capital and local knowledge through an
informal structure that relies on "horizontal systems of association, relation, and friendship to organize and mobilize community resources."⁴⁹
The organization thus developed in an informal, ad hoc manner, but it

has taken on more of an established leadership role in the community. For one thing, it has influenced government policy. In a report for the Forest Service, Su Rolle writes, "There has been a profound shift from clearcutting to selective cutting on all federal agency lands in the Applegate Watershed, and the shift was accelerated by the partnership's involvement." She also notes, "There has been a dramatic change in the average diameter of trees cut—from the larger (greater than 22 inches in diameter at breast height) to smaller trees (often 8 to 12 inches in diameter at breast height)."[50]

The Applegate Partnership's Specific Aims and Activities

In discussing the partnership's goals, political scientist and former partnership member Cassandra Moseley says, "First and foremost, the Applegate Partnership sought to open federal land management agencies to more participation. The group wanted to see citizens and stakeholders participate earlier in the planning process and have input into higher and more substantial decision-making.... Second, the group sought to integrate planning and management across the landscape," bringing together "social, economic, and ecological concerns."[51]

More substantively, the partnership pursued four key management goals, according to participant Brett KenCairn: assessing ecological conditions and available resources in the watershed; determining the social and economic challenges and opportunities facing watershed inhabitants; developing economically viable forest products projects that are also compatible with forest health (the partnership has thus promoted selective logging and of smaller-diameter trees); and improving research and monitoring activities in the watershed.[52] More specific projects have included "restoration and recovery of riparian areas, tree plantings, road reconstruction or removal, selective thinning [of tree stands], fuels reduction [to prevent uncontrollable fires], reintroduction of fire, and encouraging small landowners and the timber industry to voluntarily adopt practices that promote long-term ecological and economic health."[53] The partnership's evaluative criteria included biodiversity and old-growth protection on the one hand and community benefit on the other.[54]

The Partnership's Challenges and Accomplishments

The Applegate Partnership has faced some serious obstacles. According to KenCairn, vested interests, including the timber industry, regional and national environmental groups, and public lands agencies, felt threatened by the partnership "because it in fact began to succeed in creating a space at the table of decision making and power for local people. This fundamentally disrupted and challenged the preexisting distribution of power" as well as existing conventions that had "dictated that decisions were going to be made at higher levels in a struggle of lawyers and lobbyists."[55] At times, federal agency personnel resented the attempts of an outside board to direct their management activities.[56] In many cases, federal land managers have willingly cooperated with Applegate and other collaborative conservation groups, but a number of external factors have also undermined this cooperation: transfer or promotion of agency personnel who had been involved with the partnership, congressional pressures to increase timber harvesting, opposition to the partnership from environmental groups, and federal regulations limiting official ties between federal agencies and outside groups.[57]

Many environmental groups opposed the partnership's support even for modified timber sales. In fact, Sturtevant and Lange maintain that environmental groups that continuously hindered or resisted the process have been the biggest obstructionists because they feared that collaboration with the timber industry meant co-optation, compromise, and surrender of forest issues to local control. Environmentalist opposition thus quashed an innovative timber sale designed collaboratively with federal officials.[58] "Individuals and groups holding strong 'no commercial timber' or 'zero cut' views are a particular challenge to the partnership as it attempts to be inclusive and maintain rational discourse,"[59] Sturtevant and Lange note. In response to environmentalists' concerns, they point out, "Given the range of participation in the partnership, the potential lines of co-optation are nearly balanced," so that environmentalists might just as likely co-opt industry representatives as they might be co-opted themselves."[60]

Moseley says that members of the group were pulled this way and that by the larger political forces to which they were linked. Indeed, the partnership has had to reconcile its two roles as a meeting ground between major interests concerned with forestry issues and as way for the community to empower itself and sustainably manage its forests.[61] One major forest preservation group, Headwaters, left the Applegate Partnership because of pressure from other Northwest environmentalists.[62] Tensions also arose when groups represented in the partnership engaged in litigation against one another.[63] Over time, as newcomers have joined the group and outside actors and struggles have increased internal tensions, a good deal of the trust and cohesion has been lost.[64]

Nevertheless, the partnership has endured and become involved in a variety of activities, including a comprehensive watershed restoration strategy, grazing management, and alternatives to suburbanization and the loss of farmlands.[65] Even so, the organization has had to change. Because of environmentalist opposition to the partnership's involvement in federal land management, official collaboration with federal agencies ended and according to Hibbard and Madsen, the group has shifted its focus since 1994. It has "evolved into a forum for dialogue between valley residents and agency officials on forest management. The collaboration's on-the-ground efforts now focus on working with private landowners to develop environmentally sound land management practices."[66]

Through these activities, and despite changes in its mission, the Applegate Partnership has continued to build social capital in the region. One study found that the partnership has reduced competition for resources and overall antagonism in the Applegate. Relationships have developed among previous adversaries. These have contributed to problem-solving that extends beyond the Applegate. There is more direct communication on ecological and economic issues among watershed residents, and many landowners are integrating their management activities into the framework established by the partnership.[67] The partnership has also fostered greater civic activity and pride of place in the Applegate Watershed, "creating a proliferation of community forums for civic action regarding local economic development and reinvestment, land use zoning, watershed restoration, and stewardship of public resources and facilities.... Cattlemen, ranchers, and loggers have worked with scientists and environmentalists to preserve both riparian health and traditional land uses; self-proclaimed 'rednecks' and 'preservationists' are admitting that they have much to learn from one another."[68] Finally, the partnership has become one of several state-sponsored watershed restoration councils created by Oregon in 1994.[69]

The Promise of Collaborative Conservation
The Applegate Partnership and other efforts demonstrate several guiding principles behind collaborative conservation. First of all, it is democratic

and grassroots, drawing in members of the local community to formulate ecological and resource management strategies and get past the adversarial nature of contemporary environmental politics.

Second, collaborative conservation is regional. It works at the level of whole ecosystems, especially watersheds. As with the Applegate Partnership, approaches cut across jurisdictional, political, and agency boundaries and cover both public and private lands and a variety of land-use issues.[70] Despite jurisdictional fragmentation, regional interconnections between places are acknowledged and addressed. The Applegate Partnership's website notes, "We soon discovered that the ecological concerns were not limited to timber harvest on public lands, but included housing expansion, land use laws, agriculture, road maintenance, traffic, water quality, air quality, private land habitat loss, restoration needs, community well-being, neighbor relations and many other social issues."[71] There is a strong element of coalition building as these boundaries are bridged. For example, private landowners are brought into a deliberative, cooperative management scheme, in part through approaches that encourage participation, such as providing property owners with assistance on projects.

Third, collaborative conservation attempts to integrate science with local knowledge,[72] an approach that recognizes place-based competencies and attachments and enables local flexibility in the face of social and environmental change. Relatedly, collaborative conservation is grounded not just in participants' local knowledge but also in their "deep concern for a place close to home." It "tap[s] the creative abilities of citizens to solve the problems of a place that matters to them."[73] Among erstwhile antagonists, there is the literal common ground of shared place, as well as shared concern about threats to that place, threats to the natural environment and rural ways of life and work activities, and threats to the community in general.

Finally, collaborative conservation balances and integrates founding and preservation. In considering ecological, economic, and community concerns together, collaborative conservation focuses on the health and diversity of an ecosystem that embraces both human beings and nature. It thus aims at a comprehensive, ecosystemic perspective that cautiously approaches or even rejects ecologically risky practices like logging old growth while taking into account the survival and vitality of the rural, resource-based economy. Collaborative conservation does not seek a mere compromise between environmentalists and resource interests, but attempts to draw together ecological responsibility and concern for human social and economic needs into a unified perspective.[74] Such a perspective integrates founding activities with preservation of human communities and natural ecosystems.

As the Applegate experience shows, such community building takes time and often requires many small successes to build social capital and trust among participants and the community at large. Graham Chisolm cautions that one cannot assume a unified community exists and will simply express itself given the right forums and a change in prevailing power structures, for "in reality we are often confronted by fractious entities that are bundles of, often diverging, interests."[75] Like metropolitan regionalism, collaborative conservation arises through painstaking coalition building. Here democratic participation is important as well, enhancing knowledge of the watershed and creating a stake in the community's long-term sustainability.[76]

The creation of an actual sense of community, rather than just a coalition, is often at best only an ideal, and to many participants this ideal might be too oppressive and demanding of conformity. A more realistic goal might be Villa's "partnership in argument and conversation," discussed earlier. By virtue of their attachments to a shared place, the parties would be committed to the process and to abiding by its substantive outcomes.

Challenges Facing Collaborative Conservation

As even its supporters admit, collaborative conservation faces many obstacles. These include, as we saw, external opposition from environmental, industry, and governmental groups. Other obstacles include market forces that favor unsustainable real estate development or timber harvesting.[77] Moreover, rural communities face their own internal problems. One should not romanticize these communities. Like communities everywhere, they are often divided by continuing, intransigent factionalism.[78]

Moreover, green opponents of collaborative conservation are right that communities operating at the local or watershed level may also lack the scale and authority to deal with national or global issues. A major problem here is that of insiders versus outsiders: local forums determining policy on national assets like federal forests. George Cameron Coggins[79] says that self-appointed local mediators are usurping national concerns and assets that should remain under national, federal control. Indeed, the national forests and other federal lands were organized to serve the nation, not just those living nearby. These lands are also embedded in larger ecosystems and regions whose scope may extend beyond the purview of a stakeholder group. Coggins rightly worries that devolution to local units could fragment management of large-scale regional or national concerns, like protection of endangered salmon in the Pacific Northwest. Thus many environmentalists, as I noted in chapter 5, argue that governance of ecosystems should not be opened to local democratic deliberation but managed more or less entirely according to ecological principles. Finally, local groups may be co-opted or dominated by industry representatives. Even Donald Snow, a staunch defender of collaborative conservation, acknowledges that national or non-local interests need to be represented in collaborative conservation groups or such groups ought to be subject to formal, external oversight.[80] The tensions that stakeholders face in balancing local or regional with national concerns and in balancing collaboration with the aims of the groups they represent reflect this conflict between different scales of concern and decision making.

Collaborative conservation may also emphasize procedure itself at the expense of substantive goals. Cary Coglianese[81] maintains that such a consensus-building effort "shifts the ultimate goal away from reaching a quality decision and moves it toward reaching an agreeable one." The process may yield "policies that are based on cumbersome compromises of principles, the lowest common denominator, or the most tractable but least important issue."[82] Sturtevant and Lange note, "Collaborative groups favor broadening areas of agreement while avoiding the most contentious issues," a characteristic that marked the Applegate Partnership's reluctance to get involved in a highly contentious timber sale just outside the watershed.[83] Indeed, in their evaluation of collaborative conservation and similar efforts, Yaffee et al. say that the positive outcomes cited most often can be seen as procedural in nature. Nevertheless, such achievements may lay the groundwork for eventual ecological success.[84]

Furthermore, a consensus-based process can create sources of conflict that do not exist with other methods of policy making. Conflicts can arise over who will participate in the negotiations, the meaning of the agreement, or the extent to which the final policy decision complies with that agreement.[85]

Since they are voluntary, collaborative conservation groups more often reflect organized interests within a particular community rather than the public at large.[86] One group that has been bypassed or even excluded by collaborative conservation, Baker and Kusel point out, consists of immigrant and minority workers, particularly those that are not settled in one place. These groups are largely unrecognized in the focus on place-based, predominately white, rural forest communities. As indicated earlier, tree planters are mainly mobile, Latino workers who are poorly paid. Many are undocumented.[87]

Collaborative decision-making structures are also informal, and the groups themselves are often transient and ad hoc. As I remarked earlier about ad hoc groups, this raises serious questions of accountability and sources of conflict. Thus, in their study of the Applegate Partnership, Sturtevant and Lange note, "The hard question continues to surface: 'Who is the Applegate community, and who gets to speak for it?'"[88]

Indeed, the environmentalist criticism of collaborative conservation has some merit as long as collaborations do not have established, coherent, widely recognized mechanisms for accountability to local, regional, and national publics. Emerging coalitions may be appropriate for bridging conflicts within regions, coming up with some basis for regional cooperation, and in some cases even generating a sense of community and shared purpose. However, collaborative conservation ultimately requires more institutionalized decision-making processes and participants who are democratically elected by the community at large.

Somewhat more formalized forms of collaborative conservation have emerged with the AMAs established under the Northwest Forest Plan. The principle of local, stakeholder-based groups has also been formalized with the provision, under the 2000 Secure Rural Schools and Community Self-Determination Act, for the establishment of resource advisory committees to work with federal lands agencies. The U.S. Fish and Wildlife Service has also worked with stakeholder groups on more formalized regional plans to protect endangered species and important habitat while allowing real estate development to go through. The most notable of these plans was crafted by the Clinton administration, local governments, real estate developers, and environmentalists in the San Diego area.[89] In some cases, federal legislation has given collaborative conservation groups national forest planning authority, an approach taken most notably and controversially with California's Quincy Library Group. In all these examples, however, collaboratives fall short of direct democratic accountability to the public.

Institutionalization would sacrifice some flexibility of organizational structure, goals, and membership, but it could create more inclusive and stable processes and memberships, including representation for outsiders and for migrant workers. Formalized accountability could also help an organization weather fundamental disagreements because the losers on a particular issue would have recourse to democratic procedures through which they might prevail in future battles. Moreover, foreclosing the exit option associated with informal, voluntary membership could enable groups to address tougher issues that might otherwise drive away voluntary coalition partners. Furthermore, participants could claim more legitimacy as representatives of the community and would have clearer lines of accountability to their constituents. These considerations, however, do not mean we ought to eschew more informal, ad hoc decision making on the part of various citizens' groups. A formalized collaborative consensus group could even serve such citizen's groups by acting as a clearinghouse for organizational resources, information, and training, and as a forum for members of the community to air grievances and debate.

Unproven and problematic as it is, collaborative conservation may offer our best hope in easing the polarization and deadlock on many place-based wilderness and resource issues. The goals of national environmental groups may in fact be better served by local or regional democracy. The reliance of environmentalists on litigation and coercive regulation has only aroused resentment and backlash among rural westerners, who are essential to complying with and carrying out environmental policy, and contributed to deadlock in Washington.[90] There is also the possibility that collaborative conservation might create some approximation of a united front among westerners, from ranchers to radical greens, who are concerned about the decline of the West's beauty, ecological integrity, and way of life under the assault of unmanaged growth.[91]

The Urban/Suburban/Rural Interface

Turning to the urban/suburban/rural interface, I focus on solutions to sprawl, one of the most serious challenges discussed here. I first provide a quick overview of policies to combat sprawl and sustain a geographically diverse region and then discuss some specific policies in more detail.

An Antisprawl Program

Regional efforts to manage development, prevent sprawl, and combine founding and preservation should involve growth boundaries (which work well in combination with other growth management policies); higher-density and mixed-use development; mass-transit networks to curtail automobile-dependent development; protection, taxation, spending, and development strategies to preserve farmland, wilderness, and fragile ecosystems and bring investment back into established population centers, older suburbs, and inner cities; and corridors to connect urban green spaces and ease migration of wildlife. Regional as well as federal, state, and local governments should also eliminate regulations and incentives that promote sprawl. The most important step here—and it is admittedly controversial—would be for a regional government to take over local zoning, which is inconsistent with effective, coordinated regional planning, and eliminate zoning laws that more or less mandate sprawl. A New Urbanist-type model of high-density, pedestrian-oriented, mixed-use development—without New Urbanism's architectural orthodoxy—should be put in place of current zoning models.

Governments should also refrain from paying for infrastructure and services to accommodate new sprawling development. Many municipalities charge developers impact fees to cover the full costs of new roads, utilities, and water and sewer lines as well as additional burdens on public schools. In many states, municipalities can only impose such fees after the state government has adopted legislation enabling them to do so. Although the use of impact fees and the number of states passing enabling legislation has greatly expanded since the 1980s, impact fees have not been uniformly accepted, in part because of opposition from developers. For example, New Jersey has long faced the problem of sprawl, but it is only now, after two decades of debate in the state legislature, that the

governor and legislators have undertaken a serious effort to give municipalities significant powers to impose impact fees. In Wisconsin, a 2006
law severely *restricted* the ability of municipalities to levy such fees.[92]

Federal subsidies for private home ownership, including mortgage interest deductions, are also a major incentive for sprawl. Ideally, they
should be scaled back, particularly for more expensive or second homes,
although this would be politically challenging, to put it mildly, when
home ownership embodies the American Dream. A more realistic
approach would be to subsidize housing in higher-density and mixed-
income neighborhoods.[93]

A regional government should also work to maintain neighborhoods
and historical architecture. As Moe and Wilkie repeatedly emphasize,
neighborhood preservation does not mean just preserving buildings; it
also means revitalizing the community by providing assistance to community groups, improving local services, and nurturing or bringing in
new businesses. In a number of cities and towns, old architectural trea-
sures, including factories, warehouses, fire stations, and banks, have been
reused for housing, commercial space, and cultural venues. Older districts have been revitalized through the development of new attractions,
like baseball stadiums, especially when landmark protections are also in
place. Although sports arenas are not always a wise public investment,
in Denver, the construction of Coors Field, home of the major league
baseball Colorado Rockies, helped revive an old historic district.[94] Preservation and founding can thus work hand-in-hand in reviving older
communities. It is important, though, that revitalization not mean just
more of the same global businesses moving into an area, or that restored
areas serve tourists rather than the local community. Furthermore, revitalization should not drive out existing businesses or residents, a point I
will turn to later.

Urban Growth Boundaries

Perhaps the most direct way to combat sprawl and preserve the countryside is to stop sprawl in its tracks through urban growth boundaries. As
mentioned earlier, Oregon and most notably the Portland metro area,
have sought to stem sprawl through a regionalist approach that includes
UGBs and surrounding greenbelts. In Portland, Metro has enforced the
UGB and stringent land-use controls within it.

Portland's experience shows both the promise and limitations of UGBs. David Rusk, writing before the passage of Measure 37, said, "Portland's urban growth boundary has succeeded in protecting farmland in Oregon's rich Willamette Valley. If the Metro Council sticks to its plans, over the next forty-five years, only about four square miles of current farmland will be urbanized—as much farmland as is subdivided in the state of Michigan every ten days."[95] Though this may well change under Measure 37, Portland's developed area has thus grown at a vastly slower rate than that of other cities. The UGB has also moved investment back into urban centers, giving Portland a vibrant economy, and has prompted regulations mandating higher housing densities.

However, UGBs are not sufficient in combating sprawl, as Portland learned. Urban growth boundaries do not necessarily determine what happens within the boundary. Sprawling development within Portland's boundary caused planners and voters to adopt a new fifty-year growth plan in 1997 that includes new zoning measures to encourage more high-density development within the UGB. This was an important modification. Calthorpe and Fulton offer the contrasting lesson of Boulder, Colorado. There a UGB and greenbelt were also established, but the city did not push to increase housing within the UGB. This meant that development within the city could not accommodate job growth, and sprawl simply jumped over the greenbelt into communities beyond.[96]

Moreover, for Portland to effectively manage development, growth must be controlled not only within the UGB but on an even wider regional basis than it currently is; this is obviously a tall order, given the context created by Measure 37. A wider regional approach would include adjacent areas in Washington State, especially Vancouver. Restrictions on urban growth cannot stop at state borders. Regions that straddle state lines may require governments that cross these boundaries as well. One limited example is the Port Authority of New York and New Jersey, although it hardly fits the model of a democratic structure and is not involved in comprehensive regional land-use management but controls only certain facilities.

As it is, Portland's growth restrictions have in part pushed sprawl across the Columbia River to Vancouver. In 1997, the growth boundary itself was expanded by almost 8 square miles to accommodate more growth. Sprawl has also leapfrogged across the greenbelt surrounding Portland, and McMansions have begun sprouting in the countryside.

Finally, it has been alleged that the increasing scarcity of buildable land within the Portland metro area itself helps to drive up housing prices and reduce affordable housing. However, there may be less to this argument than commonly thought. Calthorpe and Fulton note that Portland's housing market has followed the ups and downs of Oregon's economy and that rising housing prices during the 1990s were associated with a major high-tech boom in which Portland added jobs at about twice the national average. The authors also point out that during the 1990s, home prices in Salt Lake City, which lacked growth restrictions, rose approximately 70 percent, which was slightly more than in Portland.[97]

Portland's growth-management program has on the whole been extremely promising and is far ahead of other efforts to manage sprawl. However, Measure 37 could ultimately undo Portland's model. If property owners are able to transfer land without the property losing its coverage under the new law, then significant development will start sprouting beyond the growth boundaries. Again, one lesson that might be drawn from Measure 37 is to avoid excessive zeal and rigidity in establishing growth boundaries and other regulations.

Using Development to Limit Sprawl

Controlling sprawl and managing growth do not mean shutting the door on new development. In fact, the right sorts of development can help save areas from encroachment by sprawl. A key strategy here is "smart growth," an approach undertaken most notably in Maryland in the late 1990s by former Governor Parris N. Glendening. Smart growth simultaneously limits sprawl and contributes to urban revitalization by directing state or local development funds toward existing communities and developed areas rather than greenfields and the suburban fringe.[98] New Jersey's state government has also used the distribution of funding to limit sprawl and encourage compliance with a statewide growth plan.[99]

One way of further developing areas that are already built up is through infill of currently sprawling suburbs to create higher densities and more pedestrian-friendly neighborhoods. Plenty of development opportunities exist in land occupied by abandoned malls and in the vast, often paved spaces, such as parking lots and unnecessarily wide roads, between highly dispersed structures.[100] New Urbanist designs are highly appropriate in transforming these areas. There is a double benefit to infill: less sprawl and more functional communities. Infill is being pursued throughout the nation, most notably in Washington's Puget Sound area.

Calthorpe has also long championed transit-oriented development (TOD). The aim of TOD is to cluster development around transit hubs and connect pedestrian-friendly communities through networks of rails, buses, bikeways, pedestrian routes, and other alternatives to the car. "The central notion of TODs," say Calthorpe and Fulton, "was that clustering jobs, services, and housing in areas served by transit would give people several convenient alternatives to the car: walking, biking, carpooling, buses, and rail. But the land uses needed to be more than clustered; the vision was to create interconnected neighborhoods and districts designed for the pedestrian as well as the car."[101] Transit-oriented development was incorporated into Portland's Region 2040 plan.[102]

Sustaining Rural and Wilderness Areas

Other strategies are available to stop the spread of sprawl into the countryside. Outright land purchases by public agencies or nonprofits can protect wilderness areas and working farms and forests. In several states, open space purchases have been paid for by bonds or by taxes on real estate transfers.[103] In the antisprawl measures approved in 1998, the most common measure was authorization of funding to acquire parks, farmland, and other open space. Moreover, from 1994 to 2005, states and localities approved around $31 billion in land conservation projects.[104]

In order to facilitate more government land purchases, the U.S. government should fully fund, at its $900 million annual authorization, the federal Land and Water Conservation Fund (LWCF). For one thing, the LWCF assists states and localities in making open space purchases. The LWCF has funded the acquisition of some 2.3 million acres by states and localities. In addition, the LWCF has funded the purchase of 4.5 million acres of land by federal agencies. However, appropriations for the LWCF, which was established in 1964, have rarely approached or exceeded the authorization level. Following low levels during the 1980s and most of the 1990s, appropriations were at their highest in Fiscal Year 2001, when they exceeded $900 million. However, in Fiscal Year 2002 they fell back well below the authorization level and have declined ever since. Grants for state and local land purchases have been especially shortchanged over the years, and now the Bush Administration wants to entirely eliminate this part of the LWCF.[105]

Other antisprawl policies rely on incentives. These include tax breaks for preservation or continued agricultural use, as well as conservation easements. Conservation easements enable landowners, usually farmers, to sell their development rights to a government or private land trust.[106] Landowners receive the monetary difference between selling the land for employment under its existing use—as farmland, ranchland, timberland, or other open space—and selling it to a developer.[107]

Nonprofit land trusts play an important role in land purchases and conservation easements, either by purchasing and managing land themselves or by working with governments on land acquisition; land-use and regional planning; and wilderness, habitat, and resource management. The best-known and largest land trust is the Nature Conservancy, founded in 1951. This organization, with assets of over $4.4 billion, has protected more than 117 million acres of land and 5,000 miles of river around the world.[108] The Nature Conservancy both maintains its own vast portfolio of conservation lands and also assists governments in land acquisition and planning. Another major land trust, the Trust for Public Land, operates in a slightly different manner. It eases government acquisition of open space, particularly when public agencies cannot move quickly enough to purchase a threatened area, by buying land and eventually transferring it to a public agency.[109] Two other major national nonprofits are not land trusts per se but devote themselves to land preservation. The National Trust for Historic Preservation provides financial assistance, expertise, and advocacy to help preserve downtowns and historic structures and landscapes.[110] The American Farmland Trust provides similar functions in protecting farmland from development and in promoting ecologically sound agriculture.[111]

There are also more than 1,500 local and regional land trusts throughout the United States. The Land Trust Alliance (LTA) provides funding and expertise to assist these organizations. According to the LTA, local and regional land trusts had protected more than 9.3 million acres by the end of 2003, double the amount as of 1998.[112]

Land trusts are involved not only in preservation but also in maintaining rural resource activities. Maine's Downeast Lakes Land Trust, for example, is working with other members of the Downeast Lakes Forestry

Partnership to protect 342,000 acres of forest. The land would be set aside not just for wilderness but also for working forests. The Downeast Lakes Land Trust explicitly invokes place-based values, noting that it is seeking to sustain the "local economy, linked by tradition to the natural resource base for sustenance." The organization calls the Forestry Partnership "the first northern Maine forest conservation project that is **community incubated, community supported, community led,** and designed to sustain a natural resource based, rural community economy and the lifestyle of residents in Washington County, Maine."[113]

Despite the valuable work done by land trusts, a recent study suggests that they increasingly need to consider the broader economic and ecological impact of their land purchases. Such purchases can increase land values in the surrounding area and encourage development on lands that might be even more ecologically valuable than the protected parcels.[114] Inadequately coordinated land purchases by public agencies are also vulnerable to these criticisms. Often, says Shutkin, public purchases of open space become an easy way to avoid comprehensive land-use planning and the difficult choices it involves.[115]

Sally Fairfax and the other authors of a recent volume on land trusts raise similar concerns that these organizations' land purchases may not serve important conservation priorities but may instead reflect the needs of sellers. They also point out that open space acquisition by land trusts can be costly, as buyers often overpay for land and sellers can bid up the price by threatening to sell to developers. Furthermore, reliance on private land trusts can crowd out purchases by public agencies, and such a focus on private sector efforts reinforces the notion of land preservation as a voluntary, reimbursed activity undertaken by private property owners and only if sufficient financial rewards are forthcoming. Moreover, in the vast majority of cases, the public is denied access to the protected private lands. Indeed, private land purchases often involve at best limited public accountability and transparency. Purchases also tend to reflect the priorities of wealthy citizens who support land trusts; consequently, too few resources go to the purchase of open space in urban or poor communities. Finally, preservationist measures like conservation easements may ultimately be difficult to enforce by private entities like land trusts. The authors argue that land trusts should work more closely with the local community and public agencies in planning land purchases and that government should exercise more oversight over land trusts, in part to ensure that easements are actually enforced. While not denying the importance of private land trusts, Fairfax and her co-authors also urge greater public-sector efforts to acquire land in a more coordinated fashion, including through the use of eminent domain, and a governmental role in purchasing land that serves lower-income and urban communities and provides public access.[116]

Such governmental efforts would complement the work of *community land trusts*. Community land trusts are much smaller in number than the more traditional conservation-oriented land trusts. Only about 100 exist in the United States.[117] They are urban and rural organizations concerned not so much with preserving land as with revitalizing communities. They acquire land to create affordable housing, provide space for commercial development, reduce absentee ownership, and promote homeownership, local reinvestment, and local control over land use. Community land trusts also acquire land for recreational facilities and community gardens, and oftentimes they also undertake functions served by conservation land trusts, including historic preservation and the protection of farms, working forests, ecologically sensitive areas, and other open spaces.[118]

Regional government would be well suited to mapping, targeting, and coordinating all of these public and private land protection and development efforts. Regional authorities could employ comprehensive planning in cooperation with local communities and nonprofits, pursue public land purchases and conservation easements, maintain regulatory oversight of private land purchases, and offer financial incentives to encourage preservation or redevelopment. In discharging these responsibilities, regional authorities should maximize ecological, economic, cultural, and other landscape values; pursue or encourage land purchases to benefit lower-income and urban residents; ensure public access to open space; and keep intact flourishing or otherwise important landscapes, whether urban, suburban, rural, or wild. Some governance and coordination of land purchases or other conservation activities could also take place at the local level. In Randolph, New Jersey, residents formed the Randolph Township Open Space Committee to advise the town on open space purchases. The committee's criteria for determining which parcels to purchase include environmental or habitat value, development pressure, size, and physical connection or nearness to other open space.[119]

Rural, Urban, and Suburban Agriculture

A regional government should also take advantage of potential synergies between preservation of farmland and urban revitalization. For example, establishing public or farmers' markets oriented to small, local, or regional growers can help shore up agriculture and reconnect urban and suburban residents to the local natural environment. Such markets can also help revitalize downtowns. Public markets exist in such places as Lancaster, Pennsylvania; Philadelphia; Seattle; Vancouver, Washington; and Portland, Maine. According to the U.S. Department of Agriculture, the number of farmers' markets nationwide increased from 1,755 in 1994 to 3,706 in 2004.[120]

In an effort to bring a part of the countryside back into town, many communities have cultivated urban or community gardens, often on vacant land. Such gardens can provide urban and suburban dwellers with an opportunity to grow their own food and can introduce freshly picked produce into an urban environment and contribute to a sense of place.[121]

Urban gardens have been part of the efforts of the environmental justice movement to restore environmental quality to working-class and minority communities. African-American communities in the San Francisco Bay Area and Boston, and Latino communities in New York City have planted crops in urban gardens, beautifying empty lots and median strips while reclaiming an ethnic agricultural heritage.[122] The urban garden, says Barbara Lynch, "offers respite from the pressures of urban life, produces food to share with family and neighbors, offers its cultivators ties to the rural landscapes of other times and places, and is an act of rebellion against the North American definition of urban space with its clearly defined zones and segregated land uses. In short, it transforms an alienated and alienating environment into a nurturing one."[123] Shutkin describes such an effort in Boston's Dudley neighborhood, which has suffered from poverty and pollution.[124] There the grassroots Dudley Street Neighborhood Initiative (DNSI) has cleaned up polluted and vacant sites to create a 3-acre urban farm, a greenhouse, and other food enterprises, with the products sold at local stores and a neighborhood farmers' market and distributed to food banks and shelters.

Drawing on his experience running a community farm in Weston, Massachusetts, Brian Donahue envisions combining easements, subsidies, and land purchases to create a significant "commons" of publicly and privately owned farms and working forests in each suburban community, especially newer suburbs that are in danger of destroying their agricultural land base.[125] Such a commons could employ full-time agriculturists as well as a large number of local residents as part-time workers.

Donahue argues that local, community-based forms of agriculture may in the long run move out of niche status and be economically competitive with centralized factory farming. The latter unsustainably relies on agrochemicals and extensive transportation networks, both of which are based on nonrenewable and ecologically destructive fossil fuels whose prices do not account for environmental externalities. The agrochemicals themselves are a major source of pollution. Moreover, large-scale farming, especially in the American West, frequently relies on unsustainable and subsidized irrigation systems, which might be rendered even more fragile by global warming. In addition, a growing world population could increase demand for locally grown crops. Even today, Donahue notes, locally produced fruits and vegetables can offer high quality and competitive prices compared with produce shipped long distances.[126]

Locally grown food is indeed becoming more popular, partly in reaction to what Mark Lapping calls the "globalization, corporate consolidation, and industrialization of the American food system." Lapping cites the development of "a significant number and variety of alternative agro-food models [that] counter the movement away from what remains of self-sufficiency and the trend of delocalization."[127]

The growing popularity of locally grown food is reflected in private-sector activities, such as restaurants' and supermarkets' increasing reliance on local or regional farms. The use of locally grown food to prepare restaurant or dining service meals also represents a form of regional value-added processing.[128]

Another important private sector trend is the community-supported agriculture, or CSA, movement. With CSAs, nearby residents pay an annual fee for a share of a farm's seasonal harvest and thus provide local farmers with guaranteed incomes. Customers become more familiar with local crops and more attuned to seasonal cycles. As noted on the website for the University of Massachusetts' extension program, the CSA movement is explicitly oriented to the values of place and to a regional perspective: "CSA reflects an innovative and resourceful strategy to connect local farmers with local consumers; develop a regional food supply and strong local economy; maintain a sense of community; encourage land stewardship; and honor the knowledge and experience of growers and producers working with small to medium farms." There are now 1200–1500 CSA farms in the United States.[129] Most are in rural areas, but some, like the Dudley neighborhood's urban farm, are in cities or suburbs. One role government can play in these marketplace activities is to use its own purchasing power to assist and promote local farming.[130]

Cities

Many of the antisprawl policies described above apply to cities. Here, however, I want to focus on policies that are more specifically targeted at urban revitalization. I first look at policies to reverse the decline of cities and then consider approaches to the rather different problem facing Ground Zero.

In-Place Strategies

Development targeted at urban centers and inner suburbs can bring economic opportunity back to these areas and redirect development away from the countryside. A combination of in-place and mobility strategies would be appropriate.

In-place strategies focus on revitalization of existing communities. These strategies include increased funding for affordable housing and encouraging business investment in economically distressed areas. Federal Empowerment Zone/Enterprise Community programs provide financial assistance and tax incentives to businesses investing in such places.[131]

Another, increasingly popular in-place tool is redevelopment of brownfields. Brownfields are abandoned toxic sites left fallow because of strict liability under the 1980 Comprehensive Environmental Response, Compensation, and Liability Act, or Superfund. Many of these are in low-income areas left behind by deindustrialization. Federal and state brownfields laws provide more flexible standards and tax incentives for the cleanup and redevelopment of polluted industrial sites and liability protection for owners, lenders, and developers who had no part in the original contamination. Redevelopment of brownfields benefits distressed communities and redirects development from the sprawling suburbs.

There are questions as to whether such redevelopment actually increases local employment. However, it improves the local quality of life and perhaps public health, and makes an area more attractive to business investment.[132]

Many families currently leave cities for the sprawling suburbs in search of better public schools. Consequently, another essential in-place strategy would be the equalization of school funding across localities. Such equalization would entail funding education through state or regional income taxes rather than local property taxes, as discussed earlier. As noted earlier, reliance on property taxes is inequitable and encourages sprawl.

In-place strategies are also needed in the context of growth management. Controlling sprawl, protecting open space, and even revitalizing urban areas or town centers can lead to rising property values and gentrification,[133] although the apparent experience of Portland in this regard may have been misinterpreted, as I discussed. Gentrification displaces lower- and moderate-income residents and local businesses and in doing so destroys existing neighborhoods and local character. Controls on development and measures to promote preservation must be supplemented by financial incentives or requirements for the preservation or construction of affordable housing, combined with assistance to locally owned businesses. The kind of mixed-use development favored by New Urbanists, such as locating housing over retail businesses, would also help increase the affordable housing stock.[134]

An important strategy for avoiding gentrification is reliance on grassroots neighborhood revitalization and development efforts, such as community land trusts. Moe and Wilkie show how preservation efforts in Pittsburgh involved the public sector, private foundations, and local citizens' community development organizations in rehabilitating historic structures, making them available to lower-income renters, and increasing rates of local home ownership.[135] Local activists also successfully pressured banks to increase their lending to lower-income communities. One law that helped here was the 1977 Community Reinvestment Act, which prohibited the notorious practice of "red-lining" and required lenders to do business with credit-worthy applicants in underserved urban and rural areas.[136]

The Dudley Street Neighborhood Initiative, mentioned earlier, is another grassroots neighborhood revitalization effort. As Shutkin discusses, urban agriculture is only one part of the DSNI's efforts. The organization has leveraged external funding and local support to shut down garbage transfer stations, build low-income housing, fight lead poisoning, involve local residents in comprehensive community "visioning" and planning sessions, and clean up hazardous waste sites. The initiative has taken on quasi-governmental powers. In 1988, "DSNI became the only community-based nonprofit organization in the country to be granted eminent domain power over abandoned land within its borders."[137] Thus the DSNI was able to take over and redevelop abandoned polluted sites and other vacant lots.

The Environmental Justice Movement

The Dudley Street Initiative and many other urban grassroots efforts are part of the environmental justice movement. The movement has mobilized around inequities of race and class in the siting of toxic waste dumps, polluting industries, and other noxious facilities, and in the incidence of air and water pollution. Backed by a number of studies, environmental justice activists charge that American industrial society inequitably concentrates environmental insults in relatively powerless constituencies, particularly people of color, the poor, and ethnic communities. Environmental justice activists have also accused environmentalists of disregarding the ultimate destination of noxious facilities kept out of affluent, white communities. Furthermore, they have criticized environmentalists for championing nonhuman nature while largely ignoring disenfranchised human communities.

The history of the environmental justice movement, which goes back to 1982, is documented elsewhere; I do not rehearse it here.[138] However, the movement deserves special mention for two reasons. First, it offers a grassroots strategy for in-place urban revitalization. Second, like collaborative conservation, it explicitly rejects the dichotomy between founding and preservation and works to democratize the governance of place.

The environmental justice movement expands what is commonly recognized as environmentalism. Long-standing concerns of lower-income, minority, and ethnic communities have now been recognized as "environmental." The movement addresses not only the incidence of environmental hazards but also a host of public health and quality-of-life matters: urban open space and community gardens as well as housing, homelessness, inadequate infrastructure, workplace safety, drugs, neighborhood security, and schools. Moreover, the movement belies environmentalism's traditionally white, middle- and upper-class profile. Environmental justice activists have been disproportionately lower-income women of color.[139] While such an expansion of "environmental" threatens to obscure the particular significance of ecological concerns, it also addresses the founding–preservation dichotomy that has plagued the politics of place. Moreover, the movement's expanded environmental focus joins concerns about place with democratic aspirations. The movement ties the restoration of local communities' environmental quality to the democratic empowerment of these neighborhoods.

Environmental Justice's Mixed Community
Environmental justice rejects extremes of both founding and preservation. Cynthia Hamilton and Robert Bullard, both of them activists and academics associated with the movement, are highly critical of industrialization, capitalism, and the domination of nature as fostering an imperialist ethos and leading to the ecological victimization of the poor and people of color. Bullard also criticizes the destructive aspects of competition between locales: the mobility of capital and the threat of unemployment force disadvantaged communities to accept noxious facilities and hazardous workplaces, a phenomenon termed "environmental blackmail."[140]

However, environmental justice activists are not radical preservationists. The environmental justice movement criticizes the focus of mainstream environmentalists on a "pristine" nature free of human "interference." Environmentalists, they say, end up giving higher priority to the protection of wilderness, biodiversity, and natural systems than to the health and flourishing of human communities and settled landscapes. Environmental justice instead sees humanized landscapes as legitimate parts of larger ecological systems. The human community and its actual conditions of existence, rather than an idealized preindustrial or preagricultural way of life, are as much a part of the environment as are the habitats of other organisms.

Giovanna Di Chiro says that environmental justice offers the model of the *mixed community*, in which humans and nonhumans are drawn together through diverse interactions and assemblages. The mixed community "presupposes connection to and interconnectedness with other groups, other species, and the natural environment."[141] The mixed community does not exclude human activities such as work and economic development. Rather, "the natural world [is] understood as including all aspects of daily life."[142]

The ideal of the mixed community suggests a constructive project beyond fighting pollution, as we saw with the example of urban agriculture. Groups such as Concerned Citizens of Los Angeles, in addition to protesting incinerators, have also sponsored efforts to clean up graffiti and trash and promote neighborhood redevelopment.[143] Such activism often builds on existing social networks such as church membership.[144] Overall, the environmental justice movement has sought to reaffirm and reclaim a sense of place and local community and reestablish ecological health in a distressed environment.[145]

Democratic Aims Beyond Justice and Health

Despite its name, the environmental justice movement goes well beyond distributive aims. Its emphasis on collectively restoring places and resisting the imposition of environmental inequities promotes participatory democracy. Democracy is realized through a number of activities: mobilizing and radicalizing existing social networks; cultivating local expertise on environmental issues; participating, through demonstrations or formal channels, in the planning and siting of potential environmental hazards; seeking elected office; working collectively to improve local quality of life through neighborhood cleanups, urban gardening, or community development projects; turning to lawsuits or even civil disobedience when normal channels fail; and ultimately perhaps, establishing local governance on a neighborhood level.[146] Experience in the environmental justice movement, says Hamilton, encourages participants to "start questioning the private ownership of common resources and the elite domination of modern 'democratic' politics."[147] Moreover, the democratic orientation of environmental justice has involved challenging the power of environmental groups in land-use politics. Environmental justice groups argue that the poor and people of color have long been shut out of debates over the siting of hazardous facilities, and therefore the successful efforts of environmental groups to keep such facilities out of affluent communities have meant that working-class communities and people of color end up playing the unwilling hosts.[148]

There is considerable debate over whether the inequitable distribution of environmental hazards actually translates into significant health effects.[149] However, the impulse behind the movement may not be so much actual health threats as a desire for democratic empowerment and an improved quality of life.[150] The environmental justice movement is really about democratic governance of place and the ability of a community to resist the imposition of a noxious, unpleasant, and perhaps hazardous environment. Environmental justice activists seek to counter the radical refounding of places, including their own communities, into dumping grounds for society's wastes and sacrifice zones for other undesirable land uses. Through grassroots action they seek to restore and preserve a sense of place, including a revitalization of local community and culture, connections with the land, and local quality of life and aesthetic beauty.

Policy Successes of Environmental Justice

Environmental justice activists have achieved some public policy successes,[151] although they have not revolutionized or radically democratized land-use politics. During the 1990s, the U.S. Environmental Protection Agency created a number of offices to handle environmental justice concerns, researched the distribution of environmental hazards, investigated environmental discrimination, initiated lawsuits against polluters, created advisory bodies involving activists and other stakeholders, convened a summit meeting of grassroots groups in the southeastern United States, pursued educational and outreach efforts, and recruited minority students to pursue environmental careers and work at the EPA. In 1994, President Clinton issued an executive order directing each federal agency to identify and address disproportionate public health or environmental impacts of its programs on poor or minority populations. Clinton also required that environmental and health effects on poor and minority communities be analyzed when an environmental impact statement is prepared, and that poor and minority communities have adequate access to public information on human health and environmental matters. However, since the late 1990s and especially since 9/11, the federal government, citing the need to keep dangerous information from would-be terrorists, has been rolling back regulations that give the public the right to know about hazards at chemical plants, power plants, and other nearby facilities. Despite the national security argument, the regulatory changes are also the result of pressure from affected industries.[152]

There has also been considerable activity on environmental justice at the state and local levels. A diverse range of laws, regulations, and other programs limit the geographic concentration of waste facilities; focus environmental enforcement actions on communities severely burdened by noxious or hazardous facilities; investigate citizens' environmental justice complaints; require community impact statements as part of the permitting process for potentially noxious or hazardous facilities; and require that affected communities be notified of environmental hazards. Various programs also involve citizens' advisory groups in facilities siting and waste remediation; provide environmental databases and education, as well as funding and other organizing assistance, to local communities and environmental justice groups; and facilitate communication and ease tensions between industry and local communities. State and local programs also integrate environmental justice into transportation, growth, and other land-use planning; develop interagency strategies to address and coordinate environmental justice concerns; coordinate and communicate on environmental justice issues with the U.S. Environmental Protection Agency; and gather data and establish study commissions on environmental justice. Finally, some programs provide vegetable gardens, nature trails, and other open space in urban or other under-served areas.[153]

The Challenge Facing Environmental Justice
While environmental justice will be an important movement for years to come, and while it has inspired a significant array of federal, state, and local measures, it has still not managed to fundamentally change the processes by which facilities are sited.[154] Why not? There have been a number of criticisms of the movement,[155] but I would like to offer one that is directly relevant to this book: without regional or metropolitan governance to coordinate land uses, the democratization pushed by environmental justice activists may not sufficiently address inequities in power between localities.

The environmental justice movement has, in addition to the successes noted above, admittedly gone part of the way toward addressing geographic divisions and the resulting inequities by building alliances and coalitions across racial, class, and neighborhood lines.[156] In battling a proposed incinerator, minority, working-class women in south central Los Angeles were joined by white, middle-class women from across town. In Brooklyn's Williamsburg neighborhood, an alliance of Latinos and Hasidim, joined by African-Americans, Polish-Americans, and Italian-Americans, fought against an incinerator and a radioactive waste facility.[157] Such coalitional networks are often issue-focused, strategic, and temporary, but the participants may later join together on other issues.[158]

A more institutionalized effort at interlocal coordination and fairness in siting facilities was adopted by the City of New York as part of its new charter in 1989. The city adopted a "fair share" policy to ensure that each neighborhood and borough bears its fair share of undesirable land-use facilities, such as toxic waste sites, prisons, and homeless shelters.[159] In other areas around the country, state-level measures to limit the concentration of environmentally noxious or hazardous facilities and to integrate environmental justice considerations into land-use planning should also at least begin to address geographic inequities.

However, despite these grassroots and institutional efforts, it is difficult to imagine that major differences in environmental quality, in the distribution of LULUs, and even in the availability of environmental amenities like open space will significantly ease without regional or metropolitan governance. Environmental justice groups may push for local participation in facilities siting, activists may build temporary coalitions between communities, states may try to limit concentrations of new noxious or hazardous facilities and improve their land-use planning, and large cities like New York may work to equalize conditions within their borders. However, affluent, largely white municipalities will still use their autonomy and political resources to resist LULUs, and lower-income, largely minority or ethnic communities will still face economic blackmail and have to live with relatively poor environmental conditions. What is needed is an enduring metropolitan or other regional government that is democratically run but also has significant, long-term planning powers and has the authority to compel recalcitrant communities that resist the equitable distribution of environmental burdens and amenities. The environmental justice movement, by raising concern about geographic inequities, by building coalitions, and by moving states and localities toward more equitable facilities siting and land-use planning has laid important foundations for regionalism. Now, more formal structures need to be adopted.

Mobility Strategies

In-place strategies, whether pursued through government policy or grassroots activism, should be accompanied by measures that enable mobility. As noted earlier, regions are not monocentric but have numerous population centers. Consequently, job opportunities are not concentrated in center cities but are spread across a region. Today, many lower-wage employees do not have cars and face arduous commutes across metropolitan areas to communities unfriendly to mass transit or pedestrian traffic. In order to reduce traffic and road building, establish multiple-use, mixed-income neighborhoods, and provide affordable housing near—and even within walking distance of—jobs, moderate- and low-income residences need to be built in cities and towns throughout a region, not just where lower-income populations are currently concentrated. Moreover, public policies need to reverse class and (de facto) racial segregation and the resulting concentration of poverty and provide moderate- and low-income residents with more options on where to live.

Mobility policies that provide affordable housing throughout a metropolitan area can address these issues. Calthorpe and Fulton thus call for "fair-share" housing requirements mandating that each locality provide some specified share of affordable housing. Montgomery County, Maryland, one of the nation's most affluent counties, has successfully pursued a fair share housing policy since the 1970s.[160] The creation of mixed-income, mixed-use downtowns can also help ensure that affordable housing is not segregated or relegated to marginal areas.

The failures of one major mobility program provide further clues to how mobility should be handled in a regional context. The HOPE VI Program, established by the federal Department of Housing and Urban Development under Clinton, provides money for cities to demolish and replace public housing projects that have become centers of concentrated poverty and crime. Such projects, like the notorious Cabrini-Green high-rises in Chicago, also exemplified the mid-twentieth-century phenomenon of warehousing the poor in alienating high-rises. The aim of HOPE VI was to deconcentrate and disperse poverty by providing residents with housing vouchers so they could move into other areas. Those who remained would live in more villagelike surroundings, featuring mixed-income, New Urbanist-style traditional townhouses. Although well-intentioned, the program has had a number of serious problems.[161] The demolition of existing public housing broke up communities and their social bonds and displaced thousands of low-income residents. The new housing was not sufficient to replace the number of units that had been demolished, and the vouchers had little use without significant changes in regional housing markets; displaced residents were often unable to find housing they could afford. In some ways, HOPE VI repeated the neighborhood-clearing mistakes of urban renewal. Even Calthorpe, a supporter of HOPE VI, has acknowledged that the program cannot work without broader regional provisions for affordable housing and other opportunities for lower-income urban residents.[162] Moreover, demolition of existing housing projects, however decrepit or crime ridden, should take place only when sufficient housing options already exist.

Revisiting Ground Zero

Finally, we ought to address the urban problem raised in chapter 4, that of Ground Zero. This is not an issue of urban decline, but of recovering from a disaster that was in some ways the result of bad urban planning—the building of the World Trade Center; it was also a blow to a city that was in fact flourishing economically. However, the rebuilding of Ground Zero can fit into a broader vision for New York City as itself a kind of region within the larger metropolitan area.

In chapter 4 we reviewed various proposals for Ground Zero. My own argument was that a recovery of the area, and an approach that integrated founding and preservation, entailed the creation of a mixed-use residential and retail neighborhood with a memorial component rather than rebuilding all or almost all of the lost office space or completely dedicating the area to a memorial. A mixed-use neighborhood is what local residents wanted but did not obtain.

My view of Ground Zero is in many ways consistent with a more regional approach offered by Sorkin.[163] Sorkin's proposal simultaneously addresses the needs of the Lower Manhattan neighborhoods and those of New York City as a whole. He concedes that the 10 million square feet of office space lost at Ground Zero needs to be replaced and he even maintains that additional office space eventually must be built in New York City. However, in criticizing the "hyperconcentration of the World Trade Center,"[164] Sorkin argues that none of the restored or new office space should be located at Ground Zero. It should instead be dispersed to other parts of Lower Manhattan and, importantly, to other centers throughout New York City.

Sorkin recognizes the benefits of face-to-face concentration of business operations and rejects sprawl. At the same time, though, he approaches the city as a polycentric region. He argues that the overweening centrality of Manhattan and of its individual commercial districts has sapped the economic vitality of the city's other boroughs and inflated real estate prices in Manhattan below 110th Street, increasingly making the area a monocultural haven for the rich. In a repudiation of urban renewal, the city preserved the historic architecture of Manhattan neighborhoods but at the same time it allowed extreme gentrification to destroy the cultural distinctiveness of these areas.[165]

Sorkin offers what is in effect a miniature version of the working landscape. He has called for turning all of Ground Zero into a memorial green, an excessively preservationist idea that I believe is at odds with the needs of local residents. However, his proposals in many ways add up to the mixed-use neighborhood vision favored by local residents, but on a somewhat larger scale. The key here is the shifting of office space away from the old World Trade Center site and, to a large degree, from Lower Manhattan itself. This would create a more balanced, mixed-use approach to real estate in Lower Manhattan while fostering the creation of mixed-use centers in other parts of the city. Both Lower Manhattan and other areas in the five boroughs would become mixed-use, mixed-income, pedestrian-friendly "urban villages," interspersed with and connected by greenways "for pedestrians, bikers, and nonaggressive zero-emissions vehicles."[166] His detailed vision for Lower Manhattan itself includes, in addition to these amenities, improved transit facilities; more housing; more parks; increased waterfront development; a combined set of academic quads linking local elementary and middle schools, high schools, colleges, and universities; and the provision of greater pedestrian access between Battery Park City and neighboring communities through the underground submersion of the West Street highway.[167] Aside from Sorkin's vision for the 16 acres of Ground Zero itself, this is largely consistent with what many Lower Manhattan residents themselves wanted (although a number of Battery Park City residents wanted to preserve their exclusionary isolation), and it shows how the residents' integration of founding and preservation—creating a vibrant new neighborhood while remembering the fallen—could fit into a larger regional perspective.[168]

From forests in southwestern Oregon and eastern Maine to urban gardens in Boston to regional planners' offices in Atlanta, Denver, Minneapolis, and Portland to inner cities in Pittsburgh and Los Angeles to neighborhoods in Lower Manhattan to suburbs in New Jersey and to working farms, forests, and ranches protected by conservation easements around the nation, activists, government officials, enlightened business leaders, civic organizations, and ordinary citizens are working, often unconsciously, to achieve an alternative approach to inhabiting, caring for, enjoying, and using the landscape. Their efforts suggest a realistic, promising politics that rejects the dichotomy of founding and preservation and instead tries to integrate both into a democratic practice of place by which we can simultaneously shape our spatial world and preserve its important ecological and cultural qualities enough to feel secure and at home in it. These efforts, which are in many cases pursued with scant awareness of one another, can be seen anew as the policy program for an emerging politics of place, a politics I call the working landscape.

Postscript
Place and the Lessons of Katrina

Baby, I had a beautiful home. It's hard when you lived on your own for so many years and just like you pop your finger, or in the twinkling of an eye, you're homeless.
—Seventy-one-year-old New Orleans resident Gloria Jordan, who had lost her home of 49 years to Hurricane Katrina, quoted in AP story

In the end, place still matters, even in a world of globalized networks. However, its importance does not guarantee that place, as a value or practice, will survive. We must be alert to the danger that a key human value may be lost as a result of social, economic, and political forces, a loss abetted by the intellectual apologias offered for placelessness. We ought not passively accept such a loss of place. We do face a crisis of place, and there is a need for deliberate public policies. These policies must be focused on a balancing and integration of founding and preservation as well as the democratic empowerment of localities and regions so that individuals and communities may properly care for and cultivate the places they inhabit, the places they work in, the places they visit, the places they revere or respect, and the places they love.

However, at the risk of concluding on a somber note, I must point out that much of what I advocate in this book could be for naught unless we address a global problem that is lurking in the background: the problem of climate change. The devastating landfall of Hurricane Katrina on the Gulf Coast on August 29, 2005 may be a preview of a chaotic, rootless future if steps are not taken to limit the consumption of fossil fuels and deforestation and thus mitigate the warming of the Earth's climate by carbon dioxide, methane, and other greenhouse gases.

Katrina as a Story of Displacement

The story of the Katrina disaster is in large part a story of the loss of home and of place. Katrina devastated a wide swath of the Gulf Coast. In New Orleans, the storm flooded 80 percent of the city. An estimated "700,000 or more people may have been acutely impacted by Hurricane Katrina, as a result of residing in areas that flooded or sustained significant structural damage."[1] The hurricane may have displaced as many as 1.2 million people.[2]

The Katrina disaster provided graphic testimony of the vulnerabilities of a supposedly advanced civilization to natural forces and of America's deep racial and economic inequalities and political ineptitude. The events in New Orleans were the most shocking and publicized. Thousands of mainly poor, minority, and elderly residents were trapped in the city as it was inundated. Looters roamed the streets; people were stranded on rooftops and highways; and evacuees faced appallingly inhumane conditions in the Superdome and Convention Center.

The official death toll from Katrina as of August 2006 was 1,695, with total damage estimated at $100 billion.[3] The survivors lost loved ones as well as homes and neighborhoods, i.e., places of deep personal and cultural attachment. Many Gulf Coast residents were exiled to unfamiliar communities that were often, but not always, welcoming.

The simultaneous loss of both one's house and one's neighborhood is profoundly devastating. Neighborhoods provide social networks and familiar places that can sustain someone facing the loss of a home. With the neighborhood gone as well, there is much less to fall back on. Louisiana State University sociologist Jeanne Hurlbert says, "What makes this a catastrophe isn't just the loss of physical structures. It's the phenomenal destruction of networks, the enormous loss of emotional and social support."[4]

For many, the loss of their pre-Katrina home and neighborhood may be irrevocable. In New Orleans, for example, the prospects for a more or less complete return of the city's residents remain highly uncertain. According to a survey done by the state of Louisiana and released in October 2006, only 187,525 of the pre-Katrina population of 454,863 had returned.[5] A March 2006 report by the RAND Corporation predicted that the city's population will be at only 272,000 three years after Katrina.[6]

The losses, especially in New Orleans, may be not only personal but cultural. New Orleans has in many ways been a deeply troubled city, plagued by extreme poverty, enormous crime rates, racial tensions, economic inequality, and corrupt and inept government. Yet it has also been blessed with a unique, diverse, artistic, and often eccentric culture, and has nurtured distinctive and enormously influential architectural, musical, culinary, literary, and festive traditions. This rich culture is considerably indebted to New Orleans' pre-Katrina African-American majority, and it may be doomed by undeniable ecological and geographical realities. If many of the dislocated do not return, and if flood-prone neighborhoods like the largely African-American Lower Ninth Ward and New Orleans East are not rebuilt, the city could lose much of its distinctive cultural character.[7]

Climate Change and Displacement

Whether or not Katrina's ferocity was attributable to climate change, the storm's havoc might be a preview of similar disasters. Not only are we entering a natural cycle of increased hurricane activity, but global warming may be boosting the intensity of hurricanes.[8] These trends, coupled with recent population growth and development in coastal areas, may result in a series of enormously devastating hurricanes in this century. The destructive impacts could be augmented by rising sea levels as a result of the thermal expansion of the oceans and the melting of ice caps and glaciers.[9] The United Nations Institute for Environment and Human Security warns that by 2010 there may be more than 50 million environmental refugees worldwide, with the number eventually growing into the hundreds of millions.[10]

Even if, under a highly optimistic scenario, the victims of intense hurricanes, rising sea levels, and other manifestations of global warming find new homes, neighbors, and jobs, the loss to personal and collective identities and histories and to social networks, communities, and cultures may be enormous. In other words, global warming may generate a serious worldwide crisis of forced displacement and homelessness.

Certainly New Orleans and other Gulf Coast communities have always been vulnerable to storms and flooding, given their geographic location and in many cases—most notably with New Orleans—their low elevations.[11] Irrespective of climate change, such disasters are endemic to the region. However, as the Earth warms and the ecological impacts proliferate, many other places may find themselves in a similarly vulnerable situation: places where rainfall is either scarce or excessive or where the temperature is often too hot or where potable water supplies depend on winter snow pack or where subsistence hunters seek game on frozen seas or where sewer systems are vulnerable to intrusion from rising waters or where homes are at risk from forest fires or mudslides. In other words, countless places around the world will be affected, each with its collective life and social bonds, its history, its climate and natural terrain, its plant and animal populations, its homes, its culture, and its particular ecological constraints and vulnerabilities.

The graphic images and stories of displacement caused by Katrina are profoundly sobering and could be repeated innumerable times elsewhere. Writer Tom Piazza describes his sense of trauma after having to flee New Orleans and then seeing images on television of his city "sliding into chaos."[12] He points out that he was fortunate, being able to evacuate to "a place with heat, water, medicine, food, air-conditioning at the push of a button, people to care, television to give me up-to-date news, friends and family bombarding me with calls and e-mails." He then asks, "What about the man I saw on television, walking down the street holding two young boys, his sons, by the hands, wearing only a ragged T-shirt, crying in front of the news cameras, a man like many I had spent time around, a grown man, my age, reduced to tears in front of his sons and the eyes of the world because the rickety supports that he had managed to put together for himself and his family had blown away like dust in the breeze?"[13]

In a March 1, 2005 segment on National Public Radio's *All Things Considered*, Torrie Lawson, a displaced New Orleans junior high school student, said to interviewer Michele Norris, "If you had told me I would have lived in a trailer before Katrina, I would have took it as an insult. I wouldn't have believed you. But now, it's like—it's nothing like my home. I wish I could be home *so* much, in my house."

In the end, global warming and its threats to place may be what force a realization that the founding impulse to alter and even dominate our surroundings must be tempered by preservation. If such a realization comes soon enough, it may spark serious efforts to reduce greenhouse gases and also to protect places from rampant, destructive development and environmental degradation. In many cases, as in reducing sprawl and auto dependence, these efforts will go hand-in-hand. The disaster on the Gulf Coast thus contains the small hope that the lurid images broadcast throughout the world may finally help bring home to people the importance of place and of what we stand to lose if we do not rethink our relationship to our landscape.

Notes

Introduction

1. John Cushman, "In the Utah Wilderness, A Question of Definition," *New York Times*, January 28, 1997, p. A12.

2. Lisa Levitt Ryckman, "Last, Best Wild Land," *Rocky Mountain News*, December 15, 1996, p. 30A.

3. Cushman, "A Question of Definition."

4. These criticisms have come from various philosophical directions. See, for example, William Cronon, ed., *Uncommon Ground: Toward Reinventing Nature* (New York: W.W. Norton, 1995); Neil Evernden, *The Social Creation of Nature* (Baltimore, MD: Johns Hopkins University Press, 1992); Jane Bennett and William Chaloupka, eds., *In the Nature of Things: Language, Politics, and the Environment* (Minneapolis: University of Minnesota Press, 1993); John M. Meyer, *Political Nature: Environmentalism and the Interpretation of Western Thought* (Cambridge, MA: MIT Press, 2001); Andrew Biro, *Denaturalizing Ecological Politics: Alienation from Nature from Rousseau to the Frankfurt School and Beyond* (Toronto: University of Toronto Press, 2005); Timothy W. Luke, *Ecocritique: Contesting the Politics of Nature, Economy, and Culture* (Minneapolis: University of Minnesota Press, 1997); Jane Bennett, *Unthinking Faith and Enlightenment: Nature and the State in the Post-Hegelian Era* (New York: New York University Press, 1987).

5. Iris Marion Young, *Intersecting Voices: Dilemmas of Gender, Political Philosophy, and Policy* (Princeton, NJ: Princeton University Press, 1997), pp. 151–156.

6. Michael Pollan, *Second Nature: A Gardener's Education* (New York: Bantam, 1991), pp. 223–224.

7. See Peter S. Canellos, "The Second Battle of Concord," *Boston Globe Magazine*, September 29, 1996, pp. 14–15, 32–37.

8. On practices and their distortion, or corruption, see also Alasdair MacIntyre, *After Virtue*, 2nd ed. (Notre Dame, IN: University of Notre Dame Press, 1984), especially pp. 181–203, 226–228.

9. Daniel Kemmis, "Community and the Politics of Place," in Philip D. Brick and R. McGreggor Cawley, eds., *A Wolf in the Garden: The Land Rights Movement and the New Environmental Debate* (Lanham, MD: Rowman & Littlefield, 1996), p. 242.

10. I borrow this phrase from Peter Calthorpe, *The Next American Metropolis: Ecology, Community, and the American Dream* (Princeton, NJ: Princeton Architectural Press, 1993), p. 18.

11. See John Barry, *Rethinking Green Politics: Nature, Virtue, and Progress* (London: Sage, 1999). I discuss Barry's framework in chapter 6.

12. See Kirkpatrick Sale, *Dwellers in the Land: The Bioregional Vision* (San Francisco: Sierra Club Books, 1985).

13. See, for example, Peter Calthorpe and William Fulton, *The Regional City: Planning for the End of Sprawl* (Washington, DC: Island Press, 2001); Bruce Katz, ed., *Reflections on Regionalism* (Washington, DC: Brookings Institution, 2000); Douglas S. Kelbaugh, *Repairing the American Metropolis: Common Place Revisited* (Seattle: University of Washington Press, 2002); Gerald E. Frug, *City Making: Building Communities Without Walls* (Princeton, NJ: Princeton University Press, 1999); Tony Hiss, *The Experience of Place: A New Way of Looking at and Dealing With Our Radically Changing Cities and Countryside* (Random House: New York, 1990); Iris Marion Young, *Justice and the Politics of Difference* (Princeton, NJ: Princeton University Press, 1990).

Chapter 1

1. David Harvey, *Spaces of Capital: Towards a Critical Geography* (New York: Routledge, 2001), p. 123.

2. John Rennie Short, *Global Dimensions: Space, Place, and the Contemporary World* (London: Reaktion Books, 2001), p. 168.

3. See Manuel Castells, *The Information Age: Economy, Society, and Culture: The Rise of the Network Society*, 2nd ed. (Cambridge, MA: Blackwell, 2000).

4. See Timothy W. Luke, "Governmentality and Contragovernmentality: Rethinking Sovereignty and Territoriality After the Cold War," *Political Geography*, Vol. 15, No. 6/7 (1996), pp. 491–507.

5. On the contrast between these two sorts of communities, see Calthorpe and Fulton, *Regional City*, p. 3.

6. Short, *Global Dimensions*, p. 13. Although, as I note later, Short is skeptical about the "end of geography" conceit.

7. Peter Gordon and Harry W. Richardson, "Are Compact Cities a Desirable Planning Goal?", *Journal of the American Planning Association*, Vol. 63, No. 1 (Winter 1997), pp. 95–106 (via Academic Search Premier).

8. David E. Kaplan, "The Saudi Connection: How Billions in Oil Money Spawned a Global Terror Network," *U.S. News & World Report*, December 15, 2003.

9. Steven Lee Myers, Andrew C. Revkin, Simon Romero, and Clifford Krauss, "The Big Melt: Old Ways of Life Are Fading as the Arctic Thaws," *New York Times*, October 20, 2005, p. A1.

10. David Harvey, *Justice, Nature, and the Geography of Difference* (Cambridge, MA: Blackwell, 1996), particularly pp. 323, 296, 323, and Harvey, *Spaces of Capital*, pp. 123–124. See also the latter two volumes of Castells' three-volume work, *The Information Age*. These are *The Power of Identity* (Cambridge, MA: Blackwell, 1997) and *The End of the Millennium* (Cambridge, MA: Blackwell, 1998).

11. For more extreme versions of this perspective, see George Gilder, *Telecosm: How Infinite Bandwidth will Revolutionize our World* (New York: Free Press, 2000), and Nicholas Negroponte, *Being Digital* (New York: Vintage Press, 1995).

12. Tim Cresswell, "Theorizing Place," in Ginette Verstraete and Tim Cresswell, eds., *Mobilizing Place, Placing Mobility: The Politics of Representation in a Globalized World (Thamyris/Intersecting 9)* (Amsterdam/New York: Rodopi, 2002), pp. 11–32 (quote on pp. 15–16).

13. See, for example, Bonnie Honig, "Difference, Dilemmas, and the Politics of Home," *Social Research* Vol. 61, No. 3 (Fall 1994), pp. 563–597; Teresa de Lauretis, "Eccentric Subjects: Feminist Theory and Historical Consciousness," *Feminist Studies*, Vol. 16, No. 1 (Spring 1990), pp. 115–150; Doreen Massey, *Space, Place, and Gender* (Minneapolis: University of Minnesota Press, 1994).

14. Reid Ewing, "Is Los Angeles-style Sprawl Desirable?", *Journal of the American Planning Association*, Vol. 63, No. 1 (Winter 1997), pp. 107–126 (via Academic Search Premier).

15. Lotus Development Corporation, "Conversations with Industry Innovators: Esther Dyson Interview," February, 1999 (www.lotus.com/home.nsf/welcome/interviews, accessed March 20, 1999).

16. Castells, *Network Society*, pp. 453–459.

17. See Castells, *The Power of Identity*.

18. Harvey, *Geography of Difference*, p. 246.

19. Mark Sagoff, "Settling America: The Concept of Place in Environmental Politics," in Philip D. Brick and R. McGreggor Cawley, eds., *A Wolf in the Garden: The Land Rights Movement and the New Environmental Debate* (Lanham, MD: Rowman & Littlefield 1996), pp. 249–260 (quote on p. 249).

20. Short, *Global Dimensions*, p. 12.

21. Short, *Global Dimensions*, p. 18.

22. Short, *Global Dimensions*, pp. 169–172.

23. Harvey, *Geography of Difference*, p. 261.

24. Castells says, "A place is a locale whose form, function, and meaning are self-contained within the boundaries of physical contiguity" (*Network Society*, p. 453).

25. Henri Lefebvre, *The Production of Space*, trans. Donald Nicholson-Smith (Oxford, UK: Blackwell, 1991 [1974]), pp. 93–94.

26. Castells, *Network Society*, p. 443.

27. Harvey, *Geography of Difference*, pp. 49–55, 293–294.

28. Harvey, *Geography of Difference*, pp. 49–51.

29. Much of the following draws upon Harvey's discussion of dialectics in *Geography of Difference*, pp. 48–59.

30. Harvey, *Geography of Difference*, pp. 50–51.

31. Harvey, *Geography of Difference*, p. 50.

32. Harvey, *Geography of Difference*, p. 261.

33. See *Geography of Difference*, p. 310.

34. Jane Jacobs, *The Death and Life of Great American Cities* (New York: Random House, 1992 [1961]), pp. 428–448.

35. Harvey, *Geography of Difference*, p. 53.

36. Thanks to John Barry for this insight.

37. Allan Pred, "Place as Historically Contingent Process: Structuration and the Time-Geography of Becoming Places," *Annals of the Association of American Geographers*, Vol. 74 (1984), pp. 279–297 (quote on pp. 286–287).

38. This key distinction is a major theme of Edward S. Casey's *The Fate of Place: A Philosophical History* (Berkeley: University of California Press, 1997), on whom I draw for this section. See also Yi-Fu Tuan, *Space and Place: The Perspective of Experience* (Minneapolis: University of Minnesota Press, 1977), and Robert David Sack, *Homo Geographicus: A Framework for Action, Awareness, and Moral Concern* (Baltimore, MD: Johns Hopkins University Press, 1997), p. 77.

39. Lefebvre, *Production of Space*, p. 12.

40. See Lefebvre, *Production of Space*, pp. 86–87.

41. See also Lefebvre, *Production of Space*, p. 87.

42. Lefebvre, *Production of Space*, p. 93.

43. See Tuan, *Space and Place*. Henri Lefebvre and Edward Soja both distinguish the empirical perception and study of places; the mental conceptualization of place in terms of representational categories, imagery, and symbols; and the actual lived experience of place, which is both empirical and conceptual, material and mental, subjective and objective. Soja speaks of this third category as lived space or "Thirdspace." See Lefebvre, *Production of Space*, pp. 33–34, 38–39, and Edward W. Soja, "Thirdspace: Expanding the Scope of the Geographical Imagination," in Doreen Massey, John Allen, and Philip Sarre, *Human Geography Today* (Cambridge, UK: Polity Press, 1999), pp. 260–278. For Soja, this notion of lived space opens the way to political resistance against oppressive power structures and discourses. The experience of lived space is the province of those who inhabit and use a place and it cannot be easily subordinated to dominant, hegemonic discourses ("Thirdspace," p. 276).

44. Lefebvre, *Production of Space*, p. 94.

45. On the embodied experience of place, see Tuan, *Space and Place*; Casey, *Fate of Place*; and Lefebvre, *Production of Space*, p. 162.

46. Lefebvre, *Production of Space*, p. 40.

47. Barbara Hooper, "Desiring Presence, Romancing the Real," *Annals of the Association of American Geographers*, Vol. 94, No. 4 (December 2001), pp. 703–715.

48. See Tuan, *Space and Place*, and *Topophilia: A Study of Environmental Perception, Attitudes, and Values* (New York: Columbia University Press, 1990).

49. On the significance of everyday places, see John R. Stilgoe, *Outside Lies Magic: Regaining History and Awareness in Everyday Places* (New York: Walker, 1998).

50. Tuan, *Topophilia*, pp. 63–66.

51. See also Sack, *Homo Geographicus*, p. 12.

52. On the notion of a mental, or "psychogeographic" map of the world, see also Guy Debord, "Introduction to a Critique of Urban Geography," in Ken Knabb, ed., *Situationist International Anthology* (Berkeley, CA: Bureau of Public Secrets, 1982), pp. 5–8.

53. Harvey, *Geography of Difference*, p. 305.

54. Sagoff thus speaks of "the security one has when one relies upon the characteristic aspects of places and communities one knows well" ("Settling America," p. 249).

55. Young, *Intersecting Voices*, pp. 134–164; Tuan, *Topophilia*, pp. 99–100; Sack, *Homo Geographicus*, pp. 14–17.

56. Young, *Intersecting Voices*, p. 159.

57. Tuan, *Space and Place*, p. 154.

58. See especially Honig, "Politics of Home," and de Lauretis, "Eccentric Subjects," as well as Young's critique of these authors in *Intersecting Voices*, pp. 156–160.

59. Young, *Intersecting Voices*, pp. 134–141.

60. Thanks to John Barry for this point.

61. Young, *Intersecting Voices*, pp. 157–160. Again, for an opposing perspective, see Honig, "Politics of Home."

62. bell hooks, *Yearning: Race, Gender, and Cultural Politics* (Boston: South End Press, 1990), p. 42, quoted in Young, *Intersecting Voices*, p. 160.

63. Lefebvre, *The Production of Space*, p. 93.

64. Relatedly, see Margaret Kohn's discussion of "the boundary problem" in Kohn, *Brave New Neighborhoods: The Privatization of Public Space* (New York: Routledge, 2004), pp. 156–160.

65. Gary E. Varner, "Environmental Law and the Eclipse of Land as Private Property," in Frederick Ferré and Peter Hartel, eds., *Ethics and Environmental*

Policy: Theory Meets Practice (Athens: University of Georgia Press, 1994), pp. 140–160 (quote on p. 158).

66. Young, *Intersecting Voices*, p. 142.

67. Again, as noted earlier, I adopt this typology from Young, although she does not develop these two concepts to the degree I do here and tends to favor preservation over founding.

68. Whereas ecologists once emphasized the stability and coherence of ecosystems, they now emphasize change, disturbance, and chaos in nature. Ecosystems are now regarded as mosaics of shifting "patches." On changing views of nature in ecology, see Donald Worster, *Nature's Economy: A History of Ecological Ideas*, 2nd ed. (Cambridge, UK: Cambridge University Press, 1994), and Worster, "Nature and the Disorder of History," in Michael E. Soulé and Gary Lease, eds., *Reinventing Nature: Responses to Postmodern Deconstruction* (Washington, DC: Island Press, 1995), pp. 65–85.

69. Here I leave aside the admittedly important issue of whether nonhuman organisms, specifically sentient animals, can define places. It seems evident that they do, as is suggested by the territorial behavior of animals. See also Edward S. Casey, "Between Geography and Philosophy: What Does It Mean to Be in the Place-World?", *Annals of the Association of American Geographers*, Vol. 91, No. 4 (December 2001), pp. 683–693, specifically p. 693 n. 36.

70. For a similar point, see Heidegger's discussion of how a bridge creates a place by connecting two points on opposing banks. However, as Young points out, Heidegger may be putting too much emphasis on the physical construction of places, i.e., place founding through building. See Martin Heidegger, "Building Dwelling Thinking," in David Farrell Krel, ed., *Basic Writings* (San Francisco: HarperCollins, 1977), pp. 343–363, especially pp. 353–361, and Young, *Intersecting Voices*, pp. 136–138.

71. Sack, *Homo Geographicus*, pp. 32–33, 35.

72. Yi-Fu Tuan, "Language and the Making of Place: A Narrative-Descriptive Approach," *Annals of the Association of American Geographers*, Vol. 81, No. 4 (December 1991), pp. 684–696.

73. Tuan, "Language and the Making of Place," p. 685.

74. For a contrasting view, see Lefebvre, *Production of Space*, p. 141. Lefebvre sees the production of space, or of places, as a practice that necessarily involves not just the marking of our surroundings but also the full range of social relations and material production.

75. Tuan, "Language and the Making of Place," p. 685.

76. Tuan, "Language and the Making of Place," p. 686.

77. Tuan, "Language and the Making of Place," pp. 688–689.

78. See also Sack, *Homo Geographicus*, p. 80.

79. Casey, "Between Geography and Philosophy," p. 691 n. 6.

80. Hannah Arendt, *The Human Condition* (Chicago: University of Chicago Press, 1958), p. 137.

81. The discussion that follows draws upon Pred, "Place as Historically Contingent Process," pp. 286–287.

82. Pred, "Place as Historically Contingent Process," pp. 286–287.

83. Similarly, Hiss remarks that "our ordinary surroundings ... have an immediate and a continuing effect on the way we feel and act.... These places have an impact on our sense of self, our sense of safety, the kind of work we get done, the ways we interact with other people, even our ability to function as citizens in a democracy. In short, the places where we spend our time affect the people we are and can become" (*Experience of Place*, p. xi). See also Harvey, *Geography of Difference*, pp. 304–306, 322. On the role of familiar surroundings in creating the identities of urban neighborhood dwellers, see John Logan and Harvey Molotch, *Urban Fortunes: The Political Economy of Place* (Berkeley: University of California Press, 1988). The role of place in crafting identities also fits with communitarian notions of a situated or encumbered self whose identity is at least partly constituted by its social attachments. See Michael J. Sandel, *Liberalism and the Limits of Justice* (Cambridge, UK: Cambridge University Press, 1982).

84. Young says, "The preservation of things among which one dwells give people a context for their lives" (*Intersecting Voices*, p. 153).

85. In Sack's words, "Place depends on self, and self depends on place"; "society and space are mutually constitutive, each ... altering the other" (*Homo Geographicus*, pp. 2, 34). On the mutual constitution of persons and places, see also Tuan, *Space and Place*.

86. Lefebvre thus says the "pre-existence of space conditions the subject's presence, action, and discourse, his competence and performance; yet the subject's presence, action, and discourse, at the same time as they presuppose this space, also negate it" (*Production of Space*, p. 57). See also *Production of Space*, p. 85.

87. Pred, "Place as Historically Contingent Process."

88. Casey, "Between Geography and Philosophy."

89. Casey, "Between Geography and Philosophy," p. 684; emphasis in original.

90. Casey, "Between Geography and Philosophy," p. 686.

91. Casey, "Between Geography and Philosophy," p. 686.

92. Casey, "Between Geography and Philosophy," p. 686.

93. Casey, "Between Geography and Philosophy," p. 687.

94. See Edward S. Casey, "On Habitus and Place: Responding to My Critics," *Annals of the Association of American Geographers*, Vol. 94, No. 4 (December 2001), pp. 716–723, especially p. 716.

95. Casey, "Between Geography and Philosophy," p. 688. On the importance of embodidedness in our interaction with places, see also Tuan, *Space and Place*.

96. Casey, "Between Geography and Philosophy," p. 688.

97. Casey, "Between Geography and Philosophy," pp. 688–689.

98. See chapter 6.

99. See also Harvey, *Geography of Difference*, pp. 309–310, 316, 322.

100. Doreen Massey, "Spaces of Politics," in Doreen Massey, John Allen, and Philip Sarre, *Human Geography Today* (Cambridge, UK: Polity Press, 1999), pp. 279–294 (quote on p. 279).

101. Arendt, *Human Condition*, p. 7. See also Dana R. Villa, *Arendt and Heidegger: The Fate of the Political* (Princeton, NJ: Princeton University Press, 1996), pp. 32–33.

102. See also Massey, "Spaces of Politics," p. 280.

103. See also Sack, *Homo Geographicus*, pp. 2–7.

104. Andrew Weiner, "The Taking," *Boston Phoenix*, November 30–December 7, 2000 (www.bostonphoenix.com/archive/features/00/11/30/WEST_END1.html, accessed November 6, 2006).

105. Thanks to John Barry for pointing out this example.

106. Arendt, *Human Condition*, p. 52.

107. Arendt, *Human Condition*, p. 52.

108. Hannah Pitkin says, "This world of things in which we have interest is a tangible in-between (*inter-esse*)" ["Justice: On Relating Private and Public," *Political Theory*, Vol. 9, No. 3 (August 1981), pp. 327–352 (quote on p. 342)].

109. Kemmis, "Community and the Politics of Place," pp. 244–245. See also Harvey, *Geography of Difference*, p. 310.

110. On the value of diverse urban neighborhoods, see Jacobs, *Great American Cities*.

111. Massey, "Spaces of Politics," pp. 290–291.

112. Massey, "Spaces of Politics," p. 284.

113. See Harvey, *Geography of Difference*, pp. 309–310.

114. Geraldine Pratt, "Geographies of Identity and Difference: Marking Boundaries," in Doreen Massey, John Allen, and Philip Sarre, eds., *Human Geography Today* (Cambridge, UK: Polity Press, 1999), pp. 151–167 (quote on p. 154).

115. Massey, "Spaces of Politics," p. 280.

116. Nigel Thrift says, "places must be seen as dynamic, as taking shape only in their passing" ["Steps to an Ecology of Place," in Doreen Massey, John Allen, and Philip Sarre, *Human Geography Today* (Cambridge, UK: Polity Press, 1999), pp. 295–322 (quote on p. 310)].

117. Massey, "Spaces of Politics," p. 286.

118. Massey, *Space, Place, and Gender*, pp. 120–121.

119. Massey, *Space, Place, and Gender*, p. 136. See also pp. 138, 169.

120. Pratt, "Geographies of Identity and Difference," p. 153.

121. Regarding the stressful impacts of disruptive change in places, Jonathan Kusel reviews a number of studies on "boomtowns," i.e., small communities that experience rapid growth from resource development. These studies found that boomtowns tend to experience rising crime rates and fraying social networks. See Jonathan Kusel, "Assessing Well-Being in Forest-Dependent Com-

munities," in Linda E. Kruger, ed., *Understanding Community-Forest Relations* (Portland, OR: U.S. Department of Agriculture, Forest Service, Pacific Northwest Research Station, 2003), pp. 81–103. Logan and Molotch in *Urban Fortunes* discuss the socially and personally disruptive impacts of urban redevelopment on neighborhoods, including residents' economic security, access to housing, job prospects, daily routines, and social connections.

The extreme of disruption and stress occurs when natural disasters or wars destroy places and create refugees. Recent examples include the 2005 ravaging of the Gulf Coast and flooding of New Orleans by Hurricane Katrina, the 2004 Asian Tsunami, the 1996–2003 wars in Congo, and the ongoing Israeli-Palestinian conflict. See the Postscript for a discussion of Katrina.

122. Thanks to David Schlosberg for suggesting this point.

123. See Niccolò Machiavelli, *The Prince*, Harvey C. Mansfield, trans. (Chicago: University of Chicago Press, 1998).

124. Machiavelli, *Discourses on Livy*, Bernard Crick, ed. (New York: Viking Press, 1985), Book I, chapter 9; emphasis added.

125. See Arendt, *Human Condition*.

126. Thanks to John Meyer for raising this question.

127. Jean-Jacques Rousseau, *On the Social Contract*, Book II, section 7.

128. Young, *Intersecting Voices*, p. 152.

129. Kimberly K. Smith, *Wendell Berry and the Agrarian Tradition: A Common Grace* (Lawrence: University of Kansas Press, 2003), p. 143.

130. Smith, *Wendell Berry*, p. 92.

131. Smith, *Wendell Berry*, p. 143.

132. Young, *Intersecting Voices*, p. 153.

133. Hannah Arendt, *Between Past and Future: Eight Exercises in Political Thought* (New York: Penguin Books, 1977), pp. 211–212.

134. For Arendt's views on culture involving care for nature, see also Kerry Whiteside, "Worldliness and Respect for Nature: An Ecological Application of Hannah Arendt's Conception of Culture," *Environmental Values*, Vol. 7 (1998), pp. 25–40. Heidegger, in "Building Dwelling Thinking," also emphasizes care and cultivation as central aspects of dwelling in place, although as Young points out, he is also overly focused on the creation of places through actual building. Similarly, Wendell Berry distinguishes between "nurturers" who pursue care of the land and the more dominant strain in our society—"exploiters" who see the land only in terms of efficiency and production. See Wendell Berry, *The Unsettling of America* (San Francisco: Sierra Club Books, 1977), pp. 7–8.

135. Arendt's discussion brings to mind two similar concepts. The first is the value, often stated in religious terms, of careful stewardship of the Earth. The second is explored by Smith in her account of Wendell Berry. Smith discusses Berry's emphasis on a quality he calls "grace," a term he uses in a secular sense. Grace, Smith says, "is a sensitivity to the situation combined with a

316 Notes to pp. 45–46

sense, below the level of conscious thought, of what to do—and what one can do—in this context." A graceful solution, "instead of doing violence to natural processes of growth and decay, works within those processes and turns them to human advantage." Consequently, "in acting gracefully, one accepts and responds to the physical features of the world, rather than attempting to change or overcome those features. Grace allows one to adapt to the world, rather than force the world to conform to one's own will" (*Wendell Berry*, pp. 160, 163, 164).

136. See Jim Cheney, "Postmodern Environmental Ethics: Ethics as Bioregional Narrative," in Max Oelschlaeger, ed., *Postmodern Environmental Ethics* (Albany: State University of New York Press, 1995), pp. 23–42.

137. The notion of moral obligation to a place should be readily understandable to anyone familiar with either communitarian views of the self as situated, or feminist notions of moral obligation arising through concrete relationships, as in the ethic of care. For a communitarian perspective, see Sandel, *Liberalism and the Limits of Justice*, and MacIntyre, *After Virtue*. For a feminist perspective, see Seyla Benhabib, "The Generalized and the Concrete Other," in Seyla Benhabib and Drucilla Cornell, eds., *Feminism as Critique* (Minneapolis: University of Minnesota Press, 1987), pp. 77–95; Carol Gilligan, *In A Different Voice* (Cambridge, MA: Harvard University Press, 1982); and Joan Tronto, *Moral Boundaries: A Political Argument for an Ethics of Care* (New York: Routledge, 1989).

138. One can trace these ideas in part to the land ethic of mid-twentieth-century naturalist Aldo Leopold. Leopold recognized the necessity of economic use of the land and emphasized how protection of natural systems benefits human beings. A land ethic "[e]xamine[s] each question in terms of what is ethically and esthetically right as well as what is economically expedient." However, Leopold suggests that the land is not just a good to be used, but something deserving of moral consideration. He says, "A thing is right when it tends to preserve the integrity, stability, and beauty of the biotic community. It is wrong when it tends otherwise" [*A Sand County Almanac* (New York: Oxford University Press, 1949), pp. 224–225]. Leopold also notes, "a land ethic changes the role of *Homo sapiens* from conqueror of the land-community to plain member and citizen of it. It implies respect for his fellow-members, and also respect for the community as such" (*Sand County Almanac*, p. 204).

139. Sale, *Dwellers in the Land*.

140. Val Plumwood, "Nature, Self, and Gender: Feminism, Environmental Philosophy, and the Critique of Rationalism," in Michael Zimmerman, J. Baird Callicott, George Sessions, Karen J. Warren, and John Clark, eds., *Environmental Philosophy: From Animal Rights to Radical Ecology*, 1st ed. (Englewood Cliffs, NJ: Prentice Hall, 1993), pp. 284–309 (quote on p. 297).

141. Young, *Intersecting Voices*, p. 153.

142. On the need to manage wilderness, see Roderick Nash, *Wilderness and the American Mind*, 3rd ed. (New Haven, CT: Yale University Press, 1982), p. 339, and Barry, *Rethinking Green Politics*, p. 102.

Chapter 2

1. For accounts of the Northwest forest debate, see Bill Dietrich, *The Final Forest: The Battle for the Last Great Trees of the Pacific Northwest* (New York: Penguin, 1992); Steven Lewis Yaffee, *The Wisdom of the Spotted Owl: Policy Lessons for a New Century* (Washington, DC: Island Press, 1994); Karen Arabas and Joe Bowersox, eds., *Forest Futures: Science, Politics, and Policy for the Next Century* (Lanham, MD: Rowman & Littlefield, 2004); Kathie Durbin, *Tree Huggers: Victory, Defeat, and Renewal in the Northwest Ancient Forest Campaign* (Seattle: The Mountaineers, 1996); Douglas E. Booth, *Valuing Nature: The Decline and Preservation of Old-Growth Forests* (Lanham, MD: Rowman & Littlefield, 1994); H. Michael Anderson and Jeffrey T. Olson, *Federal Forests and the Economic Base of the Pacific Northwest: A Study of Regional Transitions* (Washington, DC: Wilderness Society, 1991); James D. Proctor, "Whose Nature? The Contested Moral Terrain of Ancient Forests," in William Cronon, ed., *Uncommon Ground: Toward Reinventing Nature* (New York: W.W. Norton, 1995), pp. 269–297; Mark Bonnett and Kurt Zimmerman, "Politics and Preservation: The Endangered Species Act and the Northern Spotted Owl," *Ecology Law Quarterly*, Vol. 18, No. 1 (1991), pp. 105–171; Catherine Caulfield, "A Reporter at Large: The Ancient Forest," *New Yorker*, May 14, 1990, pp. 46–84; Judith A. Layzer, *The Environmental Case: Translating Values into Policy*, 1st ed. (Washington, DC: CQ Press, 2002), pp. 155–182; Paul Roberts, "The Federal Chain-Saw Massacre: Clinton's Forest Service and Clear-Cut Corruption," *Harper's*, Vol. 294, No. 1765 (June 1997), pp. 37–51; Ted Gup, "Owl vs. Man," *Time*, Vol. 135, No. 26 (June 25, 1990) pp. 56–63 (www.time.com/time/archive, accessed November 6, 2006).

2. John A. Kitzhaber, "Principles and Politics of Sustainable Forestry in the Pacific Northwest: Charting a New Course," in Karen Arabas and Joe Bowersox, eds., *Forest Futures: Science, Politics, and Policy for the Next Century* (Lanham, MD: Rowman & Littlefield, 2004), pp. 223–236 (quote on pp. 225–226).

3. Felicity Barringer, "Logging and Politics Collide in Idaho," *New York Times*, August 9, 2004 (www.nytimes.com, accessed August 9, 2004).

4. Joe Bowersox and Karen Arabas, "Forests Past and Forests Future—Connecting Science, Politics, and Policy," in Karen Arabas and Joe Bowersox, eds., *Forest Futures: Science, Politics, and Policy for the Next Century* (Lanham, MD: Rowman & Littlefield, 2004), pp. 280–291 (quote on p. 283).

5. Bowersox and Arabas, "Forests Past and Forests Future," p. 281.

6. Caulfield, "Ancient Forest," p. 52.

7. See Nash, *Wilderness and the American Mind*.

8. See Samuel P. Hays, *Conservation and the Gospel of Efficiency: The Progressive Conservation Movement 1890–1920* (Cambridge, MA: Harvard University Press, 1959).

9. Yaffee, *Wisdom of the Spotted Owl*, pp. 3, 260.

10. Yaffee, *Wisdom of the Spotted Owl*, p. 268.

11. Joe Bowersox and Karen Arabas, "Introduction: Natural and Human History of Pacific Northwest Forests," in Karen Arabas and Joe Bowersox, eds., *Forest Futures: Science, Politics, and Policy for the Next Century* (Lanham, MD: Rowman & Littlefield, 2004), pp. xxiii–xlii.

12. Timber is measured in board feet. A board foot is 1 foot square by 1 inch thick. A typical single-family home requires about 10,000 board feet to construct.

13. Roberts, "Federal Chain-Saw Massacre," p. 41.

14. Roberts, "Federal Chain-Saw Massacre," pp. 40–41; Glenn Hodges, "Dead Wood: Reform of the U.S. Forest Service," *Washington Monthly*, Vol. 28, No. 10 (October 1996), p. 12 (via Lexis-Nexis Academic).

15. Yaffee, *Wisdom of the Spotted Owl.*

16. Dietrich, *Final Forest*, p. 174.

17. Clear-cutting is the complete logging of an entire stand of trees, so that few trees or none remain.

18. Yaffee, *Wisdom of the Spotted Owl*, p. 241.

19. Rocky Barker, "New Forestry in the Next West," in John A. Baden and Donald Snow, *The Next West: Public Lands, Community, and Economy in the American West* (Washington, DC: Island Press, 1997), pp. 29–30.

20. Roberts, "Federal Chain-Saw Massacre," p. 47.

21. Chad Hanson and Carl Pope, "The Sierra Club Replies: Who's Really Radical?", *Christian Science Monitor*, June 13, 1996, p. 19; John J. Berger, "9 Ways to Save our National Forests," *Sierra*, Vol. 82, No. 4 (July 17, 1997), p. 38 (via Lexis-Nexis Academic).

22. Daniel Lewis, "The Trailblazer," *New York Times Magazine*, June 13, 1999, pp. 50–53.

23. Jennifer C. Thomas and Paul Mohai, "Racial, Gender, and Professional Diversification in the Forest Service from 1983 to 1992," *Policy Studies Journal*, Vol. 23, No. 2 (Summer 1995), pp. 296–309. Thomas and Mohai also argue that the agency has become more diverse in terms of gender and race. Jonathan Kusel, however, sees only limited progress in racial and ethnic diversification since the early 1990s. See Kusel, *Community Forestry in the United States: Learning from the Past, Crafting the Future* (Washington, DC: Island Press, 2003), pp. 125–126.

In 1998, Roger Sedjo noted, "[the Forest Service] has changed internally. The culture has changed as staff trained in traditional forestry has been supplemented with those trained in wildlife, ecology and the biological sciences" ["Forest Service Vision: or, Does the Forest Service Have a Future?" Resources for the Future Discussion Paper 99-03 (Washington, DC: Resources for the Future, 1998), p. 7]. However, Bowersox argues that this new perspective may not have had time to sink deep roots since federal forest policy under George W. Bush has moved back toward a commodity orientation. See Joe Bowersox, "Fire on the Hill: Using Ecological Disturbance Theory to Understand the Ambiguous Prospects of the Northwest Forest Plan," in Karen Arabas and Joe Bowersox, eds., *Forest*

Futures: Science, Politics, and Policy for the Next Century (Lanham, MD: Rowman & Littlefield, 2004), pp. 237–255.

24. Douglas Jehl, "Clinton Forest Chief Acts to Stop Logging of the Oldest Trees," *New York Times*, January 9, 2001, p. A1; Lewis, "Trailblazer"; Kathie Durbin, "A Western Showdown," *Washington Monthly*, Vol. 30, No. 5 (May 1998), pp. 15–18.

25. Douglas Jehl, "Road Ban Set for One-third of U.S. Forests," *New York Times*, January 5, 2001, p. A1; "Nearing a Forest Legacy" (editorial), *New York Times*, January 8, 2001, p. A16.

26. Jehl, "Clinton Forest Chief Acts to Stop Logging."

27. See Michael Milstein, "Bush Ready to Reshape Federal Forests," *Oregonian*, November 18, 2004, p. A1. See also William R. Lowry, "A Return to Traditional Priorities in Natural Resource Policies," in Michael E. Kraft and Norman J. Vig, eds., *Environmental Policy: New Directions for the Twenty-first Century*, 6th ed. (Washington, DC: CQ Press, 2005), pp. 311–332.

28. Michelle Cole, "Federal Forests Get Looser Rein with New Rules," *Oregonian*, December 23, 2004, p. B3; Warren Cornwall, "Forest Rules May Reframe Timber Debate," *Seattle Times*, December 24, 2004, p. B1.

29. Felicity Barringer, "Bush Seeks Shift in Logging Rules," *New York Times*, July 13, 2004, p. A1; Warren Cornwall, "Untouched National Forests Lose Clinton-Era Protections," *Seattle Times*, May 6, 2005, p. B1; Felicity Barringer, "Judge Voids Bush Policy on National Forest Roads," *New York Times*, September 21, 2006, p. 21.

30. See Bowersox, "Using Ecological Disturbance Theory."

31. Bowersox, "Using Ecological Disturbance Theory," p. 247; Mark Larabee, "'Live' Tree Dispute Kills Logging Plan," *Oregonian*, December 11, 2004, p. B1.

32. Jack Ward Thomas, "Sustainability of the Northwest Forest Plan: Still to Be Tested," in Karen Arabas and Joe Bowersox, eds., *Forest Futures: Science, Politics, and Policy for the Next Century* (Lanham, MD: Rowman & Littlefield, 2004), pp. 3–22 (see p. 21). See also Electa Draper, "Forest Service Centennial: Many Uses, Many Struggles," *Denver Post*, October 4, 2005, p. A14.

33. See Jessie McQuillan, "Thinning the Ranks," *Missoula Independent*, Vol. 17, No. 38 (June 15, 2006) (www.missoulanews.com/Archives/News.asp?no=5778, accessed September 3, 2006).

34. Michael Milstein, "Budget Cuts Rescue Some Old-Growth Trees," *Oregonian*, October 14, 2005 p. D1; Steve Lipsher, "Forest Service Centennial: Many Uses, Many Struggles Nurtured Nature," *Denver Post*, October 2, 2005, p. A1; Michael Milstein, "Budget Ax Cutting Off Access to Roads in National Forests," *Oregonian*, July 28, 2005 p. A1; Glen Martin, "New Sales Reignite Timber Battles," *San Francisco Chronicle*, December 13, 2004, p. A1.

35. Roberts, "Federal Chain-Saw Massacre," p. 47.

36. On corporate restructuring and clear-cutting, see Dietrich, *Final Forest*, p. 185. The redwood stands in California were owned by Pacific Lumber, which

had been bought out by financier Charles Hurwitz and his Houston-based MAX-XAM Corporation. Hurwitz wanted to log the trees to service debt from the takeover. His actions sparked a battle involving environmentalists, the timber industry, the federal government, and the state of California. In the end, a portion of the redwood stands was purchased as protected public land. For more on this issue, see David Harris, *The Last Stand: The War Between Wall Street and Main Street over California's Ancient Redwoods* (New York: Times Books, 1995), and Joan Dunning and Doug Thron, *From the Redwood Forest: Ancient Trees and the Bottom Line: A Headwaters Journey* (White River Junction, VT: Chelsea Green, 1998). On the Northern Forest, see David Dobbs and Richard Ober, *The Northern Forest* (White River Junction, VT: Chelsea Green, 1995).

37. Anderson and Olson, *Federal Forests*, p. 3.

38. Yaffee, *Wisdom of the Spotted Owl*, p. 215–216.

39. Bonnett and Zimmerman "Politics and Preservation," p. 114. See also Jerry F. Franklin and Thomas A. Spies, "Characteristics of Old-Growth Douglas-Fir Forests," in *New Forests for a Changing World* (Bethesda, MD: Society of American Foresters, 1984), pp. 328–334.

40. David A. Perry, "Ecological Realities of the Northwest Forest Plan," in Karen Arabas and Joe Bowersox, eds., *Forest Futures: Science, Politics, and Policy for the Next Century* (Lanham, MD: Rowman & Littlefield, 2004), pp. 23–47 (see p. 47 n. 1).

41. Yaffee, *Wisdom of the Spotted Owl*, pp. 24–26.

42. Perry, "Ecological Realities," pp. 25–28.

43. Dietrich, *Final Forest*, p. 231.

44. Anderson and Olson, *Federal Forests*, p. 13.

45. In 1991, Anderson and Olson estimated that 77 percent of the forestland area on the Westside was available and suited for commercial timber production. Of this, 26.7 percent was in the hands of the timber industry and 55 percent was under federal, state, or county ownership. Of the total timberland, 39.3 percent was in national forest hands. They add that the dominance of the industry and the national forests is unique to the Westside and results in a large number of wood-processing enterprises without a land base, a situation that has put considerable pressure on national forest lands (*Federal Forests*, p. 47). The authors note that as defined by the Forest Service, timberland is land that is capable of producing at least 20 cubic feet (240 board feet) of industrial wood per acre, per year and that is not otherwise withdrawn from commercial timber harvesting. Roberts says that in 1992, a thousand board feet of softwood, the standard pricing unit, cost $255 ("Federal Chain-Saw Massacre," p. 48).

46. Dietrich, *Final Forest*, p. 169.

47. According to Rex Storm, forest policy analyst for the Associated Oregon Loggers (the trade association for logging contractors in Oregon) in Salem, logging jobs generally pay $12–$15 per hour, although a "faller" or "cutter," someone who actually cuts timber by hand with a chain saw, can earn $28 per hour (figures as of 2000). Such salaries are not earned on a regular, full-time basis be-

cause employment in logging work is uneven owing to changes in the weather and timber demand and because of litigation and injunctions in recent years. Consequently, hourly wages are not readily extrapolated to annual income (Storm, personal communication, May 5, 2000).

48. Bowersox and Arabas, "Natural and Human History," p. xxxvii.

49. Layzer, *Environmental Case*, 1st ed., p. 158.

50. John H. Beuter, "Sustained Yield: Goals, Policies, Promises," in Karen Arabas and Joe Bowersox, eds., *Forest Futures: Science, Politics, and Policy for the Next Century* (Lanham, MD: Rowman & Littlefield, 2004), pp. 48–67 (see pp. 54–55).

51. Layzer, *Environmental Case*, 1st ed., p. 158.

52. Charles McCoy, "Cut Down: Timber Town is Bitter Over Efforts to Save the Rare Spotted Owl," *Wall Street Journal*, January 6, 1992, p. A1. Kusel, drawing on his study of forest-dependent communities in California, says that "extensive job loss in rural forest communities was devastating in both the short and long term. Economic and social turmoil led to short-term difficulties for families and communities and resulted in a long-term reduction in community capacity" (Kusel, "Assessing Well-Being in Forest-Dependent Communities," p. 85). See also Jonathan Kusel, "Ethnographic Analysis of Three Forest Communities in California," in *Well-Being in Forest-Dependent Communities*, Vol. 2 (Sacramento: California Department of Forestry, Forest and Rangeland Assessment Program, 1991).

53. Layzer, *Environmental Case*, 1st ed., p. 171.

54. Yaffee, *Wisdom of the Spotted Owl*, pp. 149–150. A 1992 analysis by the American Forestry Association compared several studies estimating job losses from protection of Northern spotted owl habitat. Projected job losses for the remainder of the 1990s varied from 12,000 to over 147,000 (Yaffee, *Wisdom of the Spotted Owl*, p. 174). Yaffee notes that what differed among the competing studies was their strategic choice of assumptions, which dramatically affected outcomes (*Wisdom of the Spotted Owl*, p. 174). Estimates are often shaped by one's political perspective in the debate and by whether one uses as a baseline industry employment during the years of particularly high and unsustainable logging levels in the 1980s, by how one calculates indirect impacts on other employment (such as employment in restaurants and stores), and by whether one expects logging restrictions on federal lands to increase or depress timber harvesting on private lands (Layzer, *Environmental Case*, 1st ed., pp. 167–168).

55. Layzer, *Environmental Case*, 1st ed., p. 176.

56. Storm, personal communication.

57. Beuter, "Sustained Yield," p. 58.

58. Jim Kadera, "Housing Revs Up Oregon Timber," *Oregonian*, June 3, 2005, p. B1.

59. Dietrich, *Final Forest*, p. 206.

60. Layzer, *Environmental Case*, 1st ed., p. 158.

61. Beverly A. Brown, *In Timber Country: Working People's Stories of Environmental Conflict and Urban Flight* (Philadelphia: Temple University Press, 1995), p. 21.

62. "Counties Face 'Cliff'" (Editorial), *Eugene Register-Guard*, September 18, 2006 (www.registerguard.com/news/2006/09/18/ed.edit.ruralcounties.phn .0918.p1.php?section=opinion, accessed September 30, 2006).

63. John W. Harman, United States General Accounting Office, "Forest Service Needs to Improve Efforts to Reduce Below-Cost Timber Sales," Testimony Before the Subcommittee on Forests, Family Farms, and Energy, Committee on Agriculture, United States House of Representatives, April 25, 1991. On discounted timber sales, see James K. Meissner, *Forest Service: Factors Affecting Bids on Timber Sales* (GAO/RCED-97-175R, Washington, DC: U.S. General Accounting Office, 1997).

64. See Ross W. Gorte, *Below-Cost Timber Sales: An Overview* (Washington, DC: Congressional Research Service, 2004); Linda M. Calbom, *Financial Management: Annual Costs of Forest Service's Timber Sales Programs Are Not Determinable* (GAO-01-1101R, Washington, DC: U.S. General Accounting Office, 2001); Sharon Nappier, *Lost in the Forest: How the Forest Service's Misdirection, Mismanagement, and Mischief Squanders Your Tax Dollars* (Washington, DC: Taxpayers for Common Sense, 2002); Southeast Alaska Conservation Council, *Taxpayer Losses and Missed Opportunities: How Tongass Rainforest Logging Costs Taxpayers Millions* (Juneau, AK: Southeast Alaska Conservation Council, 2003).

65. See, for example, Caulfield, "Ancient Forest"; Anderson and Olson, *Federal Forests*; Dietrich, *Final Forest*; Brown, *In Timber Country*, p. 19.

66. Bowersox and Arabas, "Natural and Human History," p. xxxvii.

67. Dietrich, *Final Forest*, pp. 172–177. The Cecil quote appears on p. 172.

68. Kusel, *Community Forestry*, pp. 28–29.

69. Kusel, *Community Forestry*, pp. 48–49.

70. Layzer, *Environmental Case*, 1st ed., p. 177.

71. See "Oregon Timber Towns Enjoying Renaissance; As Owl Debate Fades, Booming Economy Adds Jobs," *Chicago Tribune*, October 17, 1994, p. 6, as well as David Seideman, "Out of the Woods; Oregon Economy is Reborn after Environmental Movement Reduces Logging Industry," *Audubon*, Vol. 98, No. 4 (July 1996), pp. 66–75. Some of this recovery is also attributable to increased reliance on small woodlots.

72. Timothy Egan, "Urban Sprawl Strains Western States," *New York Times*, December 29, 1996, p. A1.

73. Stuart Wasserman, "Preserving Owl's Habitat Helps People, Expert Says," *San Francisco Chronicle*, March 30, 1992, p. A4.

74. Caulfield, "Ancient Forest"; Wasserman, "Preserving Owl's Habitat Helps People"; Seideman, "Out of the Woods."

75. Elizabeth Arnold, "Saving the Spotted Owl: Benefits of Recovery Effort Remain Complex, Controversial," *Morning Edition*, National Public Radio, August 6, 2004.

76. See Brown, *In Timber Country*; Victoria E. Sturtevant and Jonathan I. Lange, "From 'Them' to 'Us': The Applegate Partnership," in Jonathan Kusel and Elisa Adler, *Forest Communities, Community Forests* (Lanham, MD: Rowman & Littlefield, 2003), pp. 117–133; and Jared Diamond's account of Montana's Bitterroot Valley in *Collapse: How Societies Choose to Fail or Succeed* (New York: Penguin Books, 2005), pp. 27–75.

77. Layzer, *Environmental Case*, 1st ed., p. 177.

78. Washington State Department of Natural Resources, *Washington State Forest Legacy Program Assessment of Need* (Olympia: Washington State Department of Natural Resources, 2004), p. 3-1.

79. Layzer, *Environmental Case*, 1st ed., p. 177.

80. Bowersox, "Using Ecological Disturbance Theory," p. 251.

81. Ted L. Helvoigt, Darius M. Adams, and Art L. Ayre, "Employment Transitions in Oregon's Wood Products Sector During the 1990s," *Journal of Forestry*, Vol. 101, No. 4 (June 2003), pp. 42–46.

82. Brown, *In Timber Country*, pp. 20, 27–28.

83. See Caulfield "Ancient Forest"; Gup, "Owl vs. Man"; Perri Knize, "The Mismanagement of the National Forests," *Atlantic Monthly*, Vol. 268, No. 4 (October 1991), pp. 98–112; Arabas and Bowersox, "Natural and Human History"; and Perry, "Ecological Realities."

84. Arabas and Bowersox, "Natural and Human History," p. xxix.

85. Perry, "Ecological Realities," p. 28.

86. Brown, *In Timber Country*, pp. 23–30; Dietrich, *Final Forest*, pp. 74–77.

87. Spikes were hammered into trees so that the trees could not be milled lest the equipment be destroyed. Saboteurs would therefore announce that a tree had been spiked. However, the possibility that a spiked tree might be logged and milled made the practice dangerous because those operating the milling equipment could be severely injured, as at least one worker was. Earth First! has disavowed the practice since 1990.

88. Layzer, *Environmental Case*, 1st ed., pp. 164–165. A June 25, 1990 cover story in *Time* magazine was entitled "Owl vs. Man."

89. Dietrich, *Final Forest*, p. 213.

90. In this paragraph I draw upon summaries of the plan from the web sites of the U.S. Bureau of Land Management, Coos Bay District (www.or.blm.gov/coosbay, accessed May 18, 2000) and the U.S. Forest Service Region 6 office in Portland, Oregon, which posted a 1998 report on the plan (see U.S. Forest Service, "1998 Northwest Forest Plan Accomplishment Report," www.fs.fed.us/r6, accessed May 18, 2000), as well as Yaffee, *Wisdom of the Spotted Owl*, pp. 140–151; Durbin, *Tree Huggers*, pp. 203–211; and Thomas, "Sustainability of the Northwest Forest Plan."

91. Perry, "Ecological Realities," p. 37.

92. The U.S. Forest Service's "1998 Northwest Forest Plan Accomplishment Report" suggests that the targeted level of overall financial assistance was more or less met: "The Northwest Economic Adjustment Initiative has combined the resources of 12 federal agencies and 3 state governments to deliver over one billion dollars in assistance to Pacific Northwest communities since 1994." This does not necessarily mean that the targeted level was adequate to the needs of timber workers and communities.

93. Thomas, "Sustainability of the Northwest Forest Plan," p. 13.

94. Margaret A. Shannon, "The Northwest Forest Plan as a Learning Process: A Call for New Institutions Bridging Science and Politics," in Karen Arabas and Joe Bowersox, eds., *Forest Futures: Science, Politics, and Policy for the Next Century* (Lanham, MD: Rowman & Littlefield, 2004), pp. 256–279.

95. Thomas, "Sustainability of the Northwest Forest Plan," pp. 14–16.

96. Frederick J. Swanson, "Roles of Scientists in Forestry Policy and Management: Views from the Pacific Northwest," in Karen Arabas and Joe Bowersox, eds., *Forest Futures: Science, Politics, and Policy for the Next Century* (Lanham, MD: Rowman & Littlefield, 2004), pp. 112–126 (see p. 125).

97. Thomas, "Sustainability of the Northwest Forest Plan," p. 14.

98. On opposition from timber interests and environmentalists, see Mark Dowie, *Losing Ground: American Environmentalism at the Close of the Twentieth Century*, (Cambridge, MA: MIT Press, 1995), pp. 189–190; John H. Cushman, "Owl Issue Tests Reliance on Consensus in Environmentalism," *New York Times*, March 6, 1994, p. 28; Scott Sonner, "Forest Plan Inadequate, Groups Say," *Seattle Times*, February 5, 1998 (www.seattletimes.com/news/local/html98log_020598.html, accessed May 18, 2000); Scott Sonner, "Timber Rules Fail Forests?" Associated Press, February 4, 1998 (www.abcnews.go.com/sections/science/DailyNews/nwlogging0204.html, accessed May 18, 2000); Environmental News Network, "Clinton's Northwest Forest Plan Under Fire," *ENN Daily News*, July 10, 1998 (www.enn.com/enn-news-archive/1998/07/071098/nwfor.asp, accessed May 18, 2000).

99. Sam Howe Verhovek, "Judge, Faulting Agencies, Halts Logging Deals," *New York Times*, August 5, 1999, p. A1.

100. Bowersox, "Using Ecological Disturbance Theory," p. 247.

101. Kitzhaber, "Principles and Politics," pp. 231–232.

102. This figure comes from the Oregon Department of Forestry and was quoted by Storm, May 5, 2000.

103. Beuter, "Sustained Yield," pp. 54, 57.

104. Thomas, "Sustainability of the Northwest Forest Plan."

105. Layzer, *Environmental Case*, 1st ed., p. 165. The range of enterprises classified as part of the timber industry in the region include those involved in logging, log exporting, lumber manufacturing, plywood production, millwork, and production of other items ranging from cabinets to pallets (Anderson and Olson, *Federal Forests*, pp. 42–43).

106. Dietrich says that scientists "tend to split ... between the technocrats and the naturalists, between those who like the simplified order of tree farms and those more comfortable with, or appreciative of, the seemingly disordered complexity of natural systems" (*Final Forest*, p. 103).

107. The *New York Times* cites opposition to logging among local business people concerned with impacts on tourism. See Verhovek, "Judge Halts Logging Deals."

108. See, for example, Dixie Lee Ray and Lou Gozzo, *Environmental Overkill: Whatever Happened to Common Sense?* (Washington, DC: Regnery, 1993), p. 109.

109. Quoted in Yaffee, *Wisdom of the Spotted Owl*, p. 380.

110. McCoy, "Cut Down," p. A6.

111. See, for example, Dietrich, *Final Forest*, pp. 128–129, 132.

112. Gup, "Owl vs. Man."

113. Caulfield, "Ancient Forest," p. 48.

114. Quoted in Dietrich, *Final Forest*, p. 246.

115. Douglas Jehl, "Interest Groups Draw Lines in Battle Over a Proposal to Ban Road Building in Forests," *New York Times*, May 17, 2000, p. A14.

116. Douglas Jehl, "In Idaho, a Howl Against Roadless Forests," *New York Times*, July 5, 2000, p. A10.

117. Yaffee, *Wisdom of the Spotted Owl*, p. 6; Dietrich, *Final Forest*, p. 53.

118. Yaffee, *Wisdom of the Spotted Owl*, p. 6.

119. Yaffee, *Wisdom of the Spotted Owl*, p. 6; Dietrich, *Final Forest*, p. 104.

120. Yaffee, *Wisdom of the Spotted Owl*, p. 6.

121. Yaffee, *Wisdom of the Spotted Owl*, p. 260.

122. Kusel, *Community Forests*, pp. 38–41; see also Hays, *Gospel of Efficiency*. Pinchot's elitism finds an echo in contemporary notions of centralized, top-down, expert-driven approaches to resource conservation or environmental protection, including eco-managerialism and ecological modernization. For an example of eco-managerialism, see former Vice President Albert Gore's *Earth in the Balance: Ecology and the Human Spirit* (New York: Penguin, 1993). For critical overviews of ecological modernization, see John S. Dryzek, David Downes, Christian Hunold, David Schlosberg, and Hans-Kristian Hernes, *Green States and Social Movements: Environmentalism in the United States, United Kingdom, Germany, and Norway* (Oxford, UK: Oxford University Press, 2003), pp. 164–191; and Barry, *Rethinking Green Politics*, pp. 110–118. A particularly scathing critique of eco-managerialism is found in Timothy Luke, *Ecocritique* and *Capitalism, Democracy, and Ecology: Departing from Marx* (Urbana: University of Illinois Press, 1999). Critics of eco-managerialism and ecological modernization argue that these approaches tend to be antidemocratic and that they do not challenge the fundamental growth imperative of capitalism, but instead try to make the world ecologically safe for expanding consumption and continued accumulation of capital.

123. Yaffee, *Wisdom of the Spotted Owl*, p. 6.

124. Yaffee, *Wisdom of the Spotted Owl*, pp. 260–261.

125. Yaffee, *Wisdom of the Spotted Owl*, p. 6.

126. Dietrich, *Final Forest*, p. 96.

127. Nancy Langston, "Forest Dreams, Forest Nightmares: Environmental History of a Forest Health Crisis," in Char Miller, ed., *American Forests: Nature, Culture, and Politics* (Lawrence: University Press of Kansas, 1997), pp. 247–271 (quote on p. 260). This perspective descends from what John Barry calls a "perfection of nature" view, according to which "humans could use their God-given powers of creativity and ingenuity to 'perfect' nature for 'the Glory of God'." Barry notes that this early modern view "provid[ed] a religious justification for what we would now call the 'development' of the environment. This transformation of the natural world by humans in the West took many forms, from the creation of geometrically symmetrical landscape gardens ... to the straightening of rivers and the draining of swamps" [*Environment and Social Theory* (London: Routledge, 1999), p. 40]. Thanks to Barry for alerting me to this connection.

128. Quoted in Roberts, "Federal Chain-Saw Massacre," p. 44.

129. Dietrich, *Final Forest*, p. 121; See also Yaffee, *Wisdom of the Spotted Owl*, pp. 3–8 and chapter 10.

130. Berry makes a similar comment about an illustration in the February 1970 issue of *National Geographic*. An article entitled "The Revolution in American Agriculture" included a futuristic picture of a high-tech farm tended by a variety of machines. Berry, considering this vista as well as the accompanying article asks, "Where are the people?" See Berry, *Unsettling of America*, p. 73.

131. Kusel, *Community Forestry*, p. 51.

132. Yaffee, *Wisdom of the Spotted Owl*, p. 267.

133. Dietrich, *Final Forest*, p. 165. The George W. Bush Administration has, through both legislation and rule-making, worked to limit or even eliminate public comment on forest management. These efforts have sparked legal challenges, and U.S. District Judge James K. Singleton Jr. has issued several rulings against Administration attempts to limit public participation. See, for example, Michael Milstein, "Forest Work Put on Hold after Bush Rule Gets Ax," *Oregonian*, September 30, 2005, p. C1.

134. Roberts, "Federal Chain-Saw Massacre," p. 41.

135. Roberts, "Federal Chain-Saw Massacre," p. 41.

136. Dietrich, *Final Forest*, p. 33.

137. Dietrich, *Final Forest*, p. 33.

138. Quoted in Dietrich, *Final Forest*, p. 39.

139. Quoted in Betsy Carpenter, "The Light in the Forest," *U.S. News & World Report*, April 5, 1993, p. 39 (via Lexis-Nexis Academic).

140. Kusel, *Community Forestry*, p. 65; Cassandra Moseley and Stacey Shankle, "Who Gets the Work? National Forest Contracting in the Pacific Northwest," *Journal of Forestry*, Vol. 99, No. 9 (September 2001), pp. 32–37.

141. Dietrich, *Final Forest*, p. 261.

142. Theresa Satterfield, "Pawns, Victims, or Heroes: The Negotiation of Stigma and the Plight of Oregon's Loggers," *Journal of Social Issues*, Vol. 52, No. 1 (Spring 1996), pp. 71–83 (quote on p. 80).

143. Mark Baker and Jonathan Kusel, *Community Forestry in the United States: Learning from the Past, Crafting the Future* (Washington, DC: Island Press, 2003), p. 115.

144. Brown, *In Timber Country*, pp. 247–248.

145. Dietrich, *Final Forest*, p. 36.

146. Quoted in Dietrich, *Final Forest*, p. 279.

147. U.S. House of Representatives, *California Spotted Owl Recovery Plan: Hearing Before the Subcommittee on National Parks, Forests, and Lands of the Committee on Resources*, June 6, 1995 (Washington, DC: U.S. Government Printing Office, 1995), p. 33.

148. *California Spotted Owl Recovery Plan: Hearing*, p. 33.

149. Gup, "Owl vs. Man."

150. Dietrich, *Final Forest*, p. 63.

151. Dietrich, *Final Forest*, p. 65.

152. McCoy "Cut Down," p. A6.

153. Quoted in Proctor, "Whose Nature?" pp. 270–271. This of course raises the question of whether one is benefiting or harming wildlife by feeding it.

154. Dietrich, *Final Forest*, p. 144. The notion of farming practices like timber work having value as a way of life and not just as a means of income and commodity production is of course not new. It goes back to Jeffersonian notions of a virtuous yeomanry and finds contemporary expression in the writings of advocates of agricultural life like Berry. The debate in the European Union over the continuation of agricultural subsidies also involves a discussion over whether farming should be treated as a prized way of life or as simply another business (thanks to John Barry for this point). As regards the idea of attachment to nature through work, see Barry, *Rethinking Green Politics*, pp. 154–155, 176–180, 239–242.

155. Quoted in Dietrich, *Final Forest*, p. 141.

156. Dietrich, *Final Forest*, p. 211.

157. Caulfield, "Ancient Forest," p. 46.

158. Caulfield, "Ancient Forest," p. 46.

159. Christopher Manes, *Green Rage: Radical Environmentalism and the Unmaking of Civilization* (Boston: Little, Brown, 1990), p. 84.

160. U.S. Congress, 104th Congress, 2nd Session, *Congressional Record—Senate* (March 14, 1996), p. S2006.

161. Proctor, "Whose Nature?" p. 278.

162. Dietrich, *Final Forest*, p. 211.

163. Lawrence Buell, *The Environmental Imagination: Thoreau, Nature Writing, and the Formation of American Culture* (Cambridge, MA: Harvard University Press, 1995), pp. 265–266.

164. Manes, *Green Rage*, pp. 84–85.

165. Dietrich, *Final Forest*, pp. 289, 285.

166. In developing the concept of commanding presence, I am indebted to an essay by Albert Borgmann. See Borgmann, "The Nature of Reality and the Reality of Nature," in Michael E. Soulé and Gary Lease, eds., *Reinventing Nature?: Responses to Postmodern Deconstruction* (Washington, DC: Island Press, 1995), pp. 31–45.

167. Borgmann, "Nature of Reality," p. 40.

168. The quality of sublimity was articulated in the late eighteenth and early nineteenth centuries by Edmund Burke, Immanuel Kant, and others, particularly the Romantics. "Sublimity" is the aspect of force, power, and danger in nature; in religious terms, it is nature's reflection of the might and wrath of God. Nature's sublimity suggests its independence from and ability to overshadow humanity. See Mary A. McCloskey, *Kant's Aesthetic* (Albany: State University of New York Press, 1987), especially pp. 94–104; Max Oelschlaeger, *The Idea of Wilderness: From Prehistory to the Age of Ecology* (New Haven, CT: Yale University Press, 1991), pp. 110–116; and Nash, *Wilderness and the American Mind*, pp. 44–47.

169. Caulfield, "Ancient Forest," p. 46.

170. Quoted in Dietrich, *Final Forest*, p. 269.

171. Dietrich, *Final Forest*, p. 269.

172. Caulfield, "Ancient Forest"; Proctor, "Whose Nature?".

173. Caulfield, "Ancient Forest," p. 84.

174. Caulfield, "Ancient Forest," p. 84.

175. See also Brenda Peterson, "Saving the Roots of Our Family Trees," *Seattle Times*, July 7, 1996, p. B5.

176. Dietrich, *Final Forest*, pp. 160, 242; John Bellamy Foster, "The Limits of Environmentalism without Class: Lessons from the Ancient Forest Struggle in the Pacific Northwest," in Daniel Faber, ed., *The Struggle for Ecological Democracy: Environmental Justice Movements in the United States* (New York: Guilford Press, 1998), pp. 188–217 (see p. 201).

177. Proctor, "Whose Nature?", p. 284.

178. Quoted in Kim Murphy, "Differing Values Cut Through Timber Debate," *Los Angeles Times*, April 15, 1996, p. A1.

179. Quoted in Caulfield, "Ancient Forest," p. 83.

180. Thanks to Ruth Haas for alerting me to the relationship between thinning operations and increased fire danger. See Reda M. Dennis-Parks, "Healthy Forests Restoration Act: Will It Really Protect Homes and Communities?", *Ecology Law Quarterly*, Vol. 31, No. 3 (2004), pp. 639–664; Jerry F. Franklin and James K. Agee, "Forging a Science-Based National Forest Fire Policy," *Issues in Science and Technology*, Vol. 20, No. 1 (Fall 2003), pp. 59–66; and Dominick A. Della-Sala, Jack E. Williams, Cindy Deacon Williams, and Jerry F. Franklin, "Beyond Smoke and Mirrors: a Synthesis of Fire Policy and Science," *Conservation Biology*, Vol. 18, No. 4 (August 2004), pp. 976–986. On the unprofitability of salvage logging or thinning operations in federal forests, see Michael Milstein, "Biscuit Log Sales Fall Short of Forecast," *Oregonian*, November 23, 2004, p. A1; Blaine Harden, "Salvage Logging a Key Issue in Oregon," *Washington Post*, October 15, 2004, p. A4; Dennis-Parks, "Healthy Forests Restoration Act"; and Darius M. Adams and Gregory S. Latta, "Costs and Regional Impacts of Restoration Thinning Programs on the National Forests in Eastern Oregon," *Canadian Journal of Forest Research*, Vol. 35, No. 6 (June 2005), pp. 1319–1330.

181. DellaSala, Williams, Williams, and Franklin, "Beyond Smoke and Mirrors," p. 982; Franklin and Agee, "Science-Based National Forest Fire Policy," p. 61; Nicholas C. Slosser, James R. Strittholt, Dominick A. DellaSala, and John Wilson, "The Landscape Context in Forest Conservation: Integrating Protection, Restoration, and Certification," *Ecological Restoration*, Vol. 23, No. 1 (March 2005), pp. 15–23; Perry, "Ecological Realities," pp. 23–47.

182. Thomas, "Sustainability of the Northwest Forest Plan," p. 21.

183. Karen Arabas and Joe Bowersox, "Conclusion: Forests Past and Forests Future—Connecting Science, Politics, and Policy," in Karen Arabas and Joe Bowersox, eds., *Forest Futures: Science, Politics, and Policy for the Next Century* (Lanham, MD: Rowman & Littlefield, 2004), pp. 280–291 (quote on p. 283).

184. Beuter, "Sustained Yield," p. 64.

185. Brian Donahue, *Reclaiming the Commons: Community Farms and Forests in a New England Town* (New Haven, CT: Yale University Press, 1999), pp. 218–219.

186. Simon Schama, *Landscape and Memory* (New York: Random House, 1995), pp. 83, 144.

187. Durbin, *Tree Huggers*, pp. 192–193.

188. Kusel, *Community Forestry*, p. 139. For environmentalist opposition to the Applegate Partnership, a collaborative conservation group in Oregon, see Sturtevant and Lange, "From 'Them' to 'Us'," pp. 124, 130.

189. Baker and Kusel, *Community Forestry*, p. 139. See also, for example, the remarks of then-Sierra Club chair Michael McCloskey: "The Skeptic: Collaboration Has its Limits," *High Country News*, Vol. 28, No. 9 (May 13, 1996) (www.hcn.org/archives.jsp, accessed November 6, 2006).

190. Baker and Kusel, *Community Forestry*, pp. 139–140.

191. Michael Hibbard and Jeremy Madsen, "Environmental Resistance to Place-Based Collaboration in the U.S. West," *Society & Natural Resources*, Vol. 16, No. 8 (September 2003), pp. 703–718 (quote on p. 715).

192. Hibbard and Madsen, "Environmental Resistance," p. 708.

193. McCloskey virtually admits as much. He says, "this redistribution of power is designed to disempower our constituency, which is heavily urban. Few urbanites are recognized as stakeholders in communities surrounding national forests. Few of the proposals for stakeholder collaboration provide any way for distant stakeholders to be effectively represented.

... It is curious that these ideas would have the effect of transferring influence to the very communities where we are least organized and potent. They would maximize the influence of those who are least attracted to the environmental cause and most alienated from it.

Even in places where local environmentalists exist, they are not always equipped to play competitively with industry professionals. There may be no parity in experience, training, skills or financial resources" ("Collaboration Has its Limits").

194. This remark appeared in an article on the Wilderness Society's web site. See "Quincy Library Bill No Solution," *The Wilderness Society: Conservation Coast to Coast*, October 1998 (www.wilderness.org/ccc/california/quincy.html, dead link).

195. Proctor, "Whose Nature?"

196. Quoted in Yaffee, *Wisdom of the Spotted Owl*, p. 125.

197. On the simplistic thinking behind this unfortunate phrase, see also Baker and Kusel, *Community Forestry*, pp. 82–83.

198. Baker and Kusel, *Community Forestry*, p. 82.

Chapter 3

1. "The Parking Garage," *Seinfeld*, episode 23, directed by Tom Cherones, NBC, October 30, 1991.

2. Ewing, "Los Angeles-style Sprawl."

3. James Howard Kunstler, *The Geography of Nowhere: The Rise and Decline of America's Man-Made Landscape* (New York: Simon & Schuster, 1993), pp. 50, 115.

4. Kunstler, *Geography of Nowhere*, p. 116.

5. Ewing, "Los Angeles-style Sprawl."

6. Ewing, "Los Angeles-style Sprawl."

7. For an excellent discussion of the cultural and aesthetic character of sprawl, see Kunstler, *Geography of Nowhere*.

8. See Natural Resources Conservation Service, *Natural Resources Inventory: Highlights* (Washington, DC: U.S. Department of Agriculture, January 2001).

9. Lydia Savage and Mark Lapping, "Sprawl and Its Discontents: The Rural Dimension," in Matthew J. Lindstrom and Hugh Bartling, eds., *Suburban Sprawl: Culture, Theory, and Politics* (Lanham, MD: Rowman & Littlefield, 2003), pp. 5–17 (see pp. 6–7). On the rural impacts of sprawl, see also Diamond, *Collapse*, pp. 27–75; Brown, *Timber Country*; and Ralph E. Heimlich and William D. Anderson, *Development at the Urban Fringe and Beyond: Impacts on Agriculture and Rural Land* (Washington, DC: U.S. Department of Agriculture/Economic Research Service, 2001).

10. "U.S. Urban Sprawl Devours Farmland—Green Group," Reuters Limited, September 9, 1998. In many cases, development vastly outpaces population growth. The same Sierra Club report noted that between 1990 and 1996, the dimensions of Chicago's metropolitan area expanded by 40 percent, while the population grew by only 9 percent.

11. Ulf Zimmerman, Göktuğ Morçöl, and Bethany Stich, "From Sprawl to Smart Growth: The Case of Atlanta," in Matthew J. Lindstrom and Hugh Bartling, eds., *Suburban Sprawl: Culture, Theory, and Politics* (Lanham, MD: Rowman & Littlefield, 2003), pp. 275–287. The authors describe metro Atlanta, at 110 miles across, as the most rapidly expanding and largest human settlement ever constructed (p. 275).

12. "Protecting Cape Cod" (editorial), *Boston Globe*, January 25, 1998, p. E6; Michael Grunwald, "Sprawl Intrudes on Paradise: Rapid Growth Transforms Amish Country," *Boston Globe*, May 17, 1998, p. A1; Ted Koffman, "Even in Maine?" *Environment*, Vol. 41, No. 4 (May 1999), p. 30; Egan, "Urban Sprawl Strains Western States."

13. For good summaries of the environmental and social impacts of sprawl, along with some discussion of possible solutions, see Richard Moe and Carter Wilkie, *Changing Places: Rebuilding Community in the Age of Sprawl* (New York: Henry Holt, 1997); Kelbaugh, *Repairing the American Metropolis*; Robert Paehlke, "Environmental Sustainability and Urban Life in America," in Norman Vig and Michael E. Kraft, eds., *Environmental Policy: New Directions for the Twenty-first Century* (Washington, DC: CQ Press, 2002), pp. 57–77; Thomas B. Stoel, "Reining in Urban Sprawl: What Can be Done to Tackle this Growing Problem?" *Environment*, Vol. 41, No. 4 (May 1999), pp. 6–11, 29–33.

14. Reid Ewing, Tom Schmid, Richard Killingsworth, Amy Zlot, and Stephen Raudenbush, "Relationship Between Urban Sprawl and Physical Activity, Obesity, and Morbidity," *American Journal of Health Promotion*, Vol. 18, No. 1 (September/October 2003), pp. 47–57.

15. Luke, *Capitalism, Democracy, and Ecology*, p. 98.

16. Stoel, "Reining in Urban Sprawl."

17. On opposition to Wal-Mart, see, for example, Alan Ehrenhalt, "Up Against the Wal-Mart," *Governing*, September 1992, pp. 6–7; "In Two Towns, Main Street Fights Off Wal-Mart," *New York Times*, October 21, 1993, p. A16.

18. Henry R. Richmond, "Metropolitan Land-Use Reform: The Promise and Challenge of Majority Consensus," in Bruce Katz, ed., *Reflections on Regionalism* (Washington, DC: Brookings Institution, 2000), pp. 9–39.

19. For defenses of sprawl, or criticisms of antisprawl sentiment, see, for example, Gordon and Richardson, "Are Compact Cities Desirable?"; Joel Kotkin, "Get Used to It: Suburbia's Not Going Away, No Matter What Critics Say or Do," *American Enterprise*, January/February, 2005, pp. 32–37; Joel Kotkin, "Suburban Tide," *Blueprint*, Vol. 2005, No. 1 (2005), pp. 22–24; Joel Kotkin, "Will Great Cities Survive?" *Wilson Quarterly*, Vol. 29, No. 2 (Spring 2005), pp. 16–27; Gregg Easterbrook, "Suburban Myth," *New Republic*, March 15, 1999, pp. 18–21; Steven Hayward, "Suburban Legends: The Fight Against Sprawl is Based More on Anti-Suburban Animus Than on Facts," *National Review*, Vol. 51, No. 5 (March 22, 1999), pp. 35–36, 38; Steven Hayward, "Legends of the Sprawl," *Policy Review*, No. 91 (September/October 1998), pp. 26–32 (www.policyreview.com/sept98/sprawl.html, accessed May 14, 1999).

20. Lewis Mumford, who is critical of the suburbs, says that a large part of their appeal, going back to Roman times, was the promise of freedom from the unhealthy, crowded, and oppressive life of the city. See Lewis Mumford, *The City in History: Its Origins, Its Transformations, and Its Prospects* (New York: Harcourt, Brace & World 1961), pp. 482–487.

21. Easterbrook, "Suburban Myth," p. 20.

22. John Andrews of the Independence Institute, quoted in James Brooke, "Denver Calls Old Airport Ground Zero for Growth," *New York Times*, September 16, 1998, p. A13.

23. Easterbrook, "Suburban Myth," p. 19.

24. Kotkin, "Get Used to It," p. 34.

25. Gordon and Richardson, "Are Compact Cities Desirable?"

26. Gordon and Richardson, "Are Compact Cities Desirable?"

27. Mumford, *City in History*, p. 504.

28. In 2000, 50 percent of the U.S. population was living in the suburbs, up from 7.1 percent in 1910. Within metropolitan areas, the majority of the population has shifted from central cities to suburbs over the same period. In 1910, about 25 percent of metropolitan residents were living in the suburbs. Today, that figure is about 62 percent [Frank Hobbs and Nicole Stoops, *Demographic Trends in the Twentieth Century* (Washington, DC: U.S. Census Bureau, 2002), p. 33]. I do not present a comprehensive history of the suburbs and urban planning in the United States. For those interested in such an account, I recommend Mumford, *City in History*; Kenneth T. Jackson, *Crabgrass Frontier: The Suburbanization of the United States* (New York: Oxford University Press, 1987); and Kunstler, *The Geography of Nowhere*.

29. See Berry, *Unsettling of America*.

30. Heidi Hartmann, Robert E. Kraut, and Louise A. Tilly, eds., *Computer Chips and Paper Clips: Technology and Women's Employment* (Washington, DC: National Academy Press, 1986), pp. 15, 81.

31. Richmond, "Land-Use Reform," p. 10.

32. Kunstler, *Geography of Nowhere*, p. 117.

33. Matthew J. Lindstrom and Hugh Bartling, "Introduction," in Matthew J. Lindstrom and Hugh Bartling, eds., *Suburban Sprawl: Culture, Theory, and Politics* (Lanham, MD: Rowman & Littlefield, 2003), pp. xi–xxvii (see pp. xvi–xvii).

34. See, for example, Mark Edward Braun, "Suburban Sprawl in Southeastern Wisconsin: Planning, Politics, and the Lack of Affordable Housing," in Matthew J. Lindstrom and Hugh Bartling, eds., *Suburban Sprawl: Culture, Theory, and Politics* (Lanham, MD: Rowman & Littlefield, 2003), pp. 257–274.

35. Moe and Wilkie, *Changing Places*, p. 55; Elliot D. Sclar, "Back to the City," *Technology Review*, August/September 1992, p. 29; James Howard Kunstler, "Home from Nowhere," *Atlantic Monthly*, Vol. 278, No. 3 (September 1996), p. 43 (www.theatlantic.com/issues/96sep/kunstler/kunstler.htm, accessed June 1, 1999).

36. Kunstler, *Geography of Nowhere*, p. 114.

37. Henry Richmond says, "Of the many laws that prescribe or induce sprawl, municipal zoning laws are the most direct, pervasive, and important ("Land-Use Reform," p. 10).

38. There is empirical evidence that regions with higher numbers of municipalities have more sprawl [Wim Wiewel and Kimberly Schaffer, "New Federal and State Policies for Metropolitan Equity," in Wim Wiewel and Joseph J. Persky, eds., *Suburban Sprawl: Private Decisions and Public Policy* (Armonk, NY: M.E. Sharpe, 2002), pp. 256–307].

39. Richmond, "Land-Use Reform."

40. Ronald Hayduk, "Race and Suburban Sprawl: Regionalism and Structural Racism," in Matthew J. Lindstrom and Hugh Bartling, eds., *Suburban Sprawl: Culture, Theory, and Politics* (Lanham, MD: Rowman & Littlefield, 2003), pp. 137–170 (quote on p. 153).

41. Hayduk, "Race and Suburban Sprawl," p. 157.

42. Moe and Wilkie, *Changing Places*, pp. 11–12.

43. "As soon as the motor car became common, the pedestrian scale of the suburb disappeared," Mumford says. "The suburb ceased to be a neighborhood unit: it became a diffused, low-density mass" (*City in History*, p. 505).

44. Wiewel and Schaffer, "New Federal and State Policies," p. 278.

45. Jackson, *Crabgrass Frontier*, p. 204.

46. Moe and Wilkie, *Changing Places*, pp. 48–50, 54–55; Richmond, "Land-Use Reform," p. 11.

47. Kunstler, *Geography of Nowhere*, p. 102; Jackson, *Crabgrass Frontier*, pp. 197–218.

48. Lindstrom and Bartling, "Introduction," p. xii.

49. Richmond, "Land-Use Reform," p. 18.

50. Lindstrom and Bartling, "Introduction," p. xvi.

51. Kunstler, *Geography of Nowhere*, p. 104; Jackson, *Crabgrass Frontier*, pp. 234–235.

52. Jackson, *Crabgrass Frontier*, p. 233.

53. Todd W. Bressi, "Planning the American Dream," in Peter Katz, ed., *The New Urbanism: Toward an Architecture of Community* (New York: McGraw-Hill, 1994), pp. xxv–xlii (quote on p. xxviii).

54. Jackson, *Crabgrass Frontier*, pp. 234–235.

55. Hayduk, "Race and Suburban Sprawl"; Jackson, *Crabgrass Frontier*, p. 241.

56. Hayduk, "Race and Suburban Sprawl," p. 143.

57. Richmond, "Land-Use Reform," p. 17.

58. Jackson, *Crabgrass Frontier*, p. 249.

59. See Moe and Wilkie, *Changing Places*, pp. 51–54.

60. Eric Schlosser, *Fast Food Nation: The Dark Side of the All-American Meal* (Boston: Houghton Mifflin, 2001), p. 66.

61. Between 1960 and 1970, for example, the Milwaukee metropolitan area saw a 10 percent decline in available jobs in the central city and a 75 percent increase in jobs outside of Milwaukee's inner city (Braun, "Suburban Sprawl in Southeastern Wisconsin," pp. 258–259).

62. Kotkin, "Will Great Cities Survive?"

63. Hayduk, "Race and Suburban Sprawl," p. 141; also Richmond, "Land-Use Reform," pp. 27–28.

64. Gordon and Richardson, "Are Compact Cities Desirable?"

65. Ewing, "Los Angeles-style Sprawl."

66. Ewing, "Los Angeles-style Sprawl."

67. It is worth noting that Gordon and Richardson and others who defend sprawl also point out that housing in more compact areas tends to be more expensive and thus exclusionary. However, this would suggest that there is considerable consumer demand for compact neighborhoods.

68. Ewing, "Los Angeles-style Sprawl."

69. Moe and Wilkie, *Changing Places*, p. xi. Many of the residents of sprawling developments are themselves nomadic, forming a demographic the *New York Times* recently dubbed "relos." See Peter T. Kilborn's portrait of such a family: Kilborn, "The Five-Bedroom, Six-Figure Rootless Life," *New York Times*, June 1, 2005. "Relos" are members of households headed by corporate employees who move every few years. Kilborn describes their struggles to create a sense of community in the various stops along the way. Over the course of fifteen years, the family profiled by Kilborn had lived in or near Houston, Texas; Rochester, New York; Baltimore, Maryland; and Atlanta, Georgia. Shortly before the article was published, they had moved to Charlotte, North Carolina.

70. Richmond, "Land-Use Reform," p. 21.

71. Moe and Wilkie, *Changing Places*, pp. 247–248.

72. Kelbaugh, *Repairing the American Metropolis*, pp. 84–85.

73. Kelbaugh, *Repairing the American Metropolis*, p. 40.

74. Kelbaugh, *Repairing the American Metropolis*, pp. 86–87.

75. Curt Hazlett, "Taking Aim at Wal-Mart," *Retail Traffic*, February 1, 2005, p. 33 (via Lexis-Nexis Academic).

76. Kelbaugh, *Repairing the American Metropolis*, p. 40.

77. Moe and Wilkie, *Changing Places*, p. 147.

78. David Brooks, "Our Sprawling, Supersize Utopia," *New York Times Magazine*, April 4, 2004, p. 46 (via Lexis-Nexis Academic).

79. Bettina Drew, *Crossing the Expendable Landscape* (St. Paul, MN: Graywolf Press, 1998), pp. 4–5, 170.

80. Kelbaugh, *Repairing the American Metropolis*, p. 40.

81. Peter Calthorpe, *The Next American Metropolis: Ecology, Community, and the American Dream* (Princeton, NJ: Princeton Architectural Press, 1993), p. 24.

82. Robert Fishman, "Megalopolis Unbound," *Wilson Quarterly*, Vol. 14, No. 1 (Winter 1990), pp. 25–46 (via Academic Search Premier).

83. On these points see also Benjamin R. Barber, "An Architecture of Liberty?: The City as Democracy's Forge," in Joan Ockham, ed., *Out of Ground Zero: Case Studies in Urban Reinvention* (New York: Columbia University Press, 2002), pp. 184–205.

84. Lindstrom and Bartling, "Introduction," pp. xvii–xviii.

85. Calthorpe, *The Next American Metropolis*, p. 23. Moe and Wilkie describe the rise of a home-centered society as an erosion of the public landscape and associated perceptions of increasing insecurity in the streets lead to a turning inward toward the private home (*Changing Places*, pp. 72–73). For an excellent discussion of the privatized landscape, see Kohn, *Brave New Neighborhoods*.

86. Robert Messia, "Lawns as Artifacts: The Evolution of Social and Environmental Implications of Suburban Residential Land Use," in Matthew J. Lindstrom and Hugh Bartling, eds., *Suburban Sprawl: Culture, Theory, and Politics* (Lanham, MD: Rowman & Littlefield, 2003), pp. 69–83 (see p. 77).

87. Bressi, "Planning the American Dream," pp. xxix–xxx. See also Kohn, *Brave New Neighborhoods*, chapters 6 and 7.

88. In *Pruneyard Shopping Center v. Robins*, a 1980 decision regarding a California mall's ban on gathering petition signatures, the U.S. Supreme Court ruled that a mall was private property and was beyond the reach of the First Amendment, unless state laws mandated otherwise. See Kohn, *Brave New Neighborhoods*, pp. 70–74. The tee-shirt incident took place at the Crossgate Mall near Albany, New York, on March 3, 2003, just before the U.S. invasion of Iraq. See Kohn, *Brave New Neighborhoods*, pp. 1–2. On the privatization of places see also Barber, "Architecture of Liberty?", pp. 192–193.

89. Kohn, *Brave New Neighborhoods*, p. 116.

90. See Kohn, *Brave New Neighborhoods*, p. 118; Michele Byers, "Waiting at the Gate: The New, Postmodern Promised Lands," in Matthew J. Lindstrom and Hugh Bartling, eds., *Suburban Sprawl: Culture, Theory, and Politics* (Lanham, MD: Rowman & Littlefield, 2003), pp. 23–43; Susan Bickford, "Constructing Inequality: City Spaces and the Architecture of Citizenship," *Political Theory*, Vol. 28, No. 3 (2000), pp. 355–376; Gerald E. Frug, *City Making: Building Communities Without Walls* (Princeton, NJ: Princeton University Press, 1999).

91. Byers, "Waiting at the Gate," pp. 33–35.

92. Kohn, *Brave New Neighborhoods*, pp. 115–123.

93. Kohn, *Brave New Neighborhoods*, p. 116.

94. Kohn, *Brave New Neighborhoods*, pp. 115–118.

95. Kohn, *Brave New Neighborhoods*, p. 117.

96. Cited in H. William Batt, "Stemming Sprawl: The Fiscal Approach," in Matthew J. Lindstrom and Hugh Bartling, eds., *Suburban Sprawl: Culture, Theory, and Politics* (Lanham, MD: Rowman & Littlefield, 2003), pp. 239–254 (pp. 242, 252).

97. Lindstrom and Bartling, "Introduction," p. xxiii.

98. Batt, "Stemming Sprawl," pp. 240–241.

99. Batt, "Stemming Sprawl," pp. 241, 251 n3.

100. Mumford, *City in History*, pp. 492–493.

101. Mumford, *City in History*, p. 503.

102. Bressi, "Planning the American Dream," p. xxix. See also Calthorpe, *Next American Metropolis*, p. 25.

103. Kunstler, *Geography of Nowhere*, p. 120.

104. Byers, "Waiting at the Gate," p. 30.

105. Logan and Molotch, *Urban Fortunes*, p. 239. Harvey remarks that communities "end up creating a kind of serial replication of homogeneity," (*Geography of Difference*, p. 298). See also Sack, *Homo Geographicus*, p. 77.

106. Sack, *Homo Geographicus*, pp. 9, 138.

107. Tom Wolfe, *A Man in Full* (New York: Farrar Straus Giroux, 1998), p. 171.

108. Calthorpe, *Next American Metropolis*, p. 18.

109. Fishman, "Megalopolis Unbound."

110. Casey, "Between Geography and Philosophy."

111. Sack, *Homo Geographicus*, p. 16. Calthorpe says that the qualities of the landscape are easily blurred by the speed at which we move in our cars (*Next American Metropolis*, p. 18).

112. Ewing, "Los Angeles-style Sprawl."

113. Moe and Wilkie, *Changing Places*, p. 179.

114. Moe and Wilkie, *Changing Places*, p. 255.

115. Lindstrom and Bartling, "Introduction," p. xx.

116. Moe and Wilkie, *Changing Places*, p. 257.

117. Braun, "Suburban Sprawl in Southeastern Wisconsin," p. 263.

118. Patricia E. Salkin, "Smart Growth and the Law," in Matthew J. Lindstrom and Hugh Bartling, eds., *Suburban Sprawl: Culture, Theory, and Politics* (Lanham, MD: Rowman & Littlefield, 2003), pp. 213–234 (see p. 213). Richmond argues that the appeal to private property rights benefits a relatively few large developers, while the costs of sprawl depress property values for many more people ("Land-Use Reform," pp. 22–23).

119. As Logan and Molotch discuss, this ideology of progress often takes the form of boosterism on the part of urban progrowth coalitions. See Logan and Molotch, *Urban Fortunes*.

120. Moe and Wilkie offer a trenchant critique of Wright as a kind of prophet of sprawl. See Moe and Wilkie, *Changing Places*, pp. 44–46.

121. This is a major theme of Logan and Molotch, *Urban Fortunes*.

122. See Martin Heidegger, "The Question Concerning Technology," in David Farrell Krell, ed., *Basic Writings* (San Francisco: HarperCollins, 1977), pp. 311–341.

123. As John Barry has reminded me, development interests often use the concept of NIMBY to discredit their opponents as parochial and self-centered.

124. See Wende Vyborney Feller, "Urban Impostures: How Two Neighborhoods Reframed Suburban Sprawl as a New Urbanist Paradise without Changing a Thing," in Matthew J. Lindstrom and Hugh Bartling, eds., *Suburban Sprawl: Culture, Theory, and Politics* (Lanham, MD: Rowman & Littlefield, 2003), pp. 49–63.

125. Weir, "Coalition Building," p. 143.

126. On global ecological limits to economic growth, see especially Herman E. Daly, *Beyond Growth: The Economics of Sustainable Development* (Boston: Beacon Press, 1997). For a green political economy that assumes ecological constraints on growth, see Barry, *Rethinking Green Politics*, pp. 142–192.

127. Kunstler, "Home from Nowhere," and Salkin, "Smart Growth and the Law," pp. 229–230.

128. Donahue, *Reclaiming the Commons*, p. 283.

129. Richmond, "Land-Use Reform," p. 19.

130. Calthorpe and Fulton, *Regional City*, p. 198.

131. Roger K. Lewis, "Comprehensive Plan Needed in Growth Management," *Washington Post*, November 14, 1998, p. E1.

132. Lewis, "Comprehensive Plan Needed in Growth Management."

133. Richmond, "Land-Use Reform," p. 31.

134. See especially Calthorpe, *Next American Metropolis*; Calthorpe and Fulton, *Regional City*; Kunstler, "Home from Nowhere"; and Peter Katz, ed., *The*

New Urbanism: Toward an Architecture of Community (New York: McGraw-Hill, 1994).

135. See, for example, Feller, "Urban Impostures."

136. Alex Marshall, "Putting Some 'City' Back in the Suburbs," *Washington Post*, September 1, 1996, p. C1 (www.alexmarshall.org, accessed July 8, 2003). See also David Harvey, "The New Urbanism and the Communitarian Trap," *Harvard Design Magazine*, No. 1 (Winter/Spring 1997), pp. 68–69.

137. Moe and Wilkie, *Changing Places*, p. 249.

138. The problems I enumerate here do not apply to at least one branch of the New Urbanist movement: Peter Calthorpe and his regionalist program. See chapter 6.

139. Kunstler, *Geography of Nowhere*, p. 257.

140. This observation is made by Amanda Rees, "New Urbanism: Visionary Landscapes in the Twenty-first Century," in Matthew J. Lindstrom and Hugh Bartling, eds., *Suburban Sprawl: Culture, Theory, and Politics* (Lanham, MD: Rowman & Littlefield, 2003), pp. 93–114 (see p. 100).

141. These criticisms and others are catalogued in Rees, "New Urbanism." Milton Curry accuses New Urbanism, particularly when it is applied to urban public housing, of trying to impose white suburban cultural values on inner-city residents and of breaking up existing urban communities. He also argues that the replacement of old housing projects with smaller New Urbanist structures reduces the stock of affordable housing, displaces the poor, and opens inner cities up to gentrification and real estate speculation. See Milton Curry, "Racial Critique of Public Housing Redevelopment Strategies," in Matthew J. Lindstrom and Hugh Bartling, eds., *Suburban Sprawl: Culture, Theory, and Politics* (Lanham, MD: Rowman & Littlefield, 2003), pp. 119–131.

142. On this criticism of New Urbanism, see especially Harvey, "New Urbanism" and Rees, "New Urbanism."

143. Rees, "New Urbanism," p. 97.

144. Kunstler, *Geography of Nowhere*, p. 257.

145. Kunstler, *Geography of Nowhere*, p. 259; emphasis in original.

146. On lifestyle centers, see Andrew Blum, "The Mall Goes Undercover: It Now Looks Like a City Street," *Slate*, April 6, 2005 (www.slate.com/id/2116246, accessed October 2, 2006); Michael Southworth, "Reinventing Main Street: From Mall to Townscape Mall," *Journal of Urban Design*, Vol. 10, No. 2 (June 2005), pp. 151–170; Parija Bhatnagar, "Not a Mall, It's a Lifestyle Center," CNNMoney.com, January 12, 2005 (www.money.cnn.com/2005/01/11/news/fortune500/retail_lifestylecenter/, accessed October 2, 2006); and Emily Shartin, "Malls, Alfresco," *Boston Globe*, August 4, 2005 (www.boston.com/news/local/articles/2005/08/04/malls_alfresco/?page=full, accessed October 2, 2006).

147. Blum, "The Mall Goes Undercover."

148. Southworth, "Reinventing Main Street," p. 160.

149. Southworth, "Reinventing Main Street," pp. 158–161.

150. See, for example, Robert Steuteville, "Developer Fascination with Urban Centers Grows," *New Urban News*, October/November 2003 (www .newurbannews.com/whatsnew.html, accessed October 2, 2006), and an on-line discussion at the website of the Congress of the New Urbanism's New England Chapter (www.cnunewengland.org/fall-2005/listserv-topic1.php, accessed October 2, 2006).

151. Harvey, "New Urbanism."

152. Jean-Jacques Rousseau, *On the Social Contract* (1762), Roger D. Masters, ed., and Judith R. Masters, trans. (New York: St. Martin's Press, 1978), Book II, chapter vii, p. 68.

153. Rousseau, *Social Contract*, Book IV, chapter ii, p. 109.

154. Quoted in Byers, "Waiting at the Gate," p. 41 n. 27.

155. "A Conversation with Alex Morton," in Matthew J. Lindstrom and Hugh Bartling, eds., *Suburban Sprawl: Culture, Theory, and Politics* (Lanham, MD: Rowman & Littlefield, 2003), pp. 115–117 (see p. 117).

156. Kohn, *Brave New Neighborhoods*, p. 128.

157. For a fuller version of the following account, see Alex Marshall, "When the New Urbanism Meets the Old Neighborhood," *Metropolis*, May 1995 (www .alexmarshall.org, accessed July 8, 2003).

158. Ironically, this attempt to found a New Urbanist community involved a denial of New Urbanist principles. As Marshall points out, an existing urban neighborhood was destroyed in the name of New Urbanism. And in place of the existing 1,500 housing units, the city planned to put in only 400–600—which flies in the face of New Urbanist notions of higher density—and at prices unaffordable for 95 percent of the neighborhood's current residents: $200,000 to over $1 million (see Harry Minium, "Homearama Headed for Norfolk in 2004," *Virginian-Pilot*, October 19, 2003), which is inconsistent with New Urbanism's push for more diverse neighborhoods.

159. See Harvey, "New Urbanism."

Chapter 4

1. James Glanz and Eric Lipton, *City in the Sky: The Rise and Fall of the World Trade Center* (New York: Henry Holt, 2003), photograph facing p. 211.

2. See Peter Marcuse, "On the Global Uses of September 11 and Its Urban Impact," in Stanley Aronowitz and Heather Gautney, eds., *Implicating Empire: Globalization and Resistance in the Twenty-first Century* (New York: Basic Books, 2003), pp. 271–285; Sharon Zukin, "Our World Trade Center"; David Harvey, "Cracks in the Edifice of the Empire State"; Eric Darton, "The Janus Face of Architectural Terrorism: Minoru Yamasaki, Mohammed Atta, and Our World Trade Center"; and Mike Wallace, "New York, New Deal" in Michael Sorkin and Sharon Zukin, eds., *After the World Trade Center: Rethinking New York City* (New York: Routledge, 2002), pp. 13–21, 57–67, 87–95, 209–223.

3. Zukin, "Our World Trade Center," p. 14.

4. In order to focus on the redevelopment controversy at Ground Zero, I leave out another post–9/11 rebuilding effort, at the Pentagon in Washington, D.C.

5. Marshall Berman, "When Bad Buildings Happen to Good People," in Michael Sorkin and Sharon Zukin, eds., *After the World Trade Center: Rethinking New York City* (New York: Routledge, 2002) pp. 1–12 (quote on p. 6).

6. Hiss, *Experience of Place*, p. 49.

7. Mark Wigley, "Insecurity by Design," in Michael Sorkin and Sharon Zukin, eds., *After the World Trade Center: Rethinking New York City* (New York: Routledge, 2002), pp. 69–85.

8. Angus Kress Gillespie, *Twin Towers: The Life of New York City's World Trade Center* (New Brunswick, NJ: Rutgers University Press, 1999), pp. 178–179.

9. Gillespie, *Twin Towers*, p. 179.

10. See Wigley, "Insecurity by Design" for a discussion of some of these characteristics.

11. Andrew Ross, "The Odor of Publicity," in Michael Sorkin and Sharon Zukin, eds., *After the World Trade Center: Rethinking New York City* (New York: Routledge, 2002), pp. 121–130 (see p. 126).

12. Gillespie, *Twin Towers*, p. 214.

13. Gillespie, *Twin Towers*, p. 179.

14. Gillespie, *Twin Towers*, p. 4.

15. This was from my personal experience while working several blocks from the World Trade Center during the late 1980s. For a similar observation, see Hiss, *Experience of Place*, pp. 49–50.

16. Paul Goldberger, *Up From Zero: Politics, Architecture, and the Rebuilding of New York* (New York: Random House, 2004), p. 31.

17. Gillespie, *Twin Towers*, p. 4.

18. James Glanz and Eric Lipton, "The Height of Ambition," *New York Times Magazine*, September 8, 2002, pp. 32–44, 59–60, 63 (quote on p. 34).

19. Goldberger, *Up From Zero*, p. 32.

20. Goldberger, *Up From Zero*, p. 33.

21. Philip Nobel, *Sixteen Acres: Architecture and the Outrageous Struggle for the Future of Ground Zero* (New York: Henry Holt, 2005), p. 55. On the idea of the World Trade Center and its shops and services as a "village" for the surrounding neighborhood, see Conor O'Clery, "9/11 Two Years On," *Irish Times*, September 6, 2003, p. 50.

22. Lefebvre speaks of "dominated" space, i.e., space entirely transformed by technology and often having a sterilized, rectilinear aspect that displaces the organic processes of the former landscape (*Production of Space*, p. 165).

23. For discussions of urban renewal, see Jacobs, *Great American Cities*; Herbert Gans, *The Urban Villagers: Group and Class in the Life of Italian-*

Americans (New York: Free Press, 1962); John Mollenkopf, *The Contested City* (Princeton, NJ: Princeton University Press, 1983); Logan and Molotch, *Urban Fortunes*, pp. 167–170; Moe and Wilkie, *Changing Places*, pp. 56–69; Drew, *Crossing the Expendable Landscape*, pp. 8–31.

24. The classic study of the West End is Gans, *Urban Villagers*. Former residents communicate through the aforementioned quarterly newsletter, the *West Ender*. Jim Campano, the editor, now describes the West End as a "neighborhood of the mind." See Weiner, "The Taking."

25. Robert Fishman, "The Death and Life of American Regional Planning," in Bruce Katz, ed., *Reflections on Regionalism* (Washington, DC: Brookings Institution, 2000), pp. 107–123 (quote on p. 111).

26. Fishman, "American Regional Planning," p. 110.

27. Moe and Wilkie, *Changing Places*, p. 57. Often when downtowns weren't demolished, older structures, including buildings of considerable beauty, were covered in aluminum siding or stucco to look more like the new suburban strip malls (*Changing Places*, p. 159).

28. Fishman, "American Regional Planning," p. 111.

29. Quoted in Moe and Wilkie, *Changing Places*, p. 63.

30. Kunstler, *Geography of Nowhere*, p. 100.

31. See Goldberger, *Up From Zero*, pp. 28–31.

32. *Susette Kelo, et al. v. City of New London, Connecticut, et al.*, 125 S. Ct. 2655 (June 23, 2005). The case involved residents of the New London, Connecticut, neighborhood of Fort Trumbull, some of whom have roots in the area going back more than a century. The ailing City of New London adopted an economic development plan that involved seizing the neighborhood under eminent domain. The land would then be used for private residential and commercial development. Susette Kelo and other property owners sued, arguing that the city could not use eminent domain because the land would not be used for a *public* purpose. The Court upheld the use of eminent domain on the grounds that the city had a legitimate public purpose: the seizure was part of a comprehensive development plan that would benefit the whole city and not just a particular group of individuals. However, the ruling also allowed states to prohibit the use of eminent domain to transfer property to another private owner. Legislation to this effect is being considered or has been adopted in a number of states, and has been introduced in Congress as well. See Institute for Justice, *Legislative Action Since Kelo* (Arlington, VA: Castle Coalition, 2006).

33. Gillespie, *Twin Towers*, p. 24.

34. Gillespie, *Twin Towers*, p. 31.

35. My history of the World Trade Center draws chiefly upon Gillespie, *Twin Towers*, and Glanz and Lipton, "Height of Ambition" and *City in the Sky*.

36. Gillespie, *Twin Towers*, p. 33; Glanz and Lipton, "Height of Ambition," p. 36.

37. Gillespie, *Twin Towers*, p. 183.

38. Glanz and Lipton, "Height of Ambition," p. 34.

39. Glanz and Lipton, *City in the Sky*, p. 60.

40. See Glanz and Lipton, *City in the Sky*, pp. 66–67, 72–73; Gillespie, *Twin Towers*, pp. 173–178.

41. Glanz and Lipton, *City in the Sky*, esp. pp. 57–60.

42. Glanz and Lipton, "Height of Ambition," p. 38.

43. Goldberger, *Up From Zero*, p. 29.

44. Glanz and Lipton, "Height of Ambition," p. 38; Gillespie, *Twin Towers*, p. 166.

45. Glanz and Lipton, *City in the Sky*, pp. 69–70.

46. Glanz and Lipton, *City in the Sky*, p. 86.

47. Gillespie, *Twin Towers*, p. 186; Sewell Chan, "Plan to Fill Freedom Tower Stirs a Debate," *New York Times*, September 20, 2006, p. B3.

48. Clay Risen, "Memories of Overdevelopment," *New Republic*, February 23, 2004, pp. 26–32.

49. Darton, "Architectural Terrorism," p. 88.

50. Jenna Weisman Joselit, "Above and Below," *New Republic*, May 27, 2002, pp. 35–37. See also Leslie Eaton, "Visions of Ground Zero: The Plans; New York Embraces Commerce, as It Always Has," *New York Times*, July 21, 2002 (www.nytimes.com, accessed February 9, 2003).

51. Goldberger, *Up From Zero*, p. 254.

52. See John Kuo Wei Tchen, "Whose Downtown?!?," in Michael Sorkin and Sharon Zukin, eds., *After the World Trade Center: Rethinking New York City* (New York: Routledge, 2002), pp. 33–44.

53. Darton, "Architectural Terrorism," p. 91.

54. Risen, "Memories of Overdevelopment," p. 28.

55. See National Institute of Standards and Technology, *Final Report on the Collapse of the World Trade Center Towers* (Washington, DC: U.S. Department of Commerce, September 2005).

56. Glanz and Lipton, *City in the Sky*, pp. 325–326.

57. Glanz and Lipton, *City in the Sky*, p. 326.

58. Goldberger, *Up From Zero*, p. 28.

59. Risen, "Memories of Overdevelopment," p. 28.

60. For more on the meaning of the phrase, see Christine Boyer, "Meditations on a Wounded Skyline and Its Stratigraphies of Pain," in Michael Sorkin and Sharon Zukin, eds., *After the World Trade Center: Rethinking New York City* (New York: Routledge, 2002), pp. 109–120 (see p. 117).

61. Goldberger, *Up From Zero*, pp. 59–62.

62. See Ada Louise Huxtable, "No Games With Ground Zero, Please: The Profit Motive Must Yield to the Greater Good," *Wall Street Journal*, July 24, 2003 (www.opinionjournal.com, accessed July 30, 2003).

63. For a lavishly illustrated and comprehensive overview of the various proposals for Ground Zero, see Suzanne Stephens, Ian Luna, and Ron Broadhurst, *Imagining Ground Zero: Official and Unofficial Proposals for the World Trade Center Site* (New York: Rizzoli/McGraw-Hill, 2004).

64. Michael Sorkin, *Starting from Zero: Reconstructing Downtown New York* (New York: Routledge, 2003), p. 87.

65. Setha M. Low, "Spaces of Reflection, Recovery, and Resistance: Reimagining the Postindustrial Plaza," in Michael Sorkin and Sharon Zukin, eds., *After the World Trade Center: Rethinking New York City* (New York: Routledge, 2002), pp. 163–171 (quote on p. 165).

66. Herbert Muschamp, "Rich Firms, Poor Ideas for Towers Site," *New York Times*, April 18, 2002 (www.nytimes.com, accessed February 9, 2003).

67. Goldberger, *Up From Zero*, p. 54.

68. Maggie Haberman and Greg Gittrich, "Firefighters Apply Heat at Public Hearing," *New York Daily News*, May 29, 2003, p. 19 (via Lexis-Nexis Academic).

69. Nobel, *Sixteen Acres*, pp. 116–117. See also Edward Wyatt, "Pataki's Surprising Limit on Ground Zero Design," *New York Times*, July 2, 2002 (www.nytimes.com, accessed February 9, 2003).

70. Nobel, *Sixteen Acres*, pp. 116–117, 253.

71. Nobel, *Sixteen Acres*, p. 253.

72. In fact a number of them were undocumented immigrants. See Sasha Polakow-Suransky, "The Invisible Victims: Undocumented Workers at the World Trade Center," *American Prospect*, December 3, 2001 (www.prospect .org, accessed December 2, 2005).

73. Paul Goldberger, "A New Beginning: Why We Should Build Apartments at Ground Zero," *New Yorker*, May 30, 2005.

74. State Deputy Comptroller for the City of New York, *Review of the Financial Plan of the City of New York: July 2006* (New York: Office of the State Comptroller, 2006), p. 45.

75. Michael Goodwin, "Rethink Freedom Tower," *New York Daily News*, May 11, 2005, p. 33.

76. Nobel, *Sixteen Acres*, p. 102.

77. Goldberger, *Up From Zero*, p. 37.

78. Nobel, *Sixteen Acres*, p. 59.

79. Goldberger, *Up From Zero*, p. 40.

80. Nobel, *Sixteen Acres*, p. 100.

81. Patrick McGeehan. "Employees Say No to Working in Freedom Tower," *New York Times*, September 19, 2006, p. B1. Jessica Bruder, "Would You Go

to Work in a New Skyscraper at Ground Zero?", *Washington Post*, March 28, 2003, p. B1.

82. Parke Chapman, "Office Glut at Ground Zero," *National Real Estate Investor*, January 1, 2005, p. 41; David Usborne, "New York Divided Over Memorial," *Independent*, June 2, 2005, p. 24; Jonathan Mahler, "The Bloomberg Vista," *New York Times Magazine*, September 10, 2006, pp. 66–87.

83. Chan, "Plan to Fill Freedom Tower." On rising commercial rents in Manhattan, see David Lombino, "Office Rents Soar in Manhattan as Vacancies Plunge, *New York Sun*, October 5, 2006, p. 1. Just before this book went to press, supporters of building office space at Ground Zero did receive a boost, as it was reported that commercial rents and vacancies in Lower Manhattan had returned to pre-9/11 levels and that private investors want to buy the Freedom Tower. See Amy Westfeldt, "Vacancies Down Around Ground Zero," Associated Press, February 25, 2007.

84. "Rethinking Ground Zero" (editorial), *New York Times*, April 24, 2005, p. 11.

85. Goldberger, "A New Beginning"; Alexandra Marks, "Chaos to Condos: Lower Manhattan's Rebirth," *Christian Science Monitor*, May 19, 2005, p. 3.

86. Nobel, *Sixteen Acres*, p. 101.

87. Sorkin, *Starting from Zero*, p. 116.

88. On green building design, see David W. Orr, *The Nature of Design: Ecology, Culture, and Human Intention* (Oxford: Oxford University Press, 2004); Nancy Jack Todd and John Todd, *From Eco-Cities to Living Machines: Principles of Ecological Design* (Berkeley, CA: North Atlantic Books, 1993); Nicholas Low, Brendan Gleeson, Ray Green, and Darko Radovic, *The Green City: Sustainable Homes, Sustainable Suburbs* (London: Routledge, 2005).

89. Anthony DePalma, "At Ground Zero, Rebuilding With Nature in Mind," *New York Times*, January 20, 2004, p. B1 (via Lexis-Nexis Academic). Thanks to John Meyer for alerting me to this dimension of the Ground Zero story.

90. DePalma, "Rebuilding With Nature in Mind."

91. See David W. Dunlap, "Ground Zero Cooling Plant Shrinks from XL to S," *New York Times*, November 16, 2005 p. B1; David W. Dunlap, "At Ground Zero, Trying to Take Account of Ecology," *New York Times*, April 15, 2004 (www.nytimes.com, accessed January 10, 2006); Lower Manhattan Development Corporation, *World Trade Center Memorial and Redevelopment Plan: Environmental Assessment for Proposed Further Refinements to the Approved Plan* (New York: Lower Manhattan Development Corporation, September 2006); Lower Manhattan Development Corporation, *World Trade Center Memorial and Redevelopment Plan: Draft Generic Environmental Impact Statement* (New York: Lower Manhattan Development Corporation, January 2004).

92. New York City Department of City Planning, "Community District Profiles: Manhattan Community District 1" (www.nyc.gov/html/dcp/pdf/lucds/mn1profile.pdf, accessed January 4, 2005).

93. Marks, "Chaos to Condos."

94. Goldberger, *Up From Zero*, p. 61.

95. Alliance for Downtown New York, *Lower Manhattan Residents: A Community in Transition* (New York: Alliance for Downtown New York, 2004), pp. 20–21.

96. Alliance for Downtown New York, *State of Lower Manhattan 2004* (New York: Alliance for Downtown New York, 2004), p. 10.

97. Glanz and Lipton, *City in the Sky*, pp. 169–170.

98. "Downtown Construction and Rebuilding Information," Lower Manhattan .info (www.lowermanhattan.info/construction/looking_ahead/battery_park.asp, accessed January 4, 2006).

99. Philip Nobel, "The New Ground Zero: The Downtown Culture Derby Begins ...," *New York Times*, August 31, 2003 (Arts and Leisure section), p. 1 (via Lexis-Nexis Academic).

100. Nobel, *Sixteen Acres*, p. 101.

101. Edward Wyatt, "Some Neighbors Seek Greater Voice on Plans for Sept. 11 Memorial," *New York Times*, June 19, 2002 (www.nytimes.com, accessed February 9, 2003).

102. "Q & A With Madelyn Wils, Chair, Community Board 1," Lower Manhattan.info, September 9, 2002 (www.lowermanhattan.info, accessed July 15, 2004).

103. Nobel, *Sixteen Acres*, pp. 56–57.

104. Nobel, *Sixteen Acres*, pp. 56–57.

105. Nobel, *Sixteen Acres*, p. 235.

106. Nobel, *Sixteen Acres*, pp. 234–239.

107. Nobel, *Sixteen Acres*, p. 235.

108. Nobel, *Sixteen Acres*, p. 236.

109. Nobel, *Sixteen Acres*, p. 238; emphasis added.

110. Mayor Michael R. Bloomberg, "Vision for 21st Century Lower Manhattan," December 12, 2002, LowerManhattan.info (www.lowermanhattan.info/news/read_mayor_bloomberg_s_80515.asp, accessed February 27, 2003). See also Jennifer Steinhauer, "Mayor's Proposal Envisions Lower Manhattan as an Urban Hamlet," *New York Times*, December 13, 2002 (www.nytimes.com, accessed February 9, 2003).

111. Goldberger, *Up From Zero*, p. 49.

112. Goldberger, *Up From Zero*, p. 74.

113. Goldberger, *Up From Zero*, p. 251.

114. Maggie Haberman and Greg Gittrich, "Where the WTC Financing Alters Original Vision," *New York Daily News*, July 20, 2003, p. 13 (via Lexis-Nexis Academic).

115. Robin Pogrebin, "Is Culture Gone at Ground Zero?" *New York Times*, September 30, 2005, p. E33.

116. Edward Wyatt, "At Trade Center Site, A Wealth of Ideas; Competing Interests Are Fighting To Have a Say in Reviving Downtown," *New York Times*, July

28, 2002 (www.nytimes.com, accessed February 9, 2003); Ernest W. Hutton, Jr., "A Lot of Loose Ends at Ground Zero," *Newsday*, August 21, 2006, p. A33.

117. Ross, "The Odor of Publicity," p. 129.

118. Edward Wyatt, "From Political Calculation, a Sweeping Vision of Ground Zero Rose," *New York Times*, March 3, 2003, p. B1 (via Lexis-Nexis Academic).

119. Goldberger, *Up From Zero*, pp. 64–65.

120. Edward Wyatt with Charles V. Bagli, "Visions of Ground Zero: The Public; Officials Rethink Building Proposal for Ground Zero," *New York Times*, July 21, 2002 (www.nytimes.com, accessed February 9, 2003); Edward Wyatt, "Visions of Ground Zero: The Overview; Six Plans for Ground Zero, All Seen as a Starting Point," *New York Times*, July 17, 2002 (www.nytimes.com, accessed February 9, 2003); Charles V. Bagli, "6 Plans for Ground Zero Share Striking Similarities," *New York Times*, July 11, 2002 (www.nytimes.com, accessed February 9, 2003).

121. Lower Manhattan Development Corporation and the Port Authority of New York and New Jersey, *The Public Dialogue: Innovative Design Study*, February 27, 2003, p. 4.

122. Edward Wyatt, "Ground Zero: The Site; Ground Zero Plan Seems to Circle Back" *New York Times*, September 13, 2003, p. B1 (via Lexis-Nexis Academic).

123. LMDC and Port Authority, *Public Dialogue*.

124. Edward Wyatt, "Practical Issues for Ground Zero," *New York Times*, February 28, 2003, p. A1.

125. Edward Wyatt, "Political Calculation."

126. Glanz and Lipton, *City in the Sky*, p. 334.

127. Edward Wyatt, "Architect and Developer Clash Over Plans for Trade Center Site," *New York Times*, July 15, 2003, p. A1 (via Lexis-Nexis Academic).

128. Their often childish rivalry was the subject of the PBS *Frontline* documentary, *Sacred Ground*, produced by Nick Rosen and directed by Kevin Sim (aired September 7, 2004).

129. Wyatt, "Architect and Developer."

130. Wyatt, "Architect and Developer."

131. Wyatt, "Architect and Developer."

132. Maggie Haberman and Greg Gittrich, "Shaky Start Leads to Stronger Foundation," *New York Daily News*, September 11, 2003, p. 21 (via Lexis-Nexis Academic).

133. Robin Pogrebin, "The Incredible Shrinking Daniel Libeskind," *New York Times*, June 20, 2004 (Arts and Leisure section), pp. 1, 32–33 (quote on p. 33).

134. Pogrebin, "Incredible Shrinking."

135. Wyatt, "Ground Zero."

136. Wyatt, "Ground Zero."

137. Tania Padgett, "Neighbors, Others Not Yet Convinced," *Newsday*, February 28, 2003 (www.newsday.com, accessed March 14, 2003).

138. Maggie Haberman and Greg Gittrich, "Victims' Kin Rip Gov," *New York Daily News*, September 11, 2003, p. 5 (via Lexis-Nexis Academic).

139. Quoted in Haberman and Gittrich, "Victims' Kin Rip Gov."

140. Wyatt, "Ground Zero."

141. Patrick D. Healy and William K. Rashbaum, "Security Issues Force a Review at Ground Zero," *New York Times*, May 1, 2005, p. 1.

142. Nicolai Ouroussoff, "A Tower of Impregnability, The Sort Politicians Love," *New York Times*, June 30, 2005, p. B1.

143. Nicolai Ouroussoff, "For Freedom Tower and Ground Zero, Disarray Reigns, and an Opportunity Awaits," *New York Times*, May 2, 2005, p. E1.

144. Rafael Vinoly, "Master Planner or Master Builder?" *New York Times*, December 12, 2003, p. A43 (via Lexis-Nexis Academic).

145. Charles V. Bagli, "Developer Takes a Financial Deal for Ground Zero," *New York Times*, April 26, 2006, p. A1. On Bloomberg's increased role, see Mahler, "Bloomberg Vista."

146. Bagli, "Developer Takes a Deal."

147. Amy Westfeldt, "Port Authority Approves Deal with Silverstein for Ground Zero," *New York Sun*, April 26, 2006 (www.nysun.com/article/31689?page_no=1, accessed May 3, 2006).

148. Bagli, "Developer Takes a Deal."

149. Sorkin, *Starting from Zero*, p. 24.

150. Nobel, *Sixteen Acres*, p. 49; Glenn Collins, "For the Design Team, a Desperate Rush," *New York Times*, July 10, 2005, p. 25.

151. Clay Risen, "Building Model," *New Republic*, October 3, 2005, pp. 18–20 (quotes on p. 18).

152. Sorkin, *Starting from Zero*, p. 125.

153. Sorkin, *Starting from Zero*, p. 126.

154. Sorkin, *Starting from Zero*, p. 124.

155. Denise Scott Brown, "Measuring Downtown's Future," *New York Times*, August 16, 2002 (www.nytimes.com, accessed March 11, 2003).

156. Michael Abelman, "Growing New Life at Ground Zero," *New York Times*, December 21, 2002 (www.nytimes.com, accessed February 9, 2003).

157. See Michael Sorkin and Sharon Zukin, eds., *After the World Trade Center: Rethinking New York City* (New York: Routledge, 2002), especially the essays: Zukin, "Our World Trade Center"; Tchen, "Whose Downtown?!?"; Ross, "The Odor of Publicity"; and Low, "Spaces of Reflection."

158. Sorkin, *Starting from Zero*, p. 12.

159. Nobel, *Sixteen Acres*, p. 96.

160. Edward Wyatt, "The New Ground Zero: There's Nothing So Closed as an Open Competition," *New York Times*, August 31, 2003 (Arts and Leisure section), p. 18 (via Lexis-Nexis Academic).

161. Lynne Duke, "An Empty Space: Eight Finalists Chosen for Memorial at Trade Center Site," *Washington Post*, November 20, 2003, p. C1.

162. David Dunlap, "The Ground Zero Memorial: The Competition: Presenting Several Versions of the Shape of Grief and Reconstruction," *New York Times*, November 20, 2003, p. B3 (via Lexis-Nexis Academic).

163. Glenn Collins, "The Ground Zero Memorial: The Competition: Avidly Dissected, the Eight Design Finalists Provide a Blueprint for Compromise," *New York Times*, November 21, 2003, p. B1 (via Lexis-Nexis Academic).

164. "A 9/11 Memorial Without Public Input Will Have No Soul," *Engineering News-Record*, Vol. 251, No. 22, December 1, 2003, p. 68 (via Lexis-Nexis Academic).

165. David W. Dunlap, "Ground Zero Jury Adheres To a Maxim: Less Is More," *New York Times*, January 7, 2004, p. B6 (via Lexis-Nexis Academic).

166. Christopher Hawthorne, "Growing Up: Getting the Ground Zero Memorial Right, *Slate*, Jan. 15, 2004 (www.slate.com, accessed January 10, 2005).

167. David W. Dunlap and Eric Lipton, "Revised Ground Zero Memorial Will Include an Artifact Center," *New York Times*, January 14, 2004, p. B1 (via Lexis-Nexis Academic).

168. Justin Davidson, "Seeking the Meaning of 9–11," *Newsday*, September 28, 2005, p. A16. See also Goldberger, *Up From Zero*, p. 239.

169. See Debra Burlingame, "The Great Ground Zero Heist," *Wall Street Journal*, June 7, 2005, p. A14.

170. Michael McAuliff, "Pols Threaten WTC Arts Center Probe," *New York Daily News*, September 22, 2005, p. 22 (via Lexis-Nexis Academic).

171. Patrick D. Healy, "Pataki Warns Cultural Groups for Museum At Ground Zero," *New York Times*, June 25, 2005, p. B1.

172. Josh Getlin, "Zero Consensus on a Tribute," *Los Angeles Times*, July 6, 2005, p. A12.

173. Getlin, "Zero Consensus."

174. "Freedom Center's Pledge of Allegiance" (editorial), *New York Daily News*, July 7, 2005, p. 34.

175. "A Next Step for Ground Zero" (editorial), *New York Daily News*, September 25, 2005, p. 42.

176. Robert Kolker, "The Grief Police," *New York Magazine*, November 28, 2005 (www.newyorkmetro.com, accessed January 4, 2006); emphasis in original.

177. McAuliff, "Pols Threaten."

178. David W. Dunlap, "Varying Boundaries of Hallowed Ground," *New York Times*, September 8, 2005, p. B4.

179. Sheryl McCarthy, "Politics and Fear Sank the Freedom Center," *Newsday*, October 3, 2005, p. A36.

180. Nicholas Wapshott, "Ground Zilch: How Al-Qaeda Defeated New York," *New Statesman*, September 5, 2005, pp. 10–12 (quote on p. 12). See also Kolker, "Grief Police."

181. Nicolai Ouroussoff, "For the Ground Zero Memorial, Death by Committee," *New York Times*, June 19, 2005 (Arts and Leisure section), p. 1. On continued controversy over the memorial, see Deborah Sontag, "The Hole in the City's Heart," *New York Times*, September 11, 2006, p. F1.

182. Philip J. Landrigan et al., "Health and Environmental Consequences of the World Trade Center Disaster," *Environmental Health Perspectives*, Vol. 112, No. 6 (May 2004), pp. 731–739 (quote on p. 731).

183. Marc Santora, "Study Finds Lack of Data On 9/11 Dust," *New York Times*, September 8, 2004, p. B1.

184. Laurie Garrett, "Under the Plume: September 11 Produced a New Kind of Pollution, and No One Knows What to Do About It," *American Prospect*, October 21, 2002, p. 22.

185. Andrew Schneider, "N.Y. Officials Underestimate Danger," *St. Louis Post-Dispatch*, January 13, 2002, p. A1 (via Lexis-Nexis Academic).

186. Landrigan et al., "Health and Environmental Consequences," p. 731. On the composition of dust from the World Trade Center, see also Paul J. Lioy et al., "Characterization of the Dust/Smoke Aerosol that Settled East of the World Trade Center (WTC) in Lower Manhattan after the Collapse of the WTC 11 September 2001," *Environmental Health Perspectives*, Vol. 110, No. 7 (July 2002), pp. 703–714; N. L. Jeffery et al., "Potential Exposures to Airborne and Settled Surface Dust in Residential Areas of Lower Manhattan Following the Collapse of the World Trade Center—New York City, November 4–December 11, 2001," *Morbidity & Mortality Weekly Report*, Vol. 52, No. 7 (February 21, 2003), pp. 131–136; Alyssa Katz, "Toxic Haste; New York's Media Rush to Judgment on New York's Air," *American Prospect*, February 25, 2002 (www.prospect.org/web/index.ww, accessed June 1, 2006).

187. Michelle Shephard and Scott Simmie, "A Breath of Dust-Filled Air," *Toronto Star*, September 11, 2002, p. B7.

188. Landrigan et al., "Health and Environmental Consequences," p. 731.

189. For health impacts on workers, see S. M. Levin et al., "Physical Health Status of World Trade Center Rescue and Recovery Workers and Volunteers—New York City, July 2002–August 2004," *Morbidity & Mortality Weekly Report*, Vol. 53, No. 35 (September 10, 2004), pp. 807–812.

190. See Levin et al., "Physical Health Status"; Chris Bowman, "Lingering Peril of 9/11: Ground Zero Workers Ran Toxic Risk, UCD Study Says," *Sacramento Bee*, September 10, 2003, p. A1; Andrew Schneider, "Public was Never Told that Dust from Ruins is Caustic," *St. Louis Post-Dispatch*, February 10, 2002, p. A1; Sigrun Davidsdottir, "Smoke Screen," *Guardian*, June 5, 2002 (Society pages), p. 8; Kirk Johnson, "Uncertainty Lingers Over Air Pollution in Days After 9/11," *New York Times*, September 7, 2003, p. 39.

191. Katz, "Toxic Haste."

192. Katz, "Toxic Haste."

193. Fred Kaplan, "Concerns Intensify on Ground Zero Dust," *Boston Globe*, February 12, 2002, p. A1.

194. Schneider, "N.Y. Officials"; Lung Chi Chen and George Thurston, "World Trade Center Cough," *Lancet* Vol. 360, No. 9350 (December 21, 2002 supplement), pp. 37–38.

195. Garrett, "Under the Plume."

196. Schneider, "Public Was Never Told."

197. Schneider, "Public Was Never Told."

198. Schneider, "N.Y. Officials."

199. Davidsdottir, "Smoke Screen"; Edie Lau and Chris Bowman, "N.Y. Air Hazards Found," *Sacramento Bee*, February 12, 2002, p. A1.

200. Schneider, "N.Y. Officials."

201. Davidsdottir, "Smoke Screen."

202. Davidsdottir, "Smoke Screen." See also Randal C. Archibold, "A Year of Dust, Ash and Anguish," *New York Times*, September 6, 2002, p. B1. For insights drawn from the response of environmental and public health professionals and officials to 9/11, see Francesca Lyman, "Messages in the Dust: Lessons Learned, Post–9/11, for Environmental Health," *Journal of Environmental Health*, Vol. 66, No. 5 (December 2003), pp. 30–37.

203. Fred Kaplan, "Concerns Intensify on Ground Zero Dust," *Boston Globe*, February 12, 2002, p. A1.

204. *EPA's Response to the World Trade Center Collapse: Challenges, Successes, and Areas for Improvement* (Washington, DC: U.S. Environmental Protection Agency, Office of Inspector General, August 21, 2003), p. i.

205. *EPA's Response*, p. 14.

206. *EPA's Response*, p. 17.

207. Schneider, "N.Y. Officials."

208. See Suzanne Mattei, *Pollution and Deception at Ground Zero* (New York: Sierra Club, August 2004), p. 73. See also Juan Gonzalez, "Dust Must Clear on Veil of Deceit," *New York Daily News*, August 19, 2004, p. 18.

209. Quoted in Susan Q. Stranahan, "Air of Uncertainty," *American Journalism Review*, January/February 2003, pp. 26–33 (quote on p. 31).

210. Schneider, "N.Y. Officials."

211. See Johnson, "Uncertainty Lingers."

212. Kirk Johnson and Jennifer 8. Lee, "When Breathing is Believing," *New York Times*, November 30, 2003, p. 37.

213. Stranahan, "Air of Uncertainty."

214. Katz, "Toxic Haste."

215. Stranahan, "Air of Uncertainty," p. 31. See also Kirk Johnson, "Uncertainty Lingers Over Air Pollution in Days After 9/11," *New York Times*, September 7, 2003, p. 39.

216. Stranahan, "Air of Uncertainty."

217. Stranahan, "Air of Uncertainty," p. 32.

218. Luz Claudio, "Environmental Aftermath of World Trade Center Disaster," *Environmental Health Perspectives*, Vol. 109, No. 11 (November 2001), pp. A528–A536.

219. Sally Ann Lederman et al., "The Effects of the World Trade Center Event on Birth Outcomes among Term Deliveries at Three Lower Manhattan Hospitals," *Environmental Health Perspectives*, Vol. 112, No. 17 (December 2004), pp. 1772–1778; Landrigan et al., "Health and Environmental Consequences," p. 737.

220. Sierra Rayne, "Using Exterior Building Surface Films to Assess Human Exposure and Health Risks from PCDD/Fs in New York City, USA, After the World Trade Center Attacks," *Journal of Hazardous Materials*, Vol. 127, Nos. 1–3 (December 2005), pp. 33–39.

221. Philip J. Landrigan, "The WTC Disaster: Landrigan's Response," *Environmental Health Perspectives*, Vol. 112, No. 11 (August 2004), p. A607.

222. Claudio, "Environmental Aftermath," p. A531.

223. "Study Sees Increase in Pediatric Asthma after WTC Disaster," *Indoor Environmental Quality Strategies*, July 2004, pp. 6–8.

224. There was also the classic Bush administration rationale for withholding information: unspecified "national security" concerns. As the *St. Louis Post-Dispatch* editorialized, "It's hard to imagine what national security interest could be furthered by sending unsuspecting citizens back into a dangerous environment." See "The EPA Blows Smoke" (editorial), *St. Louis Post-Dispatch* August 29, 2003, p. B6.

225. Herbert Muschamp, "The New Ground Zero: … With a Dubious Idea of 'Freedom'," *New York Times*, August 31, 2003 (Arts and Leisure section), p. 1 (via Lexis-Nexis Academic).

226. Risen, "Memories of Overdevelopment" (quote on p. 26).

227. Risen, "Memories of Overdevelopment."

228. Risen, "Memories of Overdevelopment."

229. Nicolai Ouroussoff, "Freedom Tower and Ground Zero."

230. Goldberger, *Up From Zero*, pp. 253–254.

231. Goldberger, "A New Beginning," p. 54.

232. Goldberger, *Up From Zero*, pp. 257–258.

233. Goldberger, "A New Beginning."

Chapter 5

1. James Scott uses the phrase "high modernism." However, this is too suggestive of the twentieth century in particular. While many of the phenomena I discuss reached their apogee in the twentieth century, they began earlier. On high modernism, see James C. Scott, *Seeing Like a State: How Certain Schemes to Improve the Human Condition Have Failed* (New Haven, CT: Yale University Press, 1998).

2. Casey, *Fate of Place*, pp. 133–193.

3. Casey, *Fate of Place*, p. 165.

4. Casey, *Fate of Place*, pp. 137–139, 147.

5. Casey, *Fate of Place*, pp. 182–186.

6. Casey, *Fate of Place*, pp. x, 178, 183.

7. Casey, *Fate of Place*, p. 186.

8. See John Locke, *Second Treatise of Government* (1690), C. B. Macpherson, ed. (Indianapolis, IN: Hackett Publishing, 1980), chapter V, §42.

9. Scott, *Seeing Like a State*, pp. 49–51. See also Patricia Nelson Limerick, *The Legacy of Conquest: The Unbroken Past of the American West* (New York: W.W. Norton, 1987), pp. 55–77, and Richard White, *It's Your Misfortune and None of My Own: A New History of the American West* (Norman: University of Oklahoma Press, 1993), pp. 137–155.

10. Harvey, *Spaces of Capital*, p. 213.

11. Scott, *Seeing Like a State*. In his account of the modern state, Scott focuses on developing and revolutionary societies. He downplays the influence of modernism on liberal societies, where its influence was somewhat constrained by various brakes on state power: the private sphere, free enterprise, free expression, and leaders' electoral accountability. However, his account of modernism is applicable to many activities in liberal capitalist societies: urban renewal, scientific forestry and agriculture, and the planning function executed not only by the state but also by the private sector, a supposed counterweight to the modern state.

12. Barry, *Rethinking Green Politics*, p. 183. On the supposed inevitability of "progress," see also my discussion of sprawl in chapter 3, as well as Harvey, *Geography of Difference*, pp. 297–299, and Richmond, "Land-Use Reform," p. 19.

13. Scott, *Seeing Like a State*, pp. 33–52.

14. Scott, *Seeing Like a State*, pp. 51, 58.

15. See Berry, *Unsettling of America*.

16. Scott, *Seeing Like a State*, pp. 262–306; see also Berry, *Unsettling of America*, and Vandana Shiva, *Biopiracy: The Plunder of Nature* (Boston: South End Press, 1997).

17. See Scott, *Seeing Like a State*, pp. 11–22.

18. Scott, *Seeing Like a State*, pp. 53–63.

19. Scott, *Seeing Like a State*, pp. 133–134.

20. See also Scott, *Seeing Like a State*, pp. 109–110.

21. Scott, *Seeing Like a State*, pp. 55–56.

22. Michel Foucault, *Discipline and Punish* (New York: Pantheon Books, 1977), and Scott, *Seeing Like a State*, pp. 81–82.

23. The discussion in the next two paragraphs draws largely on Scott, *Seeing Like a State*, pp. 103–117.

24. Moe and Wilkie, *Changing Places*, p. 43.

25. Quoted in Scott, *Seeing Like a State*, p. 111.

26. On the relation between architectural modernism and the consolidation of state power, see also Lefebvre, *Production of Space*, pp. 123–126.

27. Scott, *Seeing Like a State*, p. 109.

28. Moe and Wilkie, *Changing Places*, p. 43.

29. For the source of this rather humorous acronym, see Frank J. Popper, "Siting LULUs," *Planning*, Vol. 47, No. 4 (April 1981), pp. 12–15.

30. Scott, *Seeing Like a State*, p. 58.

31. Scott, *Seeing Like a State*, pp. 93–94.

32. On this point as it pertains to cities, see especially, Jacobs, *Great American Cities*, as well as Scott's discussion of Jacobs in *Seeing Like a State*, pp. 132–146.

33. On Brasilia, see Scott, *Seeing Like a State*, pp. 117–130.

34. Jacobs, *Great American Cities*, pp. 435–439.

35. Darton, "Architectural Terrorism," p. 91.

36. Scott, *Seeing Like a State*, p. 93.

37. Scott, *Seeing Like a State*, pp. 96–97.

38. Darton, "Architectural Terrorism," p. 91. There is also the implication here that 9/11 masterminds Osama bin Laden, former member of a family construction enterprise, and Mohamed Atta, urban planning student, were founders, albeit of an especially malevolent and perverse sort.

39. Felicity Barringer, "Property Rights Law May Alter Oregon Landscape," *New York Times*, November 26, 2004, p. A1; Dave Hunnicutt, "Vote Yes: Measure 37 Would Restore Rights and Block New Limits that Destroy Property Land Values," *Oregonian*, October 10, 2004, p. F1.

40. For articulations of the property rights position, see especially Richard A. Epstein, *Takings: Private Property and the Power of Eminent Domain* (Cambridge, MA: Harvard University Press, 1985), as well as Bruce Yandle, ed., *Land Rights: The 1990s' Property Rights Rebellion* (Lanham, MD: Rowman & Littlefield, 1995) and Nancie G. Marzulla, "Property Rights Movement: How it Began and Where it is Headed," in Philip D. Brick and R. McGreggor Cawley, eds., *A Wolf in the Garden: The Land Rights Movement and the New Environmental Debate* (Lanham, MD: Rowman & Littlefield, 1996), pp. 39–58. Epstein maintains that "each person can do with his own land what he pleases so long as he does not physically invade the land of another" (*Takings*, p. 60).

41. Epstein, *Takings*, p. 59.

42. Varner, coming from an environmentalist standpoint, makes a strikingly similar argument to justify a position entirely opposite Epstein's. He maintains that the necessity of environmental regulation undermines the notion of land as private property. Ecological processes are public goods or even public property. "Any and every piece of land is involved in diverse ecological processes, and any and every form of land use affects these processes to some extent." Consequently, land cannot be properly regarded as private property and we must "treat it as a public resource that individuals hold only in stewardship (or trust) capacity." As Varner suggests, the hard-line property rights perspective of Epstein and others can yield the surprising conclusion that land cannot meet the standard of private

ownership under conditions of ecological interdependence ("Eclipse of Land as Private Property," p. 158).

The notion that property is embedded in a larger community and that a property owner is responsible to others for the use of property goes back at least to Aristotle. Aristotle maintained that private property must be managed with an eye toward individual virtue and the public good. He consequently advocated a combination of private ownership and common use (*Politics*, Book II, chapter 5). On Aristotle's conception of property, see also Jill Frank, *A Democracy of Distinction: Aristotle and the Work of Politics* (Chicago: University of Chicago Press, 2005).

43. See Logan and Molotch, *Urban Fortunes* for a critical view of this perspective.

44. For this view, see especially James R. Rinehart and Jeffrey J. Pompe, "The Lucas Case and the Conflict over Property Rights," and Karol J. Ceplo, "Land-Rights Conflicts in the Regulation of Wetlands," in Bruce Yandle, ed., *Land Rights: The 1990s' Property Rights Rebellion* (Lanham, MD: Rowman & Littlefield, 1995), pp. 67–150.

45. The notion of subdividing the spatial terrain into commodities and turning place into property was given theoretical support in the early modern era by John Locke. Locke saw undeveloped nature as an undifferentiated waste that human beings, seeking to satisfy their basic needs, inevitably appropriate and subdivide into individualized, cultivated private property holdings (*Second Treatise*, chapter V).

46. On this point see Karl Polanyi, *The Great Transformation: The Political and Economic Origins of Our Time* (Boston: Beacon Press, [1944] 1957), especially p. 178.

47. Plumwood, "Nature, Self, and Gender," p. 302.

48. The corrupting aspects of exchange value and commodification were noted as early as Aristotle in *Politics*, Book I, chapters 9–11. This theme was also pursued by Karl Marx, especially in his critique of money. See Marx "The Economic and Philosophic Manuscripts of 1844," in Robert C. Tucker, ed., *The Marx-Engels Reader*, 2nd ed. (New York: W.W. Norton, 1978), pp. 66–125.

49. Harvey thus says that the market tends to limit consideration of the spatial context of social action (*Geography of Difference*, p. 229).

50. A recent example concerns a development proposal by the Plum Creek Timber Company in Maine's North Woods. See Jim Collins, "Lots for Sale: A Massive Project for the Maine Woods Stirs Debate," *Wilderness* (December 2005/2006), pp. 21–24, and Tux Turkel, "Development Planned in Maine's North Woods," *Planning*, Vol. 71, No. 6 (June 2005), p. 44.

51. See Joseph Schumpeter, *Capitalism, Socialism, and Democracy* (New York: Harper, [1942] 1975), pp. 82–85.

52. Harvey, *Geography of Difference*, p. 296.

53. Harvey, *Geography of Difference*, p. 296.

54. Luke, *Capitalism, Democracy, and Ecology*, p. 219.

55. Luke, *Capitalism, Democracy, and Ecology*, p. 220.

56. Luke, *Capitalism, Democracy, and Ecology*, p. 234.

57. On the decoupling of production and consumption, see also Barry, *Rethinking Green Politics*, pp. 177–181.

58. Barry, *Rethinking Green Politics*, p. 241.

59. Harvey, *Geography of Difference*, pp. 323, 296.

60. Harvey, *Spaces of Capital*, pp. 123–124.

61. See Harvey, *Geography of Difference*, pp. 297–299.

62. Steve Lohr, "POP?: Real Estate, the Global Obsession," *New York Times*, June 12, 2005, section 4, p. 1.

63. Stan Ross, "The State of Real Estate: Consolidation and Globalization in the Industry," *Marshall Magazine* (University of Southern California/Marshall School of Business), Summer 2001, pp. 33–37 (see p. 33).

64. Harvey, *Geography of Difference*, p. 298.

65. Harvey, *Geography of Difference*, pp. 297–298.

66. See Robert R. Nelson, "Tourism as a Catalyst for Local Economic Development," Department of Hotel, Restaurant and Institutional Management, University of Delaware, May 2005 (www.chep.udel.edu/directions/articles/may05/tourism.html, accessed February 17, 2006).

67. Luke, *Capitalism, Democracy, and Ecology*, p. 60.

68. Nicolai Ouroussoff, "Outgrowing Jane Jacobs and Her New York," *New York Times*, April 30, 2006 (Week in Review section), p. 1.

69. Michael Luo, "Now a Message from a Sponsor of the Subway?" *New York Times*, July 27, 2004 (www.nytimes.com, accessed July 27, 2004). See also a July 28, 2004, news release from the public interest group Commercial Alert entitled "Coalition Asks MTA Not to Sell Naming Rights to NYC Bridges, Subway Stations" (www.commercialalert.org/news-releases.php, accessed February 17, 2006).

70. Sack, *Homo Geographicus*, p. 9.

71. Sack, *Homo Geographicus*, pp. 138–141.

72. Wigley, "Insecurity By Design," pp. 74–75.

73. Kelbaugh, *Repairing the American Metropolis*, p. 41.

74. Castells, *Network Society*, p. 449.

75. Kelbaugh, *Repairing the American Metropolis*, p. 69.

76. Kelbaugh, *Repairing the American Metropolis*, p. 70.

77. Sack, *Homo Geographicus*, pp. 138–139.

78. Sack, *Homo Geographicus*, pp. 10–11.

79. Casey, "Between Geography and Philosophy," p. 685.

80. Casey, "Between Geography and Philosophy," p. 691 n. 14.

81. Casey, "Between Geography and Philosophy," pp. 684–685.

82. Casey, "Between Geography and Philosophy," pp. 684–685.

83. Casey, "Between Geography and Philosophy," p. 685.

84. Casey, "Between Geography and Philosophy," pp. 685–686.

85. Casey, "On Habitus and Place," p. 719.

86. Casey, "Between Geography and Philosophy," p. 686.

87. Logan and Molotch, *Urban Fortunes*, p. 114.

88. Moe and Wilkie, *Changing Places*, pp. 260–261.

89. Arendt, *Human Condition*, pp. 132–134. See also the observations of Mumford, writing at roughly the same time: Mumford, *City in History*, p. 545.

90. Harvey, *Geography of Difference*, p. 296.

91. Luke, *Capitalism, Democracy, and Ecology*, p. 218.

92. Harvey, *Geography of Difference*, p. 296.

93. See Castells, *Network Society*, especially pp. 407–459.

94. Castells, *Network Society*, p. 442.

95. Castells, *Network Society*, pp. 442–448.

96. Castells, *Network Society*, p. 447.

97. Luke, *Capitalism, Democracy, and Ecology*, p. 1.

98. Castells, *Network Society*, pp. 409–410.

99. Castells, *Network Society*, p. 411.

100. Castells, *Network Society*, pp. 419, 421–423.

101. Castells, *Network Society*, pp. 415, 418.

102. Castells, *Network Society*, p. 415.

103. Castells, *Network Society*, pp. 415–416. See also Saskia Sassen, *The Global City: New York, London, Tokyo* (Princeton, NJ: Princeton University Press, 1991).

104. Castells, *Network Society*, p. 422.

105. Sclar, "Back to the City," p. 29.

106. Castells says that in European urban areas, elites are more likely to inhabit the central cities rather than move to the fringes (*Network Society*, pp. 431–434).

107. Castells, *Network Society*, p. 416.

108. Castells, *Network Society*, p. 426.

109. Castells, *Network Society*, pp. 431–432.

110. Castells, *Network Society*, p. 434.

111. Castells, *Network Society*, p. 434.

112. Castells, *Network Society*, p. 439.

113. Castells, *Network Society*, p. 436; emphasis in original.

114. Mitchell Moss, "Tracking the Net: Using Domain Names to Measure the Growth of the Internet in U.S. Cities," *Journal of Urban Technology*, Vol. 4,

No. 3 (December 1997) (www.mitchellmoss.com/articles/tracking.html, accessed April 16, 2006); emphasis added.

115. Castells, *Network Society*, pp. 439–440.

116. On flexible capitalism, see Michael J. Piore and Charles F. Sabel, *The Second Industrial Divide: Possibilities for Prosperity* (New York: Basic Books, 1984); Martin Carnoy and Manuel Castells, *Sustainable Flexibility: A Prospective Study on Work, Family and Society in the Information Age* (Paris: Organization for Economic Cooperation and Development, 1997); Richard Sennett, *The Corrosion of Character: The Personal Consequences of Work in the New Capitalism* (New York: W.W. Norton, 1998); Steven P. Vallas and John P. Beck, "The Transformation of Work Revisited: The Limits of Flexibility in American Manufacturing," *Social Problems*, Vol. 43, No. 3 (August 1996), pp. 339–361; Hartmann, Kraut, and Tilly, *Computer Chips and Paper Clips*. On flexible capitalism's emphasis on rapidly changing niche markets and the relation of this orientation to postmodern thought, see Harvey, *Spaces of Capital*, pp. 121–127.

117. Castells, *Network Society*, p. 443.

118. Castells, *Network Society*, p. 415.

119. On this point see, for example, Luke, *Capitalism, Democracy, and Ecology*, pp. 53–54, 62–63.

120. Luke, *Capitalism, Democracy, and Ecology*, p. 63.

121. Greenpeace International, *Eating Up the Amazon* (Amsterdam: Greenpeace International, 2006) (www.greenpeace.org/international/press/reports?page=2, accessed April 21, 2006). See also John Vidal, "The 7,000 km Journey that Links Amazon Destruction to Fast Food," *Guardian Unlimited*, April 6, 2006 (www.guardian.co.uk/globalisation/story/0,,1747904,00.html, accessed April 21, 2006).

122. Greenpeace, *Eating Up*, p. 22.

123. For such a criticism of local corporate power, see Logan and Molotch, *Urban Fortunes*.

124. Rosabeth Moss Kanter, "Business Coalitions as a Force for Regionalism," in Bruce Katz, ed., *Reflections on Regionalism* (Washington, DC: Brookings Institution, 2000), pp. 154–181 (pp. 164–167).

125. Kanter, "Business Coalitions," pp. 164–165.

126. Kanter, "Business Coalitions," pp. 165–166.

127. Kanter, "Business Coalitions," p. 172.

128. Castells, *Network Society*, pp. 441–442.

129. Castells, *Network Society*, p. 417.

130. For a similar point, see Luke, *Capitalism, Democracy, and Ecology*, p. 16.

131. This may also be an implication of Bonnie Honig's politics of *virtù*. See Honig, *Political Theory and the Displacement of Politics* (Ithaca, NY: Cornell University Press, 1993).

132. Luke, *Capitalism, Democracy, and Ecology*, p. 100.

133. Luke, *Capitalism, Democracy, and Ecology*, pp. 3, 5.

134. Harvey, *Spaces of Capital*, p. 124. On the affinities between postmodernism and capitalism, see also David Harvey, *The Postmodern Condition* (Oxford: Oxford University Press, 1989).

135. Castells, *Network Society*, pp. 428–429.

136. Castells, *Network Society*, p. 453.

137. Luke, *Capitalism, Democracy, and Ecology*, pp. 67–68.

138. Luke, *Capitalism, Democracy, and Ecology*, p. 68.

139. On this contrast, see also Luke, *Capitalism, Democracy, and Ecology*, especially chapter 2.

140. Barry, *Rethinking Green Politics*, p. 181.

141. Luke, *Capitalism, Democracy, and Ecology*, p. 19.

142. Luke, *Capitalism, Democracy, and Ecology*, pp. 5–6.

143. Luke, *Capitalism, Democracy, and Ecology*, p. 18.

144. Luke, *Capitalism, Democracy, and Ecology*, pp. 111–113. See also Ulrich Beck, *Risk Society: Towards a New Modernity*, Mark Ritter, trans. (London: Sage, [1986] 1992).

145. Luke, *Capitalism, Democracy, and Ecology*, pp. 111–112.

146. Luke, *Capitalism, Democracy, and Ecology*, p. 219.

147. Luke, *Capitalism, Democracy, and Ecology*, pp. 112–113.

148. On this point see Samuel Bowles and Herbert Gintis, *Democracy and Capitalism: Property, Community, and the Contradictions of Modern Social Thought* (New York: Basic Books, 1987). The political constraints on jurisdictions seeking to attract investment capital are also vividly illustrated in Paul E. Peterson, *City Limits* (Chicago: University of Chicago Press, 1981).

149. Arendt, *Human Condition*, pp. 52–53.

150. Arendt, *Human Condition*, p. 58.

151. Luke, *Capitalism, Democracy, and Ecology*, p. 113.

152. See Luke, *Capitalism, Democracy, and Ecology*, chapter 4.

153. See note 122 in chapter 2.

154. See note 138 in chapter 1. Ecocentrism sees nonhuman nature, particularly natural collectives like ecosystems, as deserving moral consideration independent of human interests.

155. The idea that radical preservationism might be a strategic stance was suggested to me by John Barry.

156. Meyer, *Political Nature*, p. 152.

157. Philip Brick and Edward P. Weber, "Will Rain Follow the Plow? Unearthing a New Environmental Movement," in Philip Brick, Donald Snow, and Sarah Van De Wetering, eds., *Across the Great Divide: Explorations in Collaborative Conservation and the American West* (Washington, DC: Island Press, 2001), pp. 15–24 (quote on p. 22).

158. Dowie, *Losing Ground*, pp. 94, 97.

159. See David Helvarg, *The War Against the Greens: The "Wise-Use" Movement, the New Right, and the Browning of America*, rev. ed. (Boulder, CO: Johnson Books, 2004).

160. Layzer, *Environmental Case*, 1st ed., pp. 241–242.

161. See Dowie, *Losing Ground*, pp. 101–103 and Foster, "Limits of Environmentalism without Class," especially pp. 204, 208–211.

162. Donald Snow, "Empire or Homelands? A Revival of Jeffersonian Democracy in the American West," in John A. Baden and Donald Snow, *The Next West: Public Lands, Community, and Economy in the American West*, Washington, DC: Island Press, 1997, pp. 181–203 (quote on p. 199).

163. Thanks to David Schlosberg for his cautions about overgeneralizing here.

164. On this point see also Barry, *Rethinking Ecological Politics*, p. 24.

165. Sale, *Dwellers in the Land*, p. 55. Bioregions range in size from the 100,000-square-mile Sonora Desert and other vegetationally defined "ecoregions," to a "georegion"—for example, a watershed—defined by "clear physiographic features such as river basins, valleys, and mountain ranges, and often some special floral and faunal traits" and on down to relatively small, also topographically defined "morphoregions," such as the roughly 30-mile stretch of the lower Connecticut River Basin from Middletown to Long Island Sound (*Dwellers in the Land*, pp. 56–58).

166. Sale, *Dwellers in the Land*, p. 43.

167. Sale, *Dwellers in the Land*, p. 55; emphasis in original.

168. Sale, *Dwellers in the Land*, p. 44.

169. Sale, *Dwellers in the Land*, pp. 44–46.

170. Barry, *Rethinking Green Politics*, p. 82.

171. Meyer, *Political Nature*, pp. 21–34.

172. John Barry, *Environment and Social Theory* (London: Routledge, 1999), p. 29. Barry is quite critical of the reading-off hypothesis. For another striking example of the reading-off view, see Edward Goldsmith, *The Way: An Ecological World-View*, rev. ed. (Athens: University of Georgia Press, 1998).

173. Sale, *Dwellers in the Land*, p. 120.

174. Robyn Eckersley, *Environmentalism and Political Theory: Toward an Ecocentric Approach*, (Albany: State University of New York Press, 1992), p. 28; emphasis added.

175. Barry, *Rethinking Green Politics*, p. 33.

176. For a similar point, see Luke's critique of deep ecology in *Ecocritique*, pp. 1–27 and especially pp. 18–20.

177. Barry, *Environment and Social Theory*, p. 30. On this point see also Evernden, *Social Creation of Nature*, and John Stuart Mill's 1874 essay, "Nature," in Mill, *Three Essays on Religion: Nature, the Utility of Religion, Theism* (Amherst, NY: Prometheus Books, 1998), pp. 3–68.

178. Barry, *Rethinking Green Politics*, pp. 88–89.

179. This remark appeared in an article on the Wilderness Society's website: "Quincy Library Bill No Solution," *The Wilderness Society: Conservation Coast to Coast*, October 1998 (www.wilderness.org/ccc/california/quincy.html, dead link).

180. Barry, *Rethinking Green Politics*, p. 19; emphasis in original. Inherent in this view is, in Barry's words, "an *a priori* position that privileges the *preservation* of nature over the human use of nature" (p. 25, emphasis in original).

181. Meyer, *Political Nature*, p. 124.

182. John Carlson, "Sierra Club Official's Cut is a Snapshot of Hypocrisy," *Seattle Times*, January 18, 1994, p. B4.

183. Keith Schneider, "Logging Policy Splits Membership of Sierra Club," *New York Times*, December 26, 1993, p. 20.

184. Bill Arthur, "Carlson and His Cronies are the Real Hypocrites," *Seattle Times*, January 21, 1994, p. B7.

185. Dobbs and Ober, *Northern Forest*, pp. 154–155.

186. Richard White, "'Are You an Environmentalist or Do You Work for a Living?': Work and Nature," in William Cronon, ed., *Uncommon Ground: Toward Reinventing Nature* (New York: W.W. Norton, 1995), pp. 171–185 (quote on pp. 171–172).

187. White, "'Do You Work for a Living?'," p. 172.

188. White, "'Do You Work for a Living?'," p. 171. See also Barry, *Rethinking Green Politics*, p. 190, n. 23.

189. Sale, *Dwellers in the Land*, pp. 44–45.

190. Sale, *Dwellers in the Land*, p. 65.

191. Sale, *Dwellers in the Land*, p. 7; emphasis added.

192. Among the slogans of Earth First! was, "Back to the Pleistocene." Earth First!er John Davis, approvingly quoted by radical environmentalist Christopher Manes, thus says, "Many of us in the Earth First! movement would like to see human beings live much more like the way they did fifteen thousand years ago as opposed to what we see now" (Manes, *Green Rage*, p. 237). For a critique of radical environmentalist primitivism and its social and political implications, see Luke, *Ecocritique*, pp. 1–27.

193. Luke, *Capitalism, Democracy, and Ecology*, pp. 157–158.

194. Berry, *The Unsettling of America*, p. 26.

195. Barry, *Rethinking Green Politics*, pp. 7–8, 57–63.

196. Donahue, *Reclaiming the Commons*, p. 222.

197. In fact, though, much of the landscape that Americans see as "pristine" or "virgin" was shaped by Native Americans through controlled burning and other agricultural practices. See Gary Paul Nabhan, "Cultural Parallax in Viewing North American Habitats," in Michael E. Soulé and Gary Lease, eds.,

Reinventing Nature?: Responses to Postmodern Deconstruction (Washington, DC: Island Press, 1995), pp. 87–101.

198. William Cronon, "The Trouble with Wilderness, or Getting Back to the Wrong Nature," in William Cronon, ed., *Uncommon Ground: Toward Reinventing Nature* (New York: W.W. Norton, 1995), pp. 69–90 (quote on p. 69).

199. Hiss, *Experience of Place*, p. 195.

200. White, "'Do You Work for a Living?'," p. 185.

201. White, "'Do You Work for a Living?'," p. 174.

202. On this point see also Barry Lopez, *About This Life: Journeys on the Threshold of Memory* (New York: Alfred A. Knopf, 1998), p. 131.

Chapter 6

1. Just as there is no clear, fixed line for determining when legitimate use of nature becomes abuse. See Barry, *Rethinking Green Politics*, p. 60.

2. Hiss, *Experience of Place*, pp. 114–115.

3. Young, *Politics of Difference*, chapter 8.

4. Barry, *Rethinking Green Politics*, p. 9.

5. Barry, *Rethinking Green Politics*, p. 255.

6. Barry, *Rethinking Green Politics*, p. 62.

7. Barry, *Rethinking Green Politics*, p. 259.

8. Barry, *Rethinking Green Politics*, pp. 125–126.

9. Barry, *Rethinking Green Politics*, p. 126.

10. See Barry, *Rethinking Green Politics*, pp. 255–259.

11. Barry, *Rethinking Green Politics*, p. 102.

12. Barry, *Rethinking Green Politics*, p. 126.

13. Barry, *Rethinking Green Politics*, p. 127.

14. Barry, *Rethinking Green Politics*, p. 140, n. 14.

15. Barry, *Rethinking Green Politics*, p. 120.

16. Barry, *Rethinking Green Politics*, p. 118.

17. Barry, *Rethinking Green Politics*, p. 134.

18. Barry, *Rethinking Green Politics*, pp. 127, 130.

19. Barry, *Rethinking Green Politics*, p. 153.

20. Barry, *Rethinking Green Politics*, pp. 202–206, 215. See also John S. Dryzek, *Rational Ecology: Environment and Political Economy* (Oxford, UK: Blackwell, 1987).

21. Barry, *Rethinking Green Politics*, p. 218.

22. William Shutkin, *The Land That Could Be: Environmentalism and Democracy in the Twenty-first Century* (Cambridge, MA: MIT Press, 2000), p. 128.

23. Shutkin, *Land That Could Be*, p. 15.

24. Shutkin, *Land That Could Be*, p. 132. See also pp. 229–232.

25. Calthorpe and Fulton, *Regional City*, p. 8.

26. Calthorpe and Fulton, *Regional City*, pp. 8, 63.

27. Calthorpe and Fulton, *Regional City*, p. 62.

28. Barry, *Rethinking Green Politics*, pp. 152–154.

29. See also Epstein, *Takings*, p. 59.

30. Villa, *Arendt and Heidegger*, p. 34.

31. Harvey, *Geography of Difference*, pp. 310–313; Kemmis, "Community and the Politics of Place," pp. 244–245. Regarding this point, see also MacIntyre's discussion of a tradition being constituted by a shared argument over time (*After Virtue*, p. 222).

32. On this point, see also my discussion of collaborative conservation in the next chapter.

33. Barry, *Rethinking Green Politics*, p. 231.

34. Villa, *Arendt and Heidegger*, 34. For conceptions of place-based community that do not entail homogeneity and transparency among members, see Harvey, *Geography of Difference* and Young, *Politics of Difference*, chapter 8.

35. On place as a field for the exercise of power, see also Lefebvre, *Production of Space*.

36. On the disciplinary, repressive use of places, see also Foucault, *Discipline and Punish*.

37. Lefebvre, *Production of Space*, p. 44. Lefebvre says that ideologies cannot survive without referring to or affirming certain places.

38. Lefebvre, *Production of Space*, pp. 46–47.

39. On the role of hegemony in constructing place, see John Harner, "Place Identity and Copper Mining in Sonora, Mexico," *Annals of the Association of American Geographers*, Vol. 94, No. 4 (2001), pp. 660–680. The notion of hegemonic discourses is, as John Barry has pointed out to me, related to Marxian notions of "false consciousness."

40. Massey, "Spaces of Politics," p. 284.

41. See Harner, "Place Identity and Copper Mining."

42. For the account that follows, see Harvey, *Geography of Difference*, pp. 316–317.

43. See, for example, Samuel R. Delany, *Times Square Red, Times Square Blue* (New York: New York University Press, 2001).

44. Harvey, *Geography of Difference*, pp. 316.

45. See Lefebvre, *Production of Space*, pp. 50–51.

46. See Lefebvre, *Production of Space*, pp. 49–51.

47. See Harvey, *Geography of Difference*, p. 54.

48. See Harvey, *Geography of Difference*, p. 55.

49. Barry, *Rethinking Green Politics*, pp. 154–155.

50. Barry, *Rethinking Green Politics*, pp. 178–179.

51. Barry, *Rethinking Green Politics*, pp. 239–242.

52. Calthorpe and Fulton, *Regional City*, p. 51. See also Moe and Wilkie, *Changing Places*, pp. 229–230, and Stoel, "Reining in Urban Sprawl," pp. 31–32.

53. Shutkin, *Land That Could Be*, pp. 218–219.

54. Wiewel and Schaffer, "New Federal and State Policies," pp. 286–287.

55. Calthorpe and Fulton, *Regional City*, p. 87.

56. See Wiewel and Schaffer, "New Federal and State Policies," pp. 284–287.

57. Shawn Allee, "School Districts Encouraging Urban Sprawl?", *Great Lakes Radio Consortium*, March 13, 2006.

58. See Harvey, *Spaces of Capital*, p. 225.

59. According to the U.S. Census Bureau, "[T]he general concept of a metropolitan or micropolitan statistical area is that of a core area containing a substantial population nucleus, together with adjacent communities having a high degree of social and economic integration with that core. Metropolitan and micropolitan statistical areas comprise one or more entire counties." See U.S. Census Bureau, "About Metropolitan and Micropolitan Statistical Areas" (www.census.gov/population/www/estimates/aboutmetro.html, accessed May 18, 2006).

60. Harvey, *Spaces of Capital*, p. 225.

61. Harvey, *Spaces of Capital*, p. 225.

62. Young, *Justice and the Politics of Difference*, p. 252.

63. U.S. Census Bureau, "About Metropolitan and Micropolitan."

64. Calthorpe and Fulton, *Regional City*, p. 6. See also Ewing, "Los Angeles-style Sprawl."

65. Calthorpe and Fulton, *Regional City*, pp. 28–29.

66. Calthorpe and Fulton, *Regional City*, pp. 16–17.

67. Barry, *Rethinking Green Politics*, p. 173.

68. On these various points, see Barry, *Rethinking Green Politics*, p. 177, and Donahue, *Reclaiming the Commons*, p. 68–75.

69. Oran R. Young, *Resource Regimes: Natural Resources and Social Institutions*, Berkeley: University of California Press, 1982), p. 78.

70. Here I offer only a cursory look at deliberative institutions for integrating founding and preservation. For a much fuller discussion of various approaches to deliberative environmental politics, see Walter F. Baber and Robert V. Bartlett, *Deliberative Environmental Politics: Democracy and Ecological Rationality* (Cambridge, MA: MIT Press, 2005).

71. john a. powell, "Addressing Regional Dilemmas for Minority Communities," in Bruce Katz, ed., *Reflections on Regionalism* (Washington, DC: Brookings Institution, 2000), pp. 218–245 (see p. 220).

72. powell, "Addressing Regional Dilemmas."

73. Young, *Politics of Difference*, p. 252.

74. Elinor Ostrom, *Governing the Commons: The Evolution of Institutions for Collective Action* (Cambridge, UK: Cambridge University Press, 1990).

75. Frug, *City Making*, pp. 86–88, 162–163.

76. Kunstler, "Home from Nowhere," p. 66.

77. See David Schlosberg, *Environmental Justice and the New Pluralism: The Challenge of Difference* (Oxford, UK: Oxford University Press, 1999).

78. This view is shared by theorists of participatory democracy like Benjamin Barber, who advocates a civic-oriented architecture, although he disdains New Urbanism. See Barber, "An Architecture of Liberty?" and *Strong Democracy: Participatory Politics for a New Age* (Berkeley: University of California Press, 1984), as well as Michael J. Sandel, *Democracy's Discontent: America in Search of a Public Philosophy* (Cambridge, MA: Harvard University Press, 1996), pp. 335–336.

79. Jacobs, *Great American Cities*, pp. 149–151.

80. On the importance of a local bar to the community of Manhasset, the Long Island town where I grew up, see J.R. Moehringer, *The Tender Bar: A Memoir* (New York: Hyperion Books, 2005).

81. Calthorpe and Fulton, *Regional City*, pp. 32–33, 37–40, 45–46.

82. See Ed Marston, "The Quincy Library Group: A Divisive Attempt at Peace," in Philip Brick, Donald Snow, and Sarah Van De Wetering, *Across the Great Divide: Explorations in Collaborative Conservation and the American West* (Washington, DC: Island Press, 2001), pp. 79–90.

83. See Thomas R. Berger, *Northern Frontier, Northern Homeland: The Report of the Mackenzie Valley Pipeline Inquiry, Vol. 2* (Ottawa: Minister of Supply and Services Canada, 1977). The pipeline inquiry is also discussed in Dryzek, *Rational Ecology*.

84. Harvey, *Spaces of Capital*, pp. 196–197.

85. Schlosberg, *Environmental Justice*, pp. 134–139.

86. Schlosberg, *Environmental Justice*, p. 143.

87. Shutkin, *Land That Could Be*, p. 132.

88. Shutkin, *Land That Could Be*, p. 131.

89. On this issue and the idea of bridges between particular and universal geographic horizons, see Harvey, *Spaces of Capital*, pp. 158–207.

90. Harvey, *Spaces of Capital*, p. 196.

91. Robert D. Yaro, "Growing and Governing Smart: A Case Study of the New York Region," in Bruce Katz, ed., *Reflections on Regionalism* (Washington, DC: Brookings Institution, 2000), pp. 43–77 (see p. 70).

92. "Preservation: Slowing the Development: Migration Pits Rural Assets, Growth," *Detroit News*, March 15, 1998 (www.detnews.com/1998/metrox/suburbs/1migrate/1migrate.htm, dead link).

93. Rusk, "Growth Management," p. 104.

94. powell, "Addressing Regional Dilemmas," p. 239.

95. Margaret Weir, "Coalition Building for Regionalism," in Bruce Katz, ed., *Reflections on Regionalism* (Washington, DC: Brookings Institution, 2000), pp. 127–153 (see pp. 130–131).

96. Stoel, "Reining in Urban Sprawl," p. 11.

97. Stoel, "Reining in Urban Sprawl," p. 29.

98. powell, "Addressing Regional Dilemmas," pp. 239–240.

99. powell, "Addressing Regional Dilemmas," p. 240.

100. Rusk, "Growth Management, p. 99.

101. Calthorpe and Fulton, *Regional City*, p. 118.

102. Hayward, "Legends of the Sprawl."

103. Richmond, "Metropolitan Land-Use Reform," p. 34.

104. Barringer, "Property Rights Law."

105. Ray Ring, "Taking Liberties," *High Country News*, Vol. 38, No. 13 (July 24, 2006), pp. 8-14 (quote on pp. 11–12).

106. Laura Oppenheimer, "Measure 37 Question: Is Land-Use Law Usable?" *Oregonian*, March 26, 2006, p. B1.

107. Barringer, "Property Rights Law."

108. Laura Oppenheimer, "As Landscape Shifts, Oregon Struggles to Protect Farmland," *Oregonian*, May 31, 2005, p. A1.

109. Judith Layzer, *The Environmental Case: Translating Values into Policy*, 2nd ed. (Washington, DC: CQ Press, 2006), p. 481.

110. Layzer, *Environmental Case*, 2nd ed., p. 486.

111. Layzer, *Environmental Case*, 2nd ed., p. 484.

112. Jonathan Walters, "Law of the Land: Voters' Challenge to Oregon's Stringent Land Use Controls May Signal a Major Shift in the Property Rights Debate Nationwide," *Governing Magazine*, May 2005 (via Lexis-Nexis Academic).

113. Layzer, *Environmental Case*, 2nd ed., p. 483.

114. Barringer, "Property Rights Law."

115. Walters, "Law of the Land."

116. "Measure 37 'Snag' Reveals the True Game" (editorial), *Oregonian*, April 3, 2006, p. C6.

117. Ring, "Taking Liberties," pp. 11, 12, 14.

118. See Ring, "Taking Liberties"; William Yardley, "Anger Drives Property Measures," *New York Times*, October 8, 2006, p. 34; John Miller, "Property-Rights Measures on Ballot in 4 Western States," *Salt Lake Tribune*, October 16, 2006 (www.sltrib.com/news/ci_4499162, accessed October 16, 2006); Jeff Brady,

"Western Voters Weigh Shift in Property Rights," *Morning Edition*, National Public Radio, September 18, 2006; Jeff Brady, "Western Voters Consider Property Rights Changes," *Morning Edition*, National Public Radio, September 19, 2006.

119. Weir, "Coalition Building," pp. 133–134.

120. Weir, "Coalition Building," p. 129.

121. Rusk, "Growth Management," p. 103.

122. Zimmerman, Morçöl, and Stich, "From Sprawl to Smart Growth," pp. 275–287 (see p. 282).

123. Zimmerman, Morçöl, and Stich, "From Sprawl to Smart Growth," pp. 282–283.

124. Zimmerman, Morçöl, and Stich, "From Sprawl to Smart Growth," pp. 283–284.

125. Zimmerman, Morçöl, and Stich, "From Sprawl to Smart Growth," pp. 283–284.

126. Zimmerman, Morçöl, and Stich, "From Sprawl to Smart Growth," p. 284.

127. Rusk, "Growth Management," pp. 100–101.

128. Calthorpe and Fulton, *Regional City*, p. 62.

129. Yaro, "Growing and Governing Smart," p. 74.

130. Salkin, "Smart Growth and the Law," p. 219.

131. See Philip G. Terrie, *Contested Terrain: A New History of Nature and People in the Adirondacks* (Syracuse, NY: Syracuse University Press, 1999), pp. 159–183.

132. Salkin, "Smart Growth and the Law," p. 217.

133. Salkin, "Smart Growth and the Law," p. 218.

134. Weir, "Coalition Building," p. 128.

135. Weir, "Coalition Building," p. 128.

136. Weir, "Coalition Building," pp. 148–150.

137. Shutkin, *Land That Could Be*, pp. 216–217.

138. Shutkin, *Land That Could Be*, pp. 222–230. See also www.njfuture.org (accessed May 25, 2006).

139. Richmond, "Metropolitan Land-Use Reform," p. 22.

140. Zimmerman, Morçöl, and Stich, "From Sprawl to Smart Growth," p. 285.

141. Zimmerman, Morçöl, and Stich, "From Sprawl to Smart Growth," p. 285.

142. Kanter, "Business Coalitions," pp. 167–168.

143. Kanter, "Business Coalitions," pp. 168–171.

144. Kanter, "Business Coalitions," pp. 171–173.

145. See powell, "Addressing Regional Dilemmas."

146. powell, "Addressing Regional Dilemmas."

147. See powell, "Addressing Regional Dilemmas."

148. powell, "Addressing Regional Dilemmas," pp. 229–230. For an example of such an argument, see Curry, "Racial Critique."

149. powell, "Addressing Regional Dilemmas," pp. 232–236.

150. powell, "Addressing Regional Dilemmas," pp. 237–239.

151. Calthorpe and Fulton, *Regional City*, p. 20.

152. Kanter, "Business Coalitions," pp. 160–164.

153. Weir, "Coalition Building," p. 129.

154. Weir, "Coalition Building," p. 139.

Chapter 7

1. Calthorpe and Fulton, *Regional City*, pp. 159–171.

2. Some residents of the Northwest think of themselves as "Cascadians." Even more fanciful, and rather dated, is Ernest Callenbach's novel *Ecotopia* (New York: Bantam, 1975), which envisions an ecologically oriented, quasi-utopian republic in Washington, Oregon, and Northern California.

3. Quoted in Steven L. Yaffee, Ali F. Phillips, Irene C. Frentz, Paul W. Hardy, Sussanne M. Maleki, and Barbara E. Thorpe, *Ecosystem Management in the United States: An Assessment of Current Experience (A Collaborative Effort of the University of Michigan and the Wilderness Society)* (Washington, DC: Island Press, 1996), p. 3.

4. Dietrich, *Final Forest*, pp. 287–288.

5. Kitzhaber, "Principles and Politics," p. 233.

6. Bowersox, "Using Ecological Disturbance Theory," p. 251.

7. Shannon, "Northwest Forest Plan," p. 265.

8. See Shannon, "Northwest Forest Plan" and Bowersox, "Using Ecological Disturbance Theory."

9. Shannon, "Northwest Forest Plan," p. 274.

10. Kitzhaber, "Principles and Politics," p. 233.

11. Jerry Franklin, University of Washington, personal communication, May 17, 2000; Perry, "Ecological Realities." For a detailed discussion of variable retention harvesting, see Jerry F. Franklin, Dean Rae Berg, Dale A. Thornburgh, and John C. Tappeiner, "Alternative Silvicultural Approaches to Timber Harvesting: Variable Harvest Retention Systems," in Kathryn A. Kohm and Jerry F. Franklin, eds., *Creating a Forestry for the Twenty-first Century: The Science of Ecosystem Management* (Washington, DC: Island Press, 1997), pp. 111–139.

12. Dietrich, *Final Forest*, pp. 110, 242–243; Proctor, "Whose Nature?", p. 289; Franklin, personal communication.

13. Proctor, "Whose Nature?" p. 289.

14. See the budget tables at the National Park Service's Budget Website (home.nps.gov/applications/budget2/tables.htm, accessed October 19, 2006).

15. White, "'Do You Work for a Living?'," p. 174.

16. White, "'Do You Work for a Living?'," pp. 172–173.

17. Kitzhaber, "Principles and Politics," p. 233.

18. Nels Hanson, personal communication, May 17, 2000.

19. Dietrich, *Final Forest*, p. 277.

20. Hanson, personal communication. See also Bill McKibben, "What Good Is a Forest?" *Audubon*, Vol. 98, No. 3 (May 1996), pp. 54–63.

21. Beuter, "Sustained Yield," pp. 64–65.

22. Oregon Small Woodlands Association, "Policy Statement" (www.oswa.org/policystatement1992.pdf, accessed May 26, 2006).

23. Barker, "New Forestry," pp. 42–43. For a detailed discussion of possible approaches to sustaining and regulating small-scale forestry, see Frederick W. Cubbage, "The Public Interest in Private Forests: Developing Regulations and Incentives," in Kathryn A. Kohm and Jerry F. Franklin, eds., *Creating a Forestry for the Twenty-first Century: The Science of Ecosystem Management* (Washington, DC: Island Press, 1997), pp. 337–356.

24. Barker, "New Forestry," pp. 39–41.

25. The quotes that follow are taken from Ryan Temple, "Value-Added Manufacturing: An Oregon Perspective," Sustainable Oregon (www.sustainableoregon.net/forestry/value_added.cfm, accessed May 4, 2006).

26. Yaffee et al., *Ecosystem Management*, p. 3.

27. Snow, "Empire or Homelands?"; Graham Chisolm, "Tough Towns: The Challenge of Community-Based Conservation," in Philip D. Brick and R. McGreggor Cawley, eds., *A Wolf in the Garden: The Land Rights Movement and the New Environmental Debate* (Lanham, MD: Rowman & Littlefield, 1996), pp. 279–292.

28. Yaffee et al., *Ecosystem Management*, pp. 21–22.

29. Brick and Weber, "Will Rain Follow the Plow?"

30. On the connections among this movement, regionalism, and Shutkin's civic environmentalism, see Baker and Kusel, *Community Forestry*.

31. Debra S. Knopman, Megan M. Susman, and Marc K. Landy, "Civic Environmentalism: Tackling Tough Land-Use Problems with Innovative Governance," *Environment*, Vol. 41, No. 10 (December 1999), pp. 24–32 (see pp. 26–27).

32. Knopman, Susman, and Landy, "Civic Environmentalism," pp. 26–27.

33. Yaffee et al., *Ecosystem Management*, p. 3.

34. Yaffee et al., *Ecosystem Management*, p. 25.

35. Snow, "Empire or Homelands?", p. 186; emphasis in original.

36. Yaffee et al., *Ecosystem Management*, pp. 16–17.

37. Baker and Kusel, *Community Forestry*, p. 213.

38. Chisolm, "Tough Towns," p. 287; Yaffee et al., *Ecosystem Management*, p. 32.

39. Knopman, Susman, and Landy, "Civic Environmentalism," p. 30.

40. Brett KenCairn, "Peril on Common Ground: The Applegate Experiment," in Philip D. Brick and R. McGreggor Cawley, eds., *A Wolf in the Garden: The Land Rights Movement and the New Environmental Debate* (Lanham, MD: Rowman & Littlefield, 1996), pp. 261–277 (quote on p. 273).

41. Cassandra Moseley, "The Applegate Partnership: Innovation in Crisis," in Philip Brick, Donald Snow, and Sarah Van De Wetering, eds., *Across the Great Divide: Explorations in Collaborative Conservation and the American West* (Washington, DC: Island Press, 2001), pp. 102–111 (see p. 108).

42. Yaffee et al., *Ecosystem Management*, p. 87.

43. KenCairn, "Peril on Common Ground," p. 267.

44. Moseley, "Applegate Partnership," pp. 103–104.

45. KenCairn, "Peril on Common Ground," p. 265.

46. Sturtevant and Lange, "From 'Them' to 'Us'," p. 121.

47. Sturtevant and Lange, "From 'Them' to 'Us'," p. 118.

48. Sturtevant and Lange, "From 'Them' to 'Us'," p. 123.

49. KenCairn, "Peril on Common Ground," p. 274.

50. Su Rolle, *Measures of Progress for Collaboration: Case Study of the Applegate Partnership* (Portland, OR: U.S. Department of Agriculture, Forest Service, Pacific Northwest Research Station, 2002), p. 3.

51. Cassandra Moseley, "Community Participation and Institutional Change: The Applegate Partnership and Federal Land Management in Southwest Oregon," unpublished paper presented at the Annual Meeting of the Western Political Science Association (San Jose, CA, March 24–26, 2000), p. 6.

52. KenCairn, "Peril on Common Ground," p. 267.

53. Yaffee et al., *Ecosystem Management*, p. 88.

54. KenCairn, "Peril on Common Ground," pp. 267–268.

55. KenCairn, "Peril on Common Ground," p. 274.

56. KenCairn, "Peril on Common Ground," pp. 268–270, 274.

57. Sturtevant and Lange, "From 'Them' to 'Us'," p. 129.

58. Sturtevant and Lange, "From 'Them' to 'Us'," pp. 124, 128.

59. Sturtevant and Lange, "From 'Them' to 'Us'," p. 130.

60. Sturtevant and Lange, "From 'Them' to 'Us'," p. 125.

61. KenCairn, "Peril on Common Ground," p. 273.

62. Moseley, "Applegate Partnership," p. 107.

63. Sturtevant and Lange, "From 'Them' to 'Us'," p. 124.

64. Sturtevant and Lange, "From 'Them' to 'Us'," p. 130.

65. KenCairn, "Peril on Common Ground," pp. 271–272.

66. Hibbard and Madsen, "Environmental Resistance," p. 710.

67. Yaffee et al., *Ecosystem Management*, p. 88.

68. Sturtevant and Lange, "From 'Them' to 'Us'," p. 130.

69. Sturtevant and Lange, "From 'Them' to 'Us'," p. 126.

70. Knopman, Susman, and Landy, "Civic Environmentalism," p. 30.

71. Applegate Partnership/Applegate River Watershed Council, "Mission Statement" (www.arwc.org/aboutus.html, accessed May 1, 2006).

72. Brick and Weber, "Will Rain Follow the Plow?", pp. 17, 19.

73. Knopman, Susman, and Landy, "Civic Environmentalism," p. 26.

74. Brick and Weber, "Will Rain Follow the Plow?"

75. Chisolm, "Tough Towns," p. 290.

76. Brick and Weber, "Will Rain Follow the Plow?"

77. For some additional obstacles, see KenCairn, "Peril on Common Ground," p. 277.

78. Chisolm, "Tough Towns," pp. 279–280.

79. George Cameron Coggins, "Of Californicators, Quislings, and Crazies: Some Perils of Devolved Collaboration," in Philip Brick, Donald Snow, and Sarah Van De Wetering, eds., *Across the Great Divide: Explorations in Collaborative Conservation and the American West* (Washington, DC: Island Press, 2001), pp. 163–171.

80. Snow, "Empire or Homelands?", pp. 198–199.

81. Cary Coglianese, "The Limits of Consensus" (review of *The Environmental Protection System in Transition: Toward a More Desirable Future*), *Environment*, Vol. 41, No. 3 (April 1999), pp. 28–33.

82. Coglianese, "Limits of Consensus," p. 31.

83. Sturtevant and Lange, "From 'Them' to 'Us'," p. 125.

84. Yaffee et al., *Ecosystem Management*, pp. 23–24, 41.

85. Coglianese, "Limits of Consensus," p. 32.

86. Coggins, "Californicators."

87. Baker and Kusel, *Community Forestry*, pp. 65, 69, 109–113, 132, 143.

88. Sturtevant and Lange, "From 'Them' to 'Us'," p. 130.

89. Layzer believes that the San Diego program has met with only mixed success. See Layzer, *Environmental Case*, 2nd ed., pp. 436–465.

90. Snow, "Coming Home"; Brick and Weber, "Will Rain Follow the Plow?", p. 20.

91. Chisolm, "Tough Towns," p. 284.

92. Moe and Wilkie, *Changing Places*, pp. 255, 257; Wiewel and Schaffer, "New Federal and State Policies," pp. 261–263; Tom Hester, "Towns May Get Right to Levy Impact Fees," *Newark Star-Ledger*, October 3, 2006 (www.nj .com/news/ledger/jersey/index.ssf?/base/news-4/115985162792400.xml&coll=1,

accessed October 22, 2006); Michele Derus, "State Hears Developers, Restricts Impact Fees," *Milwaukee Journal Sentinel*, June 1, 2006, p. D1; Arthur C. Nelson, Mitch Moody, *Paying for Prosperity: Impact Fees and Job Growth* (Washington: Brookings Institution, 2003).

93. Wiewel and Schaffer, "New Federal and State Policies," pp. 271–273; Calthorpe and Fulton, *Regional City*, pp. 97–98.

94. Moe and Wilkie, *Changing Places*, pp. 190–191.

95. David Rusk, "Growth Management: The Core Regional Issue," in Bruce Katz, ed., *Reflections on Regionalism* (Washington, DC: Brookings Institution, 2000), pp. 78–106 (see p. 98).

96. Calthorpe and Fulton, *Regional City*, p. 68.

97. Calthorpe and Fulton, *Regional City*, pp. 66–67.

98. Stoel, "Reining in Urban Sprawl," p. 11; Wiewel and Schaffer, "New Federal and State Policies," p. 267. See also Shutkin's discussion of smart growth in New Jersey's Somerset County, in *Land That Could Be*, pp. 218–222.

99. Shutkin, *Land That Could Be*, p. 219.

100. Calthorpe and Fulton, *Regional City*, p. 7.

101. Calthorpe and Fulton, *Regional City*, p. 110.

102. Calthorpe and Fulton, *Regional City*, pp. 116–121. Shifting federal funding from roads to mass transit is essential in promoting TOD. On this point see Calthorpe and Fulton, *Regional City*, pp. 72, 90–91, and Wiewel and Schaffer, "New Federal and State Policies," pp. 279–280. An increase in gasoline taxes could also help, by encouraging more use of mass transit, and could be part of an overall strategy to promote high-density, less auto-dependent development.

103. Such taxes create "land banks," which supply funds for future land purchases. See Donahue, *Reclaiming the Commons*, p. 294.

104. Stoel, "Reining in Urban Sprawl," p. 31; Dennis Farney, "Green Pieces," *Governing*, August 2006, pp. 26–33. The Clinton administration proposed an antisprawl "livability agenda," including federal funds for open-space purchases and "$700 million in tax credits to increase funding for mass transit; support local partnerships that pursue smart growth strategies across jurisdictional lines; and enable communities to issue bonds to protect green spaces, protect water quality, and clean up abandoned industrial sites" (Stoel, "Reining in Urban Sprawl," p. 31). The Bush administration did not follow up on this.

105. For more information on the Land and Water Conservation Fund, see Carol Hardy Vincent, *Land and Water Conservation Fund: Overview, Funding History, and Current Issues* (Washington: Congressional Research Service, 2006); Mike McQueen, *Land and Water Conservation Fund: An Assessment of Its Past, Present and Future* (Arlington, VA: The Conservation Fund, 2000); and the National Park Service (www.nps.gov/lwcf/, accessed November 13, 2006).

106. Donahue calls conservation easements the best tool for keeping farmers on the land (*Reclaiming the Commons*, p. 289).

107. Wiewel and Schaffer, "New Federal and State Policies," pp. 268–269.

108. www.nature.org (accessed May 23, 2006).

109. See www.tpl.org (accessed May 25, 2006).

110. Moe and Wilkie, *Changing Places*, pp. 150–151; www.nationaltrust.org (accessed May 25, 2006).

111. See www.farmland.org (accessed May 25, 2006).

112. See www.lta.org (accessed May 23, 2006).

113. www.downeastlakes.org (accessed May 23, 2006); emphasis in original. Thanks to Margie Thickstun for calling my attention to this organization.

114. Paul R. Armsworth, Gretchen C. Daily, Peter Kareiva, and James N. Sanchirico, "Land Market Feedbacks Can Undermine Biodiversity Conservation," *Proceedings of the National Academy of Sciences*, Vol. 103, No. 14 (April 4, 2006), pp. 5403–5408.

115. Shutkin, *Land That Could Be*, p. 233.

116. See Sally K. Fairfax, Lauren Gwin, Mary Ann King, Leigh Raymond and Laura A. Watt, *Buying Nature: The Limits of Land Acquisition as a Conservation Strategy, 1780–2004* (Cambridge, MA: MIT Press, 2005).

117. Fairfax, Gwin, King, Raymond, and Watt, *Buying Nature*, p. 267.

118. See the Institute for Community Economics, at www.iceclt.org.

119. See Wiewel and Schaffer, "New Federal and State Policies," p. 269; Shutkin, *Land That Could Be*, p. 215. See also www.randolphnj.org/open_space (accessed May 24, 2006).

120. www.ams.usda.gov/farmersmarkets (accessed May 23, 2006). On farmers' markets, see also Francesca Lyman, "Twelve Gates to the City," *Sierra*, Vol. 82, No. 3 (May/June 1997), pp. 28–35.

121. Paul Rauber, "Cultivating our Cities," *Sierra*, Vol. 82, No. 3 (May/June 1997), pp. 19–21.

122. Barbara Deutsch Lynch, "The Garden and the Sea: U.S. Latino Environmental Discourses and Mainstream Environmentalism," *Social Problems*, Vol. 40, No. 1 (February 1993), pp. 108–124; Giovanna Di Chiro, "Nature as Community: The Convergence of Environment and Social Justice," in William Cronon, ed., *Uncommon Ground: Toward Reinventing Nature* (New York: W.W. Norton, 1995), pp. 298–320 (pp. 318–319); Kevin Penton, "They're on Weed Patrol for an Urban Garden Project," *Boston Globe*, July 11, 1999 (City Weekly section), p. 1; Rauber, "Cultivating Our Cities"; Melody Ermachild Chavis, "Strong Roots," *Sierra*, Vol. 82, No. 3 (May/June 1997), pp. 48–51, 78.

123. Lynch, "The Garden and the Sea," p. 112; also Di Chiro, "Nature as Community," p. 319.

124. Shutkin, *Land That Could Be*, pp. 143–165. For more recent information, see www.thefoodproject.org and www.dsni.org (accessed May 23, 2006).

125. See Donahue, *Reclaiming the Commons*.

126. Donahue, *Reclaiming the Commons*, pp. 68–75.

127. Mark B. Lapping, "Toward the Recovery of the Local in the Globalizing Food System: The Role of Alternative Agricultural and Food Models in the US," *Ethics, Place & Environment*, Vol. 7, No. 3 (October 2004), pp. 141–150.

128. See Gina T. Gerbasi, "Athens Farmers' Market: Evolving Dynamics and Hidden Benefits to a Southeast Ohio Rural Community," *Focus on Geography*, Vol. 49, No. 2 (Fall 2006), pp. 1–6; April Terreri, "The Food Pipeline," *Planning*, Vol. 70, No. 3 (March 2004), pp. 4–9; Corby Kummer, "Good-bye, Cryovac," *Atlantic*, Vol. 294, No. 3 (October 2004), pp. 197–202; Mark Winston Griffith, "How Harlem Eats," *Nation*, Vol. 283, No. 7 (September 11, 2006), pp. 36–38.

129. See www.umassvegetable.org/food_farming_systems/csa/index.html (accessed October 23, 2006); Dominick Villane, "Sharing the Family Farm," *The Massachusetts Sierran*, Vol. 3, No. 2 (Spring 1997), p. 1; Beth Lucht, "Betting the Farm on Local Markets," *Progressive*, Vol. 70, No. 4 (April 2006), p. 35; Umut Newbury and Megan Phelps, "Join the Real Food Revival!", *Mother Earth News*, No. 211 (August/September 2005), pp. 40–46; and Sarah Milstein, "Creating A Market," *Mother Earth News*, No. 172 (February/March 1999), pp. 40–44, 112.

130. Leslie Teach Robbins, "Pass the Peas Please," *State Legislatures*, Vol. 31, No. 5 (May 2005), pp. 30–31.

131. Calthorpe and Fulton, *Regional City*, pp. 100–101.

132. For some questions regarding whether brownfields benefit a local community, see Christopher Foreman, The *Promise and Peril of Environmental Justice* (Washington, DC: Brookings Institution, 1998), pp. 94–99.

133. See, for example, Moe and Wilkie, *Changing Places*, pp. 100–141, on the relation between urban preservation and gentrification and on measures to prevent or mitigate gentrification.

134. Calthorpe and Fulton, *Regional City*, p. 78.

135. See Moe and Wilkie, *Changing Places*, pp. 119–138.

136. Moe and Wilkie, *Changing Places*, p. 131.

137. Shutkin, *The Land That Could Be*, p. 149.

138. On the history, politics, and ideology of the environmental justice movement, see Gerald R. Visgilio and Diana M. Whitelaw, eds., *Our Backyard: A Quest for Environmental Justice* (Lanham, MD: Rowman & Littlefield, 2003); Robert D. Bullard, *Dumping in Dixie: Race, Class, and Environmental Quality* (Boulder, CO: Westview Press, 1994); Robert Bullard, ed., *Confronting Environmental Racism: Voices from the Grassroots* (Boston: South End Press, 1993); Schlosberg, *Environmental Justice*; Dowie, *Losing Ground*, pp. 125–174; Di Chiro, "Nature as Community"; and Robert Gottlieb, *Forcing the Spring: The Transformation of the American Environmental Movement* (Washington, DC: Island Press, 1993). For an assessment of the evidence for discriminatory, either race- or class-based, siting of environmental hazards, as well as a discussion of the policy responses to environmental justice, see Evan J. Ringquist, "Environmental

Justice: Normative Concerns, Empirical Evidence, and Government Action" in Norman Vig and Michael E. Kraft, eds., *Environmental Policy: New Directions for the Twenty-first Century*, 6th ed. (Washington, DC: CQ Press, 2005), pp. 232–256. For a critique of the environmental justice movement, see Foreman, *Promise and Peril*.

139. Di Chiro, "Nature as Community," p. 300.

140. See Cynthia Hamilton, "Coping with Industrial Exploitation," in Robert Bullard, ed., *Confronting Environmental Racism: Voices from the Grassroots* (Boston: South End Press, 1993), pp. 63–76; Bullard, *Dumping in Dixie*, pp. 9–10; and Robert Bullard, "Anatomy of Environmental Racism and the Environmental Justice Movement," in Robert Bullard, ed., *Confronting Environmental Racism: Voices from the Grassroots* (Boston: South End Press, 1993), pp. 15–39.

141. Di Chiro, "Nature as Community," p. 318.

142. Di Chiro, "Nature as Community," p. 305.

143. Di Chiro, "Nature as Community," p. 319.

144. Schlosberg, *Environmental Justice*, pp. 113–115.

145. Di Chiro, "Nature as Community," pp. 313–314.

146. On this last idea, see Hamilton, "Coping with Industrial Exploitation," pp. 66–67.

147. Hamilton, "Coping with Industrial Exploitation," pp. 66, 74–75.

148. Di Chiro, "Nature as Community," p. 305.

149. Ringquist, "Environmental Justice," p. 257; Foreman, *Promise and Peril*; Layzer, *Environmental Case*, 1st ed., p. 73.

150. Foreman, *Promise and Peril*, pp. 109–136.

151. Much of the information in this section draws upon Ringquist, "Environmental Justice."

152. See Richard Dahl, "Does Secrecy Equal Security?", *Environmental Health Perspectives*, Vol. 112, No. 2 (February 2004), pp. A104–A107; Joseph A. Davis, "Environmental Hazards: What You Don't Know Just Might Hurt You," *IRE Journal*, Vol. 28, No. 1 (January/February 2005), pp. 13, 41.

153. For a comprehensive review of state environmental justice programs, see Steven Bonorris, ed., *Environmental Justice for All: A Fifty-State Survey of Legislation, Policies, and Initiatives* (San Francisco: American Bar Association and University of California Hastings College of the Law, 2004).

154. Ringquist makes this point. See "Environmental Justice."

155. See Ringquist, "Environmental Justice," and Foreman, *Promise and Peril*.

156. Schlosberg, *Environmental Justice*, pp. 107–144.

157. Schlosberg, *Environmental Justice*, pp. 115–126.

158. Schlosberg, *Environmental Justice*, pp. 139–140.

159. Ringquist, "Environmental Justice."

160. Calthorpe and Fulton, *Regional City*, pp. 73–77; Wiewel and Schaffer, "New Federal and State Policies," p. 276.

161. The following discussion draws upon Curry, "Racial Critique."

162. Calthorpe and Fulton, *Regional City*, pp. 261–262.

163. Michael Sorkin, "The Center Cannot Hold," in Michael Sorkin and Sharon Zukin, eds., *After the World Trade Center: Rethinking New York City* (New York: Routledge, 2002), pp. 197–207; Sorkin, *Starting from Zero*.

164. Sorkin, "Center Cannot Hold," p. 202.

165. Sorkin, "Center Cannot Hold," pp. 202–204.

166. Sorkin, "Center Cannot Hold," p. 207; Sorkin, *Starting from Zero*, pp. 30–50.

167. Sorkin, "Center Cannot Hold," pp. 200–201.

168. Urban historian Mike Wallace also urges thinking beyond Ground Zero itself and calls for a shift away from New York City's excessive reliance on FIRE industries and reduction of the vast inequalities in wealth associated with the 1990s boom in the FIRE sector. He urges job creation, neighborhood revitalization, and a more diversified economy through greater assistance to local manufacturers and small businesses, brownfields redevelopment, changes in the transportation infrastructure to reduce highly polluting truck traffic going through the city, increased provision of affordable housing, and revival of the city's port facilities. See Wallace, "New York, New Deal."

Postscript

1. Thomas Gabe, Gene Falk, and Maggie McCarty, *Hurricane Katrina: Social-Demographic Characteristics of Impacted Areas* (Washington, DC: Congressional Research Service, November 4, 2005), p. ii.

2. Gabe, Falk, and McCarty, *Hurricane Katrina*, p. 14.

3. "Politics May Doom New Orleans" (Editorial), *San Francisco Chronicle*, August 25, 2006, p. B10.

4. Quoted in Anna Mulrine, "The Long Road Back," *U.S. News & World Report*, February 27, 2006, pp. 44–50, 52–58.

5. Reported in Adam Nossiter, "New Orleans Population Is Reduced Nearly 60%," *New York Times*, October 7, 2006, p. A9.

6. Kevin McCarthy, D. J. Peterson, Narayan Sastry, and Michael Pollard, *The Repopulation of New Orleans After Hurricane Katrina* (Santa Monica, CA: RAND Corporation, 2006).

7. Manuel Roig-Franzia, "A City Fears for Its Soul: New Orleans Worries That Its Unique Culture May Be Lost," *Washington Post*, February 3, 2006, p. A1.

8. See Kerry Emanuel, "Increasing Destructiveness of Tropical Cyclones Over the Past 30 Years," *Nature*, Vol. 436, No. 7051 (August 4, 2005), pp. 686–688.

9. Intergovernmental Panel on Climate Change, *Summary for Policymakers: A Report of Working Group I of the Intergovernmental Panel on Climate Change* (Geneva: World Meteorological Organization and the United Nations Environment Programme, 2001).

10. United Nations University: Institute for Environment and Human Security, "As Ranks of 'Environmental Refugees' Swell Worldwide, Calls Grow for Better Definition, Recognition, Support" (press release), October 12, 2005 (www.ehs .unu.edu, accessed March 1, 2006).

11. See, for example, Craig E. Colten, *An Unnatural Metropolis: Wresting New Orleans from Nature* (Baton Rouge: Louisiana State University Press, 2005); Richard E. Sparks, "Rethinking, Then Rebuilding New Orleans," *Issues in Science & Technology*, Vol. 22, No. 2 (Winter 2006), pp. 33–39; and Peirce F. Lewis, *New Orleans: The Making of an Urban Landscape* (Santa Fe, NM: Center for American Places, 2003).

12. Tom Piazza, *Why New Orleans Matters* (New York: HarperCollins, 2005), p. ix.

13. Piazza, *Why New Orleans Matters*, p. xvi.

Bibliography

"A 9/11 Memorial Without Public Input Will Have No Soul" (editorial), *Engineering News-Record*, Vol. 251, No. 22 (December 1, 2003), p. 68.

Abelman, Michael, "Growing New Life at Ground Zero," *New York Times*, December 21, 2002, p. A21.

"A Conversation with Alex Morton," in Matthew J. Lindstrom and Hugh Bartling, eds., *Suburban Sprawl: Culture, Theory, and Politics*, Lanham, MD: Rowman & Littlefield, 2003, pp. 115–117.

Adams, Darius M., and Gregory S. Latta, "Costs and Regional Impacts of Restoration Thinning Programs on the National Forests in Eastern Oregon," *Canadian Journal of Forest Research*, Vol. 35, No. 6 (June 2005), pp. 1319–1330.

Allee, Shawn, "School Districts Encouraging Urban Sprawl?", *Great Lakes Radio Consortium*, March 13, 2006.

Alliance for Downtown New York, *Lower Manhattan Residents: A Community in Transition*, New York: Alliance for Downtown New York, 2004.

Alliance for Downtown New York, *State of Lower Manhattan 2004*, New York: Alliance for Downtown New York, 2004.

Anderson, H. Michael, and Jeffrey T. Olson, *Federal Forests and the Economic Base of the Pacific Northwest: A Study of Regional Transitions*, Washington, DC: Wilderness Society, 1991.

"A Next Step for Ground Zero" (editorial), *New York Daily News*, September 25, 2005, p. 42.

Applegate Partnership/Applegate River Watershed Council, "Mission Statement" (www.arwc.org/aboutus.html, accessed May 1, 2006).

Arabas, Karen, and Joe Bowersox, "Conclusion: Forests Past and Forests Future—Connecting Science, Politics, and Policy," in Karen Arabas and Joe Bowersox, eds., *Forest Futures: Science, Politics, and Policy for the Next Century*, Lanham, MD: Rowman & Littlefield, 2004, pp. 280–291.

Arabas, Karen, and Joe Bowersox, eds., *Forest Futures: Science, Politics, and Policy for the Next Century*, Lanham, MD: Rowman & Littlefield, 2004.

Archibold, Randal C., "A Year of Dust, Ash and Anguish," *New York Times*, September 6, 2002, p. B1.

Arendt, Hannah, *The Human Condition*, Chicago: University of Chicago Press, 1958.

Arendt, Hannah, *Between Past and Future: Eight Exercises in Political Thought*, New York: Penguin Books, 1977.

Aristotle, *The Politics*, Carnes Lord, trans., Chicago: University of Chicago Press, 1984.

Armsworth, Paul R., Gretchen C. Daily, Peter Kareiva, and James N. Sanchirico, "Land Market Feedbacks Can Undermine Biodiversity Conservation," *Proceedings of the National Academy of Sciences*, Vol. 103, No. 14 (April 4, 2006), pp. 5403–5408.

Arnold, Elizabeth "Saving the Spotted Owl: Benefits of Recovery Effort Remain Complex, Controversial," *Morning Edition*, National Public Radio, August 6, 2004.

Arthur, Bill, "Carlson and His Cronies are the Real Hypocrites," *Seattle Times*, January 21, 1994, p. B7.

Baber, Walter F., and Robert V. Bartlett, *Deliberative Environmental Politics: Democracy and Ecological Rationality*, Cambridge, MA: MIT Press, 2005.

Bagli, Charles V., "6 Plans for Ground Zero Share Striking Similarities," *New York Times*, July 11, 2002, p. B1.

Bagli, Charles V., "Developer Takes a Financial Deal for Ground Zero," *New York Times*, April 26, 2006, p. A1.

Baker, Mark, and Jonathan Kusel, *Community Forestry in the United States: Learning From the Past, Crafting the Future*, Washington, DC: Island Press, 2003.

Barber, Benjamin R., "An Architecture of Liberty?: The City as Democracy's Forge," in Joan Ockham, ed., *Out of Ground Zero: Case Studies in Urban Reinvention*, New York: Columbia University Press, 2002, pp. 184–205.

Barber, Benjamin R., *Strong Democracy: Participatory Politics for a New Age*, Berkeley: University of California Press, 1984.

Barker, Rocky, "New Forestry in the Next West," in John A. Baden and Donald Snow, *The Next West: Public Lands, Community, and Economy in the American West*, Washington, DC: Island Press, 1997, pp. 29–30.

Barringer, Felicity, "Bush Seeks Shift in Logging Rules," *New York Times*, July 13, 2004, p. A1.

Barringer, Felicity, "Logging and Politics Collide in Idaho," *New York Times*, August 9, 2004, p. 10.

Barringer, Felicity, "Property Rights Law May Alter Oregon Landscape," *New York Times*, November 26, 2004, p. A1.

Barringer, Felicity, "Judge Voids Bush Policy on National Forest Roads, *New York Times*, September 21, 2006, p. 21.

Barry, John, *Environment and Social Theory*, London: Routledge, 1999.

Barry, John, *Rethinking Green Politics: Nature, Virtue, and Progress*, London: Sage, 1999.

Batt, H. William, "Stemming Sprawl: The Fiscal Approach," in Matthew J. Lindstrom and Hugh Bartling, eds., *Suburban Sprawl: Culture, Theory, and Politics*, Lanham, MD: Rowman & Littlefield, 2003, pp. 239–254.

Beck, Ulrich, *Risk Society: Towards a New Modernity*, Mark Ritter, trans., London: Sage, 1992 (1986).

Benhabib, Seyla, "The Generalized and the Concrete Other," in Seyla Benhabib and Drucilla Cornell, eds., *Feminism as Critique*, Minneapolis: University of Minnesota Press, 1987, pp. 77–95.

Bennett, Jane, *Unthinking Faith and Enlightenment: Nature and the State in the Post-Hegelian Era*, New York: New York University Press, 1987.

Bennett, Jane, and William Chaloupka, eds., *In the Nature of Things: Language, Politics, and the Environment*, Minneapolis: University of Minnesota Press, 1993.

Berger, John J., "9 Ways to Save our National Forests," *Sierra*, Vol. 82, No. 4 (July 17, 1997), p. 38.

Berger, Thomas R., *Northern Frontier, Northern Homeland: The Report of the Mackenzie Valley Pipeline Inquiry*, Vol. 2, Ottawa: Minister of Supply and Services Canada, 1977.

Berman, Marshall, "When Bad Buildings Happen to Good People," in Michael Sorkin and Sharon Zukin, eds., *After the World Trade Center: Rethinking New York City*, New York: Routledge, 2002, pp. 1–12.

Berry, Wendell, *The Unsettling of America*, San Francisco: Sierra Club Books, 1977.

Beuter, John H., "Sustained Yield: Goals, Policies, Promises," in Karen Arabas and Joe Bowersox, eds., *Forest Futures: Science, Politics, and Policy for the Next Century*, Lanham, MD: Rowman & Littlefield, 2004, pp. 48–67.

Bhatnagar, Parija, "Not a Mall, It's a Lifestyle Center, CNNMoney.com, January 12, 2005 (www.money.cnn.com/2005/01/11/news/fortune500/retail_lifestylecenter/, accessed October 2, 2006).

Bickford, Susan, "Constructing Inequality: City Spaces and the Architecture of Citizenship," *Political Theory*, Vol. 28, No. 3 (June 1, 2000), pp. 355–376.

Biro, Andrew, *Denaturalizing Ecological Politics: Alienation from Nature from Rousseau to the Frankfurt School and Beyond*, Toronto: University of Toronto Press, 2005.

Bloomberg, Michael R., "Vision for 21st Century Lower Manhattan," LowerManhattan.info, December 12, 2002 (www.lowermanhattan.info/news/read_mayor_bloomberg_s_80515.asp, accessed February 27, 2003).

Blum, Andrew, "The Mall Goes Undercover: It Now Looks Like a City Street," *Slate*, April 6, 2005 (www.slate.com/id/2116246, accessed October 2, 2006).

Bonnett, Mark, and Kurt Zimmerman, "Politics and Preservation: The Endangered Species Act and the Northern Spotted Owl," *Ecology Law Quarterly*, Vol. 18, No. 1 (1991), pp. 105–171.

Bonorris, Steven, *Environmental Justice for All: A Fifty-State Survey of Legislation, Policies, and Initiatives*, San Francisco: American Bar Association and University of California Hastings College of the Law, 2004.

Booth, Douglas E., *Valuing Nature: The Decline and Preservation of Old-Growth Forests*, Lanham, MD: Rowman & Littlefield, 1994.

Borgmann, Albert, "The Nature of Reality and the Reality of Nature," in Michael E. Soulé and Gary Lease, eds., *Reinventing Nature?: Responses to Postmodern Deconstruction*, Washington, DC: Island Press, 1995, pp. 31–45.

Bowersox, Joe, "Fire on the Hill: Using Ecological Disturbance Theory to Understand the Ambiguous Prospects of the Northwest Forest Plan," in Karen Arabas and Joe Bowersox, eds., *Forest Futures: Science, Politics, and Policy for the Next Century*, Lanham, MD: Rowman & Littlefield, 2004, pp. 237–255.

Bowersox, Joe, and Karen Arabas, "Forests Past and Forests Future—Connecting Science, Politics, and Policy," in Karen Arabas and Joe Bowersox, eds., *Forest Futures: Science, Politics, and Policy for the Next Century*, Lanham, MD: Rowman & Littlefield, 2004, pp. 280–291.

Bowersox, Joe, and Karen Arabas, "Introduction: Natural and Human History of Pacific Northwest Forests," in Karen Arabas and Joe Bowersox, eds., *Forest Futures: Science, Politics, and Policy for the Next Century*, Lanham, MD: Rowman & Littlefield, 2004, pp. xxiii–xlii.

Bowles, Samuel, and Herbert Gintis, *Democracy and Capitalism: Property, Community, and the Contradictions of Modern Social Thought*, New York: Basic Books, 1987.

Bowman, Chris, "Lingering Peril of 9/11: Ground Zero Workers Ran Toxic Risk, UCD Study Says," *Sacramento Bee*, September 10, 2003, p. A1.

Boyer, Christine, "Meditations on a Wounded Skyline and Its Stratigraphies of Pain," in Michael Sorkin and Sharon Zukin, eds., *After the World Trade Center: Rethinking New York City*, New York: Routledge, 2002, pp. 109–120.

Brady, Jeff, "Western Voters Consider Property Rights Changes," *Morning Edition*, National Public Radio, September 19, 2006.

Brady, Jeff, "Western Voters Weigh Shift in Property Rights," *Morning Edition*, National Public Radio, September 18, 2006.

Braun, Mark Edward, "Suburban Sprawl in Southeastern Wisconsin: Planning, Politics, and the Lack of Affordable Housing," in Matthew J. Lindstrom and Hugh Bartling, eds., *Suburban Sprawl: Culture, Theory, and Politics*, Lanham, MD: Rowman & Littlefield, 2003, pp. 257–274.

Bressi, Todd W., "Planning the American Dream," in Peter Katz, ed., *The New Urbanism: Toward an Architecture of Community*, New York: McGraw-Hill, 1994, pp. xxv–xlii.

Brick, Philip D., and R. McGreggor Cawley, eds., *A Wolf in the Garden: The Land Rights Movement and the New Environmental Debate*, Lanham, MD: Rowman & Littlefield, 1996.

Brick, Philip D., and Edward P. Weber, "Will Rain Follow the Plow? Unearthing a New Environmental Movement," in Philip D. Brick, Donald Snow, and Sarah Van De Wetering, eds., *Across the Great Divide: Explorations in Collaborative Conservation and the American West*, Washington, DC: Island Press, 2001, pp. 15–24.

Brick, Philip D., Donald Snow, and Sarah Van De Wetering, eds., *Across the Great Divide: Explorations in Collaborative Conservation and the American West*, Washington, DC: Island Press, 2001.

Brooks, David, "Our Sprawling, Supersize Utopia," *New York Times Magazine*, April 4, 2004, pp. 46–51.

Brown, Beverly A., *In Timber Country: Working People's Stories of Environmental Conflict and Urban Flight*, Philadelphia: Temple University Press, 1995.

Brown, Denise Scott, "Measuring Downtown's Future," *New York Times*, August 16, 2002, p. A17.

Bruder, Jessica, "Would You Go to Work in a New Skyscraper at Ground Zero?", *Washington Post*, March 28, 2003, p. B1.

Buell, Lawrence, *The Environmental Imagination: Thoreau, Nature Writing, and the Formation of American Culture*, Cambridge, MA: Harvard University Press, 1995.

Bullard, Robert D., ed., *Confronting Environmental Racism: Voices from the Grassroots*, Boston: South End Press, 1993.

Bullard, Robert D., "Anatomy of Environmental Racism and the Environmental Justice Movement," in Robert D. Bullard, ed., *Confronting Environmental Racism: Voices from the Grassroots*, Boston: South End Press, 1993, pp. 15–39.

Bullard, Robert D., *Dumping in Dixie: Race, Class, and Environmental Quality*, Boulder, CO: Westview Press, 1994.

Burlingame, Debra, "The Great Ground Zero Heist," *Wall Street Journal*, June 7, 2005, p. A14.

Byers, Michele, "Waiting at the Gate: The New, Postmodern Promised Lands," in Matthew J. Lindstrom and Hugh Bartling, eds., *Suburban Sprawl: Culture, Theory, and Politics*, Lanham, MD: Rowman & Littlefield, 2003, pp. 23–43.

Calbom, Linda M., *Financial Management: Annual Costs of Forest Service's Timber Sales Programs Are Not Determinable* (GAO-01-1101R), Washington, DC: U.S. General Accounting Office, 2001.

Calthorpe, Peter, *The Next American Metropolis: Ecology, Community, and the American Dream*, Princeton, NJ: Princeton Architectural Press, 1993.

Calthorpe, Peter, and William Fulton, *The Regional City: Planning for the End of Sprawl*, Washington, DC: Island Press, 2001.

Canellos, Peter S., "The Second Battle of Concord," *Boston Globe Magazine*, September 29, 1996, pp. 14–15, 32–37.

Carlson, John, "Sierra Club Official's Cut is a Snapshot of Hypocrisy," *Seattle Times*, January 18, 1994, p. B4.

Carnoy, Martin, and Manuel Castells, *Sustainable Flexibility: A Prospective Study on Work, Family and Society in the Information Age*, Paris: Organization for Economic Cooperation and Development, 1997.

Carpenter, Betsy, "The Light in the Forest," *U.S. News & World Report*, April 5, 1993, p. 39.

Casey, Edward S., *The Fate of Place: A Philosophical History*, Berkeley: University of California Press, 1997.

Casey, Edward S., "Between Geography and Philosophy: What Does It Mean to Be in the Place-World?", *Annals of the Association of American Geographers*, Vol. 91, No. 4 (December 2001), pp. 683–693.

Casey, Edward S., "On Habitus and Place: Responding to My Critics," *Annals of the Association of American Geographers*, Vol. 91, No. 4 (December 2001), pp. 716–723.

Castells, Manuel, *The Power of Identity*, Cambridge, MA: Blackwell, 1997.

Castells, Manuel, *The End of the Millennium*, Cambridge, MA: Blackwell, 1998.

Castells, Manuel, *The Rise of the Network Society*, 2nd ed., Cambridge, MA: Blackwell, 2000.

Caulfield, Catherine, "A Reporter at Large: The Ancient Forest," *New Yorker*, May 14, 1990, pp. 46–84.

Ceplo, Karol J., "Land-Rights Conflicts in the Regulation of Wetlands," in Bruce Yandle, ed., *Land Rights: The 1990s' Property Rights Rebellion*, Lanham, MD: Rowman & Littlefield, 1995, pp. 102–150.

Chan, Sewell, "Plan to Fill Freedom Tower Stirs Debate," *New York Times*, September 20, 2006, p. B3.

Chapman, Parke, "Office Glut at Ground Zero," *National Real Estate Investor*, January 1, 2005, p. 41.

Chavis, Melody Ermachild, "Strong Roots," *Sierra*, Vol. 82, No. 3 (May/June 1997), pp. 48–51, 78.

Chen, Lung Chi, and George Thurston, "World Trade Center Cough." *Lancet*, Vol. 360, No. 9350 (December 21, 2002 supplement), pp. 37–38.

Cheney, Jim, "Postmodern Environmental Ethics: Ethics as Bioregional Narrative," in Max Oelschlaeger, ed., *Postmodern Environmental Ethics*, Albany: State University of New York Press, 1995, pp. 23–42.

Chisolm, Graham, "Tough Towns: The Challenge of Community-Based Conservation," in Philip D. Brick and R. McGreggor Cawley, eds., *A Wolf in the Garden: The Land Rights Movement and the New Environmental Debate*, Lanham, MD: Rowman & Littlefield, 1996, pp. 279–292.

Claudio, Luz, "Environmental Aftermath of World Trade Center Disaster," *Environmental Health Perspectives*, Vol. 109, No. 11 (November 2001), pp. A528–A536.

Coggins, George Cameron, "Of Californicators, Quislings, and Crazies: Some Perils of Devolved Collaboration," in Philip D. Brick, Donald Snow, and Sarah Van De Wetering, eds., *Across the Great Divide: Explorations in Collaborative Conservation and the American West*, Washington, DC: Island Press, 2001, pp. 163–171.

Coglianese, Cary, "The Limits of Consensus," *Environment*, Vol. 41, No. 3 (April 1999), pp. 28–33.

Cole, Michelle, "Federal Forests Get Looser Rein with New Rules," *Oregonian*, December 23, 2004, p. B3.

Collins, Glenn, "The Ground Zero Memorial: The Competition: Avidly Dissected, the Eight Design Finalists Provide a Blueprint for Compromise," *New York Times*, November 21, 2003, p. B1.

Collins, Glenn, "For the Design Team, a Desperate Rush," *New York Times*, July 10, 2005, p. 25.

Collins, Jim, "Lots for Sale: A Massive Project for the Maine Woods Stirs Debate," *Wilderness*, 2005, pp. 21–24.

Colten, Craig E., *An Unnatural Metropolis: Wresting New Orleans from Nature*, Baton Rouge: Louisiana State University Press, 2005.

Cornwall, Warren, "Forest Rules May Reframe Timber Debate," *Seattle Times*, December 24, 2004, p. B1.

Cornwall, Warren, "Untouched National Forests Lose Clinton-Era Protections," *Seattle Times*, May 6, 2005, p. B1.

"Counties Face 'Cliff'" (editorial), *Eugene Register-Guard*, September 18, 2006 (www.registerguard.com/news/2006/09/18/ed.edit.ruralcounties.phn.0918.p1.php?section=opinion, accessed September 30, 2006).

Cresswell, Tim, "Theorizing Place," in Ginette Verstraete and Tim Cresswell, eds., *Mobilizing Place, Placing Mobility: The Politics of Representation in a Globalized World (Thamyris/Intersecting 9)*, Amsterdam/New York: Rodopi, 2002, pp. 11–32.

Cronon, William, ed., *Uncommon Ground: Toward Reinventing Nature*, New York: W.W. Norton, 1995.

Cronon, William, "The Trouble with Wilderness, or Getting Back to the Wrong Nature," in William Cronon, ed., *Uncommon Ground: Toward Reinventing Nature*, New York: W.W. Norton, 1995, pp. 69–90.

Cubbage, Frederick W., "The Public Interest in Private Forests: Developing Regulations and Incentives," in Kathryn A. Kohm and Jerry F. Franklin, eds., *Creating a Forestry for the Twenty-first Century: The Science of Ecosystem Management*, Washington, DC: Island Press, 1997, pp. 337–356.

Curry, Milton, "Racial Critique of Public Housing Redevelopment Strategies," in Matthew J. Lindstrom and Hugh Bartling, eds., *Suburban Sprawl: Culture,*

Theory, and Politics, Lanham, MD: Rowman & Littlefield, 2003, pp. 119–131.

Cushman, John, "In the Utah Wilderness, A Question of Definition," *New York Times*, January 28, 1997, p. A12.

Cushman, John H., "Owl Issue Tests Reliance on Consensus in Environmentalism," *New York Times*, March 6, 1994, p. 28.

Dahl, Richard, "Does Secrecy Equal Security?", *Environmental Health Perspectives*, Vol. 112, No. 2 (February 2004), pp. A104–A107.

Daly, Herman E., *Beyond Growth: The Economics of Sustainable Development*, Boston: Beacon Press, 1997.

Darton, Eric, "The Janus Face of Architectural Terrorism: Minoru Yamasaki, Mohammed Atta, and Our World Trade Center," in Michael Sorkin and Sharon Zukin, eds., *After the World Trade Center: Rethinking New York City*, New York: Routledge, 2002, pp. 87–95.

Davidsdottir, Sigrun, "Smoke Screen," *Guardian*, June 5, 2002, p. 8 (Society pages).

Davidson, Justin, "Seeking the Meaning of 9–11," *Newsday*, September 28, 2005, p. A16.

Davis, Joseph A., "Environmental Hazards: What You Don't Know Just Might Hurt You," *IRE Journal*, Vol. 28, No. 1 (January/February 2005), pp. 13, 41.

Debord, Guy, "Introduction to a Critique of Urban Geography," in Ken Knabb, ed., *Situationist International Anthology*, Berkeley, CA: Bureau of Public Secrets, 1982, pp. 5–8.

Delany, Samuel R., *Times Square Red, Times Square Blue*, New York: New York University Press, 2001.

de Lauretis, Teresa, "Eccentric Subjects: Feminist Theory and Historical Consciousness," *Feminist Studies*, Vol. 16, No. 1 (Spring 1990), pp. 115–150.

DellaSala, Dominick A., Jack E. Williams, Cindy Deacon Williams, and Jerry F. Franklin, "Beyond Smoke and Mirrors: a Synthesis of Fire Policy and Science," *Conservation Biology*, Vol. 18, No. 4 (August 2004), pp. 976–986.

Dennis-Parks, Reda M., "Healthy Forests Restoration Act: Will It Really Protect Homes and Communities?", *Ecology Law Quarterly*, Vol. 31, No. 3 (2004), pp. 639–664.

DePalma, Anthony, "At Ground Zero, Rebuilding with Nature in Mind," *New York Times*, January 20, 2004, p. B1.

Derus, Michele, "State Hears Developers, Restricts Impact Fees," *Milwaukee Journal Sentinel*, June 1, 2006, p. D1.

Diamond, Jared, *Collapse: How Societies Choose to Fail or Succeed*, New York: Penguin, 2005.

Di Chiro, Giovanna, "Nature as Community: The Convergence of Environment and Social Justice," in William Cronon, ed., *Uncommon Ground: Toward Reinventing Nature*, New York: W.W. Norton, 1995, pp. 298–320.

Dietrich, Bill, *The Final Forest: The Battle for the Last Great Trees of the Pacific Northwest*, New York: Penguin, 1992.

Dobbs, David, and Richard Ober, *The Northern Forest*, White River Junction, VT: Chelsea Green, 1995.

Donahue, Brian, *Reclaiming the Commons: Community Farms and Forests in a New England Town*, New Haven, CT: Yale University Press, 1999.

Dowie, Mark, *Losing Ground: American Environmentalism at the Close of the Twentieth Century*, Cambridge, MA: MIT Press, 1995.

"Downtown Construction and Rebuilding Information: Looking Ahead," LowerManhattan.info (www.lowermanhattan.info/construction/looking_ahead/, accessed January 4, 2006).

Draper, Electa, "Forest Service Centennial: Many Uses, Many Struggles," *Denver Post*, October 4, 2005, p. A14.

Drew, Bettina, *Crossing the Expendable Landscape*, St. Paul, MN: Graywolf Press, 1998.

Dryzek, John S., *Rational Ecology: Environment and Political Economy*, Oxford, UK: Blackwell, 1987.

Dryzek, John S., David Downes, Christian Hunold, David Schlosberg, and Hans-Kristian Hernes, *Green States and Social Movements: Environmentalism in the United States, United Kingdom, Germany, and Norway*, Oxford, UK: Oxford University Press, 2003.

Dunlap, David W., "The Ground Zero Memorial: The Competition: Presenting Several Versions of the Shape of Grief and Reconstruction," *New York Times*, November 20, 2003, p. B3.

Dunlap, David W., "At Ground Zero, Trying to Take Account of Ecology," *New York Times*, April 15, 2004, p. B3.

Dunlap, David W., "Varying Boundaries of Hallowed Ground," *New York Times*, September 8, 2005, p. B4.

Dunlap, David W., "Ground Zero Cooling Plant Shrinks from XL to S," *New York Times*, November 16, 2005, p. B1.

Dunning, Joan, and Doug Thron, *From the Redwood Forest: Ancient Trees and the Bottom Line: A Headwaters Journey*, White River Junction, VT: Chelsea Green, 1998.

Durbin, Kathie, *Tree Huggers: Victory, Defeat, and Renewal in the Northwest Ancient Forest Campaign*, Seattle: The Mountaineers, 1996.

Durbin, Kathie, "A Western Showdown," *Washington Monthly*, Vol. 30, No. 5 (May 1998), pp. 15–18.

Easterbrook, Gregg, "Suburban Myth," *New Republic*, March 15, 1999, pp. 18–21.

Eaton, Leslie, "Visions of Ground Zero: The Plans; New York Embraces Commerce, as It Always Has," *New York Times*, July 21, 2002, p. 30.

Eckersley, Robyn, *Environmentalism and Political Theory: Toward an Ecocentric Approach*, Albany: State University of New York Press, 1992.

Egan, Timothy, "Urban Sprawl Strains Western States," *New York Times*, December 29, 1996, p. A1.

Ehrenhalt, Alan, "Up Against the Wal-Mart," *Governing*, September 1992, pp. 6–7.

Emanuel, Kerry, "Increasing Destructiveness of Tropical Cyclones Over the Past 30 Years," *Nature*, Vol. 436, No. 7051 (August 4, 2005), pp. 686–688.

EPA's Response to the World Trade Center Collapse: Challenges, Successes, and Areas for Improvement, Washington, DC: U.S. Environmental Protection Agency, Office of Inspector General, August 21, 2003.

Epstein, Richard A., *Takings: Private Property and the Power of Eminent Domain*, Cambridge, MA: Harvard University Press, 1985.

Evernden, Neil, *The Social Creation of Nature*, Baltimore, MD: Johns Hopkins University Press, 1992.

Ewing, Reid, "Is Los Angeles-style Sprawl Desirable?", *Journal of the American Planning Association*, Vol. 63, No. 1 (Winter 1997), pp. 107–126.

Ewing, Reid, Tom Schmid, Richard Killingsworth, Amy Zlot, and Stephen Raudenbush, "Relationship Between Urban Sprawl and Physical Activity, Obesity, and Morbidity," *American Journal of Health Promotion*, Vol. 18, No. 1 (September/October 2003), pp. 47–57.

Fairfax, Sally K., Lauren Gwin, Mary Ann King, Leigh Raymond, and Laura A. Watt, *Buying Nature: The Limits of Land Acquisition as a Conservation Strategy, 1780–2004*, Cambridge, MA: MIT Press, 2005.

Farney, Dennis, "Green Pieces," *Governing*, August 2006, pp. 26–33.

Feller, Wende Vyborney, "Urban Impostures: How Two Neighborhoods Reframed Suburban Sprawl as a New Urbanist Paradise without Changing a Thing," in Matthew J. Lindstrom and Hugh Bartling, eds., *Suburban Sprawl: Culture, Theory, and Politics*, Lanham, MD: Rowman & Littlefield, 2003, pp. 49–63.

Fishman, Robert, "Megalopolis Unbound," *Wilson Quarterly*, Vol. 14, No. 1 (Winter 1990), pp. 25–46.

Fishman, Robert, "The Death and Life of American Regional Planning," in Bruce Katz, ed., *Reflections on Regionalism*, Washington, DC: Brookings Institution, 2000, pp. 107–123.

Foreman, Christopher, *The Promise and Peril of Environmental Justice*, Washington, DC: Brookings Institution, 1998.

Foster, John Bellamy, "The Limits of Environmentalism without Class: Lessons from the Ancient Forest Struggle in the Pacific Northwest," in Daniel Faber, ed., *The Struggle for Ecological Democracy: Environmental Justice Movements in the United States*, New York: Guilford Press, 1998, pp. 188–217.

Foucault, Michel, *Discipline and Punish*, New York: Pantheon Books, 1977.

Frank, Jill, *A Democracy of Distinction: Aristotle and the Work of Politics*, Chicago: University of Chicago Press, 2005.

Franklin, Jerry F., and James K. Agee, "Forging a Science-Based National Forest Fire Policy," *Issues in Science and Technology*, Vol. 20, No. 1 (Fall 2003), pp. 59–66.

Franklin, Jerry F., and Thomas A. Spies, "Characteristics of Old-Growth Douglas-Fir Forests," in *New Forests for a Changing World*, Bethesda, MD: Society of American Foresters, 1984, pp. 328–334.

Franklin, Jerry F., Dean Rae Berg, Dale A. Thornburgh, and John C. Tappeiner, "Alternative Silvicultural Approaches to Timber Harvesting: Variable Harvest Retention Systems," in Kathryn A. Kohm and Jerry F. Franklin, eds., *Creating a Forestry for the Twenty-first Century: The Science of Ecosystem Management*, Washington, DC: Island Press, 1997, pp. 111–139.

"Freedom Center's Pledge of Allegiance" (editorial), *New York Daily News*, July 7, 2005, p. 34.

Frug, Gerald E., *City Making: Building Communities Without Walls*, Princeton, NJ: Princeton University Press, 1999.

Gabe, Thomas, Gene Falk, and Maggie McCarty, *Hurricane Katrina: Social-Demographic Characteristics of Impacted Areas*, Washington, DC: Congressional Research Service, November 4, 2005.

Gans, Herbert, *The Urban Villagers: Group and Class in the Life of Italian-Americans*, New York: Free Press, 1962.

Garrett, Laurie, "Under the Plume: September 11 Produced a New Kind of Pollution, and No One Knows What to Do About It," *American Prospect*, Vol. 13, No. 19 (October 21, 2002), p. 22.

Gerbasi, Gina T., "Athens Farmers' Market: Evolving Dynamics and Hidden Benefits to a Southeast Ohio Rural Community," *Focus on Geography*, Vol. 49, No. 2 (Fall 2006), pp. 1–6.

Gilder, George, *Telecosm: How Infinite Bandwidth Will Revolutionize our World*, New York: Free Press, 2000.

Gillespie, Angus Kress, *Twin Towers: The Life of New York City's World Trade Center*, New Brunswick, NJ: Rutgers University Press, 1999.

Gilligan, Carol, *In A Different Voice*, Cambridge, MA: Harvard University Press, 1982.

Glanz, James, and Eric Lipton, "The Height of Ambition," *New York Times Magazine*, September 8, 2002, pp. 32–44, 59–60, 63.

Glanz, James, and Eric Lipton, *City in the Sky: The Rise and Fall of the World Trade Center*, New York: Henry Holt, 2003.

Goldberger, Paul, *Up From Zero: Politics, Architecture, and the Rebuilding of New York*, New York: Random House, 2004.

Goldberger, Paul, "A New Beginning: Why We Should Build Apartments at Ground Zero," *New Yorker*, May 30, 2005, p. 54.

Goldsmith, Edward, *The Way: An Ecological World-View*, rev. ed., Athens: University of Georgia Press, 1998.

Gonzalez, Juan, "Dust Must Clear on Veil of Deceit," *New York Daily News*, August 19, 2004, p. 18.

Goodwin, Michael, "Rethink Freedom Tower," *New York Daily News*, May 11, 2005, p. 33.

Gordon, Peter, and Harry W. Richardson, "Are Compact Cities a Desirable Planning Goal?", *Journal of the American Planning Association*, Vol. 63, No. 1 (Winter 1997), pp. 95–106.

Gore, Albert, *Earth in the Balance: Ecology and the Human Spirit*, New York: Penguin, 1993.

Gorte, Ross W., *Below-Cost Timber Sales: An Overview*, Washington, DC: Congressional Research Service, 2004.

Gottlieb, Robert, *Forcing the Spring: The Transformation of the American Environmental Movement*, Washington, DC: Island Press, 1993.

Greenpeace International, *Eating Up the Amazon*, Amsterdam: Greenpeace International, 2006 (www.greenpeace.org/international/press/reports?page=2, accessed April 21, 2006).

Griffith, Mark Winston, "How Harlem Eats," *Nation*, Vol. 283, No. 7 (September 11, 2006), pp. 36–38.

Gup, Ted, "Owl vs. Man," *Time*, Vol. 135, No. 26 (June 25, 1990), pp. 56–63 (www.time.com/time/archive, accessed November 6, 2006).

Haberman, Maggie, and Greg Gittrich, "Firefighters Apply Heat at Public Hearing," *New York Daily News*, May 29, 2003, p. 19.

Haberman, Maggie, and Greg Gittrich, "Where the WTC Financing Alters Original Vision," *New York Daily News*, July 20, 2003, p. 13.

Haberman, Maggie, and Greg Gittrich, "Shaky Start Leads to Stronger Foundation," *New York Daily News*, September 11, 2003, p. 21.

Hamilton, Cynthia, "Coping with Industrial Exploitation," in Robert D. Bullard, ed., *Confronting Environmental Racism: Voices from the Grassroots*, Boston: South End Press, 1993, pp. 63–76.

Hanson, Chad, and Carl Pope, "The Sierra Club Replies: Who's Really Radical?", *Christian Science Monitor*, June 13, 1996, p. 19.

Harden, Blaine, "Salvage Logging a Key Issue in Oregon," *Washington Post*, October 15, 2004, p. A4.

Harman, John W., United States General Accounting Office, "Forest Service Needs to Improve Efforts to Reduce Below-Cost Timber Sales," Testimony Before the Subcommittee on Forests, Family Farms, and Energy, Committee on Agriculture, United States House of Representatives, April 25, 1991.

Harner, John, "Place Identity and Copper Mining in Sonora, Mexico," *Annals of the Association of American Geographers*, Vol. 91, No. 4 (December 2001), pp. 660–680.

Harris, David, *The Last Stand: The War Between Wall Street and Main Street over California's Ancient Redwoods*, New York: Times Books, 1995.

Hartmann, Heidi, Robert E. Kraut, and Louise A. Tilly, eds., *Computer Chips and Paper Clips: Technology and Women's Employment*, Washington, DC: National Academy Press, 1986.

Harvey, David, *The Postmodern Condition*, Oxford: Oxford University Press, 1989.

Harvey, David, *Justice, Nature, and the Geography of Difference*, Cambridge, MA: Blackwell, 1996.

Harvey, David, "The New Urbanism and the Communitarian Trap," *Harvard Design Magazine*, No. 1 (Winter/Spring 1997), pp. 68–69.

Harvey, David, *Spaces of Capital: Towards a Critical Geography*, New York: Routledge, 2001.

Harvey, David, "Cracks in the Edifice of the Empire State," in Michael Sorkin and Sharon Zukin, eds., *After the World Trade Center: Rethinking New York City*, New York: Routledge, 2002, pp. 57–67.

Hawthorne, Christopher, "Growing Up: Getting the Ground Zero Memorial Right," *Slate*, Jan. 15, 2004 (www.slate.com, accessed January 10, 2005).

Hayduk, Ronald, "Race and Suburban Sprawl: Regionalism and Structural Racism," in Matthew J. Lindstrom and Hugh Bartling, eds., *Suburban Sprawl: Culture, Theory, and Politics*, Lanham, MD: Rowman & Littlefield, 2003, pp. 137–170.

Hays, Samuel P., *Conservation and the Gospel of Efficiency: The Progressive Conservation Movement 1890–1920*, Cambridge, MA: Harvard University Press, 1959.

Hayward, Steven, "Legends of the Sprawl," *Policy Review*, No. 91 (September–October 1998), pp. 26–32.

Hayward, Steven, "Suburban Legends: The Fight Against Sprawl is Based More on Anti-Suburban Animus Than on Facts," *National Review*, Vol. 51, No. 5 (March 22, 1999), pp. 35–36, 38.

Hazlett, Curt, "Taking Aim at Wal-Mart," *Retail Traffic*, February 1, 2005, p. 33.

Healy, Patrick D., "Pataki Warns Cultural Groups For Museum At Ground Zero," *New York Times*, June 25, 2005, p. B1.

Healy, Patrick D., and William K. Rashbaum, "Security Issues Force a Review at Ground Zero," *New York Times*, May 1, 2005, p. 1.

Heidegger, Martin, "Building Dwelling Thinking," in David Farrell Krell, ed., *Basic Writings*, San Francisco: HarperCollins, 1977, pp. 343–363.

Heidegger, Martin, "The Question Concerning Technology," in David Farrell Krell, ed., *Basic Writings*, San Francisco: HarperCollins, 1977, pp. 311–341.

Heimlich, Ralph E., and William D. Anderson, *Development at the Urban Fringe and Beyond: Impacts on Agriculture and Rural Land*, Washington, DC: U.S. Department of Agriculture/Economic Research Service, 2001.

Helvarg, David, *The War Against the Greens: The "Wise-Use" Movement, the New Right, and the Browning of America*, rev. ed., Boulder, CO: Johnson Books, 2004.

Helvoigt, Ted L., Darius M. Adams, and Art L. Ayre, "Employment Transitions in Oregon's Wood Products Sector During the 1990s," *Journal of Forestry*, Vol. 101, No. 4 (June 2003), pp. 42–46.

Hester, Tom, "Towns May Get Right to Levy Impact Fees," *Newark Star-Ledger*, October 3, 2006 (www.nj.com/news/ledger/jersey/index.ssf?/base/news-4/115985162792400.xml&coll=1, accessed October 22, 2006).

Hibbard, Michael, and Jeremy Madsen, "Environmental Resistance to Place-Based Collaboration in the U.S. West," *Society & Natural Resources*, Vol. 16, No. 8 (September 2003), pp. 703–718.

Hiss, Tony, *The Experience of Place: A New Way of Looking at and Dealing With Our Radically Changing Cities and Countryside*, Random House: New York, 1990.

Hobbs, Frank, and Nicole Stoops, *Demographic Trends in the Twentieth Century*, Washington, DC: U.S. Census Bureau, 2002.

Hodges, Glenn, "Dead Wood: Reform of the U.S. Forest Service," *Washington Monthly*, Vol. 28, No. 10 (October 1996), p. 12.

Honig, Bonnie, *Political Theory and the Displacement of Politics*, Ithaca, NY: Cornell University Press, 1993.

Honig, Bonnie, "Difference, Dilemmas, and the Politics of Home," *Social Research*, Vol. 61, No. 3 (Fall 1994), pp. 563–597.

hooks, bell, *Yearning: Race, Gender, and Cultural Politics*, Boston: South End Press, 1990.

Hooper, Barbara, "Desiring Presence, Romancing the Real," *Annals of the Association of American Geographers*, Vol. 94, No. 4 (December 2001), pp. 703–715.

Hunnicutt, Dave, "Vote Yes: Measure 37 Would Restore Rights and Block New Limits that Destroy Property Land Values," *Oregonian*, October 10, 2004, p. F1.

Hutton, Ernest W., Jr., "A Lot of Loose Ends at Ground Zero," *Newsday*, August 21, 2006, p. A33.

Huxtable, Ada Louise, "No Games With Ground Zero, Please: The Profit Motive Must Yield to the Greater Good," *Wall Street Journal*, July 24, 2003 (www.opinionjournal.com, accessed July 30, 2003).

Institute for Justice, *Legislative Action Since Kelo*, Arlington, VA: Castle Coalition, 2006.

Intergovernmental Panel on Climate Change, *Summary for Policymakers: A Report of Working Group I of the Intergovernmental Panel on Climate Change*, Geneva: World Meteorological Organization and the United Nations Environment Programme, 2001.

"In Two Towns, Main Street Fights Off Wal-Mart," *New York Times*, October 21, 1993, p. A16.

Jackson, Kenneth T., *Crabgrass Frontier: The Suburbanization of the United States*, New York: Oxford University Press, 1987.

Jacobs, Jane, *The Death and Life of Great American Cities*, New York: Random House, 1992 (1961).

Jeffery, N. L., C. D'Andrea, J. Leighton, S. E. Rodenbeck, L. Wilder, D. DeVoney, et al., "Potential Exposures to Airborne and Settled Surface Dust in Residential Areas of Lower Manhattan Following the Collapse of the World Trade Center—New York City, November 4–December 11, 2001," *Morbidity & Mortality Weekly Report*, Vol. 52, No. 7 (February 21, 2003), pp. 131–136.

Jehl, Douglas, "In Idaho, a Howl Against Roadless Forests," *New York Times*, July 5, 2000, p. A10.

Jehl, Douglas, "Road Ban Set for One-third of U.S. Forests," *New York Times*, January 5, 2001, p. A1.

Jehl, Douglas, "Clinton Forest Chief Acts to Stop Logging of the Oldest Trees," *New York Times*, January 9, 2001, p. A1.

Johnson, Kirk, "Uncertainty Lingers Over Air Pollution in Days After 9/11," *New York Times*, September 7, 2003, p. 39.

Johnson, Kirk, and Jennifer 8. Lee, "When Breathing is Believing," *New York Times*, November 30, 2003, p. 37.

Joselit, Jenna Weisman, "Above and Below," *New Republic*, May 27, 2002, pp. 35–37.

Kanter, Rosabeth Moss, "Business Coalitions as a Force for Regionalism," in Bruce Katz, ed., *Reflections on Regionalism*, Washington, DC: Brookings Institution, 2000, pp. 154–181.

Kaplan, Fred, "Concerns Intensify on Ground Zero Dust," *Boston Globe*, February 12, 2002, p. A1.

Katz, Alyssa, "Toxic Haste; New York's Media Rush to Judgment on New York's Air" *American Prospect*, Vol. 13, No. 4 (February 25, 2002), p. 13.

Katz, Bruce, ed., *Reflections on Regionalism*, Washington, DC: Brookings Institution, 2000.

Katz, Peter, ed., *The New Urbanism: Toward an Architecture of Community*, New York: McGraw-Hill, 1994.

Kelbaugh, Douglas S., *Repairing the American Metropolis: Common Place Revisited*, Seattle: University of Washington, 2002.

Kemmis, Daniel, "Community and the Politics of Place," in Philip D. Brick and R. McGreggor Cawley, eds., *A Wolf in the Garden: The Land Rights Movement and the New Environmental Debate*, Lanham, MD: Rowman & Littlefield, 1996, pp. 235–248.

KenCairn, Brett, "Peril on Common Ground: The Applegate Experiment," in Philip D. Brick and R. McGreggor Cawley, eds., *A Wolf in the Garden: The Land Rights Movement and the New Environmental Debate*, Lanham, MD: Rowman & Littlefield, 1996, pp. 261–277.

Kilborn, Peter T., "The Five-Bedroom, Six-Figure Rootless Life," *New York Times*, June 1, 2005, p. A1.

Kitzhaber, John A., "Principles and Politics of Sustainable Forestry in the Pacific Northwest: Charting a New Course," in Karen Arabas and Joe Bowersox, eds., *Forest Futures: Science, Politics, and Policy for the Next Century*, Lanham, MD: Rowman & Littlefield, 2004, pp. 223–236.

Knize, Perri, "The Mismanagement of the National Forests," *Atlantic Monthly*, Vol. 268, No. 4 (October 1991), pp. 98–112.

Knopman, Debra S., Megan M. Susman, and Marc K. Landy, "Civic Environmentalism: Tackling Tough Land-Use Problems with Innovative Governance," *Environment*, Vol. 41, No. 10 (December 1999), pp. 24–32.

Koffman, Ted, "Even in Maine?", *Environment*, Vol. 41, No. 4 (May 1999), p. 30.

Kohn, Margaret, *Brave New Neighborhoods: The Privatization of Public Space*, New York: Routledge, 2004.

Kolker, Robert, "The Grief Police," *New York Magazine*, November 28, 2005 (www.newyorkmetro.com, accessed January 4, 2006).

Kotkin, Joel, "Get Used to It: Suburbia's Not Going Away, No Matter What Critics Say or Do," *American Enterprise*, January/February, 2005, pp. 32–37.

Kotkin, Joel, "Suburban Tide," *Blueprint*, March 15, 2005, pp. 22–24.

Kotkin, Joel, "Will Great Cities Survive?", *Wilson Quarterly*, Vol. 29, No. 2 (Spring 2005), pp. 16–27.

Kummer, Corby, "Good-bye, Cryovac," *Atlantic*, Vol. 294, No. 3 (October 2004), pp. 197–202.

Kunstler, James Howard, *The Geography of Nowhere: The Rise and Decline of America's Man-Made Landscape*, New York: Simon & Schuster, 1993.

Kunstler, James Howard, "Home from Nowhere," *Atlantic Monthly*, Vol. 278, No. 3 (September 1996), pp. 43–66.

Kusel, Jonathan, "Ethnographic Analysis of Three Forest Communities in California," in *Well-Being in Forest-Dependent Communities*, Vol. 2, Sacramento: California Department of Forestry, Forest and Rangeland Assessment Program, 1991.

Kusel, Jonathan, "Assessing Well-Being in Forest-Dependent Communities," in Linda E. Kruger, ed., *Understanding Community-Forest Relations*, Portland, OR: U.S. Department of Agriculture, Forest Service, Pacific Northwest Research Station, 2003, pp. 81–103.

Kusel, Jonathan, *Community Forestry in the United States: Learning from the Past, Crafting the Future*, Washington, DC: Island Press, 2003, pp. 125–126.

Landrigan, Philip J., "The WTC Disaster: Landrigan's Response," *Environmental Health Perspectives*, Vol. 112, No. 11 (August 2004), p. A607.

Landrigan, Philip J., Paul J. Lioy, George Thurston, Gertrud Berkowitz, L. C. Chen, Steven N. Chillrud, et al., "Health and Environmental Consequences of the World Trade Center Disaster," *Environmental Health Perspectives*, Vol. 112, No. 6 (May 2004), pp. 731–739.

Langston, Nancy, "Forest Dreams, Forest Nightmares: Environmental History of a Forest Health Crisis," in Char Miller, ed., *American Forests: Nature, Culture, and Politics*, Lawrence: University Press of Kansas, 1997, pp. 247–271.

Lapping, Mark B., "Toward the Recovery of the Local in the Globalizing Food System: The Role of Alternative Agricultural and Food Models in the US," *Ethics, Place & Environment*, Vol. 7, No. 3 (October 2004), pp. 141–150.

Larabee, Mark, "'Live' Tree Dispute Kills Logging Plan," *Oregonian*, December 11, 2004, p. B1.

Lau, Edie, and Chris Bowman, "N.Y. Air Hazards Found," *Sacramento Bee*, February 12, 2002, p. A1.

Layzer, Judith A., *The Environmental Case: Translating Values into Policy*, 1st ed., Washington, DC: CQ Press, 2002.

Layzer, Judith A., *The Environmental Case: Translating Values into Policy*, 2nd ed., Washington, DC: CQ Press, 2006.

Lederman, Sally Ann, Virginia Rauh, Lisa Weiss, Janet L. Stein, Lori A. Hoepner, Mark Becker, et al., "The Effects of the World Trade Center Event on Birth Outcomes among Term Deliveries at Three Lower Manhattan Hospitals," *Environmental Health Perspectives*, Vol. 112, No. 17 (December 2004), pp. 1772–1778.

Lefebvre, Henri, *The Production of Space*, Donald Nicholson-Smith, trans., Oxford, UK: Blackwell, 1991 (1974).

Leopold, Aldo, *A Sand County Almanac*, New York: Oxford University Press, 1949.

Levin, S. M., R. Herbert, J. M. Moline, A. C. Todd, L. Stevenson, P. Landsbergis, et al., "Physical Health Status of World Trade Center Rescue and Recovery Workers and Volunteers—New York City, July 2002–August 2004," *Morbidity & Mortality Weekly Report*, Vol. 53, No. 35 (September 10, 2004), pp. 807–812.

Lewis, Daniel, "The Trailblazer," *New York Times Magazine*, June 13, 1999, pp. 50–53.

Lewis, Peirce F., *New Orleans: The Making of an Urban Landscape*, Santa Fe, NM: Center for American Places, 2003.

Lewis, Roger K., "Comprehensive Plan Needed in Growth Management," *Washington Post*, November 14, 1998, p. E1.

Limerick, Patricia Nelson, *The Legacy of Conquest: The Unbroken Past of the American West*, New York: W.W. Norton, 1987.

Lindstrom, Matthew J., and Hugh Bartling, eds., *Suburban Sprawl: Culture, Theory, and Politics*, Lanham, MD: Rowman & Littlefield, 2003.

Lindstrom, Matthew J., and Hugh Bartling, "Introduction," in Matthew J. Lindstrom and Hugh Bartling, eds., *Suburban Sprawl: Culture, Theory, and Politics*, Lanham, MD: Rowman & Littlefield, 2003, pp. xi–xxvii.

Lioy, Paul J., Clifford P. Weisel, James R. Millette, Steven Eisenreich, Daniel Vallero, John Offenberg, et al., "Characterization of the Dust/Smoke Aerosol that Settled East of the World Trade Center (WTC) in Lower Manhattan after the Collapse of the WTC 11 September 2001," *Environmental Health Perspectives*, Vol. 110, No. 7 (July 2002), pp. 703–714.

Lipsher, Steve, "Forest Service Centennial: Many Uses, Many Struggles Nurtured Nature," *Denver Post*, October 2, 2005, p. A1.

Locke, John, *Second Treatise of Government*, C. B. Macpherson, ed., Indianapolis: Hackett Publishing, 1980 (1690).

Logan, John, and Harvey Molotch, *Urban Fortunes: The Political Economy of Place*, Berkeley: University of California Press, 1988.

Lohr, Steve, "POP?: Real Estate, the Global Obsession," *New York Times*, June 12, 2005 (section 4) p. 1.

Lombino, David, "Office Rents Soar in Manhattan as Vacancies Plunge," *New York Sun*, October 5, 2006, p. 1.

Lopez, Barry, *About This Life: Journeys on the Threshold of Memory*, New York: Knopf, 1998.

Lotus Development Corporation, "Conversations with Industry Innovators: Esther Dyson Interview," February, 1999 (www.lotus.com/home.nsf/welcome/interviews, accessed March 20, 1999).

Low, Nicholas, Brendan Gleeson, Ray Green, and Darko Radovic, *The Green City: Sustainable Homes, Sustainable Suburbs*, London: Routledge, 2005.

Low, Setha M., "Spaces of Reflection, Recovery, and Resistance: Reimagining the Postindustrial Plaza," in Michael Sorkin and Sharon Zukin, eds., *After the World Trade Center: Rethinking New York City*, New York: Routledge, 2002, pp. 163–171.

Lower Manhattan Development Corporation, *World Trade Center Memorial and Redevelopment Plan: Draft Generic Environmental Impact Statement*, New York: LMDC, January 2004.

Lower Manhattan Development Corporation, *World Trade Center Memorial and Redevelopment Plan: Environmental Assessment for Proposed Further Refinements to the Approved Plan*, New York: Lower Manhattan Development Corporation, September 2006.

Lower Manhattan Development Corporation and the Port Authority of New York and New Jersey, *The Public Dialogue: Innovative Design Study*, New York: LMDC/PANYNJ, February 27, 2003.

Lowry, William R., "A Return to Traditional Priorities in Natural Resource Policies," in Michael E. Kraft and Norman J. Vig, eds., *Environmental Policy: New Directions for the Twenty-first Century*, 6th ed., Washington, DC: CQ Press, 2005, pp. 311–332.

Lucht, Beth, "Betting the Farm on Local Markets," *Progressive*, Vol. 70, No. 4 (April 2006), p. 35.

Luke, Timothy W., "Governmentality and Contragovernmentality: Rethinking Sovereignty and Territoriality After the Cold War," *Political Geography*, Vol. 15, No. 6/7 (1996), pp. 491–507.

Luke, Timothy W., *Ecocritique: Contesting the Politics of Nature, Economy, and Culture*, Minneapolis: University of Minnesota Press, 1997.

Luke, Timothy W., *Capitalism, Democracy, and Ecology: Departing from Marx*, Urbana: University of Illinois Press, 1999.

Luo, Michael, "Now a Message from a Sponsor of the Subway?" *New York Times*, July 27, 2004, p. A1.

Lyman, Francesca, "Twelve Gates to the City," *Sierra*, Vol. 82, No. 3 (May/June 1997), pp. 28–35.

Lyman, Francesca, "Messages in the Dust: Lessons Learned, Post-9/11, for Environmental Health," *Journal of Environmental Health*, Vol. 66, No. 5 (December 2003), pp. 30–37.

Lynch, Barbara Deutsch, "The Garden and the Sea: U.S. Latino Environmental Discourses and Mainstream Environmentalism," *Social Problems*, Vol. 40, No. 1 (February 1993), pp. 108–124.

Machiavelli, Niccolò, *Discourses on Livy*, Bernard Crick, ed., New York: Viking Press, 1985.

Machiavelli, Niccolò, *The Prince*, Harvey C. Mansfield, trans., Chicago: University of Chicago Press, 1998.

MacIntyre, Alasdair, *After Virtue*, 2nd ed., Notre Dame, IN: University of Notre Dame Press, 1984.

Mahler, Jonathan, "The Bloomberg Vista," *New York Times Magazine*, September 10, 2006, pp. 66–87.

Manes, Christopher, *Green Rage: Radical Environmentalism and the Unmaking of Civilization*, Boston: Little, Brown, 1990.

Marcuse, Peter, "On the Global Uses of September 11 and Its Urban Impact," in Stanley Aronowitz and Heather Gautney, eds., *Implicating Empire: Globalization and Resistance in the Twenty-first Century*, New York: Basic Books, 2003, pp. 271–285.

Marks, Alexandra, "Chaos to Condos: Lower Manhattan's Rebirth," *Christian Science Monitor*, May 19, 2005, p. 3.

Marshall, Alex, "Putting Some 'City' Back in the Suburbs," *Washington Post*, September 1, 1996, p. C1.

Marshall, Alex, "When the New Urbanism Meets the Old Neighborhood," *Metropolis*, May 1995 (www.alexmarshall.org, accessed July 8, 2003).

Marston, Ed., "The Quincy Library Group: A Divisive Attempt at Peace," in Philip D. Brick, Donald Snow, and Sarah Van De Wetering, *Across the Great Divide: Explorations in Collaborative Conservation and the American West*, Washington, DC: Island Press, 2001, pp. 79–90.

Martin, Glen, "New Sales Reignite Timber Battles," *San Francisco Chronicle*, December 13, 2004, p. A1.

Marx, Karl, "The Economic and Philosophic Manuscripts of 1844," in Robert C. Tucker, ed., *The Marx-Engels Reader*, 2nd ed., New York: W.W. Norton, 1978, pp. 66–125.

Marzulla, Nancie G., "Property Rights Movement: How it Began and Where it is Headed," in Philip D. Brick and R. McGreggor Cawley, eds., *A Wolf in the Garden: The Land Rights Movement and the New Environmental Debate*, Lanham, MD: Rowman & Littlefield, 1996, pp. 39–58.

Massey, Doreen, *Space, Place, and Gender*, Minneapolis: University of Minnesota Press, 1994.

Massey, Doreen, "Spaces of Politics," in Doreen Massey, John Allen, and Philip Sarre, *Human Geography Today*, Cambridge, UK: Polity Press, 1999, pp. 279–294.

Massey, Doreen, John Allen, and Philip Sarre, eds., *Human Geography Today*, Cambridge, UK: Polity Press, 1999.

Mattei, Suzanne, *Pollution and Deception at Ground Zero*, New York: Sierra Club, August 2004, p. 73.

McCarthy, Kevin, D. J. Peterson, Narayan Sastry, and Michael Pollard, *The Repopulation of New Orleans After Hurricane Katrina*, Santa Monica, CA: RAND Corporation, 2006.

McCarthy, Sheryl, "Politics and Fear Sank the Freedom Center," *Newsday*, October 3, 2005, p. A36.

McCloskey, Mary A., *Kant's Aesthetic*, Albany: State University of New York Press, 1987.

McCloskey, Michael, "The Skeptic: Collaboration Has its Limits," *High Country News*, Vol. 28, No. 9 (May 13, 1996), p. 7.

McCoy, Charles, "Cut Down: Timber Town is Bitter Over Efforts to Save the Rare Spotted Owl," *Wall Street Journal*, January 6, 1992, p. A1.

McGeehan, Patrick, "Employees Say No to Working in Freedom Tower," *New York Times*, September 19, 2006, p. B1.

McKibben, Bill, "What Good Is a Forest?" *Audubon*, Vol. 98, No. 3 (May 1996), pp. 54–63.

McQuillan, Jessie, "Thinning the Ranks," *Missoula Independent*, Vol. 17, No. 38 (June 15, 2006) (www.missoulanews.com/Archives/News.asp?no=5778, accessed September 3, 2006).

"Measure 37 'Snag' Reveals the True Game" (editorial), *Oregonian*, April 3, 2006, p. C6.

Meissner, James K., *Forest Service: Factors Affecting Bids on Timber Sales* (GAO/RCED-97-175R), Washington, DC: U.S. General Accounting Office, 1997.

Messia, Robert, "Lawns as Artifacts: The Evolution of Social and Environmental Implications of Suburban Residential Land Use," in Matthew J. Lindstrom and Hugh Bartling, eds., *Suburban Sprawl: Culture, Theory, and Politics*, Lanham, MD: Rowman & Littlefield, 2003, pp. 69–83.

Meyer, John M., *Political Nature: Environmentalism and the Interpretation of Western Thought*, Cambridge, MA: MIT Press, 2001.

Miller, John, "Property-Rights Measures on Ballot in 4 Western States," *Salt Lake Tribune*, October 16, 2006 (www.sltrib.com/news/ci_4499162, accessed October 16, 2006).

Mill, John Stuart, "Nature," in *Three Essays on Religion: Nature, the Utility of Religion, Theism*, Amherst, NY: Prometheus Books, 1998 (1874), pp. 3–68.

Milstein, Michael, "Bush Ready to Reshape Federal Forests," *Oregonian*, November 18, 2004, p. A1.

Milstein, Michael, "Biscuit Log Sales Fall Short of Forecast," *Oregonian*, November 23, 2004, p. A1.

Milstein, Michael, "Forest Work Put on Hold after Bush Rule Gets Ax," *Oregonian*, September 30, 2005, p. C1.

Milstein, Sarah, "Creating A Market," *Mother Earth News*, No. 172 (February/March 1999), pp. 40–44, 112.

Minium, Harry, "Homearama Headed for Norfolk in 2004," *Virginian-Pilot*, October 19, 2003.

Moe, Richard, and Carter Wilkie, *Changing Places: Rebuilding Community in the Age of Sprawl*, New York: Henry Holt, 1997.

Moehringer, J. R., *The Tender Bar: A Memoir*, New York: Hyperion Books, 2005.

Mollenkopf, John, *The Contested City*, Princeton, NJ: Princeton University Press, 1983.

Moseley, Cassandra, "Community Participation and Institutional Change: The Applegate Partnership and Federal Land Management in Southwest Oregon," paper presented at the Annual Meeting of the Western Political Science Association (San Jose, CA, March 24–26, 2000).

Moseley, Cassandra, "The Applegate Partnership: Innovation in Crisis," in Philip D. Brick, Donald Snow, and Sarah Van De Wetering, eds., *Across the Great Divide: Explorations in Collaborative Conservation and the American West*, Washington, DC: Island Press, 2001, pp. 102–111.

Moseley, Cassandra, and Stacey Shankle, "Who Gets the Work? National Forest Contracting in the Pacific Northwest," *Journal of Forestry*, Vol. 99, No. 9 (September 2001), pp. 32–37.

Moss, Mitchell, "Tracking the Net: Using Domain Names to Measure the Growth of the Internet in U.S. Cities," *Journal of Urban Technology*, Vol. 4, No. 3 (December 1997) (www.mitchellmoss.com/articles/tracking.html, accessed April 16, 2006).

Mulrine, Anna, "The Long Road Back," *U.S. News & World Report*, February 27, 2006, pp. 44–50, 52–58.

Mumford, Lewis, *The City in History: Its Origins, Its Transformations, and Its Prospects*, New York: Harcourt, Brace & World, 1961.

Murphy, Kim, "Differing Values Cut Through Timber Debate," *Los Angeles Times*, April 15, 1996, p. A1.

Muschamp, Herbert, "Rich Firms, Poor Ideas for Towers Site," *New York Times*, April 18, 2002, p. E1.

Muschamp, Herbert, "The New Ground Zero: ... With a Dubious Idea of 'Freedom'," *New York Times*, August 31, 2003 (Arts and Leisure section), p. 1.

Nabhan, Gary Paul, "Cultural Parallax in Viewing North American Habitats," Michael E. Soulé and Gary Lease, eds., *Reinventing Nature?: Responses to Postmodern Deconstruction*, Washington, DC: Island Press, 1995, pp. 87–101.

Nappier, Sharon, *Lost in the Forest: How the Forest Service's Misdirection, Mismanagement, and Mischief Squanders Your Tax Dollars*, Washington, DC: Taxpayers for Common Sense, 2002.

Nash, Roderick, *Wilderness and the American Mind*, 3rd ed., New Haven, CT: Yale University Press, 1982.

National Institute of Standards and Technology, *Final Report on the Collapse of the World Trade Center Towers*, Washington, DC: U.S. Department of Commerce, September 2005.

Natural Resources Conservation Service, *Natural Resources Inventory: Highlights*, Washington, DC: U.S. Department of Agriculture, January 2001.

Negroponte, Nicholas, *Being Digital*, New York: Vintage Press, 1995.

Nelson, Arthur C., and Mitch Moody, *Paying for Prosperity: Impact Fees and Job Growth*, Washington, DC: Brookings Institution, 2003.

Nelson, Robert R., "Tourism as a Catalyst for Local Economic Development," Department of Hotel, Restaurant and Institutional Management, University of Delaware, May 2005 (www.chep.udel.edu/directions/articles/may05/tourism.html, accessed February 17, 2006).

Newbury, Umut, and Megan Phelps, "Join the Real Food Revival!", *Mother Earth News*, No. 211 (August/September 2005), pp. 40–46.

New York City Department of City Planning, "Community District Profiles: Manhattan Community District 1" (www.nyc.gov/html/dcp/pdf/lucds/mn1profile.pdf, accessed January 4, 2005).

Nobel, Philip, "The New Ground Zero: The Downtown Culture Derby Begins ...," *New York Times*, August 31, 2003 (Arts and Leisure section), p. 1.

Nobel, Philip, *Sixteen Acres: Architecture and the Outrageous Struggle for the Future of Ground Zero*, New York: Henry Holt, 2005.

Nossiter, Adam, "New Orleans Population is Reduced Nearly 60%," *New York Times*, October 7, 2006, p. A9.

O'Clery, Conor, "9/11 Two Years On," *Irish Times*, September 6, 2003, p. 50.

Oelschlaeger, Max, *The Idea of Wilderness: From Prehistory to the Age of Ecology*, New Haven, CT: Yale University Press, 1991.

Oppenheimer, Laura, "As Landscape Shifts, Oregon Struggles to Protect Farmland," *Oregonian*, May 31, 2005, p. A1.

Oppenheimer, Laura, "Measure 37 Question: Is Land-Use Law Usable?", *Oregonian*, March 26, 2006, p. B1.

Oregon Small Woodlands Association, "Policy Statement" (www.oswa.org/policystatement1992.pdf, accessed May 26, 2006).

"Oregon Timber Towns Enjoying Renaissance; As Owl Debate Fades, Booming Economy Adds Jobs," *Chicago Tribune*, October 17, 1994, p. 6.

Orr, David W., *The Nature of Design: Ecology, Culture, and Human Intention*, Oxford: Oxford University Press, 2004.

Ostrom, Elinor, *Governing the Commons: The Evolution of Institutions for Collective Action*, Cambridge, UK: Cambridge University Press, 1990.

Ouroussoff, Nicolai, "For Freedom Tower and Ground Zero, Disarray Reigns, and an Opportunity Awaits," *New York Times*, May 2, 2005, p. E1.

Ouroussoff, Nicolai, "For the Ground Zero Memorial, Death by Committee," *New York Times*, June 19, 2005 (Arts and Leisure section), p. 1.

Ouroussoff, Nicolai, "A Tower of Impregnability, The Sort Politicians Love," *New York Times*, June 30, 2005, p. B1.

Ouroussoff, Nicolai, "Outgrowing Jane Jacobs and Her New York," *New York Times*, April 30, 2006 (Week in Review), p. 1.

Paehlke, Robert, "Environmental Sustainability and Urban Life in America," in Norman Vig and Michael E. Kraft, eds., *Environmental Policy: New Directions for the Twenty-first Century*, Washington, DC: CQ Press, 2002, pp. 57–77.

Penton, Kevin, "They're on Weed Patrol for an Urban Garden Project," *Boston Globe*, July 11, 1999 (City Weekly section), p. 1.

Perry, David A., "Ecological Realities of the Northwest Forest Plan," in Karen Arabas and Joe Bowersox, eds., *Forest Futures: Science, Politics, and Policy for the Next Century*, Lanham, MD: Rowman & Littlefield, 2004, pp. 23–47.

Peterson, Brenda, "Saving the Roots of Our Family Trees," *Seattle Times*, July 7, 1996, p. B5.

Peterson, Paul E., *City Limits*, Chicago: University of Chicago Press, 1981.

Piazza, Tom, *Why New Orleans Matters*, New York: HarperCollins, 2005.

Piore, Michael J., and Charles F. Sabel, *The Second Industrial Divide: Possibilities for Prosperity*, New York: Basic Books, 1984.

Pitkin, Hanna Fenichel, "Justice: On Relating Private and Public," *Political Theory*, Vol. 9, No. 3 (August 1981), pp. 327–352.

Plumwood, Val, "Nature, Self, and Gender: Feminism, Environmental Philosophy, and the Critique of Rationalism," in Michael Zimmerman, J. Baird Callicott, George Sessions, Karen J. Warren, and John Clark, eds., *Environmental Philosophy: From Animal Rights to Radical Ecology*, 1st ed., Englewood Cliffs, NJ: Prentice Hall, 1993, pp. 284–309.

Pogrebin, Robin, "The Incredible Shrinking Daniel Libeskind," *New York Times*, June 20, 2004 (Arts and Leisure section), pp. 1, 32–33.

Pogrebin, Robin, "Is Culture Gone at Ground Zero?" *New York Times*, September 30, 2005, p. E33.

Polakow-Suransky, Sasha, "The Invisible Victims: Undocumented Workers at the World Trade Center," *American Prospect*, Vol. 12, No. 21 (December 3, 2001) (www.prospect.org/print/V12/21/polakow-suransky-s.html, accessed December 2, 2005).

Polanyi, Karl, *The Great Transformation: The Political and Economic Origins of Our Time*, Boston: Beacon Press, 1957 (1944).

"Politics May Doom New Orleans" (editorial), *San Francisco Chronicle*, August 25, 2006, p. B10.

Pollan, Michael, *Second Nature: A Gardener's Education*, New York: Bantam, 1991.

Popper, Frank J., "Siting LULUs," *Planning*, Vol. 47, No. 4 (April 1981), pp. 12–15.

powell, john a., "Addressing Regional Dilemmas for Minority Communities," in Bruce Katz, ed., *Reflections on Regionalism*, Washington, DC: Brookings Institution, 2000, pp. 218–245.

Pratt, Geraldine, "Geographies of Identity and Difference: Marking Boundaries," in Doreen Massey, John Allen, and Philip Sarre, eds., *Human Geography Today*, Cambridge, UK: Polity Press, 1999, pp. 151–167.

Pred, Allan, "Place as Historically Contingent Process: Structuration and the Time-Geography of Becoming Places," *Annals of the Association of American Geographers*, Vol. 74, No. 2 (June 1984), pp. 279–297.

"Preservation: Slowing the Development: Migration Pits Rural Assets, Growth," *The Detroit News*, March 15, 1998 (www.detnews.com/1998/metrox/suburbs/1migrate/1migrate.htm, dead link).

Proctor, James D., "Whose Nature? The Contested Moral Terrain of Ancient Forests," in William Cronon, ed., *Uncommon Ground: Toward Reinventing Nature*, New York: W.W. Norton, 1995, pp. 269–297.

"Q & A With Madelyn Wils, Chair, Community Board 1," LowerManhattan.info, September 9, 2002 (www.lowermanhattan.info/news/q___a_55197.asp, accessed July 15, 2004).

"Quincy Library Bill No Solution," *The Wilderness Society: Conservation Coast to Coast*, October 1998 (www.wilderness.org/ccc/california/quincy.html, dead link).

Rauber, Paul, "Cultivating our Cities," *Sierra*, Vol. 82, No. 3 (May/June 1997), pp. 19–21.

Ray, Dixie Lee, and Lou Gozzo, *Environmental Overkill: Whatever Happened to Common Sense?*, Washington, DC: Regnery, 1993.

Rayne, Sierra, "Using Exterior Building Surface Films to Assess Human Exposure and Health Risks From PCDD/Fs in New York City, USA, After the World Trade Center Attacks," *Journal of Hazardous Materials*, Vol. 127, Nos. 1–3 (December 2005), pp. 33–39.

Rees, Amanda, "New Urbanism: Visionary Landscapes in the Twenty-First Century," in Matthew J. Lindstrom and Hugh Bartling, eds., *Suburban Sprawl: Culture, Theory, and Politics*, Lanham, MD: Rowman & Littlefield, 2003, pp. 93–114.

"Rethinking Ground Zero" (editorial), *New York Times*, April 24, 2005, p. 11.

Richmond, Henry R., "Metropolitan Land-Use Reform: The Promise and Challenge of Majority Consensus," in Bruce Katz, ed., *Reflections on Regionalism*, Washington, DC: Brookings Institution, 2000, pp. 9–39.

Rinehart, James R., and Jeffrey J. Pompe, "The Lucas Case and the Conflict over Property Rights," in Bruce Yandle, ed., *Land Rights: The 1990s' Property Rights Rebellion*, Lanham, MD: Rowman and Littlefield, 1995, pp. 67–101.

Ringquist, Evan J., "Environmental Justice: Normative Concerns, Empirical Evidence, and Government Action," in Norman Vig and Michael E. Kraft, eds., *Environmental Policy: New Directions for the Twenty-first Century*, 6th ed. Washington, DC: CQ Press, 2005, pp. 232–256.

Ring, Ray, "Taking Liberties," *High Country News*, Vol. 38, No. 13 (July 24, 2006), pp. 8–14.

Risen, Clay, "Memories of Overdevelopment," *New Republic*, February 23, 2004, pp. 26–32.

Risen, Clay "Building Model," *New Republic*, October 3, 2005, pp. 18–20.

Robbins, Leslie Teach, "Pass the Peas Please," *State Legislatures*, Vol. 31, No. 5 (May 2005), pp. 30–31.

Roberts, Paul, "The Federal Chain-Saw Massacre: Clinton's Forest Service and Clear-Cut Corruption," *Harper's*, Vol. 294, No. 1765 (June 1997), pp. 37–51.

Roig-Franzia, Manuel, "A City Fears for Its Soul: New Orleans Worries That Its Unique Culture May Be Lost," *Washington Post*, February 3, 2006, p. A1.

Rolle, Su, *Measures of Progress for Collaboration: Case Study of the Applegate Partnership*, Portland, OR: U.S. Department of Agriculture, Forest Service, Pacific Northwest Research Station, 2002.

Ross, Andrew, "The Odor of Publicity," in Michael Sorkin and Sharon Zukin, eds., *After the World Trade Center: Rethinking New York City*, New York: Routledge, 2002, pp. 121–130.

Ross, Stan, "The State of Real Estate: Consolidation and Globalization in the Industry," *Marshall Magazine* (University of Southern California/Marshall School of Business), Summer 2001, pp. 33–37.

Rousseau, Jean-Jacques, *On the Social Contract*, Roger D. Masters, ed. and Judith R. Masters, trans., New York: St. Martin's Press, 1978 (1762).

Rusk, David, "Growth Management: The Core Regional Issue," in Bruce Katz, ed., *Reflections on Regionalism*, Washington, DC: Brookings Institution, 2000, pp. 78–106.

Ryckman, Lisa Levitt, "Last, Best Wild Land," *Rocky Mountain News*, December 15, 1996, p. 30A.

Sack, Robert David, *Homo Geographicus: A Framework for Action, Awareness, and Moral Concern*, Baltimore, MD: Johns Hopkins University Press, 1997.

"Sacred Ground," *Frontline*, produced by Nick Rosen, PBS, September 7, 2004.

Sagoff, Mark, "Settling America: The Concept of Place in Environmental Politics," in Philip D. Brick and R. McGreggor Cawley, eds., *A Wolf in the Garden: The Land Rights Movement and the New Environmental Debate*, Lanham, MD: Rowman & Littlefield, 1996, pp. 249–260.

Sale, Kirkpatrick, *Dwellers in the Land: The Bioregional Vision*, San Francisco: Sierra Club Books, 1985.

Salkin, Patricia E., "Smart Growth and the Law," in Matthew J. Lindstrom and Hugh Bartling, eds., *Suburban Sprawl: Culture, Theory, and Politics*, Lanham, MD: Rowman & Littlefield, 2003, pp. 213–234.

Sandel, Michael J., *Liberalism and the Limits of Justice*, Cambridge, UK: Cambridge University Press, 1982.

Sandel, Michael J., *Democracy's Discontent: America in Search of a Public Philosophy*, Cambridge, MA: Harvard University Press, 1996.

Santora, Marc, "Study Finds Lack of Data On 9/11 Dust," *New York Times*, September 8, 2004, p. B1.

Sassen, Saskia, *The Global City: New York, London, Tokyo*, Princeton, NJ: Princeton University Press, 1991.

Satterfield, Theresa, "Pawns, Victims, or Heroes: The Negotiation of Stigma and the Plight of Oregon's Loggers," *Journal of Social Issues*, Vol. 52, No. 1 (Spring 1996), pp. 71–83.

Savage, Lydia, and Mark Lapping, "Sprawl and Its Discontents: The Rural Dimension," in Matthew J. Lindstrom and Hugh Bartling, eds., *Suburban Sprawl: Culture, Theory, and Politics*, Lanham, MD: Rowman & Littlefield, 2003, pp. 5–17.

Schama, Simon, *Landscape and Memory*, New York: Random House, 1995.

Schlosberg, David, *Environmental Justice and the New Pluralism: The Challenge of Difference*, Oxford, UK: Oxford University Press, 1999.

Schneider, Andrew, "N.Y. Officials Underestimate Danger," *St. Louis Post-Dispatch*, January 13, 2002, p. A1.

Schneider, Andrew, "Public was Never Told that Dust from Ruins is Caustic," *St. Louis Post-Dispatch*, February 10, 2002, p. A1.

Schneider, Keith, "Logging Policy Splits Membership of Sierra Club," *New York Times*, December 26, 1993, p. 20.

Schumpeter, Joseph, *Capitalism, Socialism, and Democracy*, New York: Harper, 1975 (1942).

Sclar, Elliot D., "Back to the City," *Technology Review*, August/September 1992, pp. 29–33.

Scott, James C., *Seeing Like a State: How Certain Schemes to Improve the Human Condition Have Failed*, New Haven, CT: Yale University Press, 1998.

Sedjo, Roger A., "Forest Service Vision: or, Does the Forest Service Have a Future?", Resources for the Future Discussion Paper 99-03, Washington, DC: Resources for the Future, 1998.

Seideman, David, "Out of the Woods; Oregon Economy Is Reborn after Environmental Movement Reduces Logging Industry," *Audubon*, Vol. 98, No. 4 (July 1996), pp. 66–75.

Sennett, Richard, *The Corrosion of Character: The Personal Consequences of Work in the New Capitalism*, New York: W.W. Norton, 1998.

Shannon, Margaret A., "The Northwest Forest Plan as a Learning Process: A Call for New Institutions Bridging Science and Politics," in Karen Arabas and Joe Bowersox, eds., *Forest Futures: Science, Politics, and Policy for the Next Century*, Lanham, MD: Rowman & Littlefield, 2004, pp. 256–279.

Shartin, Emily, "Malls, Alfresco," *Boston Globe*, August 4, 2005 (www.boston.com/news/local/articles/2005/08/04/malls_alfresco/?page=full, accessed October 2, 2006).

Shephard, Michelle, and Scott Simmie, "A Breath of Dust-Filled Air," *Toronto Star*, September 11, 2002, p. B7.

Shiva, Vandana, *Biopiracy: The Plunder of Nature*, Boston: South End Press, 1997.

Short, John Rennie, *Global Dimensions: Space, Place, and the Contemporary World*, London: Reaktion Books, 2001.

Shutkin, William, *The Land That Could Be: Environmentalism and Democracy in the Twenty-first Century*, Cambridge, MA: MIT Press, 2000.

Slosser, Nicholas C., James R. Strittholt, Dominick A. DellaSala, and John Wilson, "The Landscape Context in Forest Conservation: Integrating Protection, Restoration, and Certification," *Ecological Restoration*, Vol. 23, No. 1 (March 2005), pp. 15–23.

Smith, Kimberly K., *Wendell Berry and the Agrarian Tradition: A Common Grace*, Lawrence: University of Kansas Press, 2003.

Snow, Donald, "Empire or Homelands? A Revival of Jeffersonian Democracy in the American West," in John A. Baden and Donald Snow, eds., *The Next West: Public Lands, Community, and Economy in the American West*, Washington, DC: Island Press, 1997, pp. 181–203.

Soja, Edward W., "Thirdspace: Expanding the Scope of the Geographical Imagination," in Doreen Massey, John Allen, and Philip Sarre, *Human Geography Today*, Cambridge, UK: Polity Press, 1999, pp. 260–278.

Sontag, Deborah, "The Hole in the City's Heart," *New York Times*, September 11, 2006, p. F1.

Sorkin, Michael, "The Center Cannot Hold," in Michael Sorkin and Sharon Zukin, eds., *After the World Trade Center: Rethinking New York City*, New York: Routledge, 2002, pp. 197–207.

Sorkin, Michael, *Starting from Zero: Reconstructing Downtown New York*, New York: Routledge, 2003.

Sorkin, Michael, and Sharon Zukin, eds., *After the World Trade Center: Rethinking New York City*, New York: Routledge, 2002.

Southeast Alaska Conservation Council, *Taxpayer Losses and Missed Opportunities: How Tongass Rainforest Logging Costs Taxpayers Millions*, Juneau, AK: Southeast Alaska Conservation Council, 2003.

Southworth, Michael, "Reinventing Main Street: From Mall to Townscape Mall," *Journal of Urban Design*, Vol. 10, No. 2 (June 2005), pp. 151–170.

Sparks, Richard E., "Rethinking, Then Rebuilding New Orleans," *Issues in Science & Technology*, Vol. 22, No. 2 (Winter 2006), pp. 33–39.

State Deputy Comptroller for the City of New York, *Review of the Financial Plan of the City of New York: July 2006*, New York: Office of the State Comptroller, 2006, p. 45.

Steinhauer, Jennifer, "Mayor's Proposal Envisions Lower Manhattan as an Urban Hamlet," *New York Times*, December 13, 2002 (www.nytimes.com, accessed February 9, 2003).

Stephens, Suzanne, Ian Luna, and Ron Broadhurst, *Imagining Ground Zero: Official and Unofficial Proposals for the World Trade Center Site*, New York: Rizzoli/McGraw-Hill, 2004.

Steuteville, Robert, "Developer Fascination with Urban Centers Grows," *New Urban News*, October/November 2003 (www.newurbannews.com/whatsnew.html, accessed October 2, 2006).

Stilgoe, John R., *Outside Lies Magic: Regaining History and Awareness in Everyday Places*, New York: Walker, 1998.

Stoel, Thomas B., "Reining in Urban Sprawl: What can be Done to Tackle this Growing Problem?", *Environment*, Vol. 41, No. 4 (May 1999), pp. 6–11, 29–33.

Stranahan, Susan Q., "Air of Uncertainty," *American Journalism Review*, January/February 2003, p. 26.

"Study Sees Increase in Pediatric Asthma After WTC Disaster," *Indoor Environmental Quality Strategies*, July 2004, pp. 6–8.

Sturtevant, Victoria E., and Jonathan I. Lange, "From 'Them' to 'Us': The Applegate Partnership," in Jonathan Kusel and Elisa Adler, *Forest Communities, Community Forests*, Lanham, MD: Rowman & Littlefield, 2003, pp. 117–133.

Swanson, Frederick J., "Roles of Scientists in Forestry Policy and Management: Views from the Pacific Northwest," in Karen Arabas and Joe Bowersox, eds., *Forest Futures: Science, Politics, and Policy for the Next Century*, Lanham, MD: Rowman & Littlefield, 2004, pp. 112–126.

Tchen, John Kuo Wei, "Whose Downtown?!?" in Michael Sorkin and Sharon Zukin, eds., *After the World Trade Center: Rethinking New York City*, New York: Routledge, 2002, pp. 33–44.

Temple, Ryan, "Value-Added Manufacturing: An Oregon Perspective," Sustainable Oregon (www.sustainableoregon.net/forestry/value_added.cfm, accessed May 4, 2006).

Terreri, April, "The Food Pipeline," *Planning*, Vol. 70, No. 3 (March 2004), pp. 4–9.

Terrie, Philip G., *Contested Terrain: A New History of Nature and People in the Adirondacks*, Syracuse, NY: Syracuse University Press, 1999.

"The EPA Blows Smoke" (editorial), *St. Louis Post-Dispatch*, August 29, 2003, p. B6.

Thomas, Jack Ward, "Sustainability of the Northwest Forest Plan: Still to Be Tested," in Karen Arabas and Joe Bowersox, eds., *Forest Futures: Science, Politics, and Policy for the Next Century*, Lanham, MD: Rowman & Littlefield, 2004, pp. 3–22.

Thomas, Jennifer C., and Paul Mohai, "Racial, Gender, and Professional Diversification in the Forest Service from 1983 to 1992," *Policy Studies Journal*, Vol. 23, No. 2 (Summer 1995), pp. 296–309.

Thrift, Nigel, "Steps to an Ecology of Place," in Doreen Massey, John Allen, and Philip Sarre, *Human Geography Today*, Cambridge, UK: Polity Press, 1999, pp. 295–322.

Todd, Nancy Jack, and John Todd, *From Eco-Cities to Living Machines: Principles of Ecological Design*, Berkeley, CA: North Atlantic Books, 1993.

Tronto, Joan, *Moral Boundaries: A Political Argument for an Ethics of Care*, New York: Routledge, 1989.

Tuan, Yi-Fu, *Space and Place: The Perspective of Experience*, Minneapolis: University of Minnesota Press, 1977.

Tuan, Yi-Fu, *Topophilia: A Study of Environmental Perception, Attitudes, and Values*, New York: Columbia University Press, 1990.

Tuan, Yi-Fu, "Language and the Making of Place: A Narrative-Descriptive Approach," *Annals of the Association of American Geographers*, Vol. 81, No. 4 (December 1991), pp. 684–696.

Turkel, Tux, "Development Planned in Maine's North Woods," *Planning*, Vol. 71, No. 6 (June 2005), p. 44.

United Nations University: Institute for Environment and Human Security, "As Ranks of 'Environmental Refugees' Swell Worldwide, Calls Grow for Better Definition, Recognition, Support" (press release), October 12, 2005 (www.ehs .unu.edu, accessed March 1, 2006).

Usborne, David, "New York Divided Over Memorial," *Independent*, June 2, 2005, p. 24.

U.S. Census Bureau, "About Metropolitan and Micropolitan Statistical Areas" (www.census.gov/population/www/estimates/aboutmetro.html, accessed November 6, 2006).

U.S. Environmental Protection Agency, Office of Inspector General, *EPA's Response to the World Trade Center Collapse: Challenges, Successes, and Areas for Improvement*, Washington, DC: USEPA, August 21, 2003.

U.S. Forest Service, "1998 Northwest Forest Plan Accomplishment Report" (www.fs.fed.us/r6, accessed May 18, 2000).

U.S. House of Representatives, *California Spotted Owl Recovery Plan: Hearing Before the Subcommittee on National Parks, Forests, and Lands of the Committee on Resources*, June 6, 1995, Washington, DC: U.S. Government Printing Office, 1995.

"U.S. Urban Sprawl Devours Farmland—Green Group," Reuters Limited, September 9, 1998.

Vallas, Steven P., and John P. Beck, "The Transformation of Work Revisited: The Limits of Flexibility in American Manufacturing," *Social Problems*, Vol. 43, No. 3 (August 1996), pp. 339–361.

Varner, Gary E., "Environmental Law and the Eclipse of Land as Private Property," in Frederick Ferré and Peter Hartel, eds., *Ethics and Environmental Policy: Theory Meets Practice*, Athens: University of Georgia Press, 1994, pp. 140–160.

Verhovek, Sam Howe, "Judge, Faulting Agencies, Halts Logging Deals," *New York Times*, August 5, 1999, p. A1.

Vidal, John, "The 7,000 km Journey that Links Amazon Destruction to Fast Food," *Guardian Unlimited*, April 6, 2006 (www.guardian.co.uk/globalisation/ story/0,,1747904,00.html, accessed April 21, 2006).

Villa, Dana R., *Arendt and Heidegger: The Fate of the Political*, Princeton, NJ: Princeton University Press, 1996.

Villane, Dominick, "Sharing the Family Farm," *Massachusetts Sierran*, Vol. 3, No. 2 (Spring 1997), p. 1.

Vincent, Carol Hardy, *Land and Water Conservation Fund: Overview, Funding History, and Current Issues*, Washington, DC: Congressional Research Service, 2006.

Vinoly, Rafael, "Master Planner or Master Builder?", *New York Times*, December 12, 2003, p. A43.

Visgilio, Gerald R., and Diana M. Whitelaw, eds., *Our Backyard: A Quest for Environmental Justice*, Lanham, MD: Rowman & Littlefield, 2003.

Wallace, Mike, "New York, New Deal," in Michael Sorkin and Sharon Zukin, eds., *After the World Trade Center: Rethinking New York City*, New York: Routledge, 2002, pp. 209–223.

Walters, Jonathan, "Law of the Land: Voters' Challenge to Oregon's Stringent Land Use Controls May Signal a Major Shift in the Property Rights Debate Nationwide," *Governing Magazine*, May 2005 (www.governing.com/archive/2005/may/property.txt, accessed May 2, 2006).

Wapshott, Nicholas, "Ground Zilch: How Al-Qaeda Defeated New York," *New Statesman*, September 5, 2005, pp. 10–12.

Washington State Department of Natural Resources, *Washington State Forest Legacy Program Assessment of Need*, Olympia, WA: Washington State Department of Natural Resources, 2004.

Wasserman, Stuart, "Preserving Owl's Habitat Helps People, Expert Says," *San Francisco Chronicle*, March 30, 1992, p. A4.

Weiner, Andrew, "The Taking," *Boston Phoenix*, November 30–December 7, 2000 (www.bostonphoenix.com/archive/features/00/11/30/WEST_END1.html, accessed June 3, 2006).

Weir, Margaret, "Coalition Building for Regionalism," in Bruce Katz, ed., *Reflections on Regionalism*, Washington, DC: Brookings Institution, 2000, pp. 127–153.

Westfeldt, Amy, "Port Authority Approves Deal with Silverstein for Ground Zero," *New York Sun*, April 26, 2006 (www.nysun.com/article/31689?page_no=1, accessed May 3, 2006).

Westfeldt, Amy, "Vacancies Down Around Ground Zero," Associated Press, February 25, 2007.

White, Richard, *It's Your Misfortune and None of My Own: A New History of the American West*, Norman: University of Oklahoma Press, 1993.

White, Richard, "'Are You an Environmentalist or Do You Work for a Living?': Work and Nature," in William Cronon, ed., *Uncommon Ground: Toward Reinventing Nature*, New York: W.W. Norton, 1995, pp. 171–185.

Whiteside, Kerry, "Worldliness and Respect for Nature: An Ecological Application of Hannah Arendt's Conception of Culture," *Environmental Values*, Vol. 7, No. 1 (February 1998), pp. 25–40.

Wiewel, Wim, and Kimberly Schaffer, "New Federal and State Policies for Metropolitan Equity," in Wim Wiewel and Joseph J. Persky, eds., *Suburban Sprawl: Private Decisions and Public Policy*, Armonk, NY: M.E. Sharpe, 2002, pp. 256–307.

Wigley, Mark, "Insecurity by Design," in Michael Sorkin and Sharon Zukin, eds., *After the World Trade Center: Rethinking New York City*, New York: Routledge, 2002, pp. 69–85.

408 Bibliography

Worster, Donald, *Nature's Economy: A History of Ecological Ideas*, 2nd ed., Cambridge: Cambridge University Press, 1994.

Worster, Donald, "Nature and the Disorder of History," in Michael E. Soulé and Gary Lease, eds., *Reinventing Nature: Responses to Postmodern Deconstruction*, Washington, DC: Island Press, 1995, pp. 65–85.

Wyatt, Edward, "Some Neighbors Seek Greater Voice on Plans for Sept. 11 Memorial," *New York Times*, June 19, 2002, p. B1.

Wyatt, Edward, "Pataki's Surprising Limit on Ground Zero Design," *New York Times*, July 2, 2002, p. B1.

Wyatt, Edward, "Visions of Ground Zero: The Overview; Six Plans for Ground Zero, All Seen as a Starting Point," *New York Times*, July 17, 2002, p. A1.

Wyatt, Edward, "At Trade Center Site, A Wealth of Ideas; Competing Interests Are Fighting to Have a Say in Reviving Downtown," *New York Times*, July 28, 2002, p. 25.

Wyatt, Edward, "Practical Issues for Ground Zero," *New York Times*, February 28, 2003, p. A1.

Wyatt, Edward, "From Political Calculation, a Sweeping Vision of Ground Zero Rose," *New York Times*, March 3, 2003, p. B1.

Wyatt, Edward, "Architect and Developer Clash Over Plans for Trade Center Site," *New York Times*, July 15, 2003, p. A1.

Wyatt, Edward, "The New Ground Zero: There's Nothing So Closed as an Open Competition," *New York Times*, August 31, 2003 (Arts and Leisure section), p. 18.

Wyatt, Edward, with Charles V. Bagli, "Visions of Ground Zero: The Public; Officials Rethink Building Proposal for Ground Zero," *New York Times*, July 21, 2002, p. 1.

Yaffee, Steven Lewis, *The Wisdom of the Spotted Owl: Policy Lessons for a New Century*, Washington, DC: Island Press, 1994.

Yaffee, Steven F., Ali F. Phillips, Irene C. Frentz, Paul W. Hardy, Sussanne M. Maleki, and Barbara E. Thorpe, *Ecosystem Management in the United States: An Assessment of Current Experience*, Washington, DC: Island Press, 1996.

Yandle, Bruce, ed., *Land Rights: The 1990s' Property Rights Rebellion*, Lanham, MD: Rowman & Littlefield, 1995.

Yardley, William, "Anger Drives Property Measures," *New York Times*, October 8, 2006, p. 34.

Yaro, Robert D., "Growing and Governing Smart: A Case Study of the New York Region," in Bruce Katz, ed., *Reflections on Regionalism*, Washington, DC: Brookings Institution, 2000, pp. 43–77.

Young, Iris Marion, *Justice and the Politics of Difference*, Princeton, NJ: Princeton University Press, 1990.

Young, Iris Marion, *Intersecting Voices: Dilemmas of Gender, Political Philosophy, and Policy*, Princeton, NJ: Princeton University Press, 1997.

Young, Oran R., *Resource Regimes: Natural Resources and Social Institutions*, Berkeley: University of California Press, 1982.

Zimmerman, Ulf, Göktuğ Morçöl, and Bethany Stich, "From Sprawl to Smart Growth: The Case of Atlanta," in Matthew J. Lindstrom and Hugh Bartling, eds., *Suburban Sprawl: Culture, Theory, and Politics*, Lanham, MD: Rowman & Littlefield, 2003, pp. 275–287.

Zukin, Sharon, "Our World Trade Center," in Michael Sorkin and Sharon Zukin, eds., *After the World Trade Center: Rethinking New York City*, New York: Routledge, 2002, pp. 13–21.

Websites

The American Farmland Trust: www.farmland.org

The Applegate Partnership/Applegate River Watershed Council: www.arwc.org

Congress of the New Urbanism: www.cnu.org

The Downeast Lakes Land Trust: www.downeastlakes.org

Dudley Street Neighborhood Initiative: www.dsni.org

The Food Project: www.thefoodproject.org

Institute for Community Economics: www.iceclt.org

The Land Trust Alliance: www.lta.org

Lower Manhattan Development Corporation: www.renewnyc.com

The National Trust for Historic Preservation: www.nationaltrust.org

The Nature Conservancy: www.nature.org

New Jersey Future: www.njfuture.org

Oregon Small Woodlands Association: www.oswa.org

The Randolph Township Open Space Committee: www.randolphnj.org/open _space

Sustainable Oregon: www.sustainableoregon.net

The Trust for Public Land: www.tpl.org

University of Massachusetts community-supported agriculture web page: www .umassvegetable.org/food_farming_systems/csa/index.html

Index

Founding, 3–13, 31–44, 222, 258, 305. *See also* Founding and preservation, relationship between
as collective project, 36–38, 212–213
contrast with discovery, 208
and the concept of site, 175–176
and the crisis of place, 173–204, 206–208, 210, 212–213, 215–218
and forestry politics, 46–47, 69–73, 77–78, 88–92
and speech, 31–32
and sprawl, 93, 113–115, 118, 120–122
and the World Trade Center and Ground Zero, 124–125, 130, 134–139, 141, 146–147, 159–160, 167–171
Founding and preservation, relationship between, 3–9, 12–13, 41–44, 46–47, 72, 91–92, 96–97, 114–115, 120–121, 136, 146, 170–171, 208, 213, 218, 219–221, 231–232, 244, 260, 300, 301
Frank, Jill, 354n
Franklin, Jerry, 262
Franklin, Jerry and James Agee, 85
Freedom Tower, 140, 149–153
Frug, Gerald, 239

Garrett, Laurie, 163
Gasoline taxes, 371n
Gated communities, 30, 108, 194, 230. *See also* Margaret Kohn; Private communities
Georgia Regional Transportation Authority (GRTA), 251–252, 255
Gillespie, Angus K., 126–127, 230
Gilligan, Carol, 316n
Giuliani, Rudolph, 137, 147, 151
Glanz, James, and Eric Lipton, 123, 127, 130–131, 134
Glendening, Parris N., 282
Global warming. *See* Climate change
Globalization, 15, 19–20, 39–40, 103, 174, 181–204, 219, 227–228, 237–238, 256, 288

Gold, Lou, 82, 84
Goldberger, Paul, 127, 131, 134, 135, 141, 143–144, 168–170
Gonzalez, Juan, 164–165
Goodwin, Michael, 139
Gordon, Peter, and Harry Richardson, 16–17, 97–98, 104
Grand Forks (North Dakota), 1997 flooding of, ix
Grand Staircase-Escalante National Monument, 1–3
Greenpeace International, 199
Ground Zero, 10–11, 123–125, 129, 134–171, 203, 224, 227, 239–240, 242, 244, 255, 259, 289
debate over cultural institutions at, 156–161, 170
environmental aspects of rebuilding process, 141–143
failure of democracy at, 136, 141, 147–156, 159–160, 167–169, 218
failure to integrate founding and preservation at, 125, 136, 146–147, 168–171, 217–218
as fundamentally contested, 124–125, 136–137
integrating founding and preservation at, 300
rebuilding process evaluated, 166–171
rebuilding proposals for, 148–155, 298–300
regional approach to, 298–300
as sacred, 137–138, 140, 145–146, 151, 158–159

Habitus and habitudes, 34, 191
Hamilton, Cynthia, 292–293
Hanson, Nels, 264
Harvey, David, 21, 120, 176, 201, 229–230, 243, 310n, 336n
conception of place, 21
on the geographically disruptive effects of global capitalism, 17, 19, 185–188, 194
on time-space compression, 17, 19, 187

Peggy F. Barlett and Geoffrey W. Chase, eds., *Sustainability on Campus: Stories and Strategies for Change*

Steve Lerner, *Diamond: A Struggle for Environmental Justice in Louisiana's Chemical Corridor*

Jason Corburn, *Street Science: Community Knowledge and Environmental Health Justice*

Peggy F. Barlett, ed., *Urban Place: Reconnecting with the Natural World*

David Naguib Pellow and Robert J. Brulle, eds., *Power, Justice, and the Environment: A Critical Appraisal of the Environmental Justice Movement*

Eran Ben-Joseph, *The Code of the City: Standards and the Hidden Language of Place Making*

Nancy J. Myers and Carolyn Raffensperger, eds., *Precautionary Tools for Reshaping Environmental Policy*

Kelly Sims Gallagher, *China Shifts Gears: Automakers, Oil, Pollution, and Development*

Kerry H. Whiteside, *Precautionary Politics: Principle and Practice in Confronting Environmental Risk*

Ronald Sandler and Phaedra C. Pezzullo, eds., *Environmental Justice and Environmentalism: The Social Justice Challenge to the Environmental Movement*

Julie Sze, *Noxious New York: The Racial Politics of Urban Health and Environmental Justice*

Robert D. Bullard, ed., *Growing Smarter: Achieving Livable Communities, Environmental Justice, and Regional Equity*

Ann Rappaport and Sarah Hammond Creighton, *Degrees That Matter: Climate Change and the University*

Michael Egan, *The Science of Survival: Barry Commoner and the Remaking of American Environmentalism*

David J. Hess, *Alternative Pathways in Science and Industry: Activism, Innovation, and the Environment in an Era of Globalization*

Peter F. Cannavò, *The Working Landscape: Founding, Preservation, and the Politics of Place*